Time, Change, and the American Newspaper

★ ★ ★

LEA's COMMUNICATION SERIES
Jennings Bryant/Dolf Zillmann, General Editors

For a complete list of titles in LEA's Communication Series, please contact Lawrence Erlbaum Associates, Publishers.

Time, Change, and the American Newspaper

★ ★ ★

George Sylvie
University of Texas at Austin

Patricia D. Witherspoon
University of Texas at El Paso

LAWRENCE ERLBAUM ASSOCIATES, PUBLISHERS

2002   Mahwah, New Jersey   London

Lawrence Erlbaum Associates, Inc., Publishers
10 Industrial Avenue
Mahwah, NJ 07430

Cover design by Kathryn Houghtaling Lacey

Library of Congress Cataloging-in-Publication Data

Sylvie, George.
Time, change and the American newspaper / George Sylvie,
Patricia D. Witherspoon.
    p. cm.   (LEA's communication series)
    Includes bibliographical references and index.
ISBN 0-8058-3587-3 (cloth : alk. paper)
ISBN 0-8058-3588-1 (pbk. : alk. paper)
1. Journalism—Management.   2. Newspaper publishing—
Management.   3. Journalism—Technological innovations—
United States.   4. Newspaper publishing—Technological
innovations—United States.   I. Witherspoon, Patricia D.
II. Title.   III. Series.
PN4784.M34 S98   2001
070.4´068 —dc21   2001023583
                                          CIP

Books published by Lawrence Erlbaum Associates are printed on
acid-free paper, and their bindings are chosen for strength and
durability.

Printed in the United States of America
10   9   8   7   6   5   4   3   2   1

Contents

Preface

In the 100th issue of *Human Communication Research,* E. Rogers (1999) emphasized that human communication cannot be understood fully by only those scholars in mass communication or in interpersonal communication, the two subdisciplines he identifies as the components of communication study. Indeed, he recommended that scholars from both disciplines engage in collaborative work to facilitate the understanding of human communication (pp. 627–628).

This book is a cooperative effort between two scholars who study different phenomena: The operation and management of newspapers and the leadership of change in organizations. Our separate interests inform this effort, and serve as an example of an interdisciplinary approach to studying communication and change in media organizations.

Heraclitus once wrote that "nothing endures but change." That is certainly the case in the first years of the new millenium, when newspapers, as products and as organizations, are changing because of new forms of competition, new technologies, new organizational structures, and multiple constituencies. Why focus attention on newspapers when newer media are evolving through which to disseminate information about the global society in which we live? According to Vivian (1995): "Nearly one out of two people in the United States reads a paper every day, far more than tune in the network news on television in the evening" (p. 83). He further emphasized that daily newspapers reach more than 130 million people a day in the United States, and weekly papers are read by about 200 million citizens. Additionally, more people work to gather, edit and disseminate news in newspaper offices than in other news media organizations, and more advertising dollars are invested in newspapers than in any other medium, including television.

This book is a reflection of our respect for the contributions newspapers have made to this society, and our optimism about what they may offer our citizens, in form and content, in the years ahead.

—*George Sylvie*

1

An Overview of Newspaper Change

Change is a modern-day buzzword—everybody knows about it, but no one knows what to do about it. Nowhere is this more true than in the American newspaper industry, where change, it seems, is a constant force. Not only have employees changed—in terms of what they expect from their jobs and in their demographic makeup—but the entire process of producing a paper receives daily scrutiny, from the publisher on down and from those on the outside looking in. Equipment vendors want to sell the latest technology to owners; advertisers seek more effective ways to reach customers. Of course, there are readers who are at times horrified, miffed, confused, or disappointed by the content and who—through their purchasing habits—decide whether the newspaper is worthwhile. Their opinions in that regard are always subject to change.

All this means that a newspaper must change to meet the changes of those it serves. Nobody argues this point. The problem comes in the next step: making (or not making) the change. So much—not to mention millions of dollars in profits—hangs in the balance. There are reputations at stake. In a media-rich society where word spreads almost instantaneously, no newspaper executive wants to be known as the person who stood in the way or—worse—the person who suggested the wrong change. So change has become something to be discussed, a subject of analysis and study. Can newspapers change? Will they change? More importantly, should they change?

Of course, this is not the case for every newspaper. Change happens every day and no one worriedly wrings his or her hands—it just happens. This simple assessment misses the point. Technically, someone's job is on the line every time change happens and the degree of risk varies, based on who is making the decision, the nature of the decision and its timing. Add to that the fact that events have put the industry at a crossroads in terms of how it views change and change begins to take on a life of its own. This book examines that life, starting with the ongoing industry debate over change.

PONDERING CHANGE

First, a warning: When you observe something happening over and over again, your attention naturally shifts from the phenomenon observed to the fact that it reoccurs. The same principle holds true about any debate—the question shifts from the issue at hand (in this case, change) to the issue of the debate. So the debate about change continues. As mentioned earlier, reputations, jobs, and money are obviously at stake. In the case of the change debate (and to be fair to the newspaper industry), this debate often occurs in the trade press and in academia. Both have self-interests at heart. The former shows its importance and necessity through informational training and service to the industry in various areas, one of the most important being informing managers, journalists, and other employees about trends. Academia seeks knowledge for knowledge's sake, but the academic scholar constantly pursues new knowledge, and nothing is ever newer than change (or the study of it). This book is somewhat guilty of perpetuating this debate.

We can borrow a page from newspaper methods to understand this debate. Newspapers, like most news media, gather news based on certain assumptions or values. Generally speaking, news reporters report about one or more aspects of an issue: what happened, when it happened, where and who was involved, and—if possible—why it happened. The newspaper change debate has centered around three main aspects: the impact of change (what), the methods of change (how), and the rationale for or against change (why). Each has its own set of issues, but each also illustrates the necessity for this book.

Impacts

You could call this the "doom and gloom" area of the debate. Change takes on a devilish or necessary evil persona—essentially, "Change is coming, so be prepared." This is not to belittle the respective impacts; they deserve serious consideration because they collectively represent what the industry sees when it thinks about change—the forms of change and its immediate, work-related consequences.

At this writing, the Internet and its associated ramifications posed one of the most puzzling, persistent threats to newspapers. Its capability to deliver electronic text, video, and audio to personal computers and television sets almost anywhere in the world. This caused turmoil as publishers saw traditional notions about their markets and the nature of their products rendered obsolete; in other words, they discovered that a successful online newspaper should not just be a newspaper shoveled online. How to establish a market niche and thus create a profit stirred much concern, especially since newspapers feared the loss of revenues—primarily classified advertising—to

Internet competitors who did not need huge sums of money to get established and who might be more electronically savvy when it came to understanding the inherent capabilities and attractions of the new medium (Chyi & Sylvie, 1998).

The Internet brought related problems. For example, legal and regulatory issues took on new perspectives. What was once local news became instantaneously national and international simply because of the technology. The particulars for libel, privacy, and pornography issues increased 10-fold; in short, already complicated legalities became more complex because the Internet blends two forms of expression—print and broadcast—into one, perhaps most closely resembling the telephone system but with probably 1% of the regulation and case law governing it. In other words, this has become uncharted (and thus dangerous) legal waters (Reddick & King, 1995).

For example, with the Internet, speech becomes international in scope. One of the biggest concerns may be the way American law is applied to international media or the reverse. Anything newspapers put online is now subject to the country's libel and defamation laws. Copyright issues come into play more often because of the ease with which newspapers borrow needed content and graphic elements from World Wide Web sites. Because of the proliferation of such sites and the graphics-enhancing software that make them look credible, veracity also becomes an issue.

Each impact represents a tree in a constantly growing and expanding forest. As a result, many publishers and editors can be blinded into attempting short-term solutions or quick-fixes, such as rushing to establish a web presence because of the fear of losing classified advertising to potential online competitors. In some cases, they are even encouraged to "learn to love" losing money because of the investment such new technology represents (Weaver, 1996). It is time to clear such muddled thinking.

How-To Issues

With so many impacts comes the natural question of how to deal with all of them. A more pertinent question that often arises is "How do we cope?" In short, methods of keeping up with rapid change becomes as important as— and sometimes the equivalent of—change itself.

Conventional and standard coping mechanisms often begin with the search for a model. In fact, the word model implies the existence of previous success. So newspapers often look to history—immediate or relatively ancient— for answers. One such model involves European newspapers, which are viewed as more progressive and successful in pre-press technology (Cole, 1999). Another model is the individual, "try this" approach. "This is what they did at *The Times*," is an apt description.

When models fail or do not fit, then another often-touted method of change concerns skills, that is, the new way approach, much akin to fighting change with change. For example, the increasing diversification of America (or so journalists and publishers are told) requires new methods of reporting and of thinking. As audiences become more segmented and targeted, journalists will have to accommodate them—whether via online news [by changing their styles to serve readers with short attention spans (Lanson & Fought, 1999; Yovovich, 1997)] or through more democratically inspiring content [by modifying their reporting styles to incorporate tenets of civic journalism (Merritt, 1995; Rosen & Merritt, 1994)], or through identifying and writing "diversity stories" (Aldrich, 1999).

Finally, and this may be a purely newspaper peculiarity, there is the change by not changing approach, which essentially states that newspapers will do well if they stay on course somewhat and keep doing what they do—only better, smarter, or both. Playing to such strengths necessitates awareness of surrounding change, to be sure, newspapers will prevail either because economic events will cause rivals to fall to the wayside (Bogart, 1999) or because they have something competitors do not have—brand identity, for example (Albers, 1998; Upshaw, 1995).

By no means is this a comprehensive list. You can find various approaches regularly in the trade press, which is particularly guilty of perpetuating the model approach—it provides a quick, interesting, easily mimicked idea and is journalistically do-able. However, the diversity of approaches can again muddy decision making, giving publishers too many choices and creating the forest scenario alluded to earlier. More importantly, the focus on how—on methods—clouds the issue. It takes the emphasis away from transformation and puts it into terms of coping, making do, sufficing—being adequate or normal. That is a temporal, "here and now" focus that mature industries such as newspapers cannot afford because it shifts attention away from preparing for change.

Anti-Change

Perhaps, with so much advice and with so many changes, it is not surprising that newspaper personnel often harbor a conservative (some would say contrary) attitude toward change. Newspapers often get labeled for Luddism, for being in a state of denial when it comes to change (Feola, 1997; Katz, 1998).

Researchers have given us two good examples. One study (Singer, 1997) looked at newspaper journalists' perspectives about online media. Three distinct perspectives evolved, including one "the nervous traditionalist," who is more likely to fear new technology. The "rational realist" was another type, described as believing new media will not have much near-term effect on him and as unwilling to cede control over the news product to new media. A similar study (Gade et al., 1997) examined the attitudes of journalists toward civic journalism. The researchers identified four groups, including "the concerned traditionalist" who did not see the need for a new media philosophy or civic journalism as the cure for media problems.

Nevertheless citing journalists' displeasure with innovation does not say much. Journalists, by nature and training, are cynical. So their skepticism and reluctance should not surprise. It does not stop there. Even Chris Urban, a longtime newspaper marketing master, has complained of a "culture of risk avoidance" in the industry (Hider, 1998). Another consultant (Cole, 1996) has described newspapers as "mired in the muck of tradition." Editors have been called "gutless" for not changing reporting methods to keep up with reader needs (Jennings, 1999).

Of course, complacency regarding change is a serious threat to newspapers. Publications that do not change also do not adequately monitor their markets. Without markets, there is no demand. Without demand, there is no newspaper. So simple economics dictate that newspapers must meet market challenges or die (see e.g., Johnson, 1997). Simple economics cease to enter the picture when people are confronted with change, because change usually brings about social modifications, which is what people really resist (Lawrence, 1954). So complacency and resistance constitute reactionary behavior that—much like models and other how-to approaches—once again blurs the vision of newspapers (in fact, it is akin to passive nearsightedness) and prevents them from becoming the vital, influential tools of democracy they were originally meant to become.

THE SIGNIFICANCE OF NEWSPAPERS

What is so special about newspapers? Businesses that do not change are businesses that fail, and vice versa. Why should newspapers be any different? Several things make them unique.

First, newspapers have a special role in society. For all their owners' sophisticated, corporate-style planning and centralized decision making, newspapers are local products—not only vulnerable to the whims of local economies and somewhat immune to cookie-cutter solutions, but also vital to the cultural and economic dynamic of their specific markets. In addition, newspaper markets have a unique trait in that they are two-headed entities— one function involves general reader–consumers while the other concerns advertisers. Selling local readers to advertisers makes newspapers unusually valuable and identified with their geographic area; in economic-speak, newspapers' substitutability is limited (Picard & Brody, 1997). A newspaper's contents reflect the life, character, and soul of a community; what more reason to ensure that this role continues?

Still, for all their talk of reflecting a community and its continuing evolution, newspapers themselves notoriously resist change. The First Amendment encourages newspapers to guard freedom of expression and professionally trained journalists constitute a large, vocal in-house watchdog to protect that sacred franchise. This noble standard fosters a conservative attitude regarding any potential threat. Other media have no such problems—all coexist peacefully with less-than-pure content. But when newspapers remotely hint at changing newsroom procedures—as in introducing market values or in attempting to give the public a larger voice in news selection—journalists and editors either protest the suggestions or predict the changes will lead to the eventual death of newspapers (Underwood, 1993). What makes newspapers unique also makes them change-resistant: Their unique public role has created a semi-virtuous mission or "golden rule" that essentially says anything that does not tell the public what it needs to know, in a professionally pure journalistic formula, must be inherently bad and thus is best avoided. Of course, such reasoning is ludicrous (not to mention, arrogant and, at the least, nearsighted), akin to saying, "We have the truth in our own heads; why listen to anyone else's truth?"

Newspapers' approach to the product also sets them apart. Each day (or week), the product changes. News, by definition, is timely and changing. The changing content requires a constant process—acquiring, creating, selecting, editing, and packaging processes must be coordinated, if not orchestrated. In order to report change in society and make it comprehensible (and regularly deliverable) to readers, the newspaper must have a reliable system by which to accomplish publication. As the process has become more routine, the propensity to change it has declined. Although individual newspapers do adopt new production methods, the industry's basic overall process of assembling a newspaper has changed little over the past two centuries. As a result, the newspaper has come under constant criticism. In the news-reporting sphere alone, not a week goes by without some major interest group decrying journalism's treatment of its members. But the construction of news is a systemic, complex, entrenched process (e.g., McManus, 1994; Tuchman, 1978) that cannot be changed overnight. It must change because newspapers enter the third millennium facing many more complex and subtle economic and marketing challenges. Despite continued profit, circulation prices are rising, staffs are constantly cut, space for news is declining, and market penetration is lagging—meaning the production process may have outlived its usefulness. Newspapers must change to survive.

CHANGE PROCESS AND NEWSPAPERS

Changing will not be easy. Publishers often see technology in the conventional sense of inevitable change, that is, the driving force of growth. This argument gains strength from operational history—previous successes become associated with the advent of new tools; "we did it once and we can do it again." While different tools embody change, their ties to success are not so easily established. People—particularly employees—have to embrace and adopt tools for them to become useful (e.g., Rogers, 1986). Fortunately, within the newspaper, adoption usually occurs for a variety of reasons—behavioral incentives ranging from market incentives to more income to status enhancement.

Although adoptive success often begets economic success, it also can create a paralyzing mindset. Managers and editors begin to envision technological advances with certain strategies, beliefs, and values, which then become an entrenched mode of thinking. For example, critics took delight in recounting Times-Mirror's and Knight-Ridder's fatal, multimillion-dollar forays into videotext; the lesson of the 1970s and early 1980s was that an electronic newspaper would not be accepted by consumers. It was not until the mid-1990s that the acceptance of the Internet and of personal computers made online newspapers acceptable. In addition, newspapers are just starting to discover that pagination was not the "promised land" of labor cost-effectiveness it was touted, that with its placement of page control in the newsroom's hands has come the unintended impacts of deskilling some news editors and organizational havoc (Russial, 1994; Sylvie, 1995).

As a result, "thinking out of the box" becomes a mantra to publishers who see themselves falling into predictable thought patterns about the future and the direction of change. This is especially true when new, seemingly mystifying technologies pose a challenge, prompting publishers to search for models of success. They are advised to re-learn the way they do things, to experiment and to try new things, even to the point of violating competitive common sense through alliances with other newspapers (in the case of the Internet; Albers, 1995b; Jennings, 1999). They seek to re-engineer their work processes or, redefine their jobs or, at the very least, re-tool their thinking (Pogash, 1996; Whiteside, 1996). The problem, of course, is that even such attempts to be different are themselves conformist in the sense that they emulate fads or quick-fix approaches or are done simply to be different when, in fact, trying to be different is not only reactionary but conforms to someone else's notion of accepted behavior.

Only when change is acceptably framed—as instrumental to all concerned or to those with the power to affect it—does change get due consideration. For example, some might say team reporting should not be presented to reporters as a new way of reporting, but rather as a way to make their jobs easier and more fun. Newsroom change often gets nipped in the bud because many editors forget change must be presented from the most advantageous motivational perspective of the person who will be doing the changing—in other words, "This is change you'll *want* to undertake." Of course, motivation can be negative as well, but it does not have to be.

If an editor has to be concerned about motivation, the proper mode of thought and how to accommodate change, the question rightfully becomes "How does or should change occur?" What is more, as the world's economy constantly changes and adjusts, editors and publishers rightfully may wonder whether their approach to change really matters—as if it is a simple matter of economics determining the future as always, that the politics of efficiency and of expediency will always defeat the politics of journalistic purity. This explanation oversimplifies the situation for individual newspapers, which—because of their local orientation—must be attuned to a complex web of factors, ranging from size of organization, to health and complexity of the local economy, to managerial vision and employee motivation, to lifestyles of consumers.

But what of change? How does it work? Change expert Kanter and her colleagues suggested that although different people see organizational change differently, change is not necessarily something new and different. Rather, real organizational change occurs when the organization's character—its structure, systems, and culture—changes. As organizations move toward a goal, change occurs—some of it observable, some of it smoothly unobservable (mainly because of the lack of conflict or challenge). Three things create such movement: Changes in the motion of the environment, changes in motion of the parts of the organization in relation to one another as the organization grows or ages, and changes in the organization's internal political workings (Kanter, Stein, & Jick, 1992).

Once any of those movements occur, the editor–publisher must know which role to assume in order to manage the change. When it comes to connecting the newspaper to the environment, the manager can become a strategist—anticipating change and providing direction. In the case of the newspaper progressing through its stages, the manager becomes an implementor, managing and executing projects of change. Finally, when change involves the newspaper's political dimensions, tension and conflict often arise because this is where people are most affected by the change and the implementation. The manager, too, can become change recipient—a passive beneficiary (more or less) of change and one who must overcome feelings of powerlessness (whether personal or among subordinates; Kanter et al., 1992).

In essence, Kanter and colleagues said organizational change is more complex than it sounds. The newspaper industry must begin to view change as a dynamic process that is more than just something to which it simply must react and adjust. That most newspapers do not fathom change is understandable because they live it everyday. Just as it is difficult for an individual to understand intuitively how the body must behave in order to remain healthy and alive, it is just as difficult for the average newspaper executive to comprehend how his or her newspaper must change.

Newspapers need a comprehensive understanding of change that goes beyond the advice of consultants, the dictates of corporate executives, the needs of employees, and the whims of the local market. The challenges of the new century demand a new way of thinking. There is such a way—a model from which to view change. The model sees change as a process with a scope, causes, phases, and cycles, but more importantly as not just a concern with the future but as a consideration of a newspaper's past as well. Each—past and future—constitutes a desired or preferred way of behaving, creating not only a choice but also a tension. Briefly, we will take a closer look at the first and last of these—scope and time—to get a better sense of the job ahead of newspapers.

Change consultant Nadler suggested viewing change along two dimensions, one of which is temporal positioning of the change in relation to key outer events (Nadler, 1988). Such changes can be reactive or initiated in anticipation. The other dimension, scope, can be grouped into either incremental (within the current organizational system) or strategic (addressed to changing the organization as a whole). Matching the two dimensions yield four specific types of changes: tuning (incremental and anticipatory), adaptation (incremental and reactive), reorientation (strategic and anticipatory), and re-creation (strategic and reactive). A newspaper enters its future anticipating unknown results, but also reacting based on its past behavior and expectations. So the past influences the behaviors and—significantly—the intents, postures, and beliefs of the organization. To be sure, other factors—resources, capabilities, external pressures—constrain the decision to change. Newspapers, probably more than any other industry, are time-sensitive: Meeting deadlines, obviously, but also attempting to keep pace with the constantly changing wants and needs of their readers. This sensitivity to time drives much of the change in the industry. This book contends that the newspaper that understands the role of time in change is the newspaper that succeeds; that is, that changing or not changing depends on how one views the passage of time.

More succinctly, successful newspaper managers make a rational choice between their past and future. This book contends they often do so on the basis of economics—they change when they think they will reap more benefit than harm, and they do so because they look for ways to get the most (be it profit or productivity) in the shortest amount of time. To that end, this book describes case studies of change (or the lack of it) in the newspaper industry.

EXAMINING NEWSPAPER CHANGE

To illustrate these relationships and ideas, this book tackles the issue in segments.

Part I follows the lead of this introductory chapter, that is, discussing in detail the basic tenets of the book. Chapter 2 takes the fundamental ideas of organizations—the various approaches—and advances them in a look at organization as process: The notion that people develop rules, processes, reporting relationships, and culture through interaction. The chapter examines environmental influences on newspapers and with an eye on the 21st century newspaper organization—all while placing newspapers in the general, larger context of all organizations so as to lay the groundwork for chapter 3, where the process of organizational change is analyzed in non-newspaper industries and companies. The validity of change theory will be established by looking at the nature of change, the change process, rationale for organizational changes, resistance to such changes, and initiation and implementation strategies. From that point, we think the reader will be armed to fully appreciate chapter 4, which briefly examines newspapers and change. In particular, the chapter discusses the causes of newspaper change, how newspaper change takes shape, and when it does not work. More importantly, this chapter takes a preliminary look at the role of time in approaches to newspaper change.

Part II gives those changes a more detailed analysis, beginning in chapter 5, which surveys the role of technology in effecting–preventing change. This discussion sets the stage for chapter 6, which inspects the position of the product in effecting–preventing change. Finally, chapter 7 rounds out Part II by looking at the people at *USA TODAY* and how individuals play a role as change agents in newspaper organizations.

Finally, as you might expect, all this would be for naught without Part III, which includes impacts and implications chapters. Chapter 8 discusses the impact of change (or the lack of it) on the contemporary newspaper industry and the subsequent impacts of newspaper change on society while chapter 9 discusses future directions of change and of newspaper decision-making processes as they pertain to change; suggestions for changes in newspaper structures, and thought processes that can be made.

Philosophy

Philosophy is a way of thinking, an attitude, a system of beliefs and ideas. Therefore, the first four chapters of this book express our attitude toward examining newspapers and change. However, philosophy also is a foundation for life. Likewise, Part I lays the groundwork for how we examine the newspapers that provide our food for thought in Parts II and III.

For example, chapter 1 is more than an introduction. It ponders change via impacts and how-to issues, but it also discusses the special significance that newspapers hold among industries and how these publications face a changing future that presents a complex set of problems. In short, chapter 1 presents the foundation as a mixture of intricate elements.

In chapters 2 and 3, those elements begin to take form via discussions framed in organizational terms. Newspapers are described as entities that have evolved into systems and networks, making them unique knowledge organizations. This sets the stage for chapter 3, which focuses on the change process and how newspapers are home to rare forms of change. All in all, the foundation begins to take shape.

Finally, chapter 4 seeks to smooth and solidify the foundation by generally scrutinizing how newspapers operate and, thus, how they change or do not change. Learning the causes and influences allows the reader to apply more perspective to the case studies of Part II, and in the final analysis, appreciate the role of time and vision in those situations. This foundation becomes a bridge to the rest of the book.

CHAPTER TWO

Newspapers as Organizations

Of the many voices that have addressed the history, operation, effects, or all three of American newspapers, most have spoken about them as modern organizations. That is, they focus on contemporary newspapers as pyramidal, hierarchical systems with different functional units, vertical (mostly downward) communication, and management that is predominantly task-focused rather than employee-centered. This chapter offers a different lens through which to view newspapers as organizations by suggesting the following:

• Newspapers, like a number of other industries, began as pre-modern entities, grew into more complex structures with multiple functional units, and some are now changing into organizations with post-modern components. That is, they are developing flexible, adaptable structures, with diffused, or fuzzy boundaries, focusing on the need for rapid change using multiple new technologies, and intrinsic as well as extrinsic rewards for organizational members. In a post-modern setting, environmental changes affect internal systems, on an ongoing basis, and the key to their survival is flexibility and adaptability.

• Newspapers are systems of interconnected networks, created through communication. The surveillance function of newspapers also depends on a variety of boundary-spanning activities conducted through networks established with the external environment.

• The explosion of interest in knowledge-based organizations, and knowledge workers, has focused on computer and software companies, management consulting firms, and team-based organizations in selected industries. Newspapers, however, are also forms of knowledge organizations.

The purpose of this chapter is three-fold: (a) to focus on the evolution of newspapers as organizations; (b) to consider newspapers as systems and networks; and (c) to discuss their uniqueness as knowledge organizations. In doing so, we establish how newspapers are poised to undergo the change processes found in other types of organizations. However, it is first important to understand a contemporary, and communicative, notion of organization, for organizations at the beginning of the 21st century are conceptualized as networks of relationships, not boxes and arrows depicting work units on a company chart. The study of organizational communication over the last 25 years has led us to understand that organizations are more than hierarchies of structures and functions. They are combinations of people interacting to achieve mutual goals.

THE NOTION OF ORGANIZATION

It is ironic that treatises on newspapers as organizations historically tend to focus on management, rather than communication perspectives. Indeed, a newspaper as an organization reflects the importance of communication as the critical process that coordinates the work of people to create a product. Within the last 60 years, the concept of organization has emerged as: "consciously, coordinated activities or forces of two or more persons" (Barnard, 1938, p. 73), coalitions of individuals who set goals through interaction (Cyert & March, 1963), complex social units designed to achieve specific purposes (Knight & McDaniel, 1979), and a set of processes that "consists of plans, recipes, rules, instructions, and programs for generating, interpreting, and governing behavior that are jointly managed by two or more people" (Weick, 1979, p. 235).

An organization is not a place. It is created through social construction, and is not made of concrete and glass. Through communication, an organization's tasks are accomplished and its members create and recreate social relationships. Accordingly, organizational communication is "the collective and interactive process of generating and interpreting messages" (Stohl, 1995, p. 161). From a systemic viewpoint, it is "the process of creating and exchanging messages within a network of interdependent relationships to cope with environmental uncertainty" (Goldhaber, 1993, pp. 14–15).

In a newspaper organization, communication is the process through which:

- News is gathered.
- Information is developed into stories.
- Stories are edited.
- Citizens are contacted and enrolled as subscribers.
- Photographs are selected and arranged on pages.
- Internal functions, such as accounting and advertising, are coordinated.
- Stakeholder opinions, both inside and outside the organization, are sought and used.

In short, a newspaper is an interaction-intensive organization. While communication creates and maintains the structure, functions, and culture of all organizations, in a newspaper, communication is the intended purpose of the organization's products. In order to understand the process of change as it is experienced by newspapers, it is first important to understand how newspapers have evolved as organizations. For contemporary newspapers are the products of both societal and organizational change.

THE EVOLUTION OF NEWSPAPERS AS ORGANIZATIONS

Newspaper organizations comprise an industry that began very simply, as is the case with other American industries whose development precedes the Industrial Revolution. In this society, the dairy industry began with a cow and a cart. The postal service was a man and a horse. Newspaper organizations consisted of a person and a printing press.

Such pre-modern organizations, as well as the family farm and the "mom and pop" store, have simple structures, informal reporting relationships and small social networks (Bergquist, 1993). Leadership is paternalistic—sometimes literally—as when children work in the family business. Communication is oral and face-to-face, and one's labor is rewarded with food and shelter, or the money to afford items that fulfill basic needs.

Newspapers, and shorter versions of them such as bulletins and broadsides, were only one product of printers before the New World was settled. Moreover, printing sometimes was only one component of a printer's business, which might include a coffee house, book store, or pharmacy (Ward, 1997, p. 35). In the American colonies, money was not, and could not be, a motivating factor for starting a newspaper business, for its success was uncertain. Government printing contracts helped finance attempts to publish news of the community. After the Revolutionary War, new demands for public expression, and for discussion of events and issues, fostered organizations whose primary product became the newspaper. However, subsidies to newspapers from political candidates or their backers continued into the mid-1800s. Printing contracts and extra jobs as postmasters helped editors support themselves and their businesses. Most of these individuals worked alone, perhaps employing a young apprentice, publishing news heard on the street. Over time these individuals also relied on stories from those venturing into the uncharted territories adjacent to populated areas—the first correspondents.

In the early 1830s, the penny press developed. Selling papers on the street to an increasingly urban population began to change the newspaper as an organization dramatically. Owner–editors in New York City began hiring reporters, and the increasing commerce in the young nation's developing cities and towns fostered the use of newspapers as avenues of advertising.

James Gordon Bennett of the *New York Herald* saw advertising as a necessary means for financing the news-gathering process and for serving as a channel of information about goods and services available in growing local and regional economies.

As Americans moved from their rural roots to urban centers, growth in commerce followed their migration. Advances in science and technology increased the means of production and distribution of goods. Shops became factories. Family businesses became companies. The printer and his press became a newspaper office, with reporters, an editor, and employees who separately handled circulation, accounting, and advertising. By the mid-1890s, Joseph Pulitzer's *New York World* and other metropolitan dailies were dividing newspaper organizations into functional units by hiring specialists in advertising, business, circulation, and sales (Ward, 1997, p. 265). Although the processes of gathering, arranging, and selling information were becoming sufficiently complex to warrant the creation of specialized units within larger newspaper organizations, competition for readership also was a factor. William Randolph Hearst, for instance, in his zeal to acquire readers, created a sports department with experts as writers. His worthy competitor, Pulitzer, hired the first editor of a sports department (Ward, 1997, p. 292). The newspaper as a modern organization was emerging.

Perspectives on organizations develop out of the historical contexts in which scholars live and work. Taylor (1911) studied coal shoveling at Bethlehem Steel to forge his principles of scientific management. Henri Fayol, a French industrialist, used his personal observations to develop elements and theories of management. Weber (1947), a German sociologist, was concerned about the need for his country to build a strong economy after World War I. He suggested the efficiency of bureacratization in organizations, emphasizing the importance of rules and procedures, hierarchical authority, and formal communication. In the United States, more and bigger factories, with large and complex structures, multiple functional units, organizational charts depicting reporting relationships, and the exercise of management as a science, emerged as the prototypes of the 20th century organization.

Large and growing urban areas fostered the development of newspaper organizations with multiple functional units, in addition to news reporting. Large city publishers learned about big company structures from their colleagues in other industries, and the newspaper organization began to resemble other companies that manufactured and advertised a product. Just as other corporate magnates recognized the potential (and actual) profitability of owning multiple geographically dispersed organizations, Hearst created an empire of large-city newspapers during the late 1880s.

Newspapers as modern organizations developed chains by joining a series of multi-hierarchical entities together. Today, four out of every five daily newspapers in the United States are owned by chains (Vivian, 1995, p. 85).

They also dominate ownership of weeklies. Because of newspaper profitability in the 1970s and 1980s, chains feverishly bid for and bought locally owned newspapers, particularly in communities with only one newspaper and therefore no competition (Vivian, 1995, p. 86). Chains also have purchased numerous family-owned newspaper organizations because the federal inheritance tax has made passing the business to the next generation a tax headache and economic nightmare.

As new forms of media developed in the 20th century, chains bought radio and television stations: Formal, hierarchical media structures that had developed as modern organizations in the newspaper mold. Conglomerates were created as large groups of organizations. The Gannett Corporation, for instance, consisted of six New York state newspapers in 1906, and grew to 90 medium-sized dailies by 1982. It then began to bid on large metropolitan papers in the mid-1980s, having started *USA TODAY* as a national newspaper. Gannett then acquired a company comprised of 20 broadcasting stations. As of 1995, the media conglomerate owned over 80 daily newspapers, 39 weeklies, 16 radio and 8 television stations, the largest billboard company in the nation, and the Louis Harris polling organization (Vivan, 1995, p. 86). Large metropolitan papers, as well as media conglomerates, have bureaus in other countries. The effects and pressures of a global society, therefore, affect the operations of some newspaper organizations.

Of course, not all newspapers reside in large metropolitan areas. Weekly community publications and special interest newspapers have evolved to meet specific readership needs and interests. Their structures and operations tend to be more representative of pre-modern organizations than traditional–modern organizations, making them more adaptive to changing customer interests.

As we enter a new century, indeed a new millenium, new technologies and a globalized economy are creating new forms of organizations, including team-based, networked, knowledge-based entities, or new components of traditional organizations. Small, innovative software companies, computer organizations, as well as advertising and multi-media businesses, are potentially post-modern organizations. They generally reflect decentralized power, flattened hierarchies, cultures built on trust, and the treatment of employees as their most important resources (Eisenberg & Goodall, 1993). Such organizations have flexible structures, fuzzy boundaries, transformational (change-oriented) leadership, mediated communication (e.g. voice mail, e-mail, and videoconferencing), and a focus on both intrinsic and extrinsic rewards for employees (Bergquist, 1993). Most contemporary newspaper organizations, especially the national, regional, and large city dailies, operate as traditional, modern, pyramidal organizations. There are, however, some elements of these organizations that may be post-modern, such as the advent of online editions in some traditional newspaper organizations.

Post-modern organizations operate in a constant whirlwind of change regarded as natural and expected by organizational leaders and members. While pre-modern organizations may have depended on the great man as leader, post-modern organizations thrive on diffused, distributed, emergent leadership—throughout all levels and functional units. Whereas management is a form of social control, post-modern leaders focus on social support, on collaborating and creating community through communication. Long-term visions and short-term plans are developed through interaction that flows vertically and horizontally. As Bergquist (1993) wrote: "Conversations tend to bind people together; talk is the glue in most organizations" (p. 136). As we shall see later in this chapter, knowledge-based organizations are forms of post-modern entities, and share many of their characteristics.

As is the case with organizations in other industries, inventions and events during the last 150 years have contributed to the rapid development of newspapers as an important part of American culture. The telegraph, the telephone, computers, and satellites, as well as fast modes of transportation such as the airplane, have led to the rapid transmission of information. Moreover, reporters have been witnesses to events that have provided thousands of pages of copy, including the Civil War, the Spanish-American War, the world wars, the Great Depression, nationally known crimes such as the Lindbergh baby kidnapping, not to mention presidential elections, assassinations, and fascination with entertainment and sports figures. Advertising and circulation departments have emerged, as has the business office. Copy editors and individuals in charge of the physical production of the newspaper became part of an increasingly complex process and an organization with multiple functions. Complexity was further increased when many organizations produced two editions a day, as well as advertising supplements. They also expanded into new media, such as radio and television broadcasting, cable programming, and most recently, online editions of their news products. The newspaper organization has grown from a pre-modern organization into a complex system, a network of interrelated components, affected by multiple environmental influences.

Family-owned newspapers in this country began as pre-modern organizations and some are now multi-hierarchical corporations. Like many other American businesses in the late 1800s and early 1900s, they were passed from fathers to sons (or sons-in-law). Several have stayed in the same family for several generations. According to D. Cole (1999): ". . . some of the greatest U.S. newspapers at the close of the 20th century are controlled by the families that have controlled them for generations. The companies that really care about excellence seem to be family-controlled" (online). However, the days of family-owned newspapers may be coming to an end, because of the increasing number of take-overs of papers by conglomerates, and the federal inheritance tax—a tax levied on the estate of deceased family members before assets can be transferred to their children.

In some respects, the history of the development of newspaper organizations in this country compares easily to the development of department stores and hotel chains. Many, if not most, of them have been managed in similar ways. However, newspaper organizations are also similar to computer and software companies, advertising firms, and offices of management consultants: They are knowledge-based organizations, peopled with knowledge workers, and perhaps are best managed as post-modern organizations. However, newspapers also are creatures of their histories, and have developed structures that do not fit or foster their functions. Despite their depictions on organizational charts as groups of boxes, newspapers are systems and networks, and it is important to consider them as such if we are to understand them as knowledge organizations facing a variety of changes now and in the future.

NEWSPAPERS AS SYSTEMS

As is the case with other organizations, the primary task of a newspaper organization requires interaction among its components and communication with its environment. Indeed, its survival depends on the ability to gather and organize information of interest to its audiences. The newspaper organization is a system that depends on information from its environment, in order to organize and present that information to others—as news stories, advertisements, television logs, weather information, stock market quotes, etc.

As a system, the newspaper is comprised of components, or departments, such as news–editorial, sports, advertising, and circulation. Large metropolitan dailies, and national newspapers, such as the *Wall Street Journal* and *USA TODAY,* are even more complex because of their multiple audiences and their international offices. These offices interact to keep the system working—selling ads to pay for newspace; writing editorials and stories to maintain subscriber interest, showing circulation figures to advertisers so they will place ads to sell products, etc. As the organizational components communicate, new information continually flows into the organization from its environment: Letters to the editor, comments to reporters about their stories, and advertisers' assessments of the placement or success of their ads. In the following paragraphs, we look more closely at the components and properties of organizations as systems, using a newspaper as an example.

• Systems are hierarchically-ordered. They are embedded within larger systems and consist of subsystems. The heart, for example, is a working system, embedded within a circulatory system, which is embedded in the human body—another system. A news staff is a subsystem, embedded in a newspaper organization, which may be part of a chain of newspapers in a multiple-media conglomerate.

• The components within systems are interdependent. The heart depends on oxygen provided by the power of a pair of lungs. The lungs depend on blood flow, pumped by the heart, to work at their capacity. Reporters depend on copy editors, and both depend on the advertising department to sell enough ads to keep the paper in business. They all depend on the production staff to produce the pages on which stories and ads are found. Without reporters, the production staff would have nothing but ads to put into print.

• The walls of an organization are permeable—one cannot isolate interaction or communication, or keep it out of a system. Water and nutrients, for instance, enter the body and maintain its equilibrium, or sustain its growth. Information is brought into newspapers by reporters, editors, the publisher, readers and advertisers, and these same individuals talk about the paper—its stories, problems, and strengths in conversations with people outside the system.

• Systems depend on feedback for maintenance, growth, or both. An increased temperature in a biological system may signal illness, and the need for aspirin to eliminate the fever and regulate the system's temperature. A teen-ager's continual interest in food and sleep may signal the need for more nutrients and rest because the biological system is growing and developing. If the front page of a newspaper carries news stories for several days that focus on crimes and criminals, letters to the editor from disgruntled readers serve as feedback to remind the news staff that news can be positive as well as negative.

• A system is more than the sum of its parts. Pat Witherspoon is more than a set of biological subsystems. She also encompasses experience, expertise, values, beliefs, and attitudes, and the perceptions others have of her. *The New York Times* is more than a collection of departments. It is also "all the news that's fit to print," a well-respected paper throughout the country and well-known in many countries throughout the world. It is a reputation as well as a compilation of ink and paper.

• A system has the ability to avoid decline because it is open to its environment for resources and sustenance. Entropy is the deterioration found in closed systems. A human body succumbs to a deadly disease if left on its own to recover. Medication injected or ingested may stop the deterioration and begin a healing process. Newspapers need new reporters to replace retiring ones, or the newsgathering process stops. A daily's media sales representatives must replace advertisers who choose to buy television airtime instead of space to market their products, or the newspaper shrinks in size and begins to lose important advertising dollars.

• An organization as a system receives inputs from its environment, and through its internal processes creates outputs that are sent back into the environment. For instance, potatoes arrive in railcars from Idaho at a snack food operations plant. Sacked potato chips leave the same plant in trucks bound for supermarkets. Coal ore travels to a manufacturing plant in Pennsylvania, and steel plates or sheets are produced through specialized processes. They are shipped to buyers around the world. Newsprint arrives in the production department and becomes newspapers that are loaded on trucks. A reporter interviews a political candidate on Tuesday, and a news story appears in a Wednesday morning edition, sharing the candidate's comments with the paper's readers.

• Because of its interdependence, a system can attain a goal through "a variety of paths" (Katz & Kahn, 1966, p. 30). A well-cared-for body can live to be 75 years old by eating healthy foods, exercising, driving carefully, having regular medical check-ups, or a combination of these actions. Completing a series of investigative reports about elder abuse in nursing homes can occur because of the commitment of time and money to an investigative reporter, a publisher's support of stories at the expense of advertising revenue from nursing homes, reporter access to patients through sympathetic nurses, or all of the aforementioned.

• A system must maintain sufficient internal complexity in order to cope with the complexity of its environment. An individual must develop mechanisms to cope with the physical manifestations of stress if he or she is in a high-stress occupation, such as air traffic control or politics. Large metropolitan newspapers grew in organizational complexity as their readership grew in size and diversity. Beat reporters were hired to cover different areas of the community—for example, police, the courts, the city council, sports, public schools—as that community grew into multiple sources of information.

• Elements or components of a system, as well as environmental influences, affect the work of that system, and at times may prompt organizational change.

In addition to functional units, other components of an organization include the following:

Task

While this term refers to the general purpose of an organization, such as printing and selling newspapers, it also refers to specific tasks conducted by the workforce to achieve the organization's general purpose. The need to deliver the morning editions, write the weather summary, sell advertising space, and select letters to the editor for publication, are also organizational tasks. Each has time and resource constraints, and is an influence on the organization as a system.

Structure

The structure of newspapers as organizations may be simple or complex, depending on the paper's size and purpose. It consists of policies and procedures, as well as organizational charts, and the style handbook. Many newspapers, like other organizations, have multi-hierarchical, pyramidal structures. Others are flatter operations that are team- or group-based. In addition to formal structure, organizations also have informal, emergent structures that handle different forms, and degrees, of complexity. Organizational structure affects task-related and social communication within the organization, as well as processes of decision making.

Resources

Organizations are greatly affected by the degree to which they have sufficient people, money, and materials with which to accomplish organizational tasks. Newsprint is an important resource for newspapers, as are computers, desks, and telephones. In a newsroom, the most important resource, however, are the journalists—those who develop stories using the information they obtain from the environment. A system is in continual need of resources for both maintenance and growth, and news organizations depend on a variety of sources for information and the materials needed to accomplish organizational tasks.

Components of Culture

This chapter is written with the belief that an organization is a culture. It is a composite of values, beliefs, norms, history, heroes, stories, and ceremonies, to name just a few cultural elements. Together, and individually, the components of culture are parts of a newspaper as a system. The history of the *Wall Street Journal,* the heroes at the *Washington Post,* and the values at the *Christian Science Monitor* are components that interact with other influences within these newspaper organizations to affect system functioning. Climate, or the quality of the internal organizational environment that "is experienced by organizational members and that influences their behaviors" (Tagiuri, 1968, p. 27) is also an important element of organizational culture. It is conceptualized as being either supportive or defensive, depending on the positive or negative perceptions held by the people it affects. A positive climate in a newspaper organization may be the result of: well-defined job descriptions; journalistic autonomy among reporters; an editor that supports his staff and fosters their participation in decision making; managerial concern about employee needs; and free-flowing information and open communication across functional units and hierarchical levels.

Environmental influences also affect the work of a newspaper system. These influences include the following:

Environmental Turbulence or Stability. The degree to which a newspaper operates in a stable economic environment may affect how effectively and efficiently it functions. When a daily loses advertising dollars to another medium at the same time that the cost of newsprint is increasing and it has just been bought by a regional chain, its environment is relatively turbulent. When a small-town weekly has the same editor for 25 years, a dependable advertising base, and static operational costs, it benefits from a stable environment. It may not grow, but its present functioning will not be adversely affected.

Socioeconomic–Political Influences. Newspapers may be affected by the economy of the region they serve, the demographics of their readers, the sizes of the cities they serve, and the political leanings of their editors and publishers. Indeed, newspapers face myriad environmental influences that are rooted in economic and political forces. As a result, those who lead newspaper organizations must be visionaries to the extent they are willing to prepare for environmental changes that may affect the contemporary and future life of the organization.

As we have discussed, the concept of a system is one organizational metaphor appropriate in the study of newspapers, which depends on communication among internal components and with external constituencies to accomplish its multiple tasks and goals. It is constructed and continued through "interacting individuals pursuing multiple objectives through coordinated acts and relationships" (Stohl, 1995, p. 23). This interaction depends on communication between and among individuals, who are in contact with each other on a continuing basis in the conduct of their work. Such contacts are links that comprise the social networks, another apropos metaphor, through which organizational activity emerges and is sustained.

NEWSPAPERS AS NETWORKS

Organizations do not really conduct their work in accordance with the boxes on an organizational chart, as the traditional or classical theorists would suggest. The people who comprise organizations initiate and complete tasks through short conversations and long meetings; formal memoranda and voice mail messages; computer-edited proposals; and suggestions over coffee, with a variety of organizational members. Even those individuals who work in production lines engage in quality control meetings, and informal, work-related conversations. Newspapers, like other organizations, are comprised of patterns of interactions among and between individuals and groups. The notion of networks helps us understand that organizations are webs of "*affiliations* . . . woven through the collaborative threads of communication" (Stohl, 1995, p. 18). In contemporary organizations, and certainly in newspapers, the conduct of work depends on communicative relationships. Just as a television network is comprised of linked stations, organizations are comprised of interconnected individuals whose work and social relationships are created and recreated through communication. In the following paragraphs, we discuss several properties or characteristics of networks, and provide examples of how newspapers illustrate them.

• Some networks are created and operated formally, in accordance with policies, procedures, organizational charts, or all of the aforementioned. Deans in most universities, for instance, meet regularly through some type of council, often headed by the institution's provost or president, to discuss issues of mutual interest and develop solutions to common problems. Heads of a newspaper's departments meet with the editor regularly to consider new policy and collaborate on setting the organization's revenue goals.

• Informal networks emerge in organizations in response to need, not structure. Two deans may talk over lunch about a possible joint-degree program because of student demands for interdisciplinary work involving their colleges. The heads of circulation and advertising at a weekly newspaper may meet over coffee to discuss their concerns about the increased allocation of funds to the newsroom.

• Organizational boundaries are permeable—they are open to the environment and allow information to flow in and out of the organization. There is no "iron curtain" around organizations: Communication cannot be contained within them. Reporters pick up information in places other than news briefings. Indeed, the *Washington Post's* Bob Woodward and Carl Bernstein broke the story about the Nixon White House's involvement in the Watergate break-in by interviewing sources outside established channels of information in the White House.

• The fundamental unit of a network is a link or a communicative relationship between two people. Our primary network at work may be with the three or four people in our work group. Our interactions are frequent and sustained with each of these individuals. The primary network for the editor of a weekly community paper may be comprised of two reporters, a business manager, and herself.

Individual networks are the bases of group, organizational, and inter-organizational networks. Consider the White House bureau correspondents for a major newspaper chain. They collaborate daily to cover the president. As a group they may interact frequently with their newpapers' reporters covering Congress, perhaps to work on related stories. The two groups may talk regularly with their counterparts at another newspaper in the same chain. An interorganizational network is created when representatives of two or more chains, such as Hearst and Knight-Ridder, interact to propose a renovation of White House press space. A junior White House correspondent may establish regular communication with her senior counterpart when first arriving in Washington. Gradually, however, her network expands to other White House correspondents, Washington reporters and continually widening patterns of interaction with members of other media, governmental officials, and a variety of individuals outside her own organization.

• People in the networks we create assume one or more roles in these networks. At times we may be gatekeepers, controlling the flow of information to other individuals, or liaisons, connecting two or more groups in the same system, or bridges, serving as a link between two different systems. Some individuals are isolates: They do not have many connections in a network. They do not communicate much with anyone. An assistant to a newspaper publisher, for instance, may act as a gatekeeper, controlling others' access to her boss, and may decide what daily mail the publisher will see. The circulation manager may serve as a network liaison between the head of subscriptions and the head of newspaper delivery; they each have very different connections in the same system. The editor of a small town daily may be a member of the state daily newspaper association, and serve as a bridge from his newspaper to the professional association.

A network role that all organizational members generally assume, to varying degrees, is that of boundary spanner. We are links from our families to our church network, or from our place of work to a charitable organization we serve. The editor of a paper serves as a boundary spanner when sitting on a bank's board of directors, coaching a Little League team, or teaching a journalism class during the summer.

• Networks have different sizes and degrees of interconnectedness. One family network may be comprised of four people—the people who create and share a home. Another family network may equal 25—people in one house may visit with grandparents, aunts, uncles, and cousins on a regular and frequent basis. The editorial staff in a medium-sized daily may total 10 people, and they may communicate much of every day. The same type of staff in a national newspaper may have a network size of 25—and meet in two separate groups each day. Strong ties are characteristic of highly interconnected networks. Project teams in organizations, for instance, may work for several years together, communicating side-by-side on a daily basis. If one of these individuals takes another job, that departure has a major impact on the group.

• The degree to which an individual continually and frequently communicates with others in the same network is a function of their centrality in the network. A managing editor is central in the news staff network. The publisher may be important, but not central, among the links in that network. Those who hold positions of centrality in networks tend to possess power and control within it. They are the primary receivers of information, the focal points of communication, and therefore they hold positions of power.

Newspapers, like other organizations, are systems of interconnecting parts and networks of interacting links. However, they are also organizations where information is not only raw material—it is also their primary product. Newspapers are creators and carriers of information, disseminators of knowledge. Operating from that premise, we suggest that newspapers are knowledge-based organizations. As such, the operation of these organizations, and the changes they face, must be led with different assumptions and values than may have guided them in the past.

THE NOTION OF KNOWLEDGE ORGANIZATIONS

Printing stories from the street did not create knowledge organizations in the 1600s, when the evolution of modern-day newspapers began. In contemporary society there may be printed products, such as gossip-based tabloids, that transmit words having little or nothing to do with knowledge. However, the daily and weekly metropolitan, community, regional, and national newspapers who spend considerable resources on gathering, interpreting, and using information may be considered knowledge organizations.

While there are differences of opinion about what knowledge is, consider the following definition: "*Knowledge is information laden with experience, truth, judgment, intuition, and values; a unique combination that allows individuals and organizations to assess new situations and manage change*" (Huseman & Goodman, 1999, p. 107). Knowledge is not simply information. Davenport and Prusak (1998) identified processes for generating knowledge from information, which clarify the differences between them:

- Making comparisons. Knowledge workers compare information from one situation with information obtained in other situations.

- Assessing consequences. Knowledge workers evaluate the implications that information may have for certain decisions and actions.

- Seeing connections. Knowledge workers consider how bits of knowledge relate to other bits of knowledge.

- Engaging in conversations. Knowledge workers discuss information with others to obtain their opinions and perspectives about it (p. 6).

In January 1998, the Annenberg Center for Communication at the University of Southern California released findings of a study on the emergence of knowledge organizations, and perceptions of what they are and do (Huseman & Goodman, 1999).

The emerging discipline of knowledge management has generated differing opinions about what a knowledge organization is. Several sources, however, agree that a knowledge organization focuses on continuous learning, knowledge sharing across levels and functions, and the importance of personal and professional development opportunities for people in these organizations.

Huseman and Goodman (1999) reported the following comments from respondents in their study concerning what a knowledge organization is:

- "An organization that learns from mistakes. Risk-taking is acceptable, and open communication and analysis is encouraged . . ." (p. 136).

- "An organization that is always searching for improved ways of disseminating and applying knowledge" (p. 136).

- "Empowering the individual with professional and personal development and providing them with the tools in order to do that" (p. 138).

- "In a knowledge organization, there are a variety of ways to get information. There is persistent and consistent learning throughout one's career. Learning occurs on the job" (p. 138).

Drucker (1999) emphasized that knowledge organizations are particularly adept at scanning and retrieving information from outside their own boundaries. Their network walls are not only permeable, but inviting. Knowledge organizations value the search and use of information in the knowledge-creation process, and their most important resources are the people who possess knowledge and the ability to create more of it through analysis and interaction. Moreover, sharing knowlege with others, personally and professionally, is a primary value among organizational members. We further define knowledge organizations by suggesting they:

- Act as systems of integrated social networks

- Facilitate information flow and communication both laterally and vertically
- Focus on recruitment and retention of organizational members
- Have innovative reward systems
- Invest in the personal and professional development of organizational members
- Focus on continuous learning
- Focus on bringing information into the organization, as well as working with the information they already possess
- Emphasize knowledge and power distribution, through decentralized decision making and problem solving
- Value both the quality and the quantity of organizational output.

Knowledge organizations, forms of post-modern organizations, are very different creatures than their classical–traditional ancestors. In part, they reflect the following organizational trends that have emerged during the last 40 years (Witherspoon, 1997):

- Decreased numbers of hierarchical levels. This change has been a reaction both to financial pressures and to the introduction of new technologies as instruments of information acquisition, analysis, and dissemination. The results of this change have been more fluid communication between and among organizational levels, and more timely problem solving and decision making. Networked computers in newsrooms, for instance, have changed the hierarchical relationships between reporters and copy editors.
- Emphasis on the creation and use of work groups–teams. This trend has initiated a new way of working in many organizations. While teams are often found in newer industries such as the computer industry, work groups increasingly are being used in hospitals for patient care, in schools as teachers integrate learning activities, and in automobile factories where cars are created by teams, not assembly lines. As we shall discuss later in the book, some newspapers also are now developing stories through news teams.
- Decentralization of decision making. Fewer hierarchical levels and increased use of communication technologies have given organizational members the opportunities to make decisions where knowledge about key organizational problems and issues reside in the organizational members who daily deal with those problems and issues.
- Variable organizational rewards. Knowledge organizations are particularly appropriate for the use of intrinsic, and well as extrinsic, rewards. Flexible work schedules, opportunities for advancement, sabbaticals for new product development, and designated new challenges are valuable rewards

among workers who toil in the vineyard of knowledge creation and dissemination.

• Use of new communication technologies. Knowledge workers need tools to facilitate their access to information, analyze that information, develop it into packages of knowledge, and disseminate those packages quickly to others. Group-decision support systems, teleconferencing, and intranet systems created within organizations are all ways that new technologies now facilitate work in the knowledge organization. Computers in newspaper organizations have changed multiple components of the news production process—from news writing to copy editing to page layout.

• Extensions of organizational boundaries. Mergers, acquisitions, new communication technologies, and the growth of global organizations are only a few of the reasons it is becoming increasingly difficult to determine where an organization's boundaries end and its environment begins. Where are the boundaries of the *New York Times* when it partners with a polling agency to survey political attitudes among members of the electorate? Certainly they are extended beyond the paper's subscribers. Additionally, an organization's interaction with its environment is not only through the work of its boundary-spanning individuals and groups, but through continual contact with the community in which it resides, indeed sometimes by its very presence in the community. Knowledge organizations understand the key roles that information flow and communication play in the ongoing interaction between an organization and its environment.

The legacy of these trends is an increased availability of opportunity and choice for individuals who comprise knowledge organizations. Such individuals are the most important resource in their organizations, and deserve to be treated as such in the conduct of their daily work. More specifically, these individuals are valuable because they:

• Are highly skilled, motivated, and intelligent

• Value autonomy in their work

• Are interested in the sustainability of their work, not necessarily the longevity of their presence in the same workplace

• Share some common values with each other because of their education levels

• Are concerned about boredom at work

• Value communication in general, and feedback in particular

• Regard trust as an important organizational value

• Are capable of self-leadership

• Are assets, not costs, to their organizations.

As is the case with other knowledge workers, journalists add value to the information they bring into the newsroom, in the form of experience, expertise, analytical ability, historical context, and intuition. However, they are knowledge workers in varying degrees, perhaps because their places of work are knowledge organizations in varying degrees. Indeed, Huseman and Goodman (1999) stated that, based on both subjective and objective measures related to company atmosphere, attitudes, systems, and required training, the majority of respondent companies in their study (57%) are "far from being true knowledge organizations" (p. 150).

Accordingly, the purpose of this chapter is to suggest that newspapers are a form of knowledge organizations, and that journalists are unique knowledge workers. As an industry, the written press may not be comprised of knowledge organizations to the extent software developers are. Moreover, the degree to which different print media are knowledge organizations may vary. *The Wall Street Journal* and the *Washington Post,* for instance, are knowledge organizations. The tabloids, whose sensationalism is a value antithetical to the development of knowledge, are not. Considering newspapers as knowledge organizations is important not only to understand their operations now, but to consider how they may approach the process of change in the future, which is the focus of chapter 3. As we begin the new millenium, we must conceptualize the premises and processes facing newspapers as they conduct their work in new and different ways.

NEWSPAPERS AS KNOWLEDGE ORGANIZATIONS

What are the characteristics of contemporary newspapers that reflect their evolution as knowledge organizations? A few observations about them, and those who work within them, follow:

• Increasingly, newspapers of varying size and circulation are providing internships to college students as initial steps toward recruiting highly qualified employees from university departments of journalism and communication. The interns typically work in a variety of departments, including news–editorial, sports, circulation, and sales. These newspapers understand the importance of recruitment in knowledge organizations.

• A growing number of newspapers are changing organizational structures, increasing the use of journalistic teams, and developing integrated department structures to address problems of concern to multiple functional units—the Total Newsroom Concept (Willis, 1988, p. 10).

• Newspapers tend to value "competent, highly skilled journalists who understand the history, context, and significance of stories as well as their probable interest among readers" (Willis, 1988, p. 9). These values are in concert with those characteristic of other forms of knowledge organizations.

- Newspapers are developing new packages of information—not just a daily or weekly newspaper—but online editions, Web sites with late-breaking news, and reference services—in an attempt to serve the individual informational needs of customers.

- Many newspapers attempt to develop reporting specialists, whose experience and expertise enhance attempts at infomation gathering and analysis, in order to develop higher quality knowledge products.

Newspapers increasingly are hiring knowledge workers to fulfill organizational missions, and not all are reporters or even in the news–editorial area of operation. The following are several findings about journalists, based in part on research conducted and published by Weaver and Wilhoit (1991):

- The advent, and promulgation, of specialists since the 1830s have fostered a belief that some journalists are informational experts, an evolutionary trend in knowledge organizations.

- Muckraking journalists at the turn of the 19th century, and investigative reporters in present-day America, are guided by values, such as truth, integrity, and careful reporting—values that reflect those of knowledge organizations.

- Some newspapers attempt to provide continuing education (continuous learning) that fit knowledge workers' expectations and professional goals. Newspapers sponsor workshops and seminars for practicing, and future, employees.

- Organizational members in a newspaper have higher education levels than their counterparts 20 or more years ago.

- American journalists value autonomy in their workplace, as do other knowledge workers.

- Journalists receive reactions from their audiences regularly—feedback used to improve future work.

- The work of journalists is pluralistic. They interpret as well as disseminate information—which means they add intellectual value to a product, unlike the town printer two centuries ago.

- Journalists have standards governing their work. These relate to their identification and use of sources of information, and ethics related to the use of information in general and in specific stories.

- Journalism is an intellectual occupation, requiring research and analytical skills. It "has many more standards of work, duty, and ethics" than it possessed 100 years ago (Weaver & Wilhoit, 1991, p. 218).

Contemporary theories of organization, those evolving within the last 15–20 years, generally have not been applied to newspaper organizations. Media management texts tend to focus on the classical, human relations, human resources, or both approaches to organizational behavior—eschewing mention of communication-based notions of organizations as systems and networks. This chapter emphasizes the newer conceptualizations of organizations—and even suggests that newspapers are, or are becoming, knowledge organizations. They are peopled by journalists and other organizational members who are increasingly knowledge workers, as discussed in the growing body of literature on knowlege management in a post-modern, information society. Continual, and large-scale, change is characteristic of such a society and its knowledge-based organizations. It is therefore appropriate that we now focus on the process of organizational change in general, and change in newspaper organizations in particular.

CHAPTER THREE

The Process of Organizational Change

Perhaps the most significant innovation during the last millenium is the printing press, which changed forever humankind's religious, political, and educational institutions because it made information available to many people, not just the rich.

In the last 150 years, the telegraph, telephone, and computer have prompted transformational change in the newspaper industry, specifically in the collection of information and the creation of the news product. More importantly, these technologies have changed the way people work, and the task-focused relationships among them. Reporters may always get the news to some extent, but new technologies increasingly bring more information to them. As technologies have become more complex, so has the environment in which journalists and their colleagues work (urban areas with growing populations). New technologies continue to alter the practice of journalism, but so do mergers, acquisitions, and other economic and structural changes in these organizations. The organizational and economic structure of a newspaper has become more complex, developing a variety of roles, responsibilities, and relationships within the organization, and among its external constituencies.

This chapter focuses on organizational change in general, and what the process may teach us about the nature of change in newspaper organizations in particular.

THE NATURE OF ORGANIZATIONAL CHANGE

As we enter the 21st century, change swirls around our educational, political, economic, and religious institutions. It affects our for-profit and non-profit organizations, and is an integral part of people's lives, particularly those who work in organizations that depend on the acquisition, packaging, and distribution of information. Change is an ongoing phenomenon in all organizations, but knowledge-based ones are experiencing rapid and transformative innovations in their strategies and structures, demographics, and technologies. Before analyzing change in newspaper organizations, it is important to understand the process in general:

- What concepts guide change?
- What conditions and reasons initiate change?
- What strategies and activities guide and implement change?
- What characterizes resistance to change?
- What role does communication play in its enactment?

Concepts of Change

The notion of change implies motion, preferably forward movement—an advance, not a retreat. As Kanter et al. (1992) suggested, change in organizations is "ubiquitous and multidirectional" and successful change efforts depend on "grabbing hold of some aspect of the motion and steering it in a particular direction . . ." (p. 10). While the process of change is often described as a series of stages or phases, these parts of the process overlap continuously and sometimes repetitively. Change is processual. It should not be conceived of as distinct units of activity that follow each other in an orderly fashion. The following conceptualizations help characterize the phenomenon:

- Change is perceptual and behavioral. It is a way of thinking, and a set of behaviors to enact that thinking. A reporter may be concerned about his or her paper's purchase by a media conglomerate, and ponder a variety of potential changes that may affect his or her work. In reality, the merger may, or may not, require actual changes in reportage.

- Change affects individuals in the multiple roles they assume in their lives—as individuals with personal goals and interests; as members of organizations, work groups, or both; and as members of families responsible for the welfare of others. Human beings often react negatively to change because they sense a resultant loss of control over their routines, jobs, and lives. Conner (1993) suggested that organizational members move through the following series of stages when adapting to unwanted change, such as organizational layoffs. They are similar to those articulated by Elizabeth Kubler-Ross in her research on how individuals face their own deaths:

> Stability—the present state; the status quo

> Immobilization—initial reaction and shock related to the change

> Denial—ignoring new information that does not fit into one's old frame of reference

> Anger—frustration; lashing out at co-workers, friends, and family

> Bargaining—the beginning of acceptance, and the process of negotiating to avoid the impact of change

> Depression—resigning oneself to the fact that change has taken place

> Testing—exploring ways to reenter the organizational process

> Acceptance—becoming part of the new organizational context; the change may not be liked but it is accepted. (pp. 132–135)

The purchase of a family-owned newspaper by a media conglomerate may stimulate these stages, particularly if employees feel like part of the family and must lose that identity within a larger, more impersonal, organizational structure.

• Change is natural, as is death. It is the rule, not the exception. (Of course many of us feel like comedian Woody Allen, who once was quoted as saying that he did not fear death. He just did not want to be there when it happened!) Slow change, which does not characterize many contemporary organizations, seems easier to adjust to than rapid change, which we often equate with disruption.

• Change may be planned or unplanned. Planned change is deliberately shaped by those within an organization. Unplanned change is prompted by forces outside an organization, whose response is reactive rather than proactive.

• Change may be incremental or transformational. Incremental change constitutes minor improvements or adjustments in an organization. Transformational change alters the technical, political, and cultural systems within an organization. The technical system is comprised of the resources needed to accomplish tasks, such as information, technology, and money. The political system is the web of interrelationships that influences decisions and decision makers. The cultural system is the shared values and beliefs that guide the organization (Tichy & Ulrich, 1984).

• Change may originate in response to internal needs of an organization, influences, or both, in the environment that surrounds it. An organization is part of a network of connections within this environment. Competition from other organizations, expectations of external constituencies, and a host of sociopolitical, legal, and technological developments, are examples of environmental conditions that may prompt organizational change.

• Change efforts may be initiated by decision makers unilaterally, through delegation, or via collaborative activities with cross-functional–multi-hierarchical groups and teams. Organizational change efforts generally have not been studied over the long time span needed for them to be initiated and developed. However, theoretically, and in some cases empirically, the shared approach to change seems to work best among the three alternatives because one's participation may lower resistance to the process and increase commitment to it. Understanding this commitment is important to identifying how a change process may be initiated and sustained.

The Change Process: A Look at Stages and Phases

Modeling change has been of interest to academics and organizational practitioners as a way of graphically depicting the process, in order to explain it to others, and develop prescribed steps to achieve a successful process. One of the more famous models was described by Lewin in 1952. Essentially he described three stages in the process:

> *Unfreezing,* in which motivation is used to help organizational members unlearn existing behaviors (such as typing news stories on typewriters);
>
> *Changing,* through which new behaviors are developed through new information, a new perspective, or both (such as learning to create stories on video display or computer terminals); and
>
> *Refreezing,* in which new behaviors are integrated into organizational routines and institutionalized as organizational practices (reporters become used to creating stories on computers, and this technology becomes established as a reporter's tool). (Schein, 1989, pp. 209–212)

In 1977, Beckhard and Harris suggested that organizational change consists of an organization moving from a present state, through a transition state, to a future state. For instance, a failing newspaper is in a present state. The process of merging with a media organization is a transition state, and the operation of the newspaper under new ownership is the future state. As mentioned earlier, the demarcation lines between these states is often fuzzy. One must always be ready to ask if organizations ever really attain the future state, or are they continually in transition? Also, by the time they have reached the future state, has that stage of change become the present state?

Kimberly and Quinn (1984) identified the following phases of a change effort in their discussion of corporate transformation:

- A trigger event caused by environmental pressures occurs.

- This event causes a dominant group in the organization to feel the need for change.

- This need motivates the creation of a vision of a future state by one or more organizational leaders.

- Using the vision as a guide, commitment for the change is mobilized among organizational members.

- The envisioned change is institutionalized in the culture through organizational practices and policies.

The development of online editions of newspapers illustrates these phases within newspaper organizations. The development of the Internet was a trigger event that caught the attention of some newspaper publishers and editors, and caused them to consider the development of online versions of their papers. These decision makers then involved other staff to develop strategic and operational plans, and put these plans into action.

Trigger events initiate change, as do other reasons both within, and external to, organizations. Identifying reasons for organizational change assists in understanding how change efforts are conceptualized and implemented.

Reasons for Organizational Change

The magnitude of an organizational change varies in degree, and a variety of reasons may prompt the process. A few examples include the following:

- Rapid growth or a decline in growth
- A decline in productivity
- A decline in resources
- Stakeholder pressures on management (union strikes, high customer expectations, and publisher insistence on a specific profit margin)
- Environmental crises (wars), organizational crises (death of an organizational leader), or both
- Sociopolitical influences on the organization (unionization, governmental regulations)
- Environmental turbulence (e.g., constant competition in the software industry)
- Changes in customer expectations and behaviors.

Of course, a number of these reasons may also become the results of change. In newspaper organizations, as in most organizations, change is planned to varying degrees and with different degrees of success. How the effort is planned and executed therefore becomes critical to the process.

Change Strategies and Activities

Strategies are sets of behaviors developed for a purpose or series of purposes. In the process of developing change strategies, Nanus (1992) suggested that decision makers ask several questions to assist in strategy development.

- What major changes can be expected in the needs and wants of organizational stakeholders (employees, customers, management)?
- What changes can be expected in the major stakeholders of the organization (in customer demographics? In employee expectations?)?
- What major economic, social, political, and technological changes can be expected in the organization's environment? (pp. 78–91)

These questions help organizational leaders take stock of their organizations and the environments in which they reside, and plot courses to reach desired goals, visions, or destinations. The specific steps they take along this journey may include:

- Identification of tasks (e.g., listing activities, and an accompanying timeline, in a change plan)
- Creation of structures to manage the change effort (e.g., appointment of a change team, or a series of task forces)
- Development of strategies to establish the need for change among organizational members (e.g., town hall meetings, executive forums with employees in functional areas)
- Development of strategies to initiate the change effort among opinion leaders (e.g., executive retreats)
- Development of strategies to communicate information—on an ongoing basis—about the change effort (e.g., e-mail updates, online question–answer sessions)
- Creation, assignment, or both of human, fiscal, and material resources through which to conduct the change (e.g., budget allocations, reassignment of staff)
- Rewarding behaviors that accomplish tasks (e.g., cash bonuses, gift certificates)
- Motivating organizational members to participate in, support, or both change-related activities (e.g., extra vacation days for meeting deadlines)
- Continually evaluating progress, for example, timeline and task checks on a weekly or monthly basis. (adapted from Beckhard & Pritchard, 1992, pp. 69–70 and Witherspoon, 1997, p. 135)

Successfully implementing strategies and activities requires support of change initiatives throughout the organization. Earlier we discussed the concern, even fear, that is sometimes felt by individuals affected by change efforts. That concern is often manifested in negative attitudes and behaviors exhibited toward the process itself.

Resistance to Change

There is a range of resistance to change efforts in organizations. It may be passive, exhibited as a lack of interest and cooperation. It may be active, in the form of verbal protests and actual attempts to block change activities. Such resistance, whatever the manifestation of it, is due to perceived threats to power, perceived disruption of personal and professional security, perceived breaks in comfortable task and social relationships, and a general, perhaps nonspecific, fear of the unknown. Indeed, Lewis and Seibold (1998) identified several barriers to change after summarizing a number of studies related to change implementation. Such barriers include insufficient resources to accomplish the change; a lack of commitment within the organization to effect change; and a lack of adequate justification for the change. Bryant (1989) suggested that resistance to change can be reduced if a number of principles are followed:

- Key organizational members feel that the plan for change is their plan, not one created by outsiders.
- Participants see change as reducing, not increasing, current task burdens.
- The change effort depends on values and ideals that are part of the organization's culture.
- Participants feel their autonomy and security are not threatened.
- The change effort is adopted by consensus after discussions among organizational members. (pp. 194–195)

At least one key to preventing, or decreasing, resistance to change is for that change to be initiated and implemented by people throughout an organization. Human beings need to feel they own, and control, their own destinies—particularly in the organizations where they spend much of their lives. Many, if not most, organizational change initiatives are begun, and directed, by executives at the higher levels of organizations. Indeed, many, if not most, of the studies of organizational change are conducted at this level (in part because of the inability to gain access to employees working at lower organizational levels). One interesting study, however, looked at change implementation throughout 91 service organizations (Nutt, 1986). Four strategies were used in 93% of the cases studied. Change by persuasion (characterized by little management review and independence of experts) was the most used strategy, followed by implementation by edict (which avoided participation, and depended on personal power and control by change initiators). "The third most common tactic was 'intervention' (marked by problem-solving orientation, 'selling of the change,' and involving employees in the change process), and the least-used tactic was 'participation' (marked by high-level goal-setting, low-level decision making, and high user involvement)" (Lewis & Seibold, 1998, p. 104). The success rates of change efforts were highest with intervention, then participation, persuasion, and edict. In short, telling people to change was not the most successful way to get them to do it, but including them in the change process did result in successful outcomes.

This study is just one illustration of the crucial role that communication plays in the process of organizational change. Indeed, change efforts are communication processes. They begin with the necessity of articulating a vision, engendering support for the various change-related tasks, delegating responsibilities, persuading, arguing, and praising—in other words, interacting to accomplish the task-related goals of the organization, and the personal and professional goals of its members.

The Critical Role of Communication in Organizational Change

Through interaction, organizational members identify the need for change, create a communal vision of what their organization should become, decide on ways of achieving change, and implement change strategies. Through language, symbolic action, and mediated communications, they create shared understandings of the need for change and how it should be implemented.

To this end, the notion of *framing* is integral to the process of organizational change. Framing is fundamentally a communication process—a series of rhetorical strategies through which frames of reference internal to individuals or organizations are manifested externally. Messages are given meaning by the context or frame in which they are communicated. Change agents, whether they are executives, middle managers, or members of teams in organizations with little hierarchy, use words and actions to establish a context for the change effort, create images and meanings that will focus attention on the need for change, and encourage participation in the strategies designed to achieve it. In this endeavor, they must remember that an organization consists of multiple, often conflicting, frames of reference.

To successfully initiate change, organizational members must see the need for it. This can be accomplished by the use of *reframing*, that is, using techniques that enable, or force, individuals to go beyond their existing frames of reference and establish new perspectives of organizational reality. As Bandler and Grinder (1982) observed: "The meaning that any event has depends upon the 'frame' in which we perceive it. When we change the frame we change the meaning. When the meaning changes the person's responses and behaviors also change" (p. 1). For instance, if newspaper employees have come to associate lay-offs with changes in editors, their conception of change may be negative. If new leadership also creates new opportunities for employee input in editorial and production decisions, the notion of change may be seen more positively.

There are several strategies through which communication frames, or reframes, the context for organizational change. They include:

• Using face-to-face communication among groups involved in conducting the process—there is no substitute for this form of human interaction, particularly in situations fraught with uncertainty and the resulting anxiety it causes, as in times of change.

• Using mediated communication, such as audioconferencing and videoconferencing, e-mail, newsletters, and brochures, to spread the word about the change process on an ongoing basis as well as to motivate interest and participation in the effort.

• Creating and disseminating multiple messages through multiple media, and the redundant use of both, from the beginning conceptualization of the need for change to the evaluation of change strategies and activities.

As is the case in a number of industries, newspaper organizations have become increasingly complex, due to changes in structure, technology, numbers, and types of products and functions. Information flow in organizations often becomes ineffective as it attempts to accommodate such complexity. As this complexity increases, so does the time it takes to process and disseminate information. If the information processing and distribution capabilities of the organization do not meet its needs during organizational change, uncertainty increases and the more uncertainty that exists the greater the need for information to explain, clarify, and reassure. Consequently, organizations, including those in the business of communication like newspapers, must use a variety of informal and formal communication channels among their internal constituencies to meet their informational needs. Computer-based information management systems also are of value in generating and disseminating data that is helpful in day-to-day, as well as long-term, change initiatives.

Organizational change, as a communication process, is facilitated or disrupted, by a variety of factors, in addition to messages and media. A review of the research and practitioner literatures devoted to organizational change implementation by Lewis and Seibold (1998) identified several categories of these factors.

Characteristics of Effective Change Agents. These authors summarized 16 studies of both internal and external change agents, spanning approximately 25 years. Characteristics of effective change agents, as identified in their review, include openness, responsiveness, innovativeness, trustworthiness, and sincerity. Additionally, these studies found that effective leaders had administrative abilities, relationship and leadership skills, and expertise. They were also comfortable with ambiguity and with themselves (pp. 106–107).

Elements Necessary for Successful Change Implementation. Summarizing eight studies during the 1980s and 1990s, Lewis and Seibold (1998) found that essential elements for change, as articulated in publications read by change implementors, included: the use of effective champions; the use of cross-functional teams; attention to education and training; and the proper allocation of resources needed to accomplish the change (p. 120).

Recommendations for Practitioners. Lewis and Seibold (1998) also reviewed 20 studies that focused on managerial involvement in change efforts, published during the last two decades. The following are a few of the more specific recommendations that emerged from this research:

- Set realistic goals
- Create a shared vision
- Get clear support of management
- Prepare and train users for new rules
- Anticipate needs of workers
- Communicate the status of the implementation
- Anticipate potential problems–effects
- Create interfunctional teams
- Develop reward programs
- Ensure the availability of resources
- Communicate face-to-face
- Communicate through immediate supervisors. (pp. 121–123)

Newspapers share many, if not most, of the characteristics common to all organizations. It is to their similarities and differences as loci of change that we now turn.

NEWSPAPERS AS SITES OF
ORGANIZATIONAL CHANGE

Newspapers, as is the case with other organizations, are affected by societal changes, including changes in demographics, lifestyle trends (e.g., single parent and dual career families), globalization of the economy, and the introduction of new technologies for use at home and work. All of these changes affect the information load on employees as well as the process of creating and disseminating the product. Newspapers also are knowledge-based organizations, focusing on creating packages of information in the form of written and online papers, and in some cases, information retrieval systems. The rate of change has increased dramatically in newspaper organizations during the last 100 years, because of the advent of new technologies, the increasing complexity of organizational structures, the urbanization of American society, and economic influences on the operation and content of newspapers. In order to adequately evaluate contemporary changes in newspapers, it is first instructive to consider newspaper change from an historical perspective, to understand how past and present experiences may be both similar to, and different from, each other.

Changes in Newspaper Organizations: An Historical Overview

Unlike products in for-profit organizations, the newspaper was not created as an instrument of economic gain. As Smith (1979) wrote, it "situated itself somewhere between the historian on one side and the diplomatic, financial and military courier on the other" (p. 7). Ironically, the first "news" papers, originating in Europe, published old accounts of occurrences, single stories called *relations* or *relaciouns,* and only the year might be mentioned (Smith, 1979, p. 9). They have become more temporal with the passage of time. Now dailies keep us up-to-date with knowledge about events of the world, the nation, and the city, every morning, and online editions and Web sites give us updates throughout the day.

The need for information to understand the world, and the need to use information to influence the world, were concurrent needs that prompted newsgathering. Centers of news exchange developed in the same cities as centers of trade (Smith, 1979, p. 18). The demand for news, and the advantages it yielded for those who possessed it, caused competing systems of newsgathering to develop. In the 18th century, struggling democracies depended on newspapers as agents of change, molders of opinion, and the political revolution in what became the United States was aided by the creation of a free press.

Smith wrote that the 1880s and 1890s were a golden age of journalism in the western world. In addition to their economic growth, newspapers attended to public service, to public needs. In Great Britain, he suggested: "The combined operations of a broad electorate, a free platform and a cheap newspaper were widely deemed to have created a perfect mechanism for the governance of society" (Smith, 1979, p. 143). In the United States, Smith (1979) observed, "the dynamics of the new popular journalism lay in the struggle between great city papers to be first with the news, in the pursuit of 'beats' and 'exclusives' to accompany the material provided by the cooperative news-gathering agencies" (p. 159). Moreover, the urban pace, coupled with competition, created a rapidity with which news was:

> sought, created and presented. The raw material of the modern newspaper had to be "hot," earthshaking; the world of the newspaperman seemed to consist of a succession of convulsive actions, autonomous, sudden, unanticipated, disconnected. The stunt and the crusade replaced the great liberal causes as the intellectual quest of journalism. (p. 159)

Such changes therefore affected the people, and the products, of newspaper organizations.

In the 20th century, technology brought about many of the changes faced by newspaper organizations, including offset printing and the computer. The interplay of new technologies and economic constraints and opportunities saw newspapers meet challenges of consolidations, the elimination of evening newspapers, the creation of national dailies, and the development of specialist papers, especially in the field of business. In the meantime:

> The journalistic practices worked out in Europe and American between 1865 and 1900 have been copied or exported throughout the world. It was evident to political groups in Africa, Asia, and South America that newspapers were an intrinsic element in waging social revolution or campaigning for changes in social structure . . . (Smith, 1979, p. 170)

Newspaper organizations struggle with a variety of countervailing influences. They are businesses, but they are also venues for discussion and debate. They are sources for news, and outlets for advertising. They are changing in appearance and reconstructing their methods of supply and distribution. The computer technology that now drives newspaper work continues to change journalists' perceptions of that work, the way they do it, and the way they relate to others in the news organization. The size and geographical scope of newspapers also differs dramatically within this society—contemporary newspaper organizations do not share the same degree of technological presence. Rate of change within newspaper organizations differs, as do reactions to that change. People in computer, electronics, and software companies are used to continual change, for competition's sake. Other individuals may not be as change oriented—they have not experienced the momentous and frequent change as have their colleagues in other industries. Additionally, as Smith (1979) wrote: "In the course of four hundred years the newspaper press has not finally dealt with the issues into which it was born. Its methods of production and distribution are always inadequate to the ideals and purposes which appear to rise from the activity of collecting news" (pp. 182–183). These are just a few of the reasons resistance to change emerges in newspaper organizations in the early 21st century, and why other components, processes, and strategies of change as they appear in newspapers are germane to their continuing development. While the following chapter focuses specifically on change in newspapers, the next section summarizes this discussion of organizational change by briefly reviewing some of the current conditions prompting future change in newspaper organizations.

The Contemporary Context for Change in Newspapers

Among the antecedents for change emerging in the newspaper industry are the ways it structures its work, develops products, engages new workers, introduces technology, and indeed, enacts its societal purpose or purposes. These antecedents are briefly discussed next.

Structure. Mergers and acquisitions are changing the structures of many newspaper organizations, for many of them are becoming parts of larger, more complex organizations, where those who wield organizational power are hierarchically distant from those who are affected by it. Such changes affect the politics of decision making, employee loyalty, and other aspects of organizational culture that may have characterized smaller, family-owned newspapers. Changes in structure affect multiple aspects of a newspaper, including its climate, its reporting of relationships among reporters, editors, and publishers, and its culture, including its core values, beliefs, and goals. Increasingly foreign investors also are becoming involved in U. S. media interests, and cultural differences such involvement entails also affect elements of organizational structure and culture.

New Products. A multi-page compilation of newsprint once was the only product of a newspaper organization. Now these organizations offer computer data banks of information, akin to the morgue where old newspapers gathered dust, waiting to be consulted as background for new stories. Advertising inserts, newspaper excerpts for classroom instruction, online editions, and web-based information sites, are some of the newer products of these organizations. These changes increase the need for new kinds of workers who complete tasks other than gathering and writing the news. As Lacy, Sohn and Wicks (1993) observed:

> Knight-Ridder, through such services as INFOCALL, has offered information delivery and retrieval systems for specialized customers who want to know about some 100 different categories covering the latest development on their favorite soap opera to stock prices. United Press International, a traditional news delivery system, has experimented with newspaper formats for airline commuters between New York and Washington, D. C. The search for audiences and markets is intense as electronic media explore print options and

traditional print organizations invest in cable and other nonprint delivery systems. (p. 65)

The products changing the potential customers for newspapers are related in great part to the technologies that have developed, and are developing, to revolutionize the newspaper industry.

New Technologies.   Computer technology in newspaper organizations now allows people to write, edit, typeset, crop pictures, and create ads. It also enables reporters to receive wire copy, information from the retrieval system once known as the morgue, and databases available through the Internet, subscription services, or both, and libraries. As these changes reveal, technology alters the nature of work in an organization, as well as the degree of control over the work process, and sometimes the worker, by the manager. Technology creates new markets, changes consumer use and behavior, and sometimes blurs market boundaries. For instance, as Lacy et al. (1993) recalled:

> During *USA TODAY*'s [italics added] first year or so of operation, analysts were trying to discern in which category it fell. Certainly it was printed on newsprint . . . but its splashy graphics, somewhat breezy writing style, and its advertising strategies reminded some of a magazine. In fact, some viewed it as a magazine in newspaper format and, thus, a competitor of magazines. (p. 321)

According to Ward (1997), lightweight flat panels, which gave us the laptop computer and then the Palm Pilot, "in combination with microprocessors, memory, and communication links, will constitute a new era of technology" (p. 517). These panels may make possible an electronic tabloid, "a convergence of print, moving pictures, and sound . . ." (p. 517).

Demographic Changes in the Work Force.   The U.S. Bureau of Labor Statistics projects that the work force in America's future will be older, with increasing numbers of females, and members of ethnic/racial minorities. In the early 1990s, it projected that 50% of the U. S. work force would be between 35 and 54 years of age in 2000 (Lacy et al, 1993). Newspaper organizations will need to compete with other industries for the best younger workers, and will need to invest in continuing education for existing employees, due to changes in technologies and resulting changes in work processes. The female labor force participation rate is projected to increase from 55% (1986 rate) to 61.5% by 2000 (Lacy et al., 1993). Continuing an existing trend in other organizations, some newspapers can expect to develop on-site day care, flex-scheduling, telecommuting, and other variations in work patterns, while maintaining a schedule of deadlines necessary to meet the needs of morning paper customers. Minority participation in the U. S. labor force is also increasing, and newspaper organizations are reflections, to some degree, of this increase. With increases in minority and immigrant participation in the work force, and in society in general, changes in newspaper organizations in the future will need to insure diversity in their perspectives on community and national issues, and programs that value and facilitate diversity in the newsroom and other sites of employment within the organization.

An important part of the contemporary context for change affecting newspapers is their increasing sophistication as knowledge organizations. As such, they are important venues of change for several reasons:

- The world economy is increasingly complex and interrelated, and is based on information distribution.

- Political systems around the world are changing, and newspapers have been, and can be, agents of change.

- New technologies are transmitting messages more quickly and to more people than has ever been the case. Newspapers, on newsprint or online, are regarded as major conduits of such messages.

- Newspapers are increasingly involved in creating new packages of information for use by different audiences.

Newspapers are businesses, but they are more than for-profit companies. Historically they have been agents of change—public voices on public matters. Conceiving of them as complex organizations from a contemporary and communication perspective is therefore important in any discussion of them as sites of change. Newspapers also are multi-purpose organizations, with business requirements and social responsibilities, and customers have high expectations of them and the ethics they reflect. In part, these expectations are rooted in the public perceptions of their historical purpose. Accordingly, eloquent voices are calling for a change in the major function of journalism in American society: The move from a reporter's monologue to a reporter–reader dialogue—a conversation (Gunaratne, 1998). This change is referred to by some scholars as a shift to public journalism, "a willingness to break with old routines, a desire to 'reconnect' with citizens and their true concerns, an emphasis on serious discussion as the primary activity in democratic politics, and a focus on citizens as actors within, rather than spectators to, the public drama" (Rosen, as cited in Gunaratne, 1998, p. 280). According to Charity (1995), public journalism "arose out of the conviction that something essential was lacking in American life right now; rational talk, community-based approaches, participatory discussions, communal glue, a proper emphasis on activity" (p. 281). Ironically, this notion of newspaper content is a return to journalism's roots—to change agency, to the engagement of the reader in the news creation and dissemination process. The same computer-based technology that has captured the interest of citizens who use that technology to do work, pay bills, order goods and services, and become informed about a variety of subjects, is piqueing their interest in more involvement with the journalistic process that results in daily and weekly newspapers. Passive television viewers are now interacting with each other in videoconferences, chat rooms, e-mail, and polls conducted online. This engagement is potentialy a major change in the relationship between newspapers and their readers, and has implications for the process and product associated with newspaper organizations. Chapter 4 is a specific discussion of change, as it is seen and experienced in these organizations.

CHAPTER FOUR

Newspapers and Change

When analyzing change, we look at differences—the ways objects or people vary from other objects or other people at a previous point in time. Some newspaper change can be obvious, such as the daily or weekly changing of news and advertisements. No two issues of a newspaper are alike; so the product itself embodies change. However, examining newspaper organizational change requires a more methodical approach. Organizations are multi-faceted; they are complex groups that operate in several layers, accomplishing tasks through many individuals who have varying goals and objectives. So you would not expect to be able to simply look at an organization and accurately determine where change occurs and ends or even what form that change takes.

This is even more true with newspapers. For example, say you meet a man for the first time. He tells you he has changed. Do you believe him? Perhaps, but not fully, simply because you do not know him well enough to gauge whether he is honest or because you are unable to observe any changes. Before you commit your trust, you would ask him what kind of change, how it happened, and why.

For example, *The Hartford (CT) Courant* hired a new editor in 1998. That in itself sounds like a change—of editors. Editors can change and the newspaper itself can remain the same. In the process of hiring its new editor, however, *The Courant* veered away from conventional methods, having the editor candidates meet with various staff members (as opposed to only the publisher and other, top executives). Upper management—while reserving the final decision for itself—ceded much of the operation to lower-level employees in an effort to democratize it. The real change was in the process, not the new editor who will be expected—like all editors—to create and nurture the paper's editorial vision and lead its journalists along the path set by that vision. The process left the newspaper in a disposition to do things in a changed manner, with cross-departmental groups resolving matters that were once solely the province of department heads (Jurkowitz, 1998).

So it is with newspapers. You need a sense of how newspapers operate and behave before you can say for sure whether they have changed. You also need an understanding of newspaper change—what causes it, how it does and does not work. For instance, why do some newspapers seem more open to the notion of cross-departmental management than others? How do you know if this is a change, a phase, or just a symptom of resistance to change? This chapter tries to provide answers to such questions and place them in a newspaper context. Afterward, we discuss newspapers' traditional routes to change and their consequences.

CAUSES OF NEWSPAPER CHANGE

Chapter 3 dealt with reasons for organizational change. Briefly summarized, the roots occur in the form of internal and external forces. Specifically, internal forces can be examined from many angles (Lawrence, 1989). For example, organizations such as newspapers have a basic framework of elements that allow them to function adequately. These elements include strategy, structure, systems, superordinate goals, staffing, skills, and styles (the *7-S framework*). Each element in its own right can cause change if management allows it to (e.g., circulation strategy can change how a newspaper distributes its product or what content the newspaper contains). The key—in predicting change and innovation—is to determine the newspaper's outlook or approach toward each element.

What that means is if a newspaper's strategy, for instance, is primarily low-cost, conservative, market share driven and profit oriented, it is not likely to welcome searches for new opportunities. Its general approach will be to cannibalize its product and markets for new ones. You can also see this approach in the way many newspapers are structured. With the centralized, functional orientation of operations—each department a fiefdom into its own—the chain of authority for decisions and communication is clearly vertical (top to bottom). Each department has its own clear-cut rules while the ideas of selling the paper and publishing it command most of the publisher's time. Such a structure will not foster innovation, for several reasons: This centralized decision making means anyone with a new idea will have to go through several layers of approval before the idea gets final favor. However, if a publisher were interested in creating and fostering change, he or she would put in place a decentralized structure, in which some decision making would be at lower levels in the hierarchy and where initiative would be nourished, without a myriad of rules. In addition, much work and strategy would be developed and get accomplished through employee task forces.

To be sure, these elements present a rather simplified picture of how change can arise. More often, change occurs in a more complex manner in newspapers. For example, when former *Los Angeles Times* publisher Mark Willes decided to bring the business side of the organization in on editorial development, shaping the model of cooperation and productivity became an ongoing process at the newspaper. Its business section, for example, was a focus for much of the early evolution of the model. Many of its feature stories began as ideas that would help advertising sales but instead became reader favorites, despite having little ad impact (Rappleye, 1998). Other topic concepts have succeeded in both arenas. Journalists strongly feared Willes' idea would result in business-side departments infringing on editorial autonomy (in fact, there were some conflicts of interest), although Willes continuously made the point that the newspaper revolved around its editorial quality—not its advertising. Still, he has questioned the notion of readership for readership's sake. The point is that *Times* editors and reporters are thinking more broadly (albeit, in some cases, somewhat less journalistically), as are the marketing, advertising, and circulation staff. The change is in the thought pattern and, thus, the work (Osborne, 1998).

But the *Times* story is more than just one of structure. There had to be a change in strategy for the structural change to occur. The fact that the strategy was the result of top management's leadership shows that people also play a role in newspaper change. Willes was made chair of Times Mirror Co., *The Times'* parent firm after working as vice chairman at General Mills, the packaged food company. He had not worked in news and his appointment was speculated as "almost inevitable" given the company's history of lagging profits and tradition of non-newspaper leadership (Pogash, 1995). Leaders are instrumental in change. They can be change strategists, change champions, or both, but they usually are at what many people consider the start of the change and, thus, become identified with the change. But you could also say that if it were not for the economy—that is, *The Times'* relative lack of an acceptable amount of profit—Willes would not have been hired. So newspaper change is like a set of concentric circles. On the outer rim is the environment, which affects the framework (strategy, structure, etc.), which influences the people with some personal stake in the newspaper, which then affects individuals in the organization and how well they work together (see Fig. 4.1).

The figure essentially can be read as saying that the environment contains movement that is unplanned by the organization—things that happen unexpectedly. This may be as simple as consumer reading habits or innovative reporting, or as complex as economic downturns. The environment can be internal or external. For example, as Times Mirror's profits declined since the 1980s, the company cut costs by downsizing *The Times* staff levels, deserted a chance to expand to San Diego, and reduced other local sections on the costly city outskirts (Thompson, 1995).

However, these movements by themselves do not necessarily create important change. There has to be a turning point of some kind. In *The Times* case, it was something that caused the newspaper to heed the necessity for

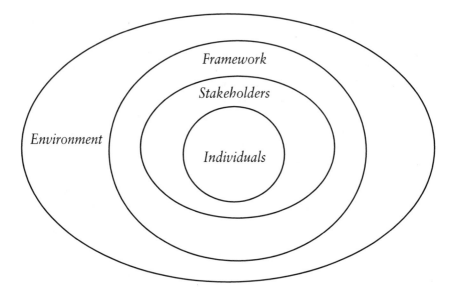

FIG. 4.1   How newspaper change occurs.

change—most likely the continuous lack of acceptable profit performance and the fact that the previous CEO had to prematurely retire for health reasons. Combined with this were the facts that the heir-apparent was an in-house candidate and that on Wall Street the company's reputation was that it made faulty use of its assets, implying that at the time it needed a conserva-tive, no-nonsense, non-emotional examination of its operations. Company officials indicated they indeed were looking for an outsider receptive to consumer tastes. From there, the company chose Willes, who began to make strategic decisions, promote change, and create devices that supported his vision (for further discussion of how this works, see Lawrence (1989) and Kanter et al. (1992). Later, that vision was scrapped when the newspaper was bought by another newspaper conglomerate.

So newspaper change is a complex process, involving many people and activities—some planned, some not. That may sound unsatisfying and impre-cise to some, but that is precisely what needs to be said: Change is not something simply accomplished. Many key elements have to be aligned and synchronized for change to occur. In newspapers, you cannot trace change to one specific thing or person. *The Times* case may seem like a one-man show of sorts, but if anything the circumstances surrounding *The Times* made Willes stand out. Before Willes, the parent company's stock was at a 10-year low of $17 per share, its New York paper was in a sea of red ink, and profit margins had declined for 5 years (Case, 1996). The scene was effectively set for transformation of some kind, though it was a multi-year process. In other words, the timing was right for Willes' arrival—just as it was for his departure.

Still, process is hard to visualize because it is everywhere, omnipresent. Just as a reader knows little of the reporting process—knowing only that the end result appears in a printed format on the lawn each morning—editors and newsroom managers are more likely to observe change (and thus understand and appreciate it more) if they can view it in some tangible form.

THE SHAPE OF NEWSPAPER CHANGE

It is the implementation of newspaper change—the activities, the trials and errors, the human behaviors, and reactions—that makes people sit up and take note of the change process. In fact, implementation is a process—a give-and-take, an ongoing dialogue, if you will, between the thing that needs changing and the person(s) expected to execute the change. The process usually has three main components: people, technology–task, and product. The following discussion centers on each of the components, providing pertinent examples, and concepts.

People

At first glance, this may seem a bit obvious. Of course, you need people if you are going to have change. However in newspapers, the people element is a diverse conceptual base from which to explore change, primarily because of the many roles they play in the change process. For example, people often are change strategists (Kanter et al., 1992). Such leaders make new approaches, assets, and arrangements that then serve as messages that the newspaper has a plan of change. Such plans, if well-crafted, lure like-minded or sympathetic employees and motivate editors and other managers to discuss the strategy among themselves and their subordinates, as Willes did at *The Times* and as Cole Campbell attempted to do at *The St. Louis Post-Dispatch*.

In late 1996, Campbell tried to change the newsroom's structure, hiring new staff and bringing in consultants to redesign the paper to help sharpen the focus of the newspaper's content. Campbell also wanted to make the newsroom culture more collaborative in an effort to produce more relevant stories for readers. So he hired outside consultants to help change how the newsroom thinks about the way it does its job. In doing so, Campbell added the extra role of change champion, that is, he pushed the idea constantly, trying to slowly re-educate mid-level editors and reporters when resistance was encountered, or when staffers were unclear on his goals and personally monitoring whether senior editors were all on the same philosophical page about the change (Shepard, 1998).

People play several, additional vital roles in change. For example, a study asked metro reporters and editors in the South, Midwest, and West their perspectives about online media. The journalists fell into three categories: benevolent revolutionary, nervous traditionalist, and rational realist. The first type, the strongest supporters of new media technology, saw change as beneficial and directly affecting journalism. Support for new media declined by varying degrees in the next two types, with the main difference being the realist liked innovations more but saw them having not much immediate impact on their jobs (Singer, 1997). With such varying outlooks, the categories suggest that support for any innovation or change differs within organization and that managers can assume each type to play a role based on how each type's members feel.

As to how this can play out in an individual newspaper, consider *The Chicago Tribune's* attempt in the mid-1980s to change its printing center. It just so happened a strike precipitated the change; the walkout centered around control over hiring selection and transfers. *Tribune* managers used the strike as an opportunity to improve the printing operations and bring the new printing plant online. Low morale—primarily because of poor supervision—had to be confronted; 1,000 new people were hired and were unfamiliar with the machinery, as well as being much younger. New supervisors had no training in future state visioning, or being able to see what top *Tribune* management wanted in the future from the printing plant. Incentive programs were developed to ensure employees did what was expected. So employee differences were recognized and dealt with (Frame, Neilsen, & Pate, 1989).

In short, people can make or break change. Successful change does not necessarily mean changed people. When *The News* in Boca Raton, FL, redesigned itself based on reader tastes in the early 1990s, those who complained the most were not readers but journalists who ridiculed the paper's new design rules, such as the fact that no story could continue (jump) from the front page (Albers, 1995a). Or consider the opposition to the formulation of reporting teams at *The Witchita Eagle*. Reporters are still trying to understand how the switch improved the paper. Flattening the managerial hierarchy meant career advancement opportunities decreased and the use of teams implied no bosses, which meant often no one took ultimate responsibility. This seeming lack of structure frustrated many *Eagle* reporters, causing some resistance (Graham & Thompson, 1997).

What roles people take often depends on their characteristics, the most crucial being what they know and their skills, needs and preferences as well as their perceptions and expectations (Nadler, Gerstein, & Shaw, 1992). When an upstate New York paper adopted audiotex personal advertisements, the staff had to be sold on the idea. Many were concerned about the unsavory image of the ads because they associated them with sex-oriented 900-telephone-number services. Those who would have to take the ad orders initially feared doing so because they thought customers would be weirdos. Status needs also entered into the fear because they felt their job was an odd way to make a living. Finally, lack of pay also was a concern until a pay plan was developed (Merskin, 1996).

Technology–Task

Change often becomes synonymous with technology in newspapers because the industry—especially since the 1960s and 1970s—constantly is undergoing adoption of more efficient means of production. Put another way: Work—the basic activities in which the newspaper is engaged—and its flow often get changed in newspapers and constitutes an important component of any change process. So it is fairly easy to cite examples of how work has changed in newspapers. In fact, anyone who has worked for a newspaper for more than a couple of years probably can cite more than one change in work processes.

The examination of work change is more than just naming new equipment or new methods of doing work. Several critical features merit examination when considering change: (a) the degree of doubt associated with the work; (b) the skill and knowledge demands of the work; (c) the built-in rewards of the work; and (d) the work's built-in performance conditions (Nadler et al., 1992). So whereas newspaper work often is the center of change, the actual change has four-fold ramifications for the newspaper employee. Analyzing these outcomes, then, enhances our potential to understand the underlying evidence and cause–inhibitor of change.

One change can have all four impacts. Take the case of electronic, computerized page design, also known as pagination. Looking at rewards, for example, the implementation of pagination at 12 newspapers unsurprisingly stirred tensions between copy desk and design desk staffs. The strain centered around territory and experience: Senior copyeditors criticized far-less-experienced page designers who they viewed as just mechanics who—because of pagination—were given plum layout assignments (Russial, 1994). At *The Beaumont Enterprise*, for example, performance conditions became an issue. Office logistics changed, pagination workstations were in short supply and often crashed, and the new technology required more work in page design because it took time away from story editing. These conditions also stirred doubt; copy editors questioned the relative advantage and compatibility of the new technology (Sylvie, 1995).

Finally, knowledge and skill demands obviously change when you alter the work process. Starting CLTV—an all-news local television station—in the early 1990s not only meant a clash of cultures at *The Chicago Tribune,* it meant a constant re-education for the newsroom editors and reporters. Being introduced to television news patterns meant not only did they have to learn to overcome their resentment of the intrusion of the 24-hour cable channel's staff in the newsroom, but they also had to create ways to showcase their work not only in print but visually as well (Sullivan, 1999).

Product

With pagination, the end result usually means well-edited, well-designed news pages—aesthetically pleasing to the consumer eye. Newspapers across the country have made such changes, primarily with a hopeful eye toward increasing readership, circulation, and advertising revenue. In short, the product often is the reason for many changes.

In the last generation, as readership penetration rates continued to decline, the industry has undergone several content-driven changes: more diverse or inclusive coverage, more consumer-oriented (less journalist-driven) news, and reader-driven content (in ads and news), among others. Typical was *The St. Louis Post-Dispatch's* 1996 attempt to take advantage of Sunday circulation—Saturday circulation was the week's worst—by creating a Saturday tabloid edition that would feature more news, sports, and religion coverage. Becoming more typical lately is the effort most newspapers are making to incorporate new media–online technology. Many newspapers simply transform the printed product onto an electronic version; some add interactive features; fewer still add exclusive news reports (Chyi & Sylvie, 1999). More to the point, publishers and editors alike theorize that such new media—if their advantages are to be fully used—will require journalists to re-evaluate and re-tool their skills (Yovovich, 1997). For example, at *The Wall Street Journal Interactive Edition,* deadline is not just daily; it is a constant. The staff never finishes because readers want up-to-the-minute news about financial markets and economic trends. Additional reporters have had to be hired to cover news readers want to see (Kirsner, 1998).

Again, it is common sense to conclude that changes in work and in people show themselves in the product. Our purpose, however, focuses on what those changes do to the organization. Whereas newspaper managers often envision the product as the consequence of change, often the product is the catalyst for additional change. In the case of unwanted change, for example, it can mean a change in staffing as in the case of the reporter who quit a Montana paper because publishers wanted to make it into a localized version of *USA TODAY* (Manning, 1991). On the other hand, content changes can spur subtle changes in other areas of content. *The Portland Oregonian* created a health-and-science reporting team in the mid-1990s in order to increase and enhance coverage and display in that area of news. Although that goal was met, other story types suffered—legislative process stories, wire stories on other states' politics, and stories on technology impact (Russial, 1997).

Such results illustrate that change does not always work, nor does it always work as intended. To fully comprehend what change means to newspapers, we must examine some typical instances and identify existing patterns. For if the shape of change makes people notice change, the absence of change commands equal attention. Both teach lessons, but the latter may be more appropriate assigned reading and more valuable for those who want to avoid failure and implement long-lasting, successful change in their newspapers.

WHEN CHANGE DOES NOT WORK WELL

It would be easy to say that change fails or falters when newspaper employees do not do what they should. There is more to it than that. A national study discovered that although newspaper managers implement high-performance managerial practices that engender change, they do so slowly, in a limited way. For example, production departments are more likely than the advertising and editorial departments to use such practices (Lewis, 1995).

Often, people resist change when they feel threatened; it is a survival mechanism. It also is difficult to make change persist because resistance takes many forms—some genuine, others are simply excuses. Table 4.1, while meant to be humorous, also is remarkably representative of comments heard in many newspaper newsrooms.

While newspaper managers should and do expect resistance, they still must be able to recognize it and understand its nature if they are to successfully engineer change. Much of the non-change at newspapers centers around four phenomena: fear, structural politics, traditional journalistic interests, and timing.

Fear

The idea of changing can stir fear in anyone. Imposed changes lessen a person's perceived autonomy and, thus, their self-control. Newspaper employees are no different than people in other industries in that they tend to view change in terms of how it will affect the technical and social aspects of their jobs. Various studies of employee satisfaction and dissatisfaction already establish this, but individual papers' experiences confirm that fear is a major change inhibitor.

Fear plays a larger part in some changes than others. Take newsroom mergers, for example. *The Pittsburgh Press* and former *Pittsburgh Post-Gazette* had different relationships to the Pittsburgh community. Much of the differences stemmed from different management styles, a union versus a non-union environment, and differences in corporate and organizational culture.

TABLE 4.1
Twenty Excuses for No Newsroom Change

1. Where are they getting the money?
2. They don't do this at *The New York Times.*
3. This was marketing's idea, wasn't it?
4. This is a *newspaper,* not a business!
5. Let's test it on sports first.
6. I want to see it on paper first.
7. When will I have time for my beat?
8. That's *absurd!*
9. How is this journalism?
10. This stinks.
11. But we've always done it this way!
12. It'll never make a profit.
13. Does this mean more meetings?
14. Isn't that a conflict of interest?
15. They *tried* that at *The Times.*
16. What consultant thought this up?
17. Quality's going to suffer.
18. If it ain't broke, . . .
19. This is just one more thing to deal with.
20. Does this mean we get a raise?

When *The Post-Gazette* bought *The Press,* there was a fear of *Press* management by reporters, who categorized *The Press* as corporate with less tolerance for peculiarities (Jurczak, 1996). Uncertainty also plagued the work of former *Raleigh Times* reporters and editors after the separate editorial staffs of the *News & Observer* and *Times* were blended, proving that "when newspaper staffs merge, one wins and one loses" (Kochersberger, 1990).

A concurrent, underlying factor involves conservative management styles. In essence, the more control-oriented and close-to-the-vest approach used, the higher the fear element. This leads to what psychologists call self-justification—when newspaper managers have to decide between a risky change and the status quo. This unpleasant cognitive situation motivates the manager to reduce the unpleasantness; as a result, fearful managers rationalize the status quo. The more he or she is committed to non-change, the more resistant that person will be to information that threatens that commitment (Festinger, 1957).

Structural Politics

Many times change cannot happen because newspapers are designed to inhibit it. Sometimes it's simply a matter of costs and resources, as in the case of managers of small-circulation newspapers who—while valuing research skills a trained librarian might provide—are less sure of the value of research done by newsroom staffers with computer access to information retrieval systems. The reason may be because the managers usually lack familiarity with such systems themselves (Martin, 1994).

Such structural elements are often deeply ingrained. Take the example of how far workplace diversity has to go in Indiana newspapers when it concerns female editorial employees. Despite the fact that large numbers reported being harassed, a study revealed very few say they will file sexual harassment complaints. They suggested that policies preventing workplace sexual harassment were token gestures lacking management backing (Flatow, 1994). Consider that mid-level managers—on whom publishers often count for marshaling support and motivating employees to change—often are the worst enemies of change. When the *Dayton Daily News* attempted to replace traditional newsroom departments with teams, editors provided the strongest resistance at times because the team structure decentralized decision making, taking power away from them and forcing them to learn to be more collaborative (Albers, 1995b).

Often structure embodies the entire newspaper's modus operandi. Beginning in the early 1980s, *The New York Daily News* was awash in red ink. Parent firm Tribune Co., dictated new work methods and hired the same law firm that handled its 1985 Chicago newspaper strike. That firm engineered a short-sighted strategy that viewed all 10 unions as one, implying to *News* journalists that the company wanted to rid the paper of unions and prompting them to go on strike in 1990. When the paper hired replacement workers, violence broke out and public sentiment sided with the unions. New York police supported the strikers, and looked the other way at those who broke the law to impede and beat replacement workers. *News* trucks were trashed and most news distributors would not sell the replacement paper. After months of mounting losses, Tribune Co. sold the *News* in March 1991.

Traditional Journalistic Interests

Reporters typically resist any change to standard reporting practices. Just as in the previous section's discussion of how journalists view new media—when the nervous traditionalist was identified as one major viewpoint—journalists are leery of new reporting trends. For example, a study of journalistic attitudes about civic journalism revealed four viewpoints: the civic journalist, the responsible liberal, the neutral observer, and the concerned traditionalist (Gade et al., 1998). Other innovations meet similar journalistic welcomes. For instance, many journalists at *The Minneapolis Star Tribune* and *The St. Paul Pioneer Press* essentially said that implementing topic news teams had hurt content quality, as well as efficiency and effectiveness of news routines (Hansen, Neuzil, & Ward, 1998). Editors, too, often warn about losing sight of core journalistic values when discussing change. Listen to what one organizational change consultant said after conducting a three-day change workshop with 40 editors:

> "I listened to them. I learned from what they said, but as a whole I found them blind to the critical realities right in front of their noses," he says. The group's consensus was that there is no such thing as radical transformational change, he recalls. (Albers, 1995b)

This phenomenon of journalistic fear often has expressed itself in reaction to corporatism in newspapers (e.g., Squires, 1993; Underwood, 1993), accusing the corporate newspaper of destroying professional journalism as it searches to emphasize profits; that is, quantity at the expense of quality. As has been shown (Demers, 1996a, 1996b), this accusation is largely overstated. Reporters and editors at corporate newspapers are more satisfied than those at non-corporate papers (Demers, 1995). However, it is not unreasonable, with the dawning of a new century and the notoriety of certain scandals calling into question the credibility of journalism (e.g., Rieder, 1999), to expect journalists to seek solace in traditional, basic values of their profession. The problem, still, is that—as mentioned previously—such a conservative attitude often impedes change.

Timing

A recent University of South Dakota journalism graduate convinced the state bureau chief of the Associated Press to hire him to expand the bureau's statewide sports coverage. Saving his money over the next two years, he then convinced investors to buy stock in *SoDak Sports,* a weekly sports tabloid for all of South Dakota. The key was to be the state's sports journalists, who were made unpaid contributing editors in return for tips for features and story ideas. Much of its content was borrowed from the state's daily newspapers, although there were many polls and reader participation items. The first issue sold out; circulation was a success—but also a key problem. *SoDak*'s sale price of 10 cents a copy did not cover production and distribution costs, and advertising income was below expectations. The more papers *SoDak* sold, the more money it lost. Twenty-two months later, Neuharth had run out of time and money (Neuharth, 1989).

The effect of time and timing cannot be underestimated when it comes to the failure of change. Too often we assign a newspaper's problem with a certain innovation to the factors previously mentioned when, in fact, the major reason is the element of time. For example, circulation problems were a key factor in the failure of *The St. Louis Sun*; the paper never recovered from mixed-up orders that prevented it from meeting the demand it had created (Mueller, 1997). Further study showed bad timing was at least partly to blame. Although editors and managers marketed the paper as emphasizing local coverage, its seven-month life saw a march of important national and international stories dominate the news: The San Francisco earthquake during the Bay area World Series, the collapse of the Soviet bloc and the opening of the Berlin Wall, and the American invasion of Panama, to name a few. This was compounded by the fact that international and national news was the *Post-Dispatch's* strong suit (Mueller, 1998).

Timing also is a double-edged sword, working to newspapers' benefits in some cases while casting doubt on other publications' efforts. A case in point was Knight-Ridder's 25/43 Project, so-named for the target audience of the plan that offered short stories, extensive and colorful graphics, and more positive news in the *Boca Raton News*. The project started in late 1990 and ended when Knight-Ridder sold the paper seven years later. Readers liked the changes but circulation figures did not dramatically reflect it. Depending on whom you speak to, the project was a failure (for the paper) or a success (for other Knight-Ridder papers, who used the findings to plan their own reader-friendly changes). Contrary to what publishers might expect, some journalists at the newspaper were excited about the project, seeing it as an enjoyable, important experience. However as a temporary project, seed money from Knight-Ridder gradually stopped coming and crucial positions went unfilled (Kodrich, 1998).

Time is more complex than that because armed with knowledge of these reasons for failure, it is still apparent that there is more to the change equation. There must be an explanation, for example as mentioned earlier, for some newspapers being more open to cross-departmental management than others. There must be a rationale for classifying some developments as a change, a phase, or just a symptom of change. This requires an analysis of newspapers' traditional routes to change and the role of time.

TIME AND APPROACHES TO NEWSPAPER CHANGE

This book is not simply about describing change. It also seeks to help newspaper managers make strategic choices regarding change. A successful change process requires understanding that—as we have shown—change is complex. Managing this complexity means realizing that there will be conflicts—in the organization's goals (as perceived by employees and managers) but also in the organization's mission. Successful change managers must clarify these goals and evaluate the newspaper's external environment as well (Beckhard & Harris, 1987).

Expediting change then requires creating a structure, that is, creating the support mechanisms, communicating the necessary vision, and helping

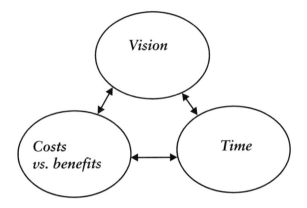

FIG. 4.2 How approaches to change are made.

establish the context that will ensure change emerges as managers would have it. Doing so requires some planning or at least an awareness of the factors surrounding change (Kanter et al., 1992). Taking action is another matter entirely. Managers—like all people—maximize their interests, according to their own internal set of tendencies and biases. When strategizing, managers try to anticipate the outcomes of their plans, often with one eye toward the past, that is, their experiences that have taught them what to expect if they take certain actions or make certain assumptions. However, time always pressures managers in any strategic situation, primarily because it is limited— either by convention (e.g., the 24-hour day) or by nature (Becker, 1993). So in making decisions to ensure or prevent change, newspaper managers weigh benefits and costs, time, and how they compare to their vision of (or desires for) the newspaper's future (see Fig. 4.2).

Time is key because it involves not just the idea of timing—that is, the idea of opportunity or chance or setting—but also the idea of duration or a stretch of time. Duration allows for evaluation of a change, a measuring stick to determine whether it truly represents a difference or if it is merely short lived. It is the latter state that determines the true test of organizational change— whether it represents transformation–reform or no more than what amounts to an organizational whim. Let us briefly see how newspapers typically handle that approach to change.

Reactive

As the name indicates, this is where newspapers adopt change as counter-move. Under this approach, the rationale for change includes any of the following: The fact that the newspaper management is disorganized, management planning is other directed (not based on the organization's own needs and behavior), or that seat-of-the-pants management rules. The reactive approach involves diametrically opposing aspects of time: It either attempts to entirely discount the role of time (because change opportunities suddenly arise) or to save time altogether (why plan when things just happen or when we are too busy to begin with?). For example, when a New England group of editors and publishers were asked why they had no plans to go online, 43% of the weeklies and 55% of the dailies said they did not have enough time (Alexander, 1997). Of course, the end result is that time is neither discounted or saved because the time between the initial, reactive decision to change and the almost surely undesired consequences mean that time needs to be taken for corrective, controlling measures.

There are myriad examples of this type of behavior, best described as "Everybody's doing it, so we should, too." This is not to imply a lack of forethought, just perhaps not as much as some other approaches. For instance, a study of community newspapers investigated their basic strategy for deciding when and why to invest in technology. Many responses were reactive—when equipment broke down or no longer performed, to stay current with the market—some even admitted they had no strategy (Massey, 1997).

Control

Newspaper managers attempt to control for several reasons, ranging from fear to invoking tradition to attempts to minimize uncertainty. The first two scenarios have been discussed previously. The final factor often is driven by a lack of confidence or clear alternative, as many publishers face when deciding what type of Internet presence they need to establish—not an easy feat in a business not known for its research and development tradition (Brown, 1998). As to time, one of the control approach's main goals is to save time by decreasing doubt. Doubt, the manager reasons, expends more time than necessary, so it must be eliminated. The folly, of course, is that nothing can be completely controlled and no one has a crystal ball that tells the future. Try as he or she might, the controlling newspaper manager winds up spending more time than planned because the newspaper world is, by nature, a complex and chaotic one that defies control.

There are many faces of control. One side involves autonomy, which one study showed affected innovativeness. Editors who scored low on an innovation measure were much more likely to perceive high publisher involvement in the newsroom (Polansky & Hughes, 1986). This is only common sense: In order to innovate, a manager must have authority to do so. Another side of control involves command, that is, the side of the person exercising control. In the case of the team-reporting approach adopted by Minnesota's Twin

Cities' newspapers, journalists there generally agreed that the team system had not given them more authority and that leaders—while advocating empowering of journalists—held on to most of their power (Neuzil, Hansen, & Ward, 1999).

Modeling

This approach might more aptly be termed the trade journal method or the networking school of change, simply because many editors and publishers get their ideas for change from colleagues at other papers—either in person or by reading accounts in newspaper-related magazines. The thinking here is fairly obvious: Not only does modeling greatly alleviate the fear of making a mistake (because newspapers, while local in nature, generally operate on many of the same principles), it also avoids redundancy—there is no chance of making the same mistakes of others—while providing the chance to adopt good (workable) ideas. In so doing, it saves time.

Of course, it does not always work that way. As any student knows, models may seem like a good fit in theory, but only when placed into practice can their value be accurately judged. That was the underlying problem with New Century Network (NCN), a joint venture of seven of the 10 largest U.S. newspaper companies aimed at making newspapers contenders in local computer information services for consumers and advertisers. The idea was to create a compatible online network that allowed affiliate papers to share information and help subscribers easily move from one to another (Garneau, 1995). NCN tried to compile a Web search–directory pact that would allow newspaper Web sites to perform like other Web search engines, allowing newspaper Web site visitors to search the entire Internet. Such search engine sites usually rank among the most heavily visited Internet sites and feature news services that directly challenge the newspaper business. However, NCN's owners could not agree on a strategy, and speculation centered around the founding companies' competing interests (Outing, 1998) as well as the fact that they had developed their own Internet advertising initiatives since NCN was formed (Snyder, 1998). Still, many newspapers use modeling when adopting a new technology or making a change of some kind.

Top-Down, Bottom-Up Strategic

This approach may seem similar to the control approach, and often the two overlap. What distinguishes this method is its dependence on communication. When there is communication, success usually follows. Recall *The Chicago Tribune's* transformation of its printing center. The employee strike opened a window that *Tribune* managers took advantage of; they decided to seize control over hiring selection and transfers by hiring new people and training them to recognize top management's vision for the plant (Frame et al., 1989). In acting this way, newspaper management takes the reins because it is their job (they get paid to do so), because they can and have the authority to do so, and because they have confidence. In doing so at the expense of communication costs time, whereas the obvious strategy is to save time.

For example, it is doubtful *The New Orleans Times-Picayune* would have won its Pulitzers in the mid-1990s had Editor Jim Amoss not been able to convey his vision of reporting excellence to the staff over an extended period of time. Amoss was a long-time staffer who ascended to the editorship via a series of steps but who marked his editorship with a commitment of resources to investigative projects. One staffer said of him, "I always had a sense that we were trying to get better and that if just stayed the course we would end up getting there" (Lisheron, 1997, p. 28).

The hallmark of this approach is participation. When *The Wichita Eagle* set its sights on improving content, editors invited the entire newsroom to brainstorm the idea and develop goals. The resulting task force examined newsroom structures and suggested converting to a team structure. The suggestion was adopted, but not without prior training—including group exercises—and the development of a blueprint that included suggestions, requirements, and questions to be considered prior to implementation. Staff members were asked for their team preferences and teams were staffed to complement the interests, needs, and skills of members. Compensation and evaluation mechanisms were adapted accordingly, and the change implemented. Adjustments were made to address whatever crisis arose, but the basic idea began to take hold and editors noticed improvement in stories. The fundamentals of teamwork and inclusiveness worked (Graham & Thompson, 1997).

SUMMARY

This chapter looked at how newspapers operate in order to give a better sense of how they change or do not change. We analyzed change and differences from obvious and not-so-obvious perspectives, each time trying to methodically enhance our understanding of newspaper change.

In terms of what causes change, we saw that factors can be complex, as in the case of *The Los Angeles Times*' move toward a market-based model. In that situation, structure and strategy went hand-in-hand, illustrating that change involves many people and activities—some planned, some not. Many key elements have to be aligned and synchronized for change to occur. In addition, the process is everywhere, omnipresent. Which brought us to the idea that newspaper change is like a set of concentric circles. On the outer rim is the environment, followed by the framework (strategy, structure, etc.), which influences the people with some personal stake in the newspaper, which then affects individuals in the organization and how well they work together.

More apparent is the process of newspaper change, which occurs through people, technology–task, and the product. Although people can make or break change, successful change does not necessarily mean changed people. What roles people take often depends on their characteristics, the most crucial being what they know and their skills, needs, and preferences as well as their perceptions and expectations. Technology–task, on the other hand, requires more than just naming new equipment or new methods of doing work. Managers must consider a work change's accompanying degree of doubt, the skill and knowledge demands of the work, the change's built-in rewards, and its built-in performance conditions. So a change in newspaper work often has four-fold ramifications for the newspaper employee. The product, in contrast, often is the ultimate reason for change.

However, it is just as important—in order to fully comprehend what change means to newspapers—to consider the absence of change. Newspaper managers must be able to recognize and understand resistance to change. Much of the non-change at newspapers centers around four phenomena: fear, structural politics, traditional journalistic interests, and timing. The latter is particularly important because it influences newspapers' traditional routes (reactive, control, modeling and top-down, bottom-up strategic) to change. Time involves not just the idea of timing—that is, the idea of opportunity or chance or setting—but also the idea of duration. Duration allows for evaluation of a change, a measuring stick to determine whether it truly represents a difference or if it is merely short-lived. It is the latter state that determines the true test of organizational change.

Armed with this more complete sense of what change means in newspapers, Part II of this book leads off with the first of three chapters that will feature extensive case studies. Chapter 5 starts the in-depth study with a look at the role of technology in newspaper change.

The Practice of Change

Chapters 5, 6, and 7 provide individual glimpses of change. They look at three different newspapers from three different perspectives. Each newspaper was chosen for study because of the successful changes it had undergone in particular areas of implementation.

According to Kanter (1983), change tends to evolve though a blend of five components: grassroots innovations, a crisis or galvanizing event, change strategists and strategic decisions, individual implementation agents and change champions, and action vehicles. When we looked for patterns in these areas, we settled on three basic components: people, technology–task, and product. Any change usually involves one or a combination of these components. Each of the following chapters scrutinizes a particular basic element.

Chapter 5 examines the role of technology. Specifically, we explore the adoption of pagination technology at *The Dallas Morning News*. The chapter defines and explains how pagination usually works, chronicles the normal adoption process, offers perspectives of the *Morning News* participants, and discusses the change that occurred.

Chapter 6 investigates the role of the product in changing a newspaper. To do so, we study the economic changes undergone by African-American weekly newspapers in Texas. The section looks at market factors and how they reflect on the advertising in the African-American press, and the resulting efforts by African-American publishers and editors to adapt to the changing demands of the market.

Chapter 7 delves into the role of people in the multiple changes occurring at *USA TODAY*. Several employees past and present give their understanding of what—besides the content—creates the national newspaper's unique working atmosphere and how people contribute to the publication's unrivaled innovative spirit.

Also, toward the end of each chapter, we use the lens of change theory to provide another perspective of the particular change or changes involved. Without such context, the chapters would be simple recordings of each paper's adventures. This text aims to provide depth beyond the facts and to illustrate how each experience can be analyzed by using organizational change theory. By so doing, we hope to furnish a model by which publishers, editors, and students may examine and guide future episodes of change.

The data for these (and later) chapters were gathered over the course of five years, most of it within 1999–2000, via telephone and personal interviews with present and former employees of the papers involved and of their competitors. In all, some 54 executives, journalists, and various employees of a number of newspapers and other institutions were interviewed—several of them multiple times. In addition, the first author visited the work facilities where possible and—with certain newspapers—on numerous occasions to observe and ask questions; twice that author conducted in-house seminars. The subjects generously shared a range of in-house communications. There were countless other interviews that informed the background sections of each of the three chapters, particularly chapter 6. Of course, the authors also relied on previously published accounts of the case study subjects. We wish to collectively thank all those who helped in this data-gathering effort.

CHAPTER FIVE

New Technology at the *Dallas Morning News*

As mentioned in chapter 4, newspaper change often is associated with technology. Since its inception as a business, but particularly in the last 30 years, the industry has sought myriad ways of enhancing technology. Newspapers are highly labor-intensive, so they have eagerly greeted most of the evolving computerization of labor (Picard & Brody, 1997; Smith, 1980).

Still, technology is but a tool in the performance of work. We earlier alluded to several critical features that merit examination when considering change (i.e., the degree of doubt associated with the work; the skill and knowledge demands of the work; the built-in rewards of the work; and the work's built-in performance conditions; see Nadler et al., 1992). So while newspaper work often is at the center of change, the change itself also has implications for the newspaper employee—analyzing these outcomes helps us understand the underlying evidence and cause–inhibitor of change.

There is no shortage of such analysis, especially in the case of pagination. For much of the last 30 years, many newspapers have sought to become paginated—the electronic assemblage of page components, including graphics, photos, type, and other art. The reasons vary, but the technology potentially yields far-reaching, cost-cutting, efficient procedures and, thereby, enhanced profits. Whereas many technologies are generally adopted with little fanfare after an acceptable breaking-in period, pagination has caused a great deal of consternation because it requires new equipment, software, and instruction (Sims, 1999). Experiences vary, but many agree with one editor who cited "system crashes, blown deadlines, chaos and frustration" during the transition to the new technology (Tarleton, 1996, p. 4).

Employee implications are numerous. For example, the implementation of pagination at 12 Western newspapers unsurprisingly stirred tensions between the copy desk and design desk staffs. The strain centered on organizational territory and experience: Senior copy editors denigrated less-experienced page designers as just mechanics who used their knowledge of pagination to gain desirable layout assignments (Russial, 1994). In addition, *The Beaumont Enterprise* had to evaluate performance conditions, change office logistics, shuffle work schedules (because pagination workstations were in short supply), and replenish morale after frequent system crashes (the new technology required more work in page design as well as took away time from story editing). All the while, doubts surfaced as copy editors questioned the relative advantage and compatibility of the new technology (Sylvie, 1995). Although pagination is seen as a plus, many editors worry about its effect on accepted editing practices (Underwood, Giffard, & Stamm, 1994).

So pagination has a checkered history in the newspaper industry. Primitive systems took extensive time to learn, called for extensive computer coding, could not manage pictures or graphics, and were sluggish and inconsistent. As a result, reports of adoption of the technology vary: One poll reported the technology—generally accepted as the next step in editing since the early 1980s—was partially or fully adopted by only 64% of newspapers in the early 1990s (Truitt, 1991). A more systematic study of the implementation of pagination in mid-size U.S. dailies found it increased demands on copy editors' time, forcing them to spend less time doing traditional word-related tasks, and more time designing and paginating pages; slightly more than half used pagination (Brill, 1994). A 1995 survey showed 20% of U.S. newspapers were paginated (Cole, 1997). Because of such an inconsistent performance record, editors and publishers continuously seek more successful models of adoption.

BACKGROUND AND THE CHANGE

Learning From History at The News

One example has been *The Dallas Morning News.* Founded in 1882, the paper has become the paper of record for Texas, a regular Pulitzer Prize finalist in the last 20 years and widely cited as one of the top 10 newspapers in the United States. However, change has not always been greeted so kindly by the paper, which was known for its abrasive conservative editorial outlook until relatively late in the 20th century (Elkind, 1985). Often criticized for catering to the rich and to the business community, the newspaper is home to several traditions (e.g., all senior editors list their home telephone numbers in the city phone book; see Gelsanliter, 1995). In fact, *The News* was a slow-growing company until the 1970s.

Much of *The News*' growth—and the successful pagination effort—was an outgrowth of the paper's battle with its previous main challenger, *The Dallas Times Herald.* The Times-Mirror Corp., at the time owners of the prestigious *Los Angeles Times* and other properties, bought the *Herald* in 1970, fully intending to do what it had done elsewhere—namely, to make *The Herald* one of the leading newspapers in the region. They instituted numerous changes in content, distribution, and marketing and, as a result, *The Herald's* circulation began to near that of its rival in 1978.

In 1979, *The News* hired a marketing consultant that indicated business, fashion, sports, arts, and entertainment—in addition to regular local and regional news—needed development, as did circulation systems (Fair, 1985). "When things were close to equal," said Ralph Langer, a one-time News editor, "we were the paper that was supposed to lose. At Times-Mirror they had four times the revenue. But the readers decided which *newspaper* they wanted. They were not deciding between companies."

To help readers decide, a change of editors in 1980 saw a resulting change in the newsroom budget, which increased by half to hire more (and better) reporters and enhance salaries (and morale). The business section staff was doubled and coverage invigorated (Reed, 1998). Meanwhile, *The Herald* also underwent changes—mostly negative ones that included, among others, readership defections to other Times-Mirror properties, increased newsprint costs, circulation discounts, and circumstances brought on by the disadvantage of being the city's No. 2 paper in a recessive economy (Fair, 1985). *The Morning News* continued to counter the *Herald* threat: When Langer became editor, he examined the various sections individually, searching for areas to improve. At one point, he had 100 new newsroom jobs to fill. "You talk about changing the culture," he said. "Here was a fairly large paper (that previously was) willing to play softball, now playing major league baseball."

By the mid-1980s, Times-Mirror sold *The Herald,* sending it into a downward spiral that eventually resulted in its closing its doors in 1991 (Gelsanliter, 1995) and selling its assets to Belo Corp., parent company of *The News.*

The sale meant the surviving paper would have to deliver an extra 100,000–150,000 newspapers—an overnight increase of nearly 30%. To do so, *The News* bought *The Herald's* three presses, its editing system, and equipment. The latter purchase seemed fortunate at the time because the paper had been looking at pagination for several years and the *Herald* system was seen as more advanced and a step in that direction. "With *The Dallas Morning News* being so large, we needed something that would work for us," said then-editor Langer. So the paper began to use its own system and that of *The Herald.* Unfortunately, the combination proved to be a disaster; it did not work most of the time and production often was stopped. So *News* management cautiously continued to look at other formats and equipment, hoping to obtain one system for the entire paper.

There was no rush to fully paginate and, indeed, only 26% of American newspapers are fully paginated (Sims, 1999). This was aided by the introduction in the 1980s of so-called desktop software—meaning computer programs that could be accessed and exploited from an individual workstation as opposed to from a large, mainframe system—that provided newsrooms the increased capability to mold pages. As a result, many newspapers—particularly smaller ones—decided to adopt such systems. Larger newspapers discovered they could do so as well (as a matter of expediency) but quickly discovered that trying to publish multiple editions on such systems was nearly impossible and highly frustrating. The systems failed to deliver a complete, digital process—one that increased production, was relatively low-cost, and on which editors could rely. There were also time issues and increased responsibilities for copy editors, who found the desktop systems often had a high learning curve and sometimes changed their job descriptions from word editors to design editors and, in the process, placed less value on actual content editing and critiquing (e.g., Sylvie, 1995).

The News, armed with knowledge of pagination's limitations, chose to wait. Instead, it combined its old advertising art and publishing technology departments into one production sub-department to join the pre-press areas that had already been combined: composing, imaging (previously part of the photo department), and news systems (previously under news). Meanwhile, the paper used and expanded the desktop approach to make better ads and to improve its electronic imaging (Konrade-Helm, 1995). "We had been looking at pagination off and on for five or six years," Langer said. "There was always a system that was 'just a year away.'"

As it pondered what to do and when, *The News* had a choice of what Cole (1995) describes as four basic approaches: do-it-yourself, almost-do-it-yourself, hire an integrator, and turnkey. In do-it-yourself, the paper self-paginates to gain more control, guarantee success, and diminish expenses. In almost-do-it-yourself, the newspaper generally will buy some hardware, software, or both, but also largely attempt to configure, assemble, and develop the system in-house. Hiring an integrator is just that: engaging an outside company to assimilate various components. Finally, turnkey involves hiring a company that manufactures both hardware and the software driving it to adapt its products to a specific newspaper's wants and needs. *The News* had tried a hybrid of the do-it-yourself and almost-do-it-yourself models after getting *The Herald's* system. There was some training, but not enough, according to Jeff Rogers, who was made head of the newsroom technology group (NTG) that would look into any new system. "They (the *Herald* terminals) were rammed down our throats and dissatisfied a lot of people," Rogers said.

Beginning in 1993–94, the paper again attempted to partly paginate using a system from Digital Technologies International for its weekly magazine, editorial–viewpoints, business, and other special sections (Konrade-Helm, 1995). However, Rogers said, "We didn't do enough training, there was no newsroom buy-in; it was more of an IT (the information technology department) thing. We just didn't do it right." Keith Campbell, assistant managing editor in charge of the news desk, said the training "didn't go extremely well because they (upper management) didn't know our needs well."

If it seems as if *The News* is deliberate and methodical in how it settled on a new system, that is just part of it. "Our guideline was we needed to assess the benefits before we adopted," Langer said. "It was such a massive project, we had to keep our eyes on the horizon." So it was not until 1996 when the newspaper began to make small moves, examining (via vendor demonstrations, discussions with peers at other papers, trade show visits, and various staffers' trips to papers in Ft. Lauderdale, San Jose, and Phoenix) state-of-the-art systems. After several meetings between interested staff and upper management (including discussion of the post-trip reports), management was convinced to go with a system bought from CCI, a European firm specializing in developing news-editorial work systems. The work had only begun.

Doing It the News Way

Rogers went to every site, wrote several extensive memos to Langer after each trip, and wound up playing a large part in engineering the change. First, the NTG was conceived and created in December 1997. The group (often called the tech team and originally consisting of former Assistant Sports Editor Rogers, the assistant business editor, the copy desk chief, two systems support technicians, and the assistant House & Garden section editor) was important because pagination was its sole concern. Therefore, management hired four new staffers to replace the journalists at their previous jobs. Deciding on the group's makeup, role, and mission took—in typical *News* fashion—six months. "It takes this place a long time to do things. . . . It took a while for people to believe it was coming," said Michael Taylor, the NTG's training point person and the former House & Garden staffer who got involved because he was ready to do something different. And the installation definitely would be different. "Our primary goal," Rogers said, "was (to have) a tool to put out a better *Dallas Morning News*. We want the system to provide efficiency."

One of the group's first discussions involved a dose of self-humility. "*We* aren't the paper," was how Rogers coined the idea. The group needed to help others reach a decision, it had to be able to communicate with the newsroom as well as represent the various areas of the newsroom. "We had to ask, 'What do *you* (other departments) think?'" Rogers said. Once that concept was driven home, the group had six months to dream about how it wanted to plan the transition, and six months to draw up specifications for the system it wanted, as well as to explain and describe to CCI the *News* workflow. It also had to communicate to the rest of the staff what it was doing—in other words, there was a realization that training actually consisted of more than just classes and lectures.

One tool (see Fig. 5.1) entailed *Interface,* a regular in-house periodical that informed employees about the system, its ramifications and requirements. The name was no coincidence, having been reached after the NTG bounced names around and reasoned the *Interface* name seemed best because the group saw itself as a bridge between the newsroom and IT. The newsletter stated there would be five key changes: desktop hardware, software, training, workflow, and redesign and web width (see Fig. 5.2). The publication also offered advice on how to prepare, and provided updates about schedules, assessments of system testing, and comparisons with efforts of other newspapers' experiences with CCI and the like. The newsletter was not just a mouthpiece for management; it often was explicitly honest and offered frank counsel. "*The Morning News* is too big a newspaper to roll out all at once, even some departments are too big to bring in CCI all at once," said one column (Rogers, 1999). "Have conversations now in your department about logical splits of work. . . . No one knows better how to do this than you and your colleagues, so don't wait until the rollout of your section approaches."

Final, pre-shipment tests were conducted in Denmark and completed in late June 1999, with the following month or so used on correcting errors and building in modifications. In August, the system was loaded and tweaked in time for a December debut. Meanwhile, behind-the-scenes adjustments continued and the NTG continued to learn from its pre-adoption visits to other newspapers, particularly the one to Ft. Lauderdale. There, *News* staffers had seen a concept called *superuser,* basically meaning a person who would teach lower-level staffers and editors how to use the new system. Such people had to be quick learners and good communicators with their peers. Newly arrived Assistant News Editor Willis (1999) described superusers at his previous paper as "standing by to answer questions and calm the masses." The NTG expanded on the idea by adding more superusers—they wound up with 12—than they had seen elsewhere. Not only would it mean more help for the adoption process, it also would eliminate a potential negative: criticism. It is not unusual to find cynics in a newspaper, especially cynics about technology or any management initiative. So if, say, a newsroom superuser reacts negatively (and publicly) to the process, that reaction does not find its way to the newsroom, but rather stays within the hierarchy of the NTG—where it is addressed and the potential problem solved.

Another important *News* wrinkle was a budget proposal to add staff to help implement the system. The plan was to create a replacement team, particularly for the copy desk, that would allow current staffers to attend training sessions and commit time to learning the system. The dozen or so replacement team members would then baby-sit those staffers' duties in the two-year process, with the hope of being hired full-time when the adoption process was completed. For example, as Keith Campbell, the Assistant

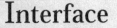

FIG 5.1   In-house bridge to pagination.

The Key Change	Related Comment
desktop hardware	"...in the end, this is not a gaggle of PCs dropped on desks...(they) bring challenges...in stability, security and backup.."
software	"CCI's software has become more stable over the past year, but it remains delicate...A change in setup in one application can drastically alter another..."
training	"we have gone to great lengths to set up a process by which you will be given enough time to be trained, and you'll be instructed by people who understand what you do..."
workflow	"the CCI system allows us to track flow of stories, graphics, photos, pages and ads; you'll be able to look at any of these and tell what stage in the workflow it's in..."
redesign and web width	"the new page design and narrow press width will require a system reconfiguration...we'll try to make the transition painless..."

FIG. 5.2   Five key changes with the CCI system.

Managing Editor for news, said, "The training is pretty intense and the superusers can't train and do their work at the same time."

Rogers said that when adopting a new pagination system, many newsrooms have the tendency to ignore copy editing and concentrate on graphic elements because the system often enhances copy editors' capabilities to improve graphics. However, it also comes with a price: The steep learning curve takes away time from copy editing itself. "So we said, 'We've got to hire people on the production desk so we keep the editing function separate from the layout function,'" he said. So Editor Ralph Langer shepherded through the budget proposal, which also included funding for restructuring and renovating parts of *News*' facilities to accommodate larger computer workstations and provide workspace for the NTG.

Probably the linchpin to the entire adoption process was the training process itself. As mentioned previously, the NTG mulled over how training went for the previous (SII) system and visited seven CCI papers to witness the various training methods. Superusers and replacement teams in place, *The News* set out to lay the groundwork for the transition.

Training 'Til It Hurts

The year 2000 was a very big news year: The Summer Olympics, and the presidential nominating conventions and subsequent elections are enough to eat up any newsroom's planning budget and time. At *The News,* however, managers in 1999 not only foresaw it as a demanding journalistic year, they saw it as all the more reason to adopt the new pagination system.

The goal was to have a computer system that would deliver information and execute tasks instantaneously, with no waiting. Editors wanted Internet access, e-mailing capabilities, intra-office messaging—all in a personal computer (PC) for each employee. For copy editors, they would no longer need to deal with intricate coding when editing stories and making up pages; they wanted to see the page as a whole—not just as a mixture of headlines, text, and graphics.

To do so would take time—lots of it. The NTG needed one person to be the guru on the training to handle scheduling problems. "We wanted to schedule way out in advance," Rogers said. At the beginning of 1999, the NTG asked department heads to schedule individual staffers in such a way as to eliminate complaining and conflicts. Michael Taylor took care of the entire process, building a scheduling database, creating preliminary training schedules, and then asking for feedback via a computerized form.

Meanwhile, Taylor began to think about the actual training. Although the NTG's visits to different newspapers were helpful, "We learned . . . more what not to do than what to do," he said. So the NTG began by finding out what kind of PC experience staffers possessed. There were many basic training exercises and sessions in the common word processing and office programs. There was training of the trainers: The superusers required five weeks of CCI training—largely in how to start a story, send it to an editor, and place it on a page—and in the process collected several training handbooks. This was to prevent them from becoming the dry, boring teachers that the NTG members had seen elsewhere.

There was a dry run in September 1999. CCI representatives and the NTG took a week to test the system on everything from developing stories to typesetting. Test pages integrated parts from all sections of the paper. Testers performed roles: Reporters, editors, layout specialists, and photo and art staffers watched to see if the system met their needs. The tests revealed few problems and all were corrected by CCI or addressed in training sessions written by the superusers.

A rollout schedule was announced—with the first department set to adopt the system in early December 1999—and training was set to begin in mid-November. As many as five locations were used for training and maps to all classrooms were posted throughout the *News* building. Most staffers would have 2½- to 4-day training sessions, while layout editors would have three-week sessions. "Other newspapers have told us we have a very aggressive training schedule," Taylor said. "But we say, 'Why not?' It's painful, but it will be shorter in the long-term." However, before training could start, more groundwork was being laid in two places.

First, each of the respective staffs was having meetings with its respective superuser representative. "We've been hearing about this for two years," said Alison Stewart, a veteran copy editor. "The method and the message have been very positive. Most of the superusers are upbeat about it and that will help a lot because they'll be teaching us (and) . . . because we'll be afraid when we have to start." Then, after discussing previous adoption methods (at Dallas and at her previous newspapers), Stewart confidently added, "Once they (the NTG) showed us it was going to be better, it was OK."

Staffers got a chance to see prototypes and have their questions answered in these meetings, which also served to buttress and clarify demonstrations by CCI reps. "The CCI guys sort of seemed like an infomercial," said Jack Pointer, a fairly new addition to the copy desk. He added, however, that a subsequent session was conducted by a superuser who "seemed confident with the system and made it seem like we were going to like this."

Second, Taylor and a 10-person group of superusers and NTG members began collaborating on an exhaustive, 21-chapter manual that discussed all aspects of the system as well as provided exercises for layout technicians and copy editors. A separate, 12-chapter manual also was prepared for reporters and editors. The NTG wanted the manuals because existing handbooks were difficult to read and often included no index. This was not an easy task and, even two weeks before training was scheduled, Taylor was nervous because the manual materials were constantly changing.

The manual also was a blessing. Taylor said the most difficult aspect was "working with the dynamic of all the different personalities." For example, with the superusers and certain members of NTG, he found that having assigned tasks for everyone was a must. The solution was the development of the training manual.

The 21 chapters reflected a simple organization style, that is each chapter discussed either a concept or an exercise or both. For example, the first chapter discussed the concept of a new environment, revolving around the following topics: desktop setup, supported software, help desk, roaming from computer to computer, e-mail, file storage, and continuing education. At the end of each chapter, there usually was an exercise. Chapter 1's exercise featured how to work within a network with the objectives of teaching about the CCI system's default configuration, how to log on to the software and how to create and save documents.

In one last written plea, the NTG asked *News* staffers to prepare for training by doing the following: First, learn the basics—how to open, edit, save, find, and retrieve files on the designated operating system. Second, learn the messaging software. Third, organize and prepare files for the move to the new system. Fourth, save Web browser bookmarks. Finally, discuss details with colleagues (J. Rogers, 1999). The publication also carried information about training locations, the rollout schedule, and miscellaneous hardware and software updates.

The typical training sessions would guide the employee through the manual for the first two weeks, with the last week being spent on hands-on exercises. The early returns on the process itself seemed promising. "This was a difficult change," said Rena Pederson, Editor of the editorial page and a *News* employee since 1973. "I've gone through (changes involving) linotype and others and this one was very complex. But it was the best job I've ever seen the paper do as far as support for the change. For example, the replacement team and the wonderful superusers all came prepared."

The editorial department, which works several days ahead of the actual publication day, had previously used Apple MacIntosh personal computers. Pederson, who had three days of training, said the CCI transition was, by comparison, much smoother than that involving the Macs. She added, however, that the CCI system was a difficult, complicated one. "Coming from SII, there's so many bells and whistles with this new system—it's faster, has more power, Internet connections and more sophisticated editing tools." She said she was especially thankful for the organized support group the paper had provided.

Jim Frisinger, who designs and edits the letters-to-the-editor page, echoed her sentiments. He was equally flattering about the training, but had reservations about the system itself. He found it "too complicated in a backward way," mentioning that the on-screen help language was not always correct or precise in its suggestions. "That made the training more difficult," he said and—at times—prompted end-runs around the system. For example, he recalled attempting to revise a late editorial concerning a primary election that day. He wanted to produce the letter Q as a *drop letter* (also known as an *initial cap*—a big capital letter set into the opening paragraph of an article's text). The system would produce other letters, but not a Q. "So rather than getting the tech person to help, we rewrote the editorial—now that's just stupid, I know, but that's what we did," he said. Still, he was willing to give the system some consideration. "In these circumstances—it's something that's evolving; it's an unfinished product—given it wasn't something that was (fully) tested, I was pretty pleased."

He felt the manual-first, exercises-second format of the training sessions was good, but at times did not meet his individual needs. As an example, he mentioned the special importance placed on graphics. He emphasized, "Charts aren't my thing." The system also was set up in a hierarchical manner, meaning once an employee completes a task on a document, the system expects (and demonstrates) how to send the material to the next-highest editor. "But I'm a one-man person in editorial," he said alluding to his letter-editing duties, "I do it all, so (with the new system), I'm sending things to myself all the time."

Still, he said the overall training structure on CCI was much better than it had been on the Macs. "There was more time to do what we had to do. I had time to do live pages. This was more structured, much more organized." As to the entire adoption process, he felt it had been handled well, given the system's quirks and the technical problems his department encountered in sending its material to the online department. "That was unfortunate . . . but they (the NTG) didn't cheat on the (backup and training) personnel, and I appreciated that."

The business news department had a somewhat different experience, in that it was experiencing considerable employee turnover at the time—a fact that even the replacement teams could not overcome. "It (the training) was good considering we were understaffed," said Business News Copy Chief Laura Ehret, "at no time have we been horribly late for deadline." She still heard "people grumbling" about having to learn a new system with "a steep learning curve," she said, but she felt the training was good. "This is a northern European system; it doesn't think like Texans think," she added.

CHANGE ANALYSIS

Thus far, we described the adoption of pagination at *The Dallas Morning News* in simple, chronological fashion. On its face, it does not sound all that exciting or unusual. To get a better understanding of the change involved, we must re-examine the *News'* efforts in this process. We previously said that newspaper change is a complex process, not something simply accomplished. In looking at how the *News* implemented this change, we merely examined the shape of change—and that shape was in the form of a technology or task. Still, our grasp of change is enhanced if we scrutinize it in the following contexts.

Vision

On the face of things, we can argue that the vision in the Dallas case was clear: The paper needed a more efficient editing system and pagination would deliver it, if properly planned. However, the real, primary change did not involve the switch to a new technology—*News* staffers have undergone such changes before. The significant change occurred in how the technological transition was engineered. There was a massive, detailed and highly coordinated planning effort. So the truly visionary element was the acknowledgment of management that it is not just what you do—changing the technology—that is important; it is how you go about doing it that also counts. A change requires resources for preparation and execution.

What caused that vision? The *News'* vision does not seem all that new or complicated. In fact, it seems simple. Management consultant and former business school dean Vaill (1993) argued that vision's power lies in its ordinariness. That, in essence, is its beauty and authority. At all times, the NTG knew what it was attempting to do, of what the end result could be and what it would mean to the people concerned. "I told the guys (in the NTG)," Rogers said, "that there was no guarantee the group would stay together. The only way is if we do what we said we needed to do in the beginning—serve a purpose." The group's task, in effect, was to create its vision by listening to and assimilating all the individual visions of the affected employees. No wonder that Vaill defined vision as "a living expression of shared meaning and commitment" (1993, p. 16).

You could argue that this aspiration in Dallas was not the result of planning so much as it was the reaction to previous experiences. After all, *News* staffers often recalled and complained of how the *Times Herald* equipment was imposed and how they did not want a repeat of that encounter, so is not a vow to do it right a reaction to having done it incorrectly? Indeed, many experts would agree that reactive planning should not be a hallmark of a visionary organization. Modern, large newspapers such as *The Morning News* are too complex and—in many cases—too bureaucratic to take a chance on letting one person or one group of people determine its fate. Reactions are one thing; what comes after the reaction is another. Vision requires more than slogans, and at the *News* the key ingredient was instilling in employees the belief that they had a stake in the process.

"Jeff (Rogers) is big on getting people to buy in," said Training Leader Michael Taylor, and it is true that most employees bought in because the CCI system was a great improvement on the previous system. When employees consider whether management is earnest in its vision, they inevitably search for concrete evidence. In short, Rogers' motivational pitches to the NTG and to the rest of the newsroom would only take him so far. Management not only had to "talk the talk," but also "walk the walk." The deliberations in choosing a system, the commitment of funds for a replacement team, and the decision to get superusers who could speak the employee's departmental language did much of the walking.

Finally, although some may view vision and strategy as the same thing, we caution against lumping them together in this case. Strategy is the planned process for achieving an organization's mission and goals. It requires the often elaborate and laborious process of assessing competitive opportunities, threats, and risks while simultaneously balancing resources and opportunities. At the *News*, as at any other newspaper, strategy entailed the long-term plans to create and increase profits and carve a market niche. An organization's vision, on the other hand, is a picture of its future state—a mental model of what it wants to be. This picture is created collectively through communication. Although some executives associate the process of visioning with top-down leadership, it is a process best shared among the internal constituencies of the organization. At the *News,* interested staffers could volunteer for the visits to paginating newspapers. The same was true for the NTG and for the superusers—there was competition among employees to gain membership. We make the distinction because many newspaper executives desperately want vision—and the entire innovation process—to be planable, to be something they can directly control. The truth (as it is with any aspect of managing) is that the manager relinquishes direct control once the employee starts working. In Dallas, editors and publishers had to trust the NTG and the superusers to know what they were doing; luckily, they did. As former Editor Ralph Langer put it: "If you hire the right people, you don't have a lot of bad things happen—You don't know they're happening."

Nanus (1992) also noted that creating a vision is a very practical process. Visions are not hallucinations, but portraits of the future developed with feet firmly planted on solid ground. To Nanus, leaders (wherever they are in an organizational hierarchy) create visions by asking several questions about the future:

- What major changes can be expected in the needs and wants of those served by the organization?

- What changes can be expected in the major stakeholders (e.g., employees, customers, clients, and management) of the organization?

- What major economic, social, political, and technological changes can be expected in the organization's environment? (p. 84)

The most successful visions are created and implemented with input from organizational members from all organizational levels and functions. Nevertheless, the impetus for the process comes from a leader with foresight—at *The News* this was Ralph Langer.

Visionary leadership was one key at *The News.* However, it would be misleading to say that the vision was an all-powerful, all-encompassing, driving force in Dallas. All visions encounter obstacles and—as previously discussed in chapter 4—change does not necessarily succeed. Many *News* staffers certainly feared the pagination system, despite its advantages. Structural politics were encountered (e.g., two departments early on became engaged in a dispute involving renovations and size of the workstations). Traditional journalistic interests reared their heads as copy editors voiced concerns about the system's potential to tax their patience and increase their workloads. These factors were mitigated by the cohesiveness and pervasiveness of the vision—the buy-in facet. "If there's one thing," said former Editor Langer, "somehow it's communicated 'This is a good thing. This is an exciting thing.' You look over there (at *The News*), at that time, we said, 'This is where we want to go' and people are invested in it, they can see where it is and they will come along.'"

Time

In the latter part of chapter 4, we said time was key in approaching change not only because it involves the idea of timing (in the sense of an opportunity), but also because of the duration aspect—whether the change represents a long-term phenomenon or a brief investment of time. Although the Dallas experience has occurred over the span of two years (and continued as this book was in press), it would be premature to describe it as long-term or permanent, since only the passage of time itself can verify that assumption. Still, time does play a role in *The News*' approach to change.

In one sense, the paper's strategy was reactive. It served as a defense of sorts to previous experiences with technology adoption—experiences that were less-than-satisfying to many employees, including members of the NTG. However, it would be a leap in logic to say the entire Dallas project was solely reactive, since that term connotes disorganized or "seat of the pants" thought. Yes, Dallas was in large part creating a change that would oppose or depart from earlier pagination trials. Rogers himself said "the DTI thing (a prior editing system) probably motivated Ralph" Langer to help the NTG sell its approach to Langer's superiors and to prevent the project from being orchestrated instead by the paper's information technology department. "There was timing," Rogers said, "It was just (that) everybody knew we had to do this."

It therefore would be fair to say this was not so much a reaction but an opportunity to learn from the past. Capturing the gains of the past, as it is called (Brown & Eisenhardt, 1998), is important for newspapers that want to create a competitive advantage in rapidly, ever-changing markets. The answer lies in a kind of regeneration: A crucial collection of employees—who possessed enough institutional memory to carry forward (unpleasant) experiences with previous technologies—and used those memories to revive or regenerate the idea of making work more efficient, and, in the long run, more profitable.

In another sense, however, the timing approach surely hinged on a top-down, bottom-up strategy. The entire effort went to great lengths to encourage participation in the training process. "The buying-in part," Langer said, "is a cultural thing that an organization either has or doesn't." For years, *The News* has taken satisfaction in its pledge to employ and keep superior people. Its salaries and employee benefits rank among the best in the industry and the newspaper attempts to create a satisfying job setting (Murphy, 1990). Reporters, for example, may become annoyed at certain newsroom restrictions, but they seldom leave the paper, which has lower-than-industry turnover rates (Gelsanliter, 1995). So it comes as no surprise that Langer, describing the staffing approach to the pagination transition, listed one of his approaches as having "a staff in place that had flexibility and attitude—the forever support system . . . I think the culture was set early on that people could buy in."

Form

Time and vision, then, provide the context and direction, respectively, of newspaper change. What of a change's form? There are three such forms: identity change, coordination change, and change in control (Kanter et al., 1992). Identity changes concern the newspaper and its environment: its assets, markets (current and potential), and its various customer–reader relationships. Coordination changes relate to the newspaper's internal mechanism, its structure and inner workings. Control changes involve politics, internal and external. Obviously, the *News* experience would most closely come under the coordination banner, for two reasons.

First, the newspaper undertook a massive training effort that would not only introduce employees to the technology, but also would incorporate the different needs and wants of the different employee types, chief among them copy editors, reporters, section editors, and department heads. One solution was the extensive manual; another involved the education effort (e.g., *Interface's* advice columns and cautionary how-to articles). Another, more difficult solution was in the training sessions, where superusers—two each from the news art, sports, lifestyles, news and metro desks and one each from business and the universal desk—had to answer questions from a staff member from any department, not simply their own departments.

Second, the organizational end-result of the pagination training was the permanent establishment of a new department, the NTG. "We're a new unit," Rogers said. "The paper always needed a bridge between the newsroom and IT (the information technology department). You've got to help them (IT) set priorities." The NTG's creation apparently is not temporary. "I've been told," Rogers said, "that creating a cost center at this newspaper is a good sign you won't go away. As far as I'm concerned, we're a department and we'll be here."

To some extent, such talk sounds political, and thereby control-oriented. Interviews with *News* staffers revealed few direct references to IT, unless methodology of previous pagination adoption efforts could be construed as political. If one makes such an assumption, then just about any task-oriented change could similarly be interpreted. At the level of end-users such as copy editors, the task issue was the focus and their concern. As copy editor, Jack Pointer commented, "There will be some intimidation (in learning the new system), but we've had system crashes and other, typical glitches. But everybody knows we need to do this because we spend too much time (worrying about headline coding and formats)."

Finally, there remains one other key aspect of form, which actually could also be considered a variant of time. This form involves the type of actions that leaders take that help encourage and prolong triumphant changes: bold strokes or long marches (Kanter et al., 1992). The former would mean the newspaper making important financial moves, such as buying another publication, closing a bureau or department, or assigning funds and staff to develop a new product, feature, or service. Long marches, on the other hand, concern procedural moves, such as combining departments, transforming relationships, or augmenting departmental efficiency. Just how long is long? The time factor is subjective, of course, but it would take a stretch of the imagination to consider the *News'* experience as a bold stroke, since that would imply a mandate from higher up in the newspaper's hierarchy. Long marches call for extraordinary commitment over a long time and, hence, are more difficult to accomplish—making the Dallas scenario all the more remarkable and noteworthy.

Still, the case for change in Dallas remains open to interrogation. Savvy editors and publishers (and cynical students of change) rightfully should inquire as to whether several criteria for change have been satisfied.

QUESTIONS (AND ANSWERS)

Change or Status Quo?

You can argue that the Dallas change was not much of a change when placed in the context of the last 25 years, when the paper began to wake up from its slumber. Murphy (1990) aptly described this pre-competition assessment by quoting one *Times Herald* executive: "Times Mirror looked at *The Morning News* as some kind of country bumpkin who was fat and dumb" (p. 4). That re-awakening set to work a huge cultural shift within the *News* and you possibly could see the pagination adoption as an incremental change in a long change initiative.

Kanter et al. (1992) suggested that "character" plays a role in determining whether change exists. Character is the "consistent, patterned behavior of an organization's members over time" and no change in character translates as a "cosmetic, temporary . . . small-c 'change'" (p. 11). Rogers and members of the NTG would argue that their strategy and methods were transformational in that they illustrated that technology did not have to be imposed on employees but, rather, could be embraced by them. You would have a tough time arguing with them that the establishment of a new organizational entity (the NTG) is a cosmetic anomaly—but it is not transformational, that is, dramatic, rapid, end-order change.

Will It Stick?

As we acknowledged in so many words, attaining change takes a great deal of effort. Often—too often, it seems—newspapers start a new project or try to undertake a shift in their culture or operations, only to back down, revise, change course, shut down, or all of the aforementioned. As we said in chapter 4, the reasons are numerous and well known. Often, the reasons (fear, politics, traditional journalistic interests and timing, chief among them) have subtler, more structural roots. For example, Brown and Eisenhardt (1998) suggested one reason involves error catastrophe—"errors accumulate, the system or vehicle of change cannot adjust because it can't differentiate errors from potentially helpful events or phenomena. Ultimately, the system won't function because too many errors prevent it from doing so" (p. 109).

To say that only time will tell if this is the case in Dallas would be too easy, almost excuse-like. Judging from the *News'* strategy, organization, and leadership in the case of pagination adoption, however, we feel fairly safe in predicting the training process and the style of learning encouraged by the NTG are in place for some time. With the adoption's continued success, it might also be safe to say that the process may be imitated in varying degrees elsewhere in the newspaper. We would not expect creation of another cost center (i.e., the NTG), but we would expect that the NTG has set a standard for department-wide technological implementation that other units would do well to study.

We would caution, however, that no change is guaranteed permanency; the NTG had better do its homework The group needs to continue its training efforts, being constantly mindful that people adopting new technologies are re-adjusting their routines and—as a result—require the drive, particulars, and ability for such re-adjustment. That means communication and education—as well as feedback—remain vital functions in the process (Kanter et al., 1992).

Will It Work for Anyone?

This is an important question, because it suggests that not all organizations—indeed, not all newspapers—are alike. On the one hand, it would seem that if a large paper such as the *News*—with its many departments, employees, and its status as one cog (albeit a large one) in a complex corporation—can get this change accomplished, then anyone can do it. On the other hand, such a statement oversimplifies what is at stake. For example, larger newspapers need to remember that previous history played a large part in the Dallas case and that not every paper's experience is similar or has the same intensity level. Smaller papers also should recognize that the *News*—because of its size—has an unusual amount of resources at its disposal.

Other, non-size factors to consider include the individuals responsible for championing the change—the so-called change agents. Jeff Rogers seemed uniquely suited to lead the cause in Dallas. His unsatisfactory experience with the previous technology, his keen sense and recognition that he needed substantial employee buy in, his eagerness to communicate that requirement to senior management, his propensity to organize, and willingness to build coalitions to assure the process' smooth transition—all helped make him capable of infusing the NTG with the same missionary fervor.

In fact, a more important question about the suitability of a proposed change may be "Will anyone work for it?"—meaning that the editor or publisher or management student must not ignore the role of people in any change. Employees, as an established part of the newspaper's structure and operational routines, create and develop norms that constitute their work environment. It is quite possible that these same *News* employees—when placed at another, similar-sized newspaper—would acquire different work habits and, thus, a markedly dissimilar reaction to the NTG's strategy than that which occurred in Dallas. That is because newspapers, like any organization, take their cue from their customers. Since customers vary by location, it is reasonable to expect that Dallas readers have diverse needs and wants in a newspaper than those in Boston. Their sense of news differs, as do their economic needs—which impacts the advertising content.

What's the Management Lesson?

Editors and publishers are, at their core, decision makers. They get paid to assess a situation, gauge available resources, balance the risks against the benefits, and commit the newspaper's resources in one direction or another. As the business and publishing worlds grow more complex and revolve at faster speeds, newspaper managers must be able to make multiple decisions more quickly. The Dallas situation may not be generalizable to newspapers of a different size, in different locations.

However, we believe *The Morning News* case has much to offer the study of change in newspaper organizations. Not only does it provide a window on the operations of one of the country's more prestigious organizations, it reveals several common truths: First, a great deal of work goes into making a change. Dallas' effort had taken two years (and counting) when this text went to press—in no way constituting a quick, bold stroke. Second, leadership often must follow if it is to succeed. The NTG's success resided in its willingness to listen to employees. Third, change cannot be divorced from the past. The *News* effort obviously capitalized on the mistakes of previous endeavors; the foundation was built on experience. Fourth, the change had someone to push it, promote it, and place it on the agenda of managers and their subordinates. Former Editor Ralph Langer and Jeff Rogers fulfilled those roles in Dallas. Fifth, there was a viable way to implement the change. The NTG prepared an in-depth, ongoing training process that took into account a large part of employee needs and questions.

In addition, the case shows that need, not uncertainty, should drive change. Successful change agents show organizational members the problems, concerns, and issues existing in an organization that should be addressed. Understanding a need for change, as Rogers did in Dallas, is one of the first steps toward employee buy in to the change and participation in change activities. As a result: Successful change, in part, depends on the early involvement of multiple participants; and adequate resources (time, people, and financial resources) are needed to implement a change initiative.

Too, successful adoption in Dallas depended on continuous communication among and between organizational members, and the free flow of information to and among the various internal constituencies. Both uncertainty and ambiguity are reduced through information-sharing, as in the case of *Interface,* as well as the numerous training sessions, memos, and feedback mechanisms involved in the Dallas effort. That the campaign created a community within the newspaper was not unintended. This is an important function within organizations, where people spend many hours of their lives, and where they obtain social support through important relationships— social relationships that are hard to create outside the work setting because of a lack of time and energy. This is particularly true for newspapers.

Finally, the Dallas change process showed that time plays an immensely important role in such initiatives. Not only did managers capitalize on discontent with previous training efforts, they considered present-day needs and habits in preparing the training manual, in scheduling training sessions, and in hiring replacement editors. Nowhere was this concern more apparent than in the recruitment and training of superusers who could relate to the employees' previous habits and connect them to their future needs, even if the employees themselves did not know what those needs would be. In the process, the *News* laid the foundation for their workflow of the future—a process that would not only be faster (and thus allow *The Morning News* to compete with quicker competitors), but more efficient and meet the communication needs of employees for some time in the future. In short, the paper's change agents looked beyond the immediate horizons and—in so doing— surveyed several horizons simultaneously.

CHAPTER SIX

Product and the Black Press

No industry can succeed if it does not meet changing needs. This is doubly true for the African-American press, which finds itself in an economic quandary. African-American newspaper advertising levels are troublesome and economic self-sufficiency always has been a struggle. Prior to the 1970s, corrective strategies included local forums for advertisers, cash incentives, agencies specializing in acquiring advertising for African-American newspapers and, ultimately, the formation of a national association to focus on the problem. Some individuals ventured so far as to conduct market research and readership studies (Pride & Wilson, 1997).

Additionally, beginning with the Civil Rights Movement, mainstream media took advantage of a more integrated society. Papers were no longer seen as relevant by a new generation of African Americans and several African-American newspapers did not survive (Bernstein, 1989; Pride & Wilson, 1997). It has been suggested (Black & Woods, 1994) that advertisers and prospective advertisers knew little about black newspapers, but that African-American newspaper sales professionals were not helpful in that regard. This echoed an earlier finding proposing African-American newspaper publishers were not assertive enough, that is, they did not consistently reinvest in their papers and did not reflect good management. It seemed as if few black newspapers had taken the time to prove their vitality as advertising media (La Brie, 1979).

However, any effort on the part of black newspapers would have been difficult to detect, since little is known about specific economic survival strategies of these newspapers. To understand these strategies, the economic background of black newspapers must be discussed and the appropriate context introduced.

THE STRUGGLE FOR SURVIVAL

Modern-Day Woes

Since their humble beginnings in 1827 as servants of, spokesmen for, and defenders of the African-American minority population of the United States

(Wolseley, 1990), African-American newspapers—as small businesses—typically struggled. No battle has been more serious, however, than in the last 30 years (since the 1970s). As conditions improved for some black citizens in the 1970s and the African-American middle class began to grow (Landry, 1987; Rose, 1976), the black press suddenly found itself facing new competition from mainstream media. For example, after the Kerner Commission's report on civil disorders in the 1960s highlighted the absence of black faces working in the general media, black newspapers experienced an acute workforce depletion, with one poll showing a seven-person average loss per paper (Pride & Wilson, 1997).

The Civil Rights Movement also helped to enlarge the black middle class, which prompted the creation of magazines that competed with black newspapers for this group's attention and advertising patronage. The black press' traditional middle class focus meant that other publications could target younger black adults and teens—and flourish. This made the black press seem old-fashioned and inappropriate to some in the black community (Pride & Wilson, 1997); television also has played an increasingly important role in attracting black audiences (e.g., see Perry, 1996).

In addition, the accelerated African-American migration to suburbs (Logan & Schneider, 1984) meant a shift from reliance on subscriber support to dependence on advertising. At the same time, African-American newspapers began to decline. Critics blamed outdated and irrelevant content and the increasing need to depend on White advertisers for revenue (Higgins, 1980; Ward, 1973). Meanwhile, African-American newspaper publishers noticed declining advertising sales and talk of an African-American newspaper identity crisis arose (Joseph, 1985). African-American newspaper publishers faced the 1990s threatened with extinction because of the loss of readers, journalists, and advertisers to other media (Fitzgerald, 1990).

In fairness, we should note that African-American newspaper trade group officials in the 1990s pointed to increased circulation and renewed determination to attain a larger share of local advertising (Stein, 1990). There were supportive examples—historical awareness campaigns, economic brokering, journalistic training, and molding public opinion—of how the black newspaper still served the African-American community (Boyd, 1991; Hatchett, 1991), but editors and publishers still were concerned about advertising support (Lacy, Stephens, & Soffin, 1991). Nearly two-thirds of the managers agreed or strongly agreed that lack of reader support was a reason that African-American newspapers fail. One content analysis showed African-American newspapers had a lower percentage of advertising from local sources than did mainstream weekly newspapers (Lacy & Ramsey, 1994). Increased costs have forced many publishers to rely on national advertising because they perceive such advertisers as having bigger advertising budgets than that of smaller, local companies (Pride & Wilson, 1997).

Questions remain as to why advertisers do not buy more ads in African-American newspapers and what black newspaper publishers have done or can do to solicit additional advertising support. Personnel limitations—a common problem in most African-American newspapers because of limited financial resources (Lacy et al., 1991)—make developing sales strategies a challenge for the African-American press. A study of African-American newspaper advertising in Texas (Sylvie & Brown-Hutton, 1999) found, for example, that the newspapers averaged only 26% of the ad employees staffing levels for mainstream weekly newspapers. In addition, advertising constituted some 41% of the space in the African-American newspapers—nowhere near mainstream weekly averages. The study concluded that black publishers have yet to convince local advertisers they reach the most people in the desired target market—problematic in that many such publishers cannot afford the price of marketing studies, appropriate circulation auditing services, or both that can document their reach, its quality and reliability. These findings confirmed an earlier study's (Black & Woods, 1994) assessment: "What we have is a double-barreled lack of understanding. Advertisers and prospective advertisers know little about black newspapers, their penetration, and the types of readers they attract. Newspaper sales professionals are not in touch with the needs of prospective advertisers and do poorly at contacting them" (p. 31).

As a result, many African-American newspaper publishers have felt a need to improve their product to attract more readers that appeal to advertisers. That usually means hiring additional staff and purchasing more efficient equipment. Without large readerships, these newspapers have difficulty getting the advertising revenues that would further improve operations and the product. Consequently, publishers have had to think either creatively or resign themselves to a continually smaller piece of the advertising pie. However, thinking creatively has been easier said than done. Many publishers are not only the chief financial officers for their publications, they also are the primary advertising point person, or the editor, or both. Finding time to think—let alone creatively think—can be a problem. In such situations, hiring inventive personnel always helps, but black newspapers must compete for such employees with the rest of the business world and the publications typically find themselves at a disadvantage in such competition. Not surprisingly, because black newspapers generally are small businesses, their salaries (for most job positions) typically are not as high as those in the mainstream press, nor are their working conditions as spacious or accompanied by the trappings of many labor-saving technologies. Unless a person was highly motivated to work for a black newspaper, these issues probably would inhibit him or her from even applying. Second, the black press still carries the stigma of any minority-owned business in the United States. Because the newspapers are perceived by the general public (and even some African

Americans) as "black"—owned and operated by African-Americans, producing content of interest largely to African Americans, or both—their product often is seen as inferior to what is in mainstream newspapers. Rightly or wrongly, public perception of a company plays a significant part in a potential employee's desire to work for that company. As a result, employing innovation via brainpower often is not that simple for many members of the black press.

Many publishers turn to their own inventiveness for support, and we examine this resourcefulness in this chapter. However, this examination needs to be put in the perspective of what black newspapers typically do about such problems and why. Only by looking at the everyday norm can we appreciate the extraordinary.

The Current Business of Black Texas Newspapers

It is a sunny December day in a large Texas city. The editor of one of the city's more respected black weeklies (we will call it *The Times*) is discussing the function of black newspapers. "The role of the black newspaper is much like it was 125 years ago," he says. "Our audience has changed, no question about it. But our audience has adjusted." The fact that there are at least four other black newspapers in town is of no consequence to him. "We try to inform, educate and entertain. I don't worry about competition . . . We don't call them (the other newspapers) 'competition.' We call them 'our peers' . . . We help each other."

That is not the attitude the general manager took in an interview for this study. There may not have been any ill will toward the other papers, he said, but the competition weakens the advertising base from a money standpoint. "Advertisers say, 'Why buy from you if I can go to Joe Blow?' If the group (of black newspapers) would stay solid, they (advertisers) couldn't do that. But not everybody's got the same bottom line." As to *The Times*' content, he acknowledged that "Our audience is a little older than average. (The editor) has been around and is known for a longer time, so the older generation can relate to him. He has a loyal following." That helps in selling ads, he said. "I can go to an advertiser if they're looking for a more stable crowd, property owners. The younger crowd doesn't have that yet. Our readers have got roots established." Still, he admitted, selling ads is a struggle.

"We're working toward trying to see what we can put together" to turn the corner, he said of the paper's efforts. He envisioned a campaign "trying to capture the upcoming market for major corporate sponsors, because they're the ones that will spend the money." Local businesses, on the other hand, "will try to put the heat on you. You have to go in and educate them about marketing your product. But our staff's small and we need to spend our time wisely and [so] we can go to Anheuser Busch (a large beer conglomerate)—the larger corporations that want to get involved." A current issue at the time showed 16 ads—only five of which could be considered purely local. National or regional companies figure prominently, from a clothing store, a bank, a grocery store, a cigarette company, and a coupon from a food company.

Local businesses pit one black newspaper against another, he said, adding such tactics make it difficult to shun corporate advertisers. "For example, (a large department store chain) takes an ad in the paper every week. You can't turn your back on that money or (the chain) will go to other (black) newspapers," he said. Still, not all of the large advertisers are as savvy. "(National retailer) Penney's thinks they've bought the African-American market if they've got our black newspaper . . . but the large, potential (black) market is virtually untapped," the general manager said. "Either they (large companies) know nothing and you have to educate them, or else they know what they're doing and want to know if *you* do."

The Times is unusual among black weekly publications in its circulation methods because it heavily relies on subscriptions (which costs between $30 and $40 a year), as opposed to community drop-off points. This is significant in that many black newspapers are free, and drop-offs give some publishers the opportunity to claim a wider readership than they actually possess. While many such publications claim to be audited, some auditing services require minimal information to perform an audit and greatly depend on the publishers' self-reports to conduct the audit. As a result, the general manager claims drop-offs are not as exact as subscription data. The idea of drop-offs versus paid circulation is a sensitive one for minority publications in Texas, particularly the black press.

The problem resides in the definition of a newspaper. The state of Texas—in awarding legal advertising (legals are announcements concerning local or state government action, e.g., the letting of bids, election notices, changes in ordinances, and the like)—requires the publication seeking the legal ads to be a bona fide newspaper. Section 2051.044 of the Texas state administrative code defines such newspapers as devoting not less than 25% of its total space to general interest items, publishing at least weekly, being entered as second-class postal matter in the county where published, and publishing regularly and continuously for at least 12 months before the governmental entity publishes the legal notice.

In order to attain second-class (also known as periodicals) status, the newspaper must be so classified by the U.S. Postal Service (USPS). However, USPS will not grant such status to freely circulated papers, of which there are many black publications. Such papers must have a list of subscribers, in effect meaning that they agree to be audited at any time and must furnish sales receipts, canceled checks, and any other information to prove they have valid subscription orders. In addition, the periodicals designation must be renewed every year. If a newspaper uses bulk or standard rates, it usually indicates it is not audit-able in the Postal Service's eyes. Black Texas newspapers have tried (and continue) to lobby legislators to change the law, without much success. Thus, *The Times* general manager's opinion: "I'd rather have 5,000 paid versus 20,000 non-paid (because) traditionally auditing and paid circulation have been used (by advertisers) as a screening device."

Nearly 200 miles away and five months later, another editor sits in the small, one-story, wood-frame former residence that houses the paper he also owns. The newspaper (we will call it *The Journal*) is low tech: There is a copying machine, an ancient word processor that actually looks like a typewriter, a telephone, and a fax machine. The office is empty at the moment, the part-time office staff member has not yet arrived. The operation definitely is a one-man effort, by and large.

A group of correspondents who get paid by the article provide the bulk of the non-syndicated editorial content of the paper, which typically runs 10 pages, two more than the summer run. The editor writes, sells ads, and lays out the paper. Another person handles delivery to the 120 or so drop-off points. Of the 6,000 circulation, he estimates that there are 250 subscribers— usually a business, a politician, or someone outside the city who is a former resident. What ads he sells are usually the result of a long-standing arrangement. "I'm on the list of a number of businesses who routinely send ads. I'm fortunate," he said.

His paper has tried other means. "We (the Texas Publishers Association, a trade group of black publishers established in 1986 to help increase advertising levels) get a deal with an advertiser, but the advertiser checks on the rates of other members and finds out some local rates were different (lower) than the state TPA rate." There have been TPA breakthroughs, most notably with the state's banks and state agencies (e.g., the Texas Lottery Commission). A few TPA members rely on cigarette and liquor ads, he said. "Those (advertisers) are people who saw we were very effective selling our product. Blacks are brand loyal and they (advertisers) were able to sustain brand loyalty . . . I was in the business for 10 years before I got a national ad, beer or liquor ad or a bank ad," he added.

Part of the reason, he theorized, is the shortage of black ad staffers. "I don't have people in the field. For our first eight years, we survived totally on black ads. I don't think anybody would have that problem if they had people in the field." This situation is compounded, he believes by the attitudes of current black newspaper advertising staff members and ignorance on the part of local advertisers. "Staffers don't want to sell ads to small businesses because they're told small businesses aren't worth the time. And advertising identity works over the long haul, not just on a specified week. But the advertiser doesn't understand that." Fostering such understanding takes time, although having three local competitors helps. "We're associates, not competitors. We try to convince advertisers to do it (run ads) like they do radio and TV ads. There, you often see or hear the same commercial on the various channels and stations," he said.

Despite the cooperation, the associates try to produce different products— each with a different focus born out of the experience of each publisher: One conservative, one progressive, and one aiming at younger readers and students in area colleges. Even with these distinctions, it is difficult to publish a consistent product. "In your editorial copy, you have to do two newspapers. The middle class wants different content than lower class blacks," he said. "The audience is dispersed. With the advent of the '80s, the community started splintering. The upper middle class is the one you cater to for ads, but you still cover the rest of the community." Try as it might to be two newspapers, *The Journal* largely caters to the traditional black middle class: Church news, civil rights updates, school district political activities, and stories about inequities in police behavior typically dominate the coverage.

Somewhat different coverage can be seen just two blocks away in the product of an associate publisher, who described himself as "a political activist across cultural lines" and as inspired by politics to create his publication, which we will call *The Planet*. The paper is unusual for a black newspaper in that it deals with issues of interest not just to blacks, but to Nicaraguans, Native Americans, liberated women, gays, lesbians, and the disabilty community. The idea was not all that altruistic, because in research-ing his idea to publish the paper, "I discovered that (people who share) the city's progressive nature and multicultural perspective have the most dispos-able income . . . I didn't want to create another black newspaper. I wanted a creative newspaper."

Despite his plans, however, the publication's still perceived as a black newspaper. With a drop-off circulation of around 8,000, his advertising strategy has been one of growth, to look at new markets for revenue. Still, he often hears, "We can't deal with you because we'll have to deal with all of them." He said the White power structure is "afraid blacks will turn a nickel into a dollar" and develop power. As a result, he cannot get continuous business. "Even African-American businesses won't advertise," he said. The ad agencies he uses, he added, "do a good job. They don't aggressively solicit clients for me, but some will recommend (the paper) to their clients . . . Advertisers don't consider us in their ad budget; they consider us in their *PR (public relations)* budget." Other black weekly employees echoed these sentiments. "They (advertisers) don't say this to us, but we know that African-American newspapers are lumped into a category," said a Dallas advertising manager. "They've set aside X-dollars for minority newspapers and divvy it up among all the newspapers in the minority community. It's like they're saying, 'I've done my duty' . . . It makes no business sense. They're not approaching us as a business, but as an *obligation*." She said she had approached local grocery store chains with a cooperative advertising idea, but she was told, "If we do it for you, we've got to do it for the others."

In summary, the business of journalism at black newspapers is about survival. Publisher–editors generally run small shops that routinely feature at least one one-employee departments, whether in editorial, advertising, or circulation. Advertising obviously is a major concern, as publishers try to determine how to maintain a steady revenue stream while balancing that need against the need to improve the editorial product. The whole issue often takes on chicken-and-egg proportions: Which do you do first—improve the content so you can sell more advertising? Or, sell more advertising so you can hire more capable, qualified staffers who will make the product something with which advertisers want to be affiliated? Often, many black newspapers end up *satisficing,* that is, making decisions that meet previously established minimum standards and, as a result, continuing to be subject to the same budgetary constraints.

For example, one Dallas weekly had no established advertising manager. "Everybody's responsible for getting ads," was how the office manager described the situation. In the office, the phone constantly rings, with 20 to 25 calls concerning advertising. The paper had no direct strategy regarding advertising. The one sales representative whose job is solely concerned with selling ads (the publisher and the general manager also are officially listed as sales representatives) worked on a commission basis, doing cold calls—most of them rejections. The position is one of high turnover because, in the words of its general manager: "Nobody's willing to work on commission." Paying that person a salary and a commission "is economically unfeasible. We can't afford it." The paper had no regular, established advertising accounts but primarily relied on drop-in service and advertising agencies. So satisficing had become a way of doing business. It did not have to be.

CHANGING THE BLACK PRESS

Objectively Black

From its beginning, *The Dallas Examiner* strove to be different. Fred J. Finch Jr., a Harvard graduate and Dallas attorney, was affiliated with *The Dallas Post-Tribune* in the 1980s and—depending on the source—either was not a successful manager there or was unpersuasive in getting *The Post-Tribune* to commit to a program of journalistic quality. So he started *The Examiner,* using the name as inspiration and aiming to feature "an in-depth look at local news." When Finch founded the paper, he wanted it to feature "breaking news and relevant issues instead of covering formal debuts and church anniversaries" (Anonymous, 1998). The first issue included four-color photos, a first for a black weekly. The paper started modestly, in a small, three-room house.

Her father "wanted to see a quality product," said Mollie Finch Belt, who became publisher when Finch died and eventually became involved in the daily operations in 1994. Up until 1996, however, *The Examiner* was probably no different than any other black weekly in Dallas. Its advertisers, for example, fell into three categories. First (and most lucrative) were national accounts, which the newspaper generally received through two or three placement agencies. Next came local, non-African-American institutional accounts, such as banks, the Dallas transit system, the City of Dallas, and the local utility companies. Finally, the newspaper had very small African-American accounts whom Faye Davis, a previous *Examiner* Advertising Manager, described as having "very little, sometimes no money in their (ad) accounts . . . They don't often understand the way ads work. They won't advertise and then don't understand why they don't grow."

There were signs that *The Examiner* was different from other black weeklies. For instance, in its promotional advertising material back then, the paper publicized itself as "overcoming the stereotypic expectation of an African-American weekly." It touted its various journalistic awards and recognition, including four Katie Awards from the mainstream Dallas Press Club. The advertising manager boasted that the paper's ad rates were the highest of any black weekly in the city—despite the difficulties of selling ad space in an environment in which some competitors were 75% cheaper. "But we have journalistic quality," she said.

The paper also had a savvy business manager trying to help *The Examiner* re-position its assets: improve the cash flow, handle cash disbursements, negotiate with vendors, and develop creative financing ideas. In short, "I have to try to get more money into the doors," said Willie Mae Hughey, who agreed to the consulting position at the request of her longtime friend, the publisher. Hughey, too, mentioned the paper's content as a key to her mission. "We want to make it heavy reading," she said. "We didn't want it to be 'just a black newspaper.' It's still written from the black perspective, but we didn't want to compete just with African-American newspapers."

She said she felt the paper had achieved its African-American niche and "We wanted to go above that." The newspaper brain-trust—Hughey, Mollie Belt and her attorney–husband–co-publisher James Belt—did not just want to compete with other black newspapers (in fact, the Belts had a one-third share in another black Dallas weekly, *The Post-Tribune*). They wanted to make the paper more visible by increasing its circulation and its exposure. They sought out joint ventures and sponsorships with other Dallas-based companies in an effort to "develop different programs for indirect advertising dollars" from other industries. Hughey said that *The Examiner's* greatest need at the time was to obtain "more capital to put into the newspaper, to get equipment and more personnel."

In short, the newspaper was going to attempt to be a black paper and something entirely different. "The (black) middle class area is out there," Hughey said, "and we're giving it strong consideration. We want a mixed audience, though." That attitude of difference had filtered down to the news staff. Anyika McMillan, Editor and Lead Reporter at the time, said, "We're objectively black." Hughey added that the Belts had "put a lot of money back into the newspaper—that makes them different." She pointed out that the Belts "have their own professions" (Mrs. Belt was a civil rights claims investigator with a Dallas branch office of the federal government), so the newspaper was "not just a way to make money." She said *The Examiner* was going to be different and contrasted it with the two other leading Dallas black weeklies, *The Dallas Weekly* and *The Dallas Post-Tribune*. The former, a tabloid-formatted publication chock-full of ads, was the most widely distributed of the three and at the time (in 1996) featured extensive use of opinion columns, syndicated materials, and press releases on subjects ranging from local politics, business, and health to sports and entertainment. "It wants to keep you on the go, a *USA TODAY*-type newspaper," Hughey said. *The Post-Tribune,* on the other hand, featured standard fare for a black weekly: church news, sorority–fraternity announcements, "man-on-street" reactions, and notable achievements by local residents, scattered among brief news reports and myriad columns featuring commentary on civil rights issues. "A traditional newspaper," was how Hughey described the broadsheet publication. At the time, *The Examiner* was, indeed, different. The format was a hybrid—two broadsheet sections folded to look like a tabloid, the cover of which usually featured a local African-American newsmaker. The tabloid opened into the front page, which was Associated Press wire copy mixed with local news about black and caucasian area residents. Inside the first section there was religion news, society features, and opinion columns—all dealing with black issues, institutions, or celebrities. The second section similarly dealt with sports, entertainment, and lifestyle issues. It was apparent *The Examiner* had a long way to go, in terms of editing, design, and layout: The content might have bordered on different, but the presentation definitely was an old school, black newspaper.

The same state still described *The Examiner's* advertising situation at the time. Co-publisher James Belt lamented the so-called PR phenomenon mentioned earlier. "It's not that black businesses won't advertise, it's that they can't; they don't have the money to buy advertising. . .How long can African-American newspapers survive on non-local ads?" he asked rhetorically. "We tried to do business with various local businesses, but they won't do it like you do with regular businesses—on a regular basis." So, in 1996, *The Examiner* seemed poised for a change.

Getting There

By Mollie Belt's own estimation, since *The Examiner* started in 1986, there have been anywhere from a half-dozen to 10 editors, most of them since 1994. Transforming the paper amidst such turmoil "has been hard to do because we have competitors" who only care about selling ads. "If you want journalism, you ask *us* to cover it. The others won't even send a reporter," she added.

The Examiner has put its money where its mouth is: In 1995, the paper was runner-up in the best newspaper category in the annual Texas Publishers Association awards contest judged by The University of Texas at Austin Department of Journalism; from 1996–1998, the paper won the award. In 1998, *The Examiner* also won best special section, best sports feature, best religion section, best design–layout, and best use of color. Although the circulation remained unchanged in 2000, the paper boasted a readership of 100,000—up from 80,000 in 1996. The paper now is almost totally done in-house; that means the 30-plus freelancers and the commission-only workers who produced the paper in 1996 were replaced by a regular, full-time staff of eight. "We really want a good product," Mollie Belt said. "We leave our folks alone so the creative juices can take hold and flow."

An extra creative maneuver occurred in the introduction of *Future Speak,* a tabloid insert that trains high school students in the basics of journalism, using the talents of Cheryl Smith, a longtime Dallas journalist and a regional director for the National Association of Black Journalists (NABJ). The newspaper recruits a dozen or more students from the Dallas area Urban Journalism Workshop and—with the help of co-sponsor AT&T—teaches students how to cover events, interview sources, write headlines, proofread, and design and layout copy. As a bonus, Smith and Mrs. Belt accompany the students on educational field trips, such as the regional and national NABJ conventions. Unfortunately, *Future Speak* demands considerable time in terms of grant writing and seeking available funds; occasionally, *The Examiner* will dip totally into its own reserves to fund the publication. When that is not an option, *Future Speak* has to go on hiatus until funding is obtained. Mrs. Belt constantly searches for funding sources for the project, which runs $50,000 annually. "We're not making any money on it. We're putting money *into* it," she said of the publication, which typically includes very few ads.

A slightly different—if still resourceful development—involves the establishment of an Internet site. *The Examiner* happens to be one of the few black papers in Texas with such a site—and they have done so without any extra expense. James Belt has managed to trade his legal expertise for the technical know-how and advice of one of his clients. Belt works on the Web as a hobby, furnishing some traditional and not-so-traditional content. The site carries conventional material in its slightly repackaged, nearly verbatim stories that run in the print edition of *The Examiner* and of *Future Speak*. Occasionally, when coverage warrants it, the online edition publishes unique content— daily coverage of the bribery trial of a black city councilman was one such incident. The novel material involves its sub-site, The Internet Open Records Project, "made up of educators, political activists, and computer professionals who believe access to public information is essential to a free and open democratic society." In essence, the site provides information about Dallas County individual voting records, Dallas schools' test scores and financial records, insurance complaints, and Texas sex offender records and locations. The site gets 250 hits a day on average, and up to a million if there is a related news event. Belt said he one day hopes the site will turn a profit and that he plans to market it to soccer moms—White females ages 24–37—by selling merchandise such as compact discs and music. "Nobody wants to do advertising with black newspapers, so 'Open Records' may be the way," Mrs. Belt said. The hopes remain dreams until the Belts can devise a way to develop a middleman role for the site, which to date carries advertising only by getting print ad clients to take an added-value option with their *Examiner* accounts. "We have all these great ideas," James Belt said, "but no money."

All this creativity has its drawbacks. As previously mentioned, the paper has had turnover in many key positions—particularly editor. Attempts to fill the position (which, while having the managing editor title, actually also was the paper's primary—and sometimes only full-time—reporter while doubling as the chief news editor) have been an exercise in frustration. "We tried through the years," Mrs. Belt said. Since the original editor left a couple years after she took over as publisher, she has seen a steady stream of editors. One previous editor falsely claimed he had journalistic experience. Another, more recently departed editor left because of what he claimed were personality conflicts with Smith, the *Future Speak* Advisor and Editorial Consultant. Staffers have said they felt Mrs. Belt did not handle such conflicts adequately and that staffers were left to their own devices. They also blamed a lack of clear hierarchy, with no one (save the publisher) with ultimate decision-making authority in editorial matters.

As a result, the paper experienced frequent breakdowns in the pre-press production process, ranging from story idea generation to page layout and resulting in missed deadlines and a few hurt feelings. Matters came to a head in late 1999 and the staff had an in-house workshop (conducted by one of this text's co-authors) to clear the air and make the process more efficient. "Now, we've got what we consider a training program. Before, we were trying to hire editors—people with journalism experience—but it just wasn't working out." The paper revamped its editorial department organization, with the publisher taking the lead in idea generation and eliminating the editor– managing editor position in favor of dividing the reporting responsibilities between two full-time reporters.

Making money also has required more creativity. "Ads are hard to come by," Mrs. Belt said. "We've just now (in 2000) got our first grocery chain ad." She hoped "*Examiner* on the Scene," a new, photo-filled society-type page will help more people in the Dallas black community be more accepting of the paper. She planned on parlaying that acceptance into more economic awareness that would attract more advertisers. "We're covering banquets, taking lots of pictures and increasing our (circulation) drop spots. More people are coming to us to co-sponsor events and we're asking them, 'Are the people you patronize advertising in this paper?' We feel once the community grasps the paper, advertisers won't have any choice." Diversifying content is a must, she added—not only because "black people like pictures" but because they "will not pick up a paper with just news in it—everybody wants to be entertained and we have to make sure we give our people what they want."

CHANGE ANALYSIS

In illustrating the evolution of *The Dallas Examiner,* we concentrated on the newspaper's attempts to make itself a more attractive and viable product. As we said in the previous chapter, simple description does not suffice if we want to understand the below-the-surface issues involved with change. The following discussion will attempt to present those issues in their appropriate contexts.

Product Vision

Whereas *The Dallas Morning News* situation featured a change in style (i.e., it is how you pursue change that counts), its black counterpart is undergoing a change in product, the end result. The difference rests in the cause. At *The News,* the collective vision of managers and subordinates helped enact the change, while *The Examiner's* vision clearly originated with management. Mollie Belt had a clear dream, one she inherited from her father, of what a black newspaper should be. Again drawing on Management Consultant Peter Vaill (1993), executives should want something and Mollie Belt certainly wanted *The Examiner* to be a good product. "We're more serious—more substantive—than other black papers in Dallas," she said. "We are a more serious newspaper. We're the only paper people can depend on to cover the things that need covering." She structured her staff to see to it that the coverage reflected that desire. Her commitment to the vision—through her retirement from her federal government position to concentrate on the paper ("I caught myself more and more at work thinking about the paper.") and her assumption of responsibility for news ideas—paved the way for achieving the vision.

Small businesses expect vision from the owner, to be sure. When the owner is the de facto editor, it is not difficult to foresee the product being shaped in the owner's image. A newspaper is not just any small business. Unlike most companies, newspapers possess dual markets: one in advertising and one in information. Each market affects the other (Picard & Brody, 1997). In many modern-day black newspapers—in Texas and across America—the sensitivity to that fact has quickly evolved. Mrs. Belt described it: "There's a fear among African-American publishers," she said, "that controversial news will affect advertising." She added that, traditionally, the "old-line" conventional black newspapers had "someone already established" as their publishers— usually a lawyer or doctor or other professional. As a result, the paper's profits were not the publisher's primary source of income, meaning that such publishers could afford to publish controversial material without fear of loss of livelihood. However such publishers—who put the Civil Rights Movement squarely on their agendas and in their newspapers—eventually grew older. In time, they turned over the reigns to family members who not only were less gifted in running the paper, but also felt less obliged to the traditional sense of mission regarding the civil rights crusade that black newspapers had felt (Pride & Wilson, 1997). The Belts said this lack of commitment and managerial adeptness leads to a lack of ability to report on the more subtle forms of racism and, conversely, a dependence on sin advertising accounts offered by the liquor and tobacco industries. "But we (*The Examiner*) have a *serious* editorial section every week," Mrs. Belt offered.

As the Belts continued to seek ways to achieve their vision, they realized it is an ongoing struggle. Mollie Belt persists in attempts to require, cajole, and conjure historical context out of the staff's editorial work—often with success, but more often after many trials and exasperating failures—frequently centering on shortcomings of staffers. There was the time when a managing editor attended an appreciation dinner for a famous, wealthy Dallas black businessman and did not interview anyone; the same staff member also left a protest rally an hour before protesters were set to speak. If anything, this shows that vision can take the newspaper only so far; the execution must be there. A product still results from a process. Vision simply provides—at most—the instructions or—at the least—the mandate. In either case, vision alone cannot produce change. We saw this in the case of *The Morning News* as well: Editors and publishers had to rely on the Newsroom Technology Group and the superusers to know what they were doing. So change occurs when this collective vision exists and is implemented. It is difficult to attain such vision if the members of the collective frequently change—as is the case here.

Time and Form

We have said that change at *The Examiner* is ongoing—implying that time does not comprise much of a factor here; indeed, in almost all organizations, change is a long-term phenomenon, with incremental changes emerging but no great, one-time transformation. In this light, it might be best to say that the newspaper is in transition toward major change.

Put another way, time is important because it involves the notion of timing and the idea of duration. Whereas the latter permits us to evaluate a change in context, the former incorporates benefits and costs in a short-term, comparative context. The whole phenomenon is akin to examining the growth of a living object, for example, a blade of grass. If you look at the blade, depending on its hue, you can either say it is grown or it is growing. You would be hard-pressed to say which is accurate without knowing several other factors: when it was planted, its maximum capacity for growth, the length of its growing season, the weather conditions and inherent probabilities, and so on. So it goes with time and *The Examiner*. It is difficult to say with authority that the paper has grown, that is, changed.

To help determine what state is proper, we can look to Brown and Eisenhardt's (1998) discussion of growing strategy. They list four basics of growth: First, grow—do not assemble; that is, a company that creates a proper strategy develops into something different over time, as part of a system and not as part of a piecemeal approach. Second, the starting position matters in that the company should start from a growable point. Third, the order matters. As a chef follows a recipe to create a proper blend of ingredients, this implies that the proper order of events or actions creates growth. Finally, watch for missing links. In other words, managers should know or search for what their companies temporarily lack. It might appear that looking for missing links signifies an assembly approach; rather, the search indicates a recognition that the growth strategy is insufficient.

Applying these growth fundamentals to *The Examiner,* then, we can see the paper is, indeed, growing—slowly and incrementally. Mollie Belt realizes that the product—indeed, that her performance as a publisher—is a work in progress. She has frequently lamented, for example, her time-management skills as a publisher. The question is whether a typical small business, because of its relatively small resources, can ever completely grow strategy in the long-term, durable sense. It would seem that black newspapers are doomed to forever be searching for missing links. Since every big business at one time was a small business, there is at least hope, as long as small businesses are able to make sound cost-benefits analyses and take advantage of timing issues—as *The Examiner* continuously attempts to do with its journalistic product.

To do so also would mean this change is of the long march variety—not in a procedural or march context, however, but a long sense of time. Again, the question of how long is long arises, but—unlike in the previous chapter—the changes experienced by *The Examiner* have been mandated by upper management. We first began looking at the paper in 1996 and, given the prior rapid employee turnover, the last five years could be considered long in one sense. Moreover, given the difficulty the Belts have had in broadening the advertising base, more editorial changes may be forthcoming as the paper continues its push to attract the right audience.

Perhaps the newspaper's main problem concerning timing is that it has been financially unable to create a time cycle or pace that makes it less dependent on national advertising. One reason has been the Belts' inability until recently to keep an advertising manager and thus create a comprehensive strategy in that regard. As a safeguard, they promoted their son and former Distribution Manager, James Belt III, to the position in 1999. However, he had no formal training in sales techniques at the time and was learning the business as he went along. Listening to the Belts, it was obvious they felt that at times they were struggling to find this time-pacing, or rhythm (Brown & Eisenhardt, 1998). In that regard, they are not alone. Many publishers and editors desire to be in a position where they can choreograph the change, rather than react to it.

The closest *The Examiner* has come is its editorial creativity, which has set a journalistic and editorial pace for other black weeklies. The increased in-depth coverage, the innovative Web site, *Future Speak*, and the introduction of a weekly radio show ("Dallas Examiner *Live*") all prove the staff's creative bent. Of course, the vision has been strictly to emphasize editorial content to this point. The paper must somehow establish the same pace on the business side. To do so will take determination, discipline, and an extended search for missing links.

The paper's business plan attempts to take this into consideration. Mrs. Belt took the first steps, joining a neighborhood Chamber of Commerce and taking weekend small business management classes. "This will help me be able to see things, to not get off on tangents," she said. As a result, when this book went to press in mid-2000, the newspaper was beginning to implement a marketing program (a marketing specialist was hired) that would examine its outreach among readers, advertisers, and non-readers. "I want to know exactly who are we here to serve," she said. In addition, the newspaper has started to target its efforts more, putting *Future Speak* on hiatus until its content can be refined and until more students can be trained take over its day-to-day operation. These and other ideas, Ms. Belt said, will be part of an overall, comprehensive approach to marketing the newspaper in the most efficient, effective way possible.

Until then, the form of the change described in this is largely one of identity, in that it concerns *The Examiner* and its environment—particularly how its readers perceive its news- and information-gathering capabilities.

Again, the changes in content reflect that identity transformation and the Belts hope it will translate into additional credibility with readers and, as a result, with advertisers. First, the newspaper went to extensive efforts to look like a mainstream, credible publication. There is plenty of color and graphics, particularly on the front page. Second, the 1999 workshop enhanced the staff's ability to meet deadlines and thus produce a more professional-looking product. Third, the creation of *Future Speak* was as an attempt to diversify the content and appeal to a broader portion of the black community (while also constituting an effort to assure a potential journalistic talent pool for the paper). Finally, the radio show and the Web site give the paper a change to discuss leading stories in detail and expose viewers and listeners to a variety of issues not in the paper. All these efforts basically extend a brand—the journalistic one. This emphasis begs for closer inspection and gives rise to additional questions about the nature of *The Examiner's* change.

QUESTIONS (AND EXPLANATIONS)

Can Objectivity Work?

On the face of it, the answer to this would seem obvious. In fact, we might be tempted to ask, "Could it hurt?" There does not seem to be an argument against making the content more credible. Credibility certainly makes the newspaper more respectable in the eyes of many customers—advertisers and readers. Such journalistic respectability creates a niche for *The Examiner* that other black newspapers in Dallas do not have.

The dual-market nature of newspapers (Picard & Brody, 1997) makes it difficult to predict that improving the editorial product alone will make the paper turn around its financial situation. Advertisers respond to more than just news; they need information about the product—its reach, viability, the audience's purchasing habits, and the like. *The Examiner,* until it gets either a larger subscriber base or performs a thorough audit of its readership, will find it difficult to get the ear of the serious, continuous advertiser. Advertisers' eagerness to advertise and buy ads directly relates to the newspaper's skill in the circulation area. So *The Examiner* will have to address its circulation methods, which many advertising agencies and their clients deem somewhat unreliable.

In addition, the newspaper must face the major business question confronting many unwilling editors in the mainstream press: How much news should there be? How much should readers' desires dictate the newspaper's content? What is the right balance between news and entertainment and how will that affect the newspaper's bottom line? Mollie Belt has begun to make concessions to this fact, acknowledging that blacks resemble other audiences

in their fancy for entertainment-oriented content. Granted, a weekly probably would not witness the journalistic hue and cry that other papers have
seen concerning fears that business values would undermine journalistic
content (Underwood, 1993). Weekly reporting staffs tend to be smaller and
their journalistic professionalism not as strongly established—not to mention
the fact that weekly newspaper working conditions generally do not encourage much thought or time to considering matters of an indirect nature, such as
matters of journalistic purity. Still, the urge to, and appeal of, publishing soft
news could distract *The Examiner* from its mission of being a heavy reading
newspaper of depth and insight.

Does Race Matter?

This is a separate, distinct concern from objectivity's ability to attract
advertisers. The uncertainty lies in determining *The Examiner's* ability to
promote and position itself as a regular or mainstream publication from a
professional standpoint. This goes far beyond the circulation idea, although
the newspaper's reliance on drop-offs continues to hamper its capabilities in
meeting advertisers' normal informational requirements. The issue, rightly or
wrongly, remains a question of race.

"Only a few advertisers are interested in 'minority markets' per se," said
Sara Martinez, a media buyer with an advertising agency in Austin. "They
want major markets and that requires auditing. Minority publications need
to put their product in a positive light," she said. "They need to say, 'Let me
show you how I can help your business.'" The solution is one of making a
business grow—even if that means reaching out toward other audiences, she
said. While auditing legitimizes the product, she added, minority publishers
have to "see beyond that (traditional mission) to be able to grow." For
instance, simply saying that your product reaches the black community
unless it reaches a large segment of that group, she said. While some
advertisers think in terms of race in promoting their products, "Seasoned
advertisers don't see 'ethnic' as 'ethnic market *only*." This calls into question
whether black newspaper publishers are accurate in their perceptions concerning their abilities to garner more advertising.

So when we ask if race matters, the question is not a moral or political one,
but an economic one. It begs the question, "Matters to whom?" At least one
study has shown that more viable black businesses do not specialize in
delivering services to largely black consumers (Smith & Moore, 1985). With
questions as to whether the black middle class can adequately finance black
businesses (Davidson, 1989), and the uncertainty about what determines
middle class blacks' sense of community (Durant & Louden, 1986), "Matters
to whom?" is, indeed, a fair question. Are black publishers following the
wrong audience? Is there truly such a workable economic idea as a black

newspaper any more? Does trying to produce one actually represent a change or more of the same?

Perhaps race has become a crutch for some publishers, but—if that is so—the Belts have demonstrated an indomitable spirit. Their editorial and financial plans exhibit a desire to grow their product and to avoid getting caught in the traditional trappings that many black newspapers find comfortable. Whether they will become successful is a question of time, of course. It also is a question of audience tastes and advertisers' perceptions.

What Is the Management Lesson?

This case proves instructive on several fronts as it concerns managing change. First, size matters in certain situations; change in a small organization has a greater chance of working if it comes from the top-down, indeed, if the editor–publisher is a role model for the process. At *The Examiner,* the Belts have personally seen to it that their vision gets implemented, despite turnover problems. Second, a change in identity requires simultaneous effort on several fronts. This weekly publication found itself extending its own vision of journalism into two other media in order to show its sincerity about its intent to become the black paper of authority in Dallas. Third and particularly true for media, implementing comprehensive, revolutionary change in the editorial product requires examining the advertising product as well. The publishers realized that in order to make money they had to spend money—paying competitive salaries, hiring specialists, and developing a business plan.

The study of product change at *The Examiner* also is an excellent illustration of a critical issue that leaders face in times of organizational change: the identification and acquisition of resources. As Pfeffer and Salancik (1978) explained in their work on resource dependence theory, environments possess resources on which organizations depend for survival. Consequently, they are constantly in the process of negotiating for resources and competing with other organizations in the search and acquisition of them. Organizational leaders, such as publishers and editors, are responsible for managing the organization's dependent relationship with its environment, and they are affected continually by the availability of resources and the competing relationships that scarcity or abundance creates. As we have seen, *The Examiner's* leaders have spent considerable effort in finding and acquiring advertising dollars to meet the paper's ongoing needs.

Finally, no change can survive without good timing and a sense of pacing or planning where it concerns time. *The Examiner* was performing adequately without the daily influence of Mollie Belt, but it was not changing or accomplishing the vision of its founder. Only when Mrs. Belt increased her involvement did momentum begin to build. Once timing kicked in, the paper then needed the benefit of a plan to implement its vision. The brand extensions, the improved quality of the product, the hiring and training of proven specialists in journalism and marketing—all contributed to a sense that the company was finally on the road to making its mark and becoming a leader in black journalism. In the process, *The Examiner* has started to set a standard for other black weeklies to follow: The proof is in a product that is readable, reliable, fair, and in the process of becoming more entertaining. Change in process showed the way for change in product, which in turn will lead to a change in a much more important sociological and political process—how to run a black newspaper.

CHAPTER SEVEN

People at *USA Today*

As mentioned earlier—and we do not consider it belaboring the obvious—people can make or break change. Organizations clearly need employees to carry out the corporate mission. So people must enact any proposed changes in order for the change to become reality. As a result, exploring change from a people perspective means examining the respective roles that individuals are capable of playing. Because organizations are people, not places, change—be it reactive or proactive, incremental or transformational—emerges or is initiated through organizational members. In this chapter, we look at the roles that individuals are capable of playing as change agents in organizations.

American corporate entities increasingly are team-based, although many still focus on individual work in departmental or similar structures, organized by function. Such is the case in newspaper organizations. As labor-intensive businesses, most newspapers group employees into departments, according to function. Managing and developing newspaper employees requires skill in motivating, communicating, organizing, and planning. In addition, editors and publishers have to recognize—and use—the paper's work culture (Sohn, Ogan, & Polich, 1986). Such cultures are comprised of people in a group who create, realize, acquire, and then use fundamental notions or processes of how to behave and think in their particular area of the workplace (Schein, 1985). In other words, the group has its own, unique ways of behaving and thinking. Getting acquainted with a newspaper's culture or cultures helps managers understand a variety of employee behavior, for example, how they withstand change (Petersen, 1992). Understanding a newsroom's culture, then, is akin to understanding how a car works—knowing how each does its job helps explain how each gets where it is going.

Newsrooms—also known as editorial departments—constitute one of the more distinctive departments in the newspaper. As the division responsible for planning, securing, and producing the nonadvertising (editorial) subject matter, the newsroom is viewed by other departments as the most difficult department to get along with (e.g., Sylvie, 1995). Part of this reputation comes from its reluctance to join other departments in becoming market-driven (Underwood, 1993), when another significant reason resides in the

CHAPTER EIGHT

The Impact of Change on Newspapers

In previous chapters, we analyzed several concepts regarding newspaper change. For example, in chapter 4, we examined causes and shapes of change. As to the former, we suggested key antecedents that initiate change. In exploring processes of newspaper change, we identified the significant areas of people, technology–task, and the product. We also briefly discussed the role of time in this arena, distinguishing between the ideas of timing and duration. Throughout the discussion, we emphasized the need to understand how individual newspapers operate and behave. We looked at three newspapers in detail in chapters 5 through 7.

Managing, of course, is more than knowing basic concepts and terminology involved. As editors and publishers attempt to make informed decisions, they must include other factors in the process. Managers require a sense of context—a well-versed wisdom based on their experience and the experience of others. It is not unusual, for example, for savvy newspaper editors to often discuss or be aware of how other newspapers have handled a particular problem or issue. Others' experiences provide perspective and a benchmark that help managers make decisions. Purely analyzing an issue without context—whether it is change or something else entirely—excludes questions of meaning and values. A good editor knows that to coldly evaluate circumstances outside their human context is an invitation to disaster or, at the least, additional problems. As every situation demands context, so, too, does our discussion of newspaper change. Context, in this case, is the perspective provided by changes experienced by the large majority of newspapers.

This chapter identifies the major reasons for change facing newspapers at the beginning of the 21st century. Furthermore, it addresses the impacts of these changes as well as their significance.

NEW TECHNOLOGIES

As labor-intensive organizations, newspapers constantly seek efficiencies and cost savings in production. Machinery and equipment of varying kinds constitute a large part of the each paper's yearly budget. So it is no surprise that technology represents an ongoing concern in all newspaper departments as they continually seek to improve the accessibility to customers and the upgrading of content. That they have succeeded in varying degrees is itself one measure of impact.

Contemporary newspapers, with the advent of computerization, have seen a relatively continuous flow of innovative journalistic tools with multiple, ripple effects. Computers and computer-related technologies have replaced some workers, caused others to be re-trained, others to be removed to other departments and some to resign or retire. The impact on workers has been detailed at great length (e.g., Picard & Brody, 1997; Smith, 1980) and to imply that one, over-arching impact occurs would be foolish.

Our purpose here is to mention some of the more subtle results of technology-related change. For example, technology impacts can be undesirable, indirect, and unanticipated as well as the more obvious desirable, direct, and anticipated (Rogers, 1986). The first grouping is by far the more interesting (and potentially damaging) set of implications. With that as our goal, we begin our discussion with four of the more recent—and controversial—technologies or ways of conducting journalistic work: electronic pagination, computer-assisted reporting, the online newspaper, and team reporting. Each promised substantial cost savings, increased effectiveness, and enhanced capabilities, but none have fully delivered on any of those promises. Such mixed results not only enable us to compare success with failure, but also allow us to more easily determine reasons for the performance of each technology.

Pagination

As mentioned in the *Dallas Morning News* case study, electronic pagination has received intense analysis from both newspaper professionals and media scholars. Since the 1970s, many newspapers have sought pagination—the electronic assemblage of page components, including graphics, photos, type, and other art—because of the promised lower costs, increased efficiency, and higher profits. However, pagination requires new equipment, software, and instruction (Sims, 1999). It has been cited as falling short on reliability and performance (Tarleton, 1996), while increasing tensions among departments and causing employees to malign co-workers (J. Russial, 1994). It has created changes in how newspapers operate, infused some editors with doubts as to its worth and reliability (Sylvie, 1995), and made editors worry about its effect on accepted editing practices (Underwood et al., 1994).

Pagination, however, also has had more subtle effects. With the exception of newspapers that plan for it, pagination has turned the newsroom copy desk from a center of editing to a center of production. Simple logic indicates that when you eliminate one group of employees (the composing room, where most page assembly occurred prior to pagination) and give their jobs to another group, then the second group will have more work to do. When the added work is tied to the sensitive, deadline-focused latter end of the production cycle, it is logical to assume that the second group will become more susceptible to the pressures inherent in that cycle. As a result, it is no surprise to see that group's morale suffer and stress increase; copy editors are more pessimistic about their careers and more critical of their papers and supervisors than others in the newsroom (Voakes, 1997). The ironic significance is that many newspapers—in their search for greater (automated) control over the production process—can no longer fully exert the level of control that made them what they once were: A careful, selective medium of record that could be relied upon more than other, more time-sensitive media.

In the process, pagination also has created a new, different type of employee: a journalist with a production mentality. Such paginators have had to wrestle with a heretofore unheard of dilemma: How to balance the need for updating the news (and hence redesigning a page) with the cost (J. Russial, 1994). This dilemma creates varying levels of anxiety, depending on a paginator's expertise level, and his or her newspaper's resources and constraints. The paginator knows, for example, that the best newspaper is one that includes as many viewpoints and detail as possible. On the other hand, space and time constrain the desire for quality news; there is only so much space on a page and stories compete for it. Pagination complicates matters by forcing the paginator to be mindful of production values, such as appearance (page makeup) and traditional editing functions. Using pagination affects copy editors' attitudes about their jobs. When combined with frequent understaffing, increased work volume, and unappreciative bosses, pagination can lead to burnout (Cook, Banks, & Thompson, 1995). Not only does this dual identity have its own internal set of conflicts, it also means that the newsroom has lost some of its journalistic purity—the economics of production have seeped into the editorial process. Pagination has muddled the traditional function of the newsroom, adding the mechanistic chore of page makeup to the journalistic task of news production. The result has been a tradeoff, as better-looking pages co-exist with less-closely edited stories.

In short, pagination has lead to basic restructuring—newsroom responsibilities and functions have been increased to take up the slack from the disappearing composing room, which previously handled page makeup. The question has to be asked: Was it wise to install a device that requires more people, time, and patience than previously necessary? The answer varies according to whom you ask. Pagination seems to have been, by and large, a tool imposed by management on the rank and file to provide added power and control—to management. From the standpoint of management, this is a plus because it allows for later-breaking news and sports; there are fewer visual gaffes—copy editors now get what they see on the screen; the faster process allows for multiple pages to be completed at once. The mechanization of copy editing also has aggravated attempts to recruit and retain copy editors. Not only must copy desks work late hours and in relative anonymity, their increasingly computerized function—while helpful in that it provides a faster, easier way to handle page makeup—adds to the technical mystique and the stereotypically negative image of the copy editor. Attempts to increase copy editor pay and benefits and to enhance their working conditions have made minimal impact, particularly at smaller newspapers.

Computer-Assisted Reporting

The computer has had profound changes throughout the newsroom, including computer-assisted reporting (CAR). In one sense, CAR can be the use of any computer in any way that helps a reporter accomplish his or her text. In another, it can mean the specified use of a particular software program in order to generate original information, that is, computer-generated journalism. Either way, CAR has the potential to change the basic makeup of journalism. It promises reporters quicker access to documentary and human sources, and provides the chance to reveal basic trends of human behavior, making it a particularly powerful—and thus, attractive—tool. It also makes it possible for smaller newspapers to improve the depth of their reporting for a relatively modest investment. However, there are indications that CAR has met with mixed success.

For example, University of Miami journalism researcher Bruce Garrison's national surveys in the 1990s regarding newspaper journalists' adoption of online newsgathering tools show usage consistently increased, although smaller newspapers' usage fell significantly behind (Garrison, 1997a). Most recently, he found that the Internet was the primary online research tool in newsrooms, particularly state and federal government Web sites. Yet inaccurate information was a pervasive problem, as was useless or bad content, outdated links, and non-attributed sites; the most widely cited common problem was lack of verification. So while the Web is helpful in researching stories, finding obscure data and sources, and improving government coverage, credibility problems rendered the quality of much data in doubt (Garrison, 1999b). In addition, as newsroom computer use swells toward 100%, questions linger about computers' time-saving abilities (Garrison, 1999a). Indeed, Garrison noted (1996) that journalism often cannot control its own destiny in this area because the computer industry develops what software journalists can use. Larger news organizations occasionally create their own software, but the expense prohibits most newsrooms from doing so. This is less of a problem as more software developers produce customizable applications.

As for the hope that CAR balances the reporting resources of large and small newspapers, Garrison's data (1996) indicated substantial differences in CAR resources in the two groups' CAR usage. Although it may be obvious that newspapers with more assets will use computers more than their less-fortunate colleagues, Garrison (1998), observed that the differences are extensive. Not only is there a disparity in general use of computers in newsgathering, but smaller papers have fewer reporters assigned to work with computers, taking CAR training and using online resources. Such papers also spend less for online services and tend to have less of a Web presence. It is too early to tell whether these differences will remain, as small newspapers typically begin to use technological innovations later than larger papers (Garrison, 1998).

Conversely, as larger newspaper newsrooms have more than tripled their use of computers in their newsgathering efforts in the past five years, one of the more understated impacts has been the decreasing reliance of reporters on news librarians. Journalists at larger papers have gained greater control over the research process by learning to use the Internet (Garrison, 2000b). In addition, the widespread usage has lead to the development of differences in that use. Garrison (2000a) called them the computer elite (possessing greater skill and schooling), who tend to be news researchers, CAR experts, and technical specialists. They differ from other reporters and editors in that they report advanced use of search engines and related tools. They tend to have different, more sophisticated search habits than others in the newsroom (Garrison, 2000a).

Although some dispute Garrison's numbers, there is no doubt that CAR has prompted change at varying paces in many newsrooms. For example, nobody questions that CAR enhances quality reporting (Boyer, 1999), thanks to the details that computerization make available. The practice of reporting remains basically unchanged in that it is still reliant on individual reporters searching for—and subsequently accessing—sources of information. CAR advocates (e.g., DeFleur, 1997) quickly stress that CAR does not fundamentally change the process, although you can argue that sophisticated CAR allows the reporter to generate stories where none may have obviously revealed itself. For example, a reporter can mine census data for population trends that might not be immediately revealed by his or her human sources. CAR also gave rise to innovative treatments of old subjects, changing anecdotal data into statistics and making available a wide array of public records (Garrison, 1997b). Still, in such instances, CAR is only reliant on the journalist's ability to analyze and detect patterns, which is not a change from traditional reporting methods.

There are concerns, however, that CAR might encourage ethical lapses such as plagiarism and lax confirmation of computer-delivered information (Steele & Cochran, 1995). Organizationally, CAR presents a challenge from the standpoint of staffing and support: Editors must budget the resources to not only provide computers and software, but also to supply training and the time needed—not only for training but for data analysis. In fact, the lack of equipment and education has combined with the inflexibility of many reporters to discourage CAR in several ways.

For instance, the different levels of computer expertise among reporters discourage some of those fearful of anything remotely considered scientific, numbers-oriented, or both. Others have enough computer know-how to do one or two things well, but often do not see the Internet as a viable resource because of the time it takes unsophisticated users (such as themselves) to narrow a search. Because of the already-stringent demands on time, many journalists are content to restrict their CAR skill to Internet glancing (Ciotta, 1996). Finally, some editors no doubt are apprehensive about the increasing use of CAR, particularly in the sense that its occasionally time-consuming nature may result in reporters spending less time with human sources related to the information they retrieved. In other words, personal interviews—whether face-to-face or telephone-based—may be getting short shrift. In fact, CAR may require additional training—in how to balance computer-generated work with shoe leather (Davenport, Fico, & Weinstock, 1996).

So CAR is comparable to pagination in that both have enhanced capabilities of their intended users by enabling quantity and quality to be improved. Both technologies also create concern because of side effects, most notably the training of users to perform job tasks previously done by other employees. Organizationally, each technology requires managerial commitment of time and resources and some restructuring of workflow. Unlike pagination, however, CAR has not yet been shown to have as many negative ramifications. In fact, CAR is no longer regarded as an alien tool, but rather a necessary tool to the journalistic technique (Ciotta, 1996).

The end result is that CAR and pagination—while promoted as providing more control in some job aspects—do not deliver equal and balanced content control in all respects. Pagination enhances control over design and layout but indirectly decreases control over text and editing. CAR boosts reporters' work with information, but at a cost of time and the use of non-documentary, human sources. In essence, each technology has had difficulty in its compatibility with existing, journalistic values, beliefs, and practices. That is not to say that these difficulties are insurmountable or that either technology is undesirable, but only that in attempting to manipulate and exercise greater control, newspapers have paid a potentially high journalistic price.

Online Newspapers

Whereas pagination and CAR have largely centered on newspaper's journalistic activities, online technology has had more extensive ramifications, although those impacts may change by the time you read this. The Internet—through a compilation of various computerized technologies that provide video, the ability to interact with audiences, and the chance for immediate feedback—allowed newspapers to have an online presence, usually an electronic version of the printed product that users can read via computer. Yet the Internet's nature as a relatively young, dynamic, and continuously evolving medium makes newspapers' role and effectiveness a more difficult read.

For example, there is some question about the newspaper's function with the advance of the Internet. While newspapers traditionally fill a concierge-like role for their audiences—showing them where to go for information, and telling them necessary things about local events and politics—the Internet has enabled consumers to usurp that role for themselves. With its library-like capabilities, the Internet provides readers with direct access to a large amount of information, much of it raw, not interpreted, and unedited. This poses a threat to the newspaper's audience base, albeit largely theoretical since no one knows for sure whether an online newspaper will provide a suitable substitute for a printed one. Online newspapers, for instance, are not portable in large measure and reading from a computer screen still is not the ingrained habit that newspaper reading has become. Some evidence suggests that newspaper use will remain the same, the Internet notwithstanding (Bromley & Bowles, 1995). Despite such assurances, however, newspapers have felt a compulsion to keep pace with the development of the Internet because of the fear of becoming extinct, not to mention the opportunity to reach more readers, generate additional revenue, and promote the print product (Peng, Tham, & Xiaoming, 1999).

Still, their pace of success has varied and sometimes stumbled. For example, a study of six Colorado papers found about only one-ninth of the stories appeared only in the online product and not in print (Singer, 1999), although electronic cannibalization of the product has been encouraged by some (Zollman, 1999b). Although the Internet is known for enhancing two-way, interactive conversation, another study of 100 U.S. newspapers (Schultz, 1999) showed only token interactive choices. The inability to get exact measurements of online readership (Kirsner, 1997) has made newspapers' task of keeping pace more daunting. Despite the fact that only about a fourth of the online newspapers have been making an online profit (Casale, 2000), few people have denied change has occurred.

Economically, the industry continues to search for a viable model. Advice abounds. Some experts suggest that each newspaper should follow the dictates of its individual market (e.g, Zollman, 1999b); others have elaborate plans that usually include optimizing the appropriate levels of good journalism and business daring (e.g., Stone, 1999a). For example, one prototype advocates building a *portal*, a highly chosen site that steers visitors to other, partnered sites based on users' habits, expertise, and a common market area

(Noth, 1999). Such a market allows advertisers to promote their products and services while the newspaper is just one of many available channels. In that sense, content changes its meaning to include everything the portal offers—advertising, news, vacation sites, search engines, and transaction capabilities—so that newspapers can address advertisers' needs for specific, tailored audiences.

If nothing more, the Internet has shown that newspaper managers must rethink—or more completely understand—a number of elements involving electronic newspapers' revenue-producing capabilities, particularly as it concerns advertising. For example, managers have had to learn how to advance from a defensive stance (e.g., protecting classified advertising from other online sources), to one of strength (e.g., searching for opportunities provided by current content; Zollman, 1999a). They have learned that the least-used sites are those that put only the newspaper online and that they must create new ways to bring advertisers and consumers together, either by building sites for others, providing Internet service, offering various modes of electronic commerce, or partnering with other companies (Casale, 2000). Although such lessons permeate the industry, some old practices are hard to change.

For example, we can look more closely at the cannibalization or shovelware issue, in which editors and publishers must wrestle with what is an acceptable level of duplication in the print and the online editions. Obviously, newspapers with more resources can afford less duplication, but even such smaller papers take this issue seriously, since it involves a crucial economic element. Newspaper markets are contained within a specific geographic area, the boundaries of which are determined by access to the newspaper. Since the Web is globally accessible, online newspapers theoretically have a number of markets—either local or long-distance, advertising or information–news (Chyi & Sylvie, 1998). In order to serve those markets, it would seem logical that the product for each would differ. However, we know that newspapers do not provide much unique online content. For instance, one study found newspapers provide an average of 22% unique online content, which 75% of Web users found unappealing (Chyi & Lasorsa, 1999).

Some experts (e.g, Zollman, 1999b) would argue that—in some markets—a majority of the online readers are new to the paper, meaning they do not know the duplicated content is available in the print edition. Despite the fact that industry data shows the overwhelming majority of users come to a newspaper Web site for local news, such users usually find that news of dubious quality (Phipps, 1999a). Still others (e.g., Lee, 1999) would say that in some cases—especially those involving smaller newspapers—access fees cannot be charged for viewing stories and advertising revenues are not sufficient to financially support the site, so Web-only stories are not cost-effective. In the end, many small newspapers—when they see that paid subscriptions and advertising do not provide enough revenue—try walking the fine line between putting too much online and taking away from their print product (Alexander, 1997; Mueller, 1999). The crucial point is there is still no conventional wisdom on shovelware (the automatic transfer of print content to online without much editing or repackaging); editors and publishers usually must rely on the economically expedient solution (i.e., shovelware), even when economic theory suggests otherwise.

Still, the world is becoming more digital, including newsrooms. In the journalistic sphere, online change also has found its share of successes and failures. Online reporting requires slightly different skills and techniques; reporters have to have a combination of routine and online abilities—much of them multimedia-oriented. For example, some online reporters need to know how to record sound and video as well as think graphically. Online writing and editing places emphasis on visually complementing the written word and, as such, requires people who value new technology, who quickly adapt to the online voice and writing approach and who willingly invite readers–users to interact with them and the story (Stepp, 1996). The Internet also has effectively changed the news cycle for most news organizations. Whereas previously newspapers published once a day, online newspapers offer the ability to deliver breaking news around the clock.

Not surprisingly, journalists have developed three mindsets in regard to online technology: They either strongly support online media, are concerned about its negative effects, or do not see it as relevant to their jobs (Singer, 1997). Supporters believe journalists will play vital roles in online media and will directly affect them, while traditionalists (those concerned about negative impacts) fear online media are elitist and will force journalism to lose its quality and value. The remainder fall somewhere in between, recognizing technology will change things but also believing it to be just another tool (Singer, 1997). Online newspaper journalists themselves, however, feel their job is more that of an editor or copy editor. Compared to those working in print newspapers, they see themselves less as interpreters of information and more as disseminators of information. In addition, they are marketers of a sort, placing high value on reaching and understanding the largest possible audience (Brill, 1999).

While traditional newsroom practices of selecting and editing news tend to remain the same, whether it be online or in the print newsroom (Martin, 1998), many newspapers grapple with how to organize and staff their online entities to take full advantage of the all-day, everyday, wire-service-like deadline cycle. As was the case with the advent of videotext (Sylvie & Danielson, 1989), resistance from traditional journalists has complicated the online journalists' job and newsrooms are slowly coming to grips with how to assimilate print and online reporters (Stone, 1999b). Some newspapers create separate departments with their own budgets, then integrate them into the regular newsroom; others have online divisions distinct from the print product. Either way, publishers have had to devote considerable thought to the issue, much of it predicated on what type of advertising is more attractive and, consequently, how adaptable the print advertising staff must be (Moses, 1999). Despite such advertising-driven concerns, some insist that online newspapers will foster such things as the birth of a new form of writing, that the Internet's more educated audiences will allow more lively writing (Pogash, 1996). More radical predictions (e.g., Phipps, 1999b) envision journalists being equipped with mobile, cyber workstations that will allow for multi-layered reporting (linking databases to readers, editors, and journalists alike).

Of course, no one can say for certain whether any journalistic transformations will occur because of online technology. As we mentioned earlier, the Internet's fluid, ever-changing nature prohibits any accurate attempt to classify change. That does not mean that editors and publishers have stood still. In fact, it might be instructive to examine typical concerns of each group as they have evolved over time. In doing so, we can begin to make some general assessment of the impact of online technology (see Fig. 8.1)

Certainly, as more has become known about the technology, concerns have become more focused. In addition to having been appropriately for-ward-thinking on the subject, editors early on realized that new media require breaking away from long-established mindsets, and asking tough questions, such as whether stories should be run online before they appear in print (Ritt, 1995). Other commandments as propagated by the American Society of Newspaper Editors' New Media Committee also include: paying attention to training and staffing levels, recognizing newsroom structures must change, exercising caution with resources since keeping technologically aware was a must, and managing uncertainty over content ownership. The more recent editor concerns (see Murdock, 2000), while undoubtedly more refined, also indicate less caution and a more courageous assertion about what will work. Such confidence suggests that the Internet has become more familiar to editors, who now see it as another editorial objective among many. On closer inspection, the earlier list (Ritt, 1995) is one of preparation and a guarded call for change—a change that now must be managed, judging by the more recent items. As a result, the latter listing also places a premium on leadership. So editors have, in one sense, become more familiar with the technology to the point that it requires standard management control in the sense of staffing and structure. In another sense, however, editors have not changed because they continue to manage, to attempt to control. They persist in their professional roles as arbiters of what is fair—witness the fact that ethical considerations and the knowledge that the Internet complicates matters maintains a place among editors' concerns.

So perhaps what has changed is editors' knowledge and skill and how much more prudently they apply it. We know, for example, that editors are

Publishers	Editors
Choice of content	Commitment from the top
Choice of web language	Leadership quality
Anticipating classified ad changes	Choice of content
Creating synergy with e-commerce	Creating regular site traffic
Connecting with community	Providing more than local news
Anticipating the convergence of media	Adusting to continuous publishing cycle
	Anticipating ethical dilemmas

FIG. 8.1   Concerns regarding online technology.

aware that the reading public has become more and more alienated from the press. As many newspapers continue to lose readers, the pressure mounts on editors to challenge their journalistic instincts and try new things. When they are accused of not being attentive to readers' needs (e.g., Jennings, 1999), sensitive editors begin to examine their news values and search for solutions. For example, a study (Gade, 1999) of various editors at 18 newspapers found three basic types: those who believe changes in newspapering make the industry more market-driven (at the expense of journalism values); those who see a clear link between the added weight given to market values, variations in news values, and better newspapers; and finally, those who feel sandwiched and conflicted by journalism and market values. Indeed, closer comparison of Fig. 8.1 with the previous (Ritt, 1995) listing of concerns shows an increased awareness of market forces. Editors do seem more business-minded—maybe not solely because of the Internet, but the Internet certainly plays a part.

As to publishers, when compared to editors, the Internet remains a strategic worry. In 1995, for example, the Internet (more specifically, the Web) represented a confusing maze of choices and threats to most publishers. First, its data-oriented nature makes information readily accessible. Second, the interconnection of sites makes travel or surfing fairly easy. Third, its multimedia capabilities far exceed those of other media. Fourth, the traditional newspaper revenue model does not neatly fit the Web. Fifth, the Web offers an additional—if troublesome—revenue stream via its transactional capabilities. Finally, newspapers—as a print medium—were unfamiliar with the mechanics and infrastructure of the Web (Conniff, 1995). As a result, publishers have considered several, somewhat radical ideas, even to the point of entertaining the *push model,* in which the electronic newspaper is delivered (in varying degrees) via e-mail to users with minimal effort on the user's part (Toner, 1997). Just as editors' concerns have become less strident, the disquieting alternatives facing publishers have seemingly been distilled to those listed in Fig. 8.1. The items, while less ominous, still indicate that publishers continue to face strategic, make-or-break choices, particularly as it pertains to convergence and all it implies. As broadband capabilities evolve, newspaper Web sites will have to adapt in order to compete with other news media. Publishers face the task of deciding how to allocate resources to their online staffs as well as providing a direction for their efforts. So, the essence of managing remains unchanged for publishers as well.

This analysis reveals much about online technology's impact. Although the Internet presents a challenge to newsrooms and newspaper organizations as a new method of delivering news and advertising and thus requires new ways of packaging them, it has not transformed (i.e., created a bold stroke of change in) the ways newspapers operate. Editors still edit and plan accordingly and publishers still provide direction for editors, advertising managers and other department heads. The long march has just begun and the much-ballyhooed new era of publishing that many predicted for newspapers has yet to occur or, if it has, it is in its fetal stages. If anything, the Internet has simply provided another publishing venue for the newspaper. No one argues the Internet's boundary-blurring capabilities in terms of the newspaper's contents, but the basic processes of packaging those contents remain unaltered. Even the newspaper's role—as an interpreter and organizer of raw information—has kept constant or even become stronger.

Team Reporting

Finally, to contrast computer and non-computerized technologies, we offer some insight into the example provided by newsrooms' ventures into team methods, specifically, and changing structures in general. For example, newsrooms traditionally delegate certain areas of coverage to particular, individual reporters. Such beats (Rich, 2000) normally include local government, education, crime, and legal (courthouse) news, among others. Yet, the 1990s saw a resurgence and a renewal for the concept of team reporting, in which reporters are placed in groups of two or more for the purpose of covering a traditional beat area or special topic, such as health. Such teams assure the flow of quality news ideas. Newspapers have used teams in various ways, whether it be cross-departmental teams to study obstacles that face the entire newspaper, or intradepartmental teams to tackle some specific problem such as circulation delivery or marketing concerns. Teams develop in order to work efficiently and effectively to identify opportunities and problems but employees often see them as top-down efforts at stifling creativity and autonomy (Sohn, Wicks, Lacy, Sylvie, 1999). Still, teams can be used successfully; in times of crisis teams are the best way for managers to get things done, as was the case in the merger of the Pittsburgh newspapers. In that situation, *The Post-Gazette* formed several groups of reporters and editors to ease the transition in several ways—from the actual, physical merging of staffs and their supplies to the emotional, sentimental gestures that made new staffers feel at home (Jurczak, 1996).

As to impact, teams—besides their obvious ability (or lack thereof) to accomplish their objectives—have become an accepted (if not pervasive) way of doing work at newspapers. It is no great change or radical departure from the norm for a department manager to assemble a team of her subordinates for whatever purpose. There is no denying that, in many cases, the "two heads are better than one" adage holds true. Team reporting, for example, has been shown—in individual cases—to produce: better coverage and better play for certain topics (Russial, 1997); better writing, more story perspectives, increased flexibility in planning, and more autonomy (Morgan, 1993); and less pressure and more community-based coverage (Johnson, 1993). However, not all departments have welcomed the concept; production departments tend to be more hostile to teams than advertising sections or the newsroom, for example (Lewis, 1997). In fact, it appears that advertising departments are in the forefront among the various units in newspapers in their support of teams (Lewis, 1995). Part of the reason may lie in the resistance to change inherent in the mechanized nature of the production department's job. Still, some evidence suggests that circulation is perceived by other departments as the most cooperative (Sylvie, 1996). So impact of teams can be described at best as—considering the conflicting evidence—mixed.

That mixed reaction is clear in the example of newsroom reporting teams. Managing editors at larger newspapers with teams disagree, for instance, on whether management and staff like newsroom teams: They showed strongest accord with the statement that top management liked the team concept, but less agreement on whether middle management and line staff liked the system. They tended to agree that the positive effects were that staff members interact more, the paper is better planned, readers get a better paper, and that news is better packaged. Whereas editors at such papers saw an improvement in quality, their business counterparts saw teams as a tool to primarily enhance productivity. Finally, newsrooms that have teams are not fully loyal to them and maintain elements of the traditional newsroom. These attitudes, gleaned from a national survey (Endres, Schierhorn, & Schierhorn, 1999), represent the ground floor of efforts to evaluate the overall impact of reporting teams. Much of what is known pertains to how teams work at a specific newspaper; no one knows of any trends. However, we do know that teams require changes in certain ways that journalists and editors behave.

Teams attempt to improve on an existing system and represent a departure from the norm. Inherent in the team approach to reporting is the restructuring of duties, either to achieve greater productivity and creativity or to eliminate layers of hierarchy within the newsroom. In many cases, reporters see teams as a business-oriented mandate, so editors not only face the challenge of organizing such teams, but also of selling them to reporters as journalistically sound endeavors that will improve quality of work life. At least two newspapers have not been able to do so (Hansen et al., 1998). The prevailing perception among journalists at the *Minneapolis Star Tribune* and the *St. Paul Pioneer Press* was that journalistic quality declined with teams and that they had more responsibility but less authority than before (Neuzil et al., 1999).

This raises the question: Why do some editors seem to think teams are effective while some journalists do not? The varying perceptions probably stem from the different perspectives of editors and reporters and from the fact that teams are a structurally oriented tool; in fact, most industries consider teams as a structural—rather than technological—element. Although the purported end result of teams is to improve the product (and, by implication, the job of the journalist), what is actually being improved is the beat system. That system typically relies on the journalist to perform routine, daily canvassing of the people and information relevant to a certain area of local life. For example, an education reporter typically must attend school board meetings, read schools-related materials, and regularly speak with school executives, teachers, parents, and students. Often one reporter performs this job; in the case of two or more, the duties classically tend to be sharply defined and divided. To an editor's way of thinking, the team concept improves on beats in that it gets more people involved at the idea stage and in helping to execute (report) the idea. Yet as a reporter sees it, when a team structure is used, the authority and responsibility for a story are not as clear, resulting in lack of cohesion and lack of obvious lines of decision making about story elements. Teams also mean that the individual reporter cedes or shares control with others and, with it, a large measure of autonomy. If it is one thing we know, it is that autonomy is a necessary component of reporting from the standpoint of it enhances reporter satisfaction (Weaver & Wilhoit, 1996). Without autonomy—a sense of being able to do what you feel is necessary when you feel the need to do so—reporters feel somewhat powerless. The fact that team reporting takes longer in many cases aggravates such feelings.

In summary (and in returning to our question about impact), teams change structure and improve coordination, but at the expense (or risk) of alienating reporters and adding time (via extra meetings and conferences). Story subjects likely receive different, more in-depth treatment. The number of general assignment reporters and those available for other duties tends to dwindle (Stepp, 1995). In short, the nature and face of news gets a makeover and newsroom structure gets redesigned. On the grand scale, newspapers are not flocking to the new method; in many cases, they retain fragments of the old beat system or refuse to use teams altogether. Teams are not for every newspaper; many are doing fine without them. The issue boils down to one of content: Teams change the substance of stories. That is true of all the technologies we discussed to this point: They all attempt to change content.

In the process, the locus of control changes. We have seen that control shifts either into the hands of employees who previously had little or no control (e.g., with pagination and teams) or that more control is given to those who need it (in the case of CAR). With online technology, the control issue revolves not at the organizational level, but at the production level—the consumer, by virtue of the uncertain nature of the Internet, is in control. The basic question then becomes: Why does control shift and change?

For one reason, there is the economic necessity of pleasing audiences and advertisers. For another, journalism—like all professions—evolves as it seeks to improve. Each of the changes discussed has been heralded as enhancing content in some form or fashion. Journalism not only is concerned with method but also with the end result because, after all, the technology's ultimate purpose is the product. Just as doctors cede much of the control over health to individual patients—via their lifestyle and eating habits—journalists, too, must cede some control over the product. Because publishers and editors see audiences changing and demanding that newspapers change with them—while reporters, as all professionals do, seek to grow in their craft—newspapers change. Whether this change is revolutionary is up for debate; after all, reporters still report and news still is news. As we see in the next section, audience demands for change in American newspapers indicate that change has not occurred fast enough to suit some readers. As a result, newspapers have felt obligated to respond.

DEMOGRAPHY—INSIDE AND OUT

The populations pertinent to newspapers wield influence. Because newspapers are primarily designed to serve mass audiences, we focus on those audiences. The internal demographics of a newspaper also play a significant role in their operation and in the changes they both initiate and experience. We begin by analyzing the external constituency of newspapers.

Reader Demographics and Other Market Factors

Since the 1980s, any time newspapers and audiences are mentioned in the same breath, the discussion turns to what some perceive as the increasing market orientation of newspapers. The use of market research to target readers and, thus, attract advertisers has been criticized as covert managerial attempts to arrange newsroom principles in line with those of readers (Squires, 1993; Underwood, 1993). Editors have been warned that if they do not take the lead, the advertising department or other unit of the newspaper will (Johnson, 1997). There is no shortage of evidence to illustrate that editors are, indeed, more business-conscious in how they approach their jobs. It is not uncommon for market considerations to enter into discussions of journalism; for example, when *The St. Louis Post-Dispatch* wanted to launch a new Saturday edition, a tabloid format was adopted by the cross-departmental planning committee because the new paper had to sell alongside the early edition (Weil, 1996).

The decline of newspaper readership has definitely impacted newspapers. Although newspaper revenues and profits continue to reach record levels, their readership numbers continue to fall in respect to where they were in the 1960s and earlier. In a sense, newspapers have had to become more efficient in order to maintain or enhance profit levels (Bogart, 1999) and the result has been a constant battle on the part of publishers to stem the readership slide. Every trade magazine, conference, seminar, or workshop are ultimately built around increasing readership to some extent. Figure 8.2 provides a sampling of the efforts (and the resulting impacts).

Another market element focuses on the external structure of the industry, particularly ownership. In that case, newspapers have been the subject of intense scrutiny, much of it taking its cue from Bagdikian (1997), who warned about the ill effects of corporate ownership and increasing concentration of newspaper ownership. Bagdikian contended that the news gives preferential treatment to large corporations, largely because of what he described as advertising-dependent chain ownership. He claimed that such news poses a direct danger to democracy and encourages increasing concentration of ownership and monopolies, particularly in the newspaper industry.

Other evidence suggests the opposite. Chain-owned and monopoly newspapers generally do not differ much from independent newspapers; for example, one study (Demers, 1996a) found few differences in editorial page content between chain and non-chain newspapers. Instead, the more a newspaper shows the corporate form, the more editorials, letters to the editor, and local staff-written stories it has. Being market-oriented does not necessarily equate to poor quality in everyone's eyes. For example, senior editors at newspapers with low market orientations feel their organizations seem slightly less committed to providing traditional content—from international news to local government and sports coverage (Beam, 1998).

In fact, one-newspaper cities seem to be an economically driven, foregone conclusion (Compaine & Gomery, 2000). As newspapers' circulations continue to fall among all newspapers and as advertisers see their options for

Problem/Effort	Impact
Exodus of Affluent Readers/Zoning	Readers expect and receive more localized news, sometimes to exclusion of news of the metro centre; reporters cover news not normally covered; advertisers reach more affluent readers; juvenile carriers replaced by adults; pagination adopted to improve deadline capabilities and enhance product image.
Loss of Advertising Share/More Aggressive Recruitment of Advertisers	Computerization and other technologies to give newspapers insertion and targeting capabilities; reliance on classified advertising; bolstering of Web sites to retain classified ads; greater emphasis on Sunday edition as main advertising vehicle; smaller, more efficient news staffs and smaller space for news
Competition from Other News Media/Customizing the News	Reliance and emphasis on softer, more in-depth news, redesign efforts to mimic other media; greater focus on local news; segregation of the news (news, sports, features, etc.); newsroom cooperation with other departments to promote the news
Loss of Advertising Revenue/Cutting Costs	Less money spent (percentage-wise) on the newsroom and the production department; more money spent on marketing and technology; editors learn to speak in business terms; management by objectives introduced on wide scale; walls between newsroom and other departments start to crack
Loss of Readers/Circulation Strategies	Focus on more affluent groups (often in outlying zones), regional newspaper concept challenged; focus on groups more likely to read via telemarketing and varying content emphases (journalism and marketing begin to blend)

FIG 8.2 Newspaper readership problems and their influences.

delivering their message increase, these advertisers grow more reluctant to place their ads in two competing newspapers when one usually can provide the coverage they need. Add to this the competition from the choices provided by online technology, and you can see that the markets for most newspapers are already saturated. As towns and cities grow more complex, the more likely newspapers are to show traits of corporate organizations and thus a much greater capacity to promote controlled social change. (Demers, 1996b).

However, that capacity likely will be muted by newspapers' declining market share. Bogart (1999) argued that—with the exception of smaller papers—such market realities will force most papers to face a choice: Either they will have to join ranks with the more cosmopolitan newspapers and become more elitist media (thus narrowing their market potential), or adhere to their traditional duty of educating the masses and admit much of their market share (and more lucrative advertising accounts) will go elsewhere. The choice should be obvious, when you consider that—from a pure market view—most companies do not see their market role as altruistically as newspapers do (Ureneck, 1999). In other words, the fact that newspapers look at their market as needing to be provided with citizen-capable skills (via news) is a bit unusual, since markets function to give consumers what they want, not necessarily what they need; that is, a market is not a democracy.

Yet that is exactly what newspapers seem to be saying when they attempt such things as civic or public journalism. Seen as a corrective tonic for journalism, civic journalism started as a movement to fill the gap between news media, the democratic process, and a continually disenchanted public. As seen by Merritt, one of the movement's leading proponents, journalism has an obligation to public life (Merritt & Carter, 1996). In civic journalism, news media try to re-engage the public on issues of public life by holding public forums, focus groups, and various meetings in which members of the public air their frustrations and concerns. In the process, journalists either have low (simply listening and reporting) or high participation (actively working to solve problems). No one, absolute method defines how to do public journalism; the results and techniques vary wherever it occurs. Whatever the involvement level, the idea is to help the community strengthen its ability to articulate its concerns and re-establish its trust in self-government (Rosen, 1996).

For their part, journalists are not quite sure what to make of the movement. For example, two newsrooms with different public journalism experiences were surveyed, yielding four perspectives. They included: those who embrace the movement; concerned traditionalists who believe journalism must be socially responsible but who do not think making democracy work is a journalist's job; neutral types who believe in objective and detached reporting; and a civic-leaning class that sees objectivity as working but are still open-minded toward civic journalism (Gade et al., 1998). As it is, the movement has been portrayed in three lights: as a new reporting technique, as civic activism, and as a financial blessing to the sagging bottom line of troubled news organizations (McMillan et al., 1996). Even proponents have admitted that the movement is still evolving and, as a result, cannot be clearly defined (Shepard, 1994).

As a result, critics complain that public journalism—while having lofty, noble goals—brings journalists to forbidden ground in that it requires participation in the news process (Stein, 1997). They also see public journalism as a covert desire to increase circulation and make editors popular, not to mention that it appears like old wine in new bottles—just good journalism. Advocates say that in civic journalism, the public asks more pointed, practical questions than journalists; they add that civic journalism also results in positive, helpful government action to solve problems (Shepard, 1994). One study has shown that the content of public journalism stories is different. Newspapers practicing public journalism while covering election campaigns not only decreased their use of horse-race polls, they also used a writing tone imitating the virtues, moral qualities, and social and political ideas of the public journalism movement (Verykoukis, 1998). Supporters note that public journalism is just as objective as other forms in that standard objectivity allows journalists to tell the truth and let the chips fall where they may. Public journalism provides a disciplined method that allows us to ask a question of the data in a way that we will not be fooled by answer (Meyer, 1995). Those who practice civic journalism feel they are not setting the public agenda, nor turning over their pages to unskilled readers, nor pandering to reader cravings for good news. "Beneath it all," wrote one editor, "public journalism is just journalism that remembers its purpose—namely, to report about public life more for the spectators than for the players in the arena" (Floyd, 1997, p. 63). Another civic journalist in a different city agreed that the process worked, "but a few days later, after the project was completed, it was business as usual in our newsroom. We had dusted off our Rolodexes and were back into conflict journalism, bringing our readers their old diet of controversy and misunderstanding" (Jennings, 1999, p. 70).

The controversy surrounding civic journalism serves as an example of the larger debate concerning the market impact on the practice of journalism. While journalists more and more concur with public concerns about their work's performance, they say that growing financial and business pressures are to blame—particularly corporate ownership and particularly at the local level. Newsroom staffers are more than twice as likely as executives to perceive that the influence has been greatest in news content (Pew Research Center, 1999). Combined with what some see as the industry's catering to those who have not traditionally read papers (and thus making itself less attractive to its traditional market), the public journalism–readers-as-writers innovation may indicate that serious consequences lie ahead for newspapers

(Picard & Brody, 1997). Despite evidence to the contrary—for example, enterprise and investigative journalism have shown signs of being more important than ever (Bernt & Greenwald, 1999). There are those (Stepp, 2000) who offer anecdotal evidence to suggest that public journalism—and its related, market-driven initiatives—has permanently changed the daily culture of the newsroom because journalists now cannot think and act without having readers in mind, as the next section shows in detail.

Diversity

In 1968, the National Advisory Commission on Civil Disorders (NACCD) blamed news organizations for reporting from a White perspective and for being lax (shockingly backward) about diversifying their reporting staffs. Although specifically referring to African Americans, the NACCD report said if news media are to comprehend and then cover minority communities, it must have the help of those communities, especially in the form of employment (NACCD, 1968).

More recently, as urban demographics change, the call for diversity has taken on renewed importance. For example, minority households' after-tax disposable income continues to increase and minorities make up a growing part of many newspaper markets, creating potential for circulation gains (Pease, 1989). Newspaper marketing researchers have begun to develop a strategic approach, targeting African-American and Hispanic groups that are least likely to be regular daily newspaper readers (Woods, 1998). Newspapers have to overcome perceptions that they undercover poor neighborhoods while overcovering their problems (and thus making it seem that minority groups are problems), as well as perceptions that their circulation and advertising departments seek to purposively exclude minority neighborhoods and businesses, and that minority coverage mirrors too many festivals and athletic events. As a result, a diverse workforce is seen as a tool for more diverse coverage, which in turn will appease and attract more readers.

The numbers of employed minorities in newspapers still is small, but not from total lack of effort. In 1978 (10 years after the NACCD's report), studies showed that only 4% of newspaper employees were minorities, and the American Society of Newspaper Editors (ASNE) approved a recommendation that by 2000 minority employment should equal the percentage of minorities in the U.S. population. By 1995, it became apparent that the 2000 goal was too optimistic (Najjar, 1995), so ASNE set a similar goal for 2025. Much of the blame has been placed on ineffective (or no) recruitment techniques and an inability to convey the goal's importance (Demo, 1999). With better, more efficient methods, the number of minority journalists at daily newspapers grew nearly 12% from 1999 to 2000, the largest percentage increase in five years. The percentage of women grew to slightly more than 37%, and women represented 34% of all newsroom supervisors (ASNE, 2000).

The case has been effectively made for such a change. For example, a 28-year study of *The New York Times* showed that from 1966 to 1994 the newspaper's increased number of female bylines correlated with increasing usage of women in pictures and in story references, although some items—such as obituaries, letters to the editor, or op-ed pieces—still lagged. The study also showed that *Times'* women writers wrote about women more than men did, but that the men increasingly wrote about women when more of their newsroom colleagues were women (Dorsher, 1997). Additonally, there is proof that this will continue with future journalists, who show that men and women judge stories differently, as do Whites and minorities; and minorities differ among themselves in news judgment (Fedler, Smith-Marzoff, & Hines, 1995).

Newspapers, however, have had trouble retaining minorities. Since the mid-1990s, minority journalists have left newspapers at nearly twice the rate of Anglo journalists. The departing journalists say the leading influences include interest in another field, lack of advancement prospects, and burnout. Most cite the perception that they feel they have to work harder than their White peers to advance, suggesting that newspapers have to improve workplace conditions to keep these journalists in journalism (McGill, 2000). As a result, newspapers have tried a myriad of programs, initiatives, and experiments at varying levels, ranging from the newsroom to the high school classroom in an attempt to grow their own journalists (e.g., see Stolberg, 1989). Results have largely been mixed and there are concerns that—particularly in higher education—much remains to be done (Manning-Miller & Dunlap, 1999). Meanwhile, coverage anxiety continues, so much so that ASNE has instituted such efforts as National Time Out for Diversity and Accuracy Day, in which papers across the country stop to reflect on how they apply diversity in their news coverage as an aspect of accuracy (Shearer, 1999). Individual newspapers have gone so far as to create specialized publications (e.g., Spanish-language weeklies, special-interest sections), conduct content audits, institute community advisory groups or tie diversity to monetary reward systems. Newspaper owners and corporations also have paid increased attention to nurturing and supporting minority managers (Terry, 1993). Diversity worries continue with the advent of the Internet and other new technologies in the newspaper industry, as the number of women and people of color who attend new media meetings and conferences remains few (Williamson, 1998).

Despite the vigilance and good intentions of the industry, however, the connection between minority staffing and the minority market needs closer examination as to its validity and value in the future of newspapers, for several reasons. For one, potential minority reader groups differ among themselves. For example, racial and ethnic minority readers are often more satisfied than White readers of the newspaper. In addition, differences among minority groups exist regarding opinions about fair coverage. For example, Hispanics feel newspapers are more fair (when compared to their expectations about fairness) than do African Americans, who also feel (more so than Hispanics) that newspapers do not sufficiently help the local community deal with problems (Woods, 1998). Differences also exist among minority journalists in terms of their religious affiliations, marital status, average age, income, job titles, job satisfaction, intention to stay in journalism, ratings of their news organizations, and opinions on acceptable reporting practices (Weaver & Wilhoit, 1996). The differences also pertain to recruitment. For instance, African-American journalists were more likely than journalists of other races to have majored in journalism in college.

Secondly, journalism news values are so entrenched as to question whether merely changing the color or gender of journalists will change their values, especially objectivity. Professional values that journalists assimilate during their schooling and formative years can be difficult to change. For example, although some (Robinson, 1991) might contend that diversity of management leads to diversity of actual content, there are others (Greenwald, 1990) who would argue just the opposite. It also is deceptive to assume that diversity of sources (presumably brought on by diversity of reporters) would then lead to diversity of content. This is not to say that workforce diversity is not important and that hiring diverse groups has no impact, but that impact has been shown in one case (female newsroom managers) to be negligible (e.g., Lacy, Davenport, & Miller, 1998). There simply is no assurance that it will lead to diverse content. This is particularly troublesome considering that minority newspaper journalists—especially males—report less autonomy than White reporters and that perceived autonomy decreases as newsroom diversity increases (Liebler, 1994).

Thirdly, the idea of hiring minority journalists presupposes that minority journalists can do a better job of covering minority issues by virtue of the fact that they are a minority. This assumes that minority journalists have somehow been trained differently than non-minority journalists when, in fact, their educational backgrounds and journalistic values are not significantly different from non-minority journalists. Both groups are just as likely, for example, to have a college degree, to have majored in journalism, and to have similar views as to how they rank the importance of media roles (Weaver & Wilhoit, 1996). As to what prompted them to enter journalism, minorities and non-minorities are fairly close in listing the desire to write and working on a college or high school newspaper (McGill, 2000). With such similarities, it is reasonable to assume that these two groups will research and produce stories in much the same manner, bringing the same values and pre-conditions to their work.

Fourthly, there is an assumption that minority journalists can somehow help newspapers better relate to minority readers. This is no more reasonable than assuming that all journalists can help newspapers relate to all readers. If years of the lack of minorities in the newsroom has resulted in continually declining circulation, why should we assume that minorities—who will be similarly trained as the non-minorities—have a magic touch with their larger communities? Why would minority managers have any more expertise at targeting minority audiences when they themselves are not typical of those audiences? For example, in 1998, only 2 million or so of the nearly 23 million African-American, non-Hispanic U.S. citizens had a college degree (U.S. Department of Commerce, 1999). That would mean that more than 90% of this country's African Americans have a different educational experience than their college-degreed counterparts. Also in 1998, about 1.1 million bachelor's degrees were awarded across the United States; of that total, only about 7,600 were in journalism (Becker et al., 1999). One can hardly argue that these 7,600 African-American journalism graduates have much in common with the readers that newspaper managers hope they will help the newspaper recruit.

Even with the ideal audience, this hoped-for influence is questionable in some respects. For example one might think that African-American professionals—because of their education and income—would be more assimilated into American society and thus predisposed to make greater use of news media than non-professionals. However, a study of a Midwest university's African-American faculty and professional staff showed their media use (including newspapers) varied little from that of area non-professionals. Instead of local media, these professionals say interpersonal networks (such as community church and neighborhood organizations) are more effective in helping them become better citizens (Mastin, 2000). This indicates newspapers should either give up or try harder with this particular audience. In fact, some evidence suggests that non-readers are a bit of a lost cause. For example, a New York study (Masullo, 1997) found that people less motivated to seek information spend less time reading newspapers; that is, there is a strong positive correlation between a desire to keep up with current events and reading newspapers several days per week. People highly motivated to seek information through newspapers read newspapers more often and longer than those without such motivation. The study also found relationships between income, education, and a desire to keep up with current events, and between age and income and spending more time with newspapers. The latter finding is of concern considering the fact that one of the primary drivers of diversity is immigration; many immigrants are illiterate, poor, or uneducated (Kees, 2000).

Finally, when you consider the socialization process inherent in being a journalist, why would you expect journalists to have much in common with their readers? For example, when compared to the general population, mass communication students such as journalism majors tend to agree with one another—or, to be less diverse—in their news judgment (Fedler et al., 1995). Compared to other women, women mass communication majors tend to agree with one another (to be less diverse), as do male mass communication majors. The same holds for minority mass communication majors. Even if women and minorities held different values, then they would have to get others in the newsroom to listen to them in order to be able to create change in content. In fact, if the civic journalism experience teaches anything, it is that editors and publishers feel that journalists have to temporarily discard their notions of objectivity and to engage the public in order to hear just what the public values, implying that journalists have, indeed, lost touch with their audiences. This in itself is no great revelation, but instead shows the fallacy involved in much of the stated motivation (i.e., to increase and diversify the readership base of newspapers) behind the move toward diversity in the workforce.

When it comes to market influences, the newspaper industry obviously has attempted to change its audience reach. External and internal demographics change work methods simply because newspaper managers feel the change is needed in order to keep pace and survive financially. The risks, again, involve alienating employees who operate on long-held assumptions that emanate from the mass media business model of operation. Whereas faithful readers get a more diverse, relevant product, their numbers are—at best—stagnant and newspapers are hard-pressed to find a new model that will prolong a mass readership. Whereas the rise of the Internet has fueled much of the change, fears about the Internet may be somewhat unfounded, as research has shown that Internet users are more likely than non-users to be newspaper readers (Stempel, Hargrove, & Bernt, 2000). Meanwhile, as publishers try to re-educate and retrain their staffs—particularly in the newsroom—they are more and more likely to notice that they are fighting an uphill battle. Journalists will do as they are educated and trained to do and until the training changes or other options are explored, the editorial content of newspapers will not significantly transform itself.

That does not mean that stories and story types will not change. For instance, a systematic but informal study (Stepp, 1999) found that since the 1960s, news space in newspapers had doubled, and that stories and front pages were more feature-oriented and longer. Papers are trying to focus on human-interest news, particularly local news. Yet to no avail. It is as if newspapers—in trying to gain control via technologies that deliver increased speed and efficiency—have actually lost control of readership. We have to remember, however, that attempts to stay the course have been inconsistent. The most obvious site is the newsroom, where journalists still exercise a large degree of autonomy regarding what they produce and what should be produced. No amount of new technology or market changes has forced journalists to abandon in large part their journalistic principles.

The basic question then emerges: Why do newspapers continue to follow the same model of doing business? Part of the reason has been because there is no immediate need to change. The growth economy of the latter 1990s and of the early stages of the new millennium has allowed newspapers to use technologies, mergers, consolidations, and other efficiencies to improve their profits to levels acceptable to shareholders. Timing has not cooperated in that newspapers feel no sense of urgency. In addition, much innovation is driven by immediate, conspicuous competition. Most newspapers, however, do not compete with another newspaper and have not done since 1970. This dominant publication model, as *USA TODAY* Publisher Tom Curley said, "brings with it a set of whole new challenges and assumptions." Newspapers with a major share of their market are essentially "playing defense," he said. Only when there is a substantial market erosion "do you soberly reflect and you see opportunities to take advantage of," he said.

To be fair, newspapers continue to try harder to improve their readership connections. Methods include: matching readers' and advertisers' needs with enhanced distribution capabilities, improving customer service to readers and advertisers, re-examining subscription models (and offering specific-day delivery), integrating print and online businesses, and using circulation databases as a channel to extra revenue, to name a few efforts. Of course, not all newspapers are created equal. For instance, although most newspapers conduct readership research, they do so at varying levels and in varying ways. Larger newspapers do more kinds of research than smaller papers, publicly held groups do the widest variety, and readership research influences some content changes, especially general content decisions (e.g., graphic design or story play), more than others (Beam, 1995).

Organizational politics also plays a part in the lack of effective change. Not only do the continued high profits of newspapers make it difficult for change from a timing standpoint, they also make it difficult for newspaper publishers to propose wholesale changes; stockholders want to see continued profits and anything but continuous improvement is considered risky. So from an organizational view, newspapers have to be concerned with the interests of their external publics. Another example involves newspaper credibility, which managers consider an obvious extension of readership woes. Newspapers believe that public perception of newspaper performance is a vital element in the fight for readership retention. In 1998, editors' early research revealed six basic reasons that the public held media in low esteem. First, readers say they see too many factual errors and spelling or grammar mistakes in newspapers. Second, the public feels that newspapers do not consistently demonstrate respect for, and knowledge of, their readers and communities. Also, the public suspects that journalists' points of view and biases influence what stories are covered and how. Fourth, the public believes newspapers chase and overcover sensational stories for dramatic and monetary purposes (they do not believe these stories deserve the attention and play they get). Fifth, the public believes newsroom values and practices sometimes conflict with their own priorities (e.g., less government news, more entertainment) for their newspapers. Finally, members of the public with actual encounters with the news process are the most critical of media credibility (ASNE, 1998).

However, after three years of study and tests of varying sorts, editors discovered that knowing the root problems of credibility and doing something about them were separate matters. Acknowledging that improving credibility takes a long-term commitment and that change is slow to be noticed by readers, newspapers have come to realize there is no formula for building such trust. The solution involves such basic work as listening better, paying more attention to basics of news coverage, and informing readers when the newspaper attempts to improve (Christie, 2000). This may sound simple, but many newsrooms are unaccustomed to explaining how they do their jobs and—as the discussion on civic journalism indicated—listening to the public in some organized fashion (even for the sake of a story) is not something journalists routinely do. Editors and reporters often tend to become defensive and argumentative in such situations and, even if they were open to such discussion, beat reporting and news values are such entrenched routines that many reporters are likely to view any changes as disruptive.

In summary, market and demographic concerns cause much reason for pause among newspaper industry leaders, more so than technologies. The reason, again, is that technologies are controllable and create leverage for editors and publishers. Technologies help form and dictate content. More importantly, readers and potential readers can only be manipulated so far. The world—even in the form of the more familiar local markets—changes constantly and its behavior is difficult (if not impossible) to predict. The stress of change, when compounded by the daily stress of the various forms of newspaper work, can overwhelm some. The sheer volume of information about change—especially in its technological forms—can be daunting. Some theorize that all these factors combined—life's unpredictability, stress, and information overload—may foster analysis paralysis, in which a manager reserves judgment because the more he or she knows, the less clear things become (Shenk, 1999). Collectively, it may seem as if the newspaper industry finds itself in such a paralysis. To be sure, there are individuals and groups consciously and aggressively working to prepare their newspapers for change. Yet there are just as many in industry publications who suggest that all newspapers have to do is stay the course, stick to what they know, and success will continue. They imply that the future's unpredictability is cause enough, that things change too quickly and that it is more prudent to market and mine the familiar themes and tools of newspapers—content that the franchise newspapers have developed and the advantages they have in connecting members of their communities.

Of course, they are partly right. There are alternatives and none need be chosen in fear. None need be perceived as losing control. Lack of control can be compensated for by preparation. Thus change can be planned and planned for (Witherspoon, 1997), if newspaper managers simply take the time to do so. Some envision doing this through technology, others through consolidation and by letting the market dictate developments. The great debate on how to change will continue because permanent change never arrives; change is processual, with no end state. This is part of the ongoing ambiguity and uncertainty that causes newspapers stress about change. In the meantime, newspapers must continue to seek new ideas. In the next chapter, we make some recommendations as to how best to plan and prepare for the changes to come, as well as how to foster the innovative environment necessary to incubate those changes.

CHAPTER NINE

Newspaper Organizations of the Future

This chapter attempts to put the previous chapters into perspective, helping the reader to not only make sense of the entire text, but also to act as a bridge: We want to end this text by discussing ways to facilitate meaningful change in newspaper organizations.

We started by paying homage to newspapers' special societal role. As local products, they serve two masters—advertisers and readers—while trying to reflect a local community. The nobility placed on newspapers' mission by the First Amendment makes adapting to (and creating) change a daunting task. This chapter meets the challenge set forth in the first chapter: suggesting a new way of thinking about change in newspaper organizations.

Recall that this book views change as occurring within an organization's framework, its overall strategy, structure, systems, goals, staffing, and so on. The framework includes the various stakeholders and individuals who are a newspaper's constituencies. The framework itself is included in the newspaper's overall environment, characterized by social, technological, economic, and political change (Lawrence, 1989).

Organizational change requires creation of support mechanisms, communicating the necessary vision and helping establish the context that will ensure change emerges. This requires some planning or at least being aware of change-inducing factors. As managers seek to maximize their interests in planning, they also try to foresee the outcomes of their plans, often with an eye on the past, that is their experiences. Because of the competition faced by news organizations, the deadlines inherent in the process of reporting news, and the continuing adoption of new technologies used to cover and report news, time is an important environmental variable in the process of change within news organizations, surrounding the process like the atmosphere. So in making decisions to create or to prevent change, newspaper managers weigh benefits and costs, time, and how they compare to the vision of (or desires for) the newspaper's future (see Fig. 9.1). When strategizing, managers try to anticipate the outcomes of their plans, often with one eye toward the past, that is their experiences that have taught them what to expect if they take certain actions or make certain assumptions. However, time always

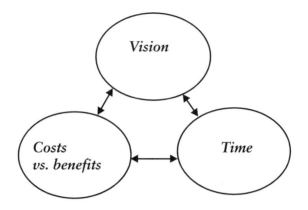

FIG 9.1 How approaches to change are made.

pressures managers in any strategic situation, primarily because it is limited—either by convention (e.g., the 24-hour day) or by nature.

Time involves not just the idea of timing—that is, the idea of opportunity or chance or setting—but also the concept of duration, or a stretch of time. Duration allows for evaluation of a change, a measuring stick to determine whether it truly represents a difference or if it is merely short-lived—and it determines the true test of organizational change. Timing, alternatively, involves the ability to gauge when a change will be accepted, needed, or wanted. The question, then, is how to gain the vision and take the most advantage of timing?

Newspaper change takes shape in three forms: people, process, and product. As elements in the framework we mentioned earlier, they typically interact. Before a change occurs or is considered, their interaction takes the shape of potential—what an editor, for example, must consider before adopting team reporting. In such a situation, the editor must not only train reporters in new team reporting methods, but must evaluate his or her staff to see if the methods are suitable and discuss the methods' potential and intricacies with the reporters. Knowing such elements helps the editor know the degree of the interaction, as well as giving him or her some insight into what other factors to consider when attempting the change. Just as the elements factor into the planning, they also usually embody the change.

The editor—and his or her staff—also has to recognize that there are varying degrees of resistance confronting any purported change. In the newspaper, these obstacles include fear, structural politics, traditional journalistic interests, and timing. Obstacles to team reporting could include fear of the technique itself, fear of how it will change journalistic techniques, and unwieldy reorganization of newsrooms to accommodate new team structures, journalists who lobby the city editor so that they can continue to cover their current beats (because they may find them either rewarding or psychologically comforting to do so). Perhaps readers may not have enough faith in the newspaper to put much stock in its team efforts, or they may value traditional beat coverage more. Each factor can be an obstacle in itself or work in tandem with the other obstacles.

In any event, newspaper employees must consider resistance to see if the change elements can—with the help of vision and time—surmount it and take the shape of the desired change or if the change can occur at all (see Fig. 9.2). Of course, employees ideally want to avoid reactive, or control-oriented, or model-based change and, instead, forge a change that's strategic. But all these occur; they may not be the best reasons for change, but in reality these often are ways change gets accomplished. The question becomes how to create the vision, properly communicate it and how to decide when?

CREATING VISION

Too often we think of vision as something that is created by pondering clouds on a mountaintop. In fact, vision is simply gaining foresight about a situation or circumstance, based on experience and a careful assessment of current and projected issues and needs. Nanus (1992) noted that creating a vision is a very practical process. Visions are not hallucinations, but portraits of the future developed with feet firmly planted on solid ground. To Nanus, leaders (wherever they are in an organizational hierarchy) create visions by asking questions about the future, by assessing the needs and wants of various constituencies of the organization. Management experts often talk about "getting out of the box," or stepping back from scenarios that the manager knows all too well, as if the metaphorical distance will provide perspective and help the manager gain clarity of thought. In newspapers, such talk may be foreign to publishers and editors, given many newspapers' assertive, or aggressive, internal communication style. For example, although most male editors go to work dressed in a suit, it is common for them to loosen their ties and roll up their shirt sleeves—an act symbolizing getting in the trenches with the reporters and connoting a desire to make oneself part of the process. When an editor stares into the newsroom, he or she sees several free, independent thinkers who have their own visions. In fact, good newsroom managing often means allowing those individuals' visions to occur. Consequently, managerial-speak on such subjects as vision often is met with a healthy dose of skepticism.

However, editors and publishers do not operate in a vacuum. They and their employees interact and attempt to publish the best newspaper they can. In the process, they develop many ideas, notions, and hunches. Still, most of

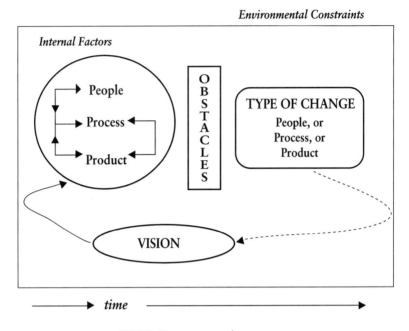

FIG 9.2   How newspaper change occurs.

what we discussed in the previous chapter seems to point out that newspapers—because of their declining credibility with the public and market share—are not creating the visions needed to help them adequately grow.

Part of the reason is the newspaper's role as a democratic institution, a representative of the free press, the fourth estate. To be fair, editors increasingly are learning the language of business and becoming aware of the other departments of the newspaper. Yet, keeping pace with changing markets takes extra effort that many newspaper managers find elusive. In addition—as alluded to in the previous chapter—the dearth of ideas partly stems from a lack of motivation. For example, newspapers have been accused of becoming complacent by one industry insider who suggests that the economic good times of the late 1990s has lulled newspapers into a smugness that prevents them from taking advantage of opportunities or investing further in the product (Nicholson, 2000). Rather than dwell on negative rationales, we suggest newspapers examine them in order to do something about the dilemma—there are ways to enable the process of visioning.

First, one has to understand what an organizational vision truly is—a mental picture of the future developed through analysis of current and projected demographic, social, economic, and technological trends and anticipated needs of the organization's internal and external constituencies.

Practicality and creativity are the parents of an organizational vision. Newspapers are no strangers to creativity—the newspaper itself is the creation of a symbolic representation of the ideas and activities particular to a local community. To produce such symbols, newspapers hire creative people—reporters, sales persons, carriers, and press operators, to name a few. Each production cycle (day or week), the newspaper challenges its employees to be creative, to develop something that did not exist in the previous production cycle. Such short-range creativity requires employees to think about what they are doing and visualize what it should become. However to be creative, a person must not only be obviously original and process many ideas simultaneously, but also exhibit signs of nonconformity and independence. When you consider that newspapers (even in their creativity of producing unique content) tend to deliver the same formatted product each time, they are not reinventing the wheel every day so much as they are changing the spokes. Any creativity is controlled or constrained by practicality—including the format and structure with which a newspaper has become associated. Newspapers do not practice creativity on a massive, transformational scale.

Vision also is another aspect of innovation, the ability to be original while simultaneously improving or advancing the newspaper in some new or novel way. A key requirement for innovation is autonomy—the feeling that you are independent and will suffer no negative ramifications or ill consequences for your actions. This feeling allows you to brainstorm, to play "what-if?" and to throw caution to the wind, but it does not guarantee you will do so. Autonomy should not be confused with creativity. Although creativity is a requirement for the journalistic function of taking chaos and creating order, autonomy does not guarantee creativity. An advertising saleswoman can have great autonomy in how she pursues an account in the sense of being left to her own devices. However, this does not necessarily mean she will exhibit creativity in that pursuit. She may, instead, court the advertiser the way she has seen other advertisers courted. Creativity would enter into the picture when the saleswoman takes a new approach and deviates from the normal methods of sales pursuits. This is as much an individually influenced decision as it is organizationally influenced; that is, the decision to exhibit new behaviors is up to the saleswoman, but the organization can encourage, or discourage those behaviors.

Such encouragement can come in a number of ways. The easiest method is to hire creative people. Another direct technique is to inform employees that autonomy is expected, although many managers fear this will lead to insubordination. The latter 1980s and 1990s have seen a push toward more participatory management, in which the manager gives direction but decisions are made by consensus based on participation by people in the work group. The hope is that the involvement of others in the decision-making process will encourage brainstorming, which will lead to more confidence and, thus, a greater capacity for creative thinking. The bigger, more practical task for most publishers or editors is to assure that the organization does not encourage conformity; routines and structure become ingrained in employees' work habits. In newspapers, the routines particularly encourage a certain mindset, with which employees identify or internalize because it has been rewarded and encouraged—particularly considering that newspaper work is divided so closely along functional lines (Sohn et al., 1986) that it is very rarely anyone's job to be a non-conformist. This can be especially true of newspapers that are owned by conglomerates or chains, although those newspapers also have the resources that they can commit to fostering creativity and encourage innovation (Polansky & Hughes, 1986).

The newspaper industry needs to find a balance between conformity and variation. Editors and publishers must find ways to provide an environment that assures a constantly expanding and open atmosphere. Colleges and universities attempt to create such an atmosphere because that is their purpose: to stimulate new thought. Some information-based or computer-based companies also have this approach because their businesses are in a turbulent industry and are based on the staple of information, which—by its nature of being fluid and ever changing—requires an openness to change. Newspapers would do well to borrow ideas from other industries and institutions that will help them institutionalize the creation of visions and change. Suggestions on how to do this have permeated the trade press and typically range from one-time, case-specific ideas (e.g., Cole, 1996) to a sweeping, radical proposal of bypassing the assembly-line production approach (e.g., Cole, 1998). As usual, a better proposal lies in between the two ideas.

Newspapers should develop structures and processes to initiate or implement visionary behaviors. Owners and publishers cannot expect journalists, advertising salespeople, carriers, and press operators (or the people who supervise them) to come up with ideas when that is—functionally speaking—not their job. They cannot rightfully expect consultants or think tanks or press associations (whose functions and missions do not coincide with that of an individual newspaper) to come up with specific, workable plans since they are not as intimately familiar with the market. They should institutionalize self-learning and self-awareness; One way is by creating a research and development department.

Traditionally in newspapers, research and development (R&D) has been the province of either the affluent newspaper, the vendor who wants to use research as a persuasive tool, the consultant whose primary interest is to be seen as unique and valuable, the press association that wants to be seen as indispensable to members, or the think tank that has an agenda—not always reliable sources for the typical newspaper. By creating an R&D component, a newspaper would make a statement that says it supports intuitive thinking, creativity, variety, and a sense of flexibility heretofore unseen in the organization. R&D departments are not part of the typical newspaper organization chart (e.g., Picard & Brody, 1997). For example, in mid-2000 there were nearly 1,500 newspapers, but only about 500 members of the major American newspaper research trade association.

As to how this could help newspaper managers distance themselves or think "out of the box," publishers—by creating a research department—effectively say that they will seek more feedback about their product and how it interacts with its customers (readers and advertisers). A properly focused research department sends the message that the newspaper will be no longer be simply looking for ideas about declining readership and competition but instead will concentrate more on how the newspaper functions—as an organization, and as a product. When a newspaper begins to direct its analysis to these areas, its managers can then focus more on the things that matter: the models they use and the rules they follow and why.

Newspapers are complex systems: There are many entities within and outside the organization that help it work. For example, newspapers interact with readers, adapt to reader and advertiser needs, have a complex set of mechanisms (relationships) that helps them interact at various levels with the public. Newspaper employees also have the ability to create. In short, newspapers are deep, intricate things, but with predictable forms and patterns—almost everyone can describe a newspaper. Therein lies the problem—newspapers are somewhat predictable and have reached a stage in which many consumers know what to expect and—if declining readership patterns are to be believed—more and more are finding more interesting leisure activities. Ironically, newspapers' complexity has reached a level in which they are perceived as mechanistic, sequential, and linear—in a word, conventional. Thus they may be less likely to be innovative in a changing, dynamic, different world.

Organizations prepare for the future through strategic planning. Newspaper organizations are in need of such planning. It represents the innovative thinking the industry and individual newspapers need. How an organization relates to its market relies on the degree of interaction and adjustment among its principles, models, rules, and behaviors; it also depends on how the organization sees those relationships and how questioning the organization is of them (Sherman & Schultz, 1998).

Values provide a newspaper with its ideals, such as informing its readers. Norms are values, indeed, the embodiment of values. Creating news, for example, is a norm because it is the theory or concept by which newspaper publishers believe they inform their readers. Rules are brief, inexact methods by which a newspaper adapts to its environment; ways in which norms are executed. Objectivity would be an example of a rule of news. Behaviors, finally, are how newspaper employees actually do their jobs. In the case of the news norm, the behaviors involve collecting and interpreting information. Norms are effective when they continually adjust to each other, meaning as one changes, so does the other (Sherman & Schultz, 1998). Norms are important because as the embodiment of rules, they set the standard for how people behave; subsequently, behavior helps clarify the model. Rules, meanwhile, are the ways the newspaper operates the model. In a newspaper, the news norm is made operational by, among other rules, objectivity. Objectivity, in turn, determines how reporters and editors behave and, as a result, how the newspaper reads.

In the modern American newspaper, however, there are other norms interacting with the rules. One such norm involves the dual nature of the newspaper's audience; advertisers and readers are essential and each needs the other, resulting in revenue for the newspaper. The key question is which norm—news or revenue—is more dominant? Obviously revenue has some primacy because without revenue, newspapers would cease to exist. Yet generating revenue is constrained by the need to identify and report the news because news is seen as one of the driving agents for readership, which then drives advertising. So newspapers' norms co-exist in tense equilibrium. In addition, newspapers cannot bear to seriously question the news norm for all the reasons that go along with questioning change. To do so would go against traditional journalism; it would place newspapers in unexplored territory, it would wreak havoc on the conventional newspaper structure and all signs (mostly those involving revenue and public necessity for reliable information) point to the fact that news still sells. So newspapers persist in attempting to fill new wine in old bottles—the rules of journalism bind newspapers to their old norm.

An R&D department would allow newspapers to more closely examine their rules, norms, values, and behaviors. It would provide data for managerial decision making. Readership data have consistently shown that news is not all that readers want, yet tweaking news rules (to more broadly define news) creates upheaval in the newsroom. Rule-based behaviors do not challenge rules (Sherman & Schultz, 1998); many newsrooms still have such rules as objectivity, reform, monitoring government, and the inverted pyramid even as they switch to behavioral tools such as computer-assisted reporting and public journalism. Neither can the vast resources and the pressure of a large corporation always change those rules; Gannett Co. Inc. tried with its NEWS 2000, a plan that attempted to merge readership, penetration, and readership satisfaction goals with journalism by redefining news. The 1991 plan sought to force Gannett papers to mirror their communities' diversity, provide information people needed, evoke emotions, and foster interaction with readers while producing public service journalism in a compelling format. However the company decided to modify the plan, admitting the plan was too complex, did not help in some readership groups and did not stem declines in readership (Moses, 2000b). At the least, this shows that newspapers need to more fully understand the pervasiveness of their values before they attempt any changes. It also illustrates that newspapers need to change the norm and that the model may be only changeable at the local level (and not at the corporate level). More importantly, it shows that change will not come easily to newspapers unless they are open to change.

This suggestion is not an anti-journalism stance. The contrary is true. Journalism is a valid and noble endeavor, with proven worth and a worthwhile mission. As mentioned earlier, newspapers—as a rule—require journalists to exhibit short-range creativity, a task that does not fully equip them to be truly creative in the long-term sense. To do so, there would have to be journalistic signs of nonconformity and independence. Independence implies to journalists only a sense of autonomy, a professional value to which journalists are honor-bound. Professionalism requires like-minded thinking, so it should come as no surprise that newspapers have turned to what they derisively refer to as MBA types—classically trained business school-type managers—to infuse the newsroom with readership-oriented creativity and innovation. The problem has been, however, that newsrooms also are professionally driven; journalists consider themselves professionals and their work thus governed by their professional norms. Newspapers would have to change the training of the profession if they wanted to change the type of content the newsroom produces. Since that is not a practical solution—even the accreditation standards that govern journalism schools' curricula are determined in large part by current and former journalists—then newspapers need to turn elsewhere for innovative thinking. Turning elsewhere means creating an R&D department that is encouraged to explore the boundaries of journalism and of the changing lifestyles of readers. Doing so might be able to help newspapers settle the conflict with business and journalistic norms. An R&D department could play "what if?" in its approach, help newspapers to learn to more adequately converse with readers and advertisers and simultaneously create an atmosphere in which newspapers voluntarily can inspect, challenge, or modify ideas without the fear of losing their uniqueness.

In the final analysis, however, an R&D department is but one way through which newspapers can attain visionary capabilities. Such a department simply represents a newspaper's willingness to consider organizational change, or a series of changes. The R&D department could work with other departments to gain continuous feedback (Lallande, 2000). The department itself would be helpless to change anything; it would need the support of the publisher, who could then direct the various departments to adjust their behavior and rules accordingly. What is needed is a reinstatement of the idea of trust: Newspapers must begin to trust the feedback they receive from readers (via such tools as an R&D department) and use the feedback to try new ideas. Those ideas need not involve only the newsroom since the idea of a newspaper should not be solely tied to having a newsroom. As the Internet continues to develop and its capacities multiply, newspapers will be forced to compete and thus take advantage of those capacities. This suggests that newspapers will become more than simply conveyors of news. There will be multimedia delivery of news, to be sure. Newspapers also will engage in other activities. They will forge links with television stations so that professionally produced video may be shown on their Web sites (Williams, 2000). Or they will continue to develop portal sites that have nothing to do with journalism and everything to do with building a sense of community, listing neighbor-hood events, school news, homework assignments, and the like (Moses, 2000a). In short, newspapers may be more like magazines, television, or books—none of it with journalists' help. Newspapers will have to resist forcing journalists to become part of the act—which means limiting attempts to retrain journalists to make them "jacks of all trades," asking them to cover non-news items, making them into recorders instead of journalists. Not only have journalists shown they will resist the pressure, but readers have shown journalism alone will not help increase readership. In the end, the new ideas will require new money for a new classification of employees—which will mean lower profits in the short term as newspapers recycle profits into a revitalized, different product. Newspapers will no longer be only "news"-papers because they will have learned to eagerly generate feedback—through the development of entertaining, non-news content—while learning to trust their instincts and experiment with change.

That will not be an easy process, however. With the pressure to perform—to attract readers and advertisers, to maintain circulation, to keep the paper interesting to readers, and to create profit in other words—newspaper employees will be hard-pressed to change their attitudes. With work routines, there is always the temptation to concentrate on the daily or weekly mission, to conduct business as usual. Listening to feedback—or to anything, for that matter—requires work and focus. That is not all. Reporters, for instance, know that good interviewing requires listening, but not listening to every-thing the person being interviewed says. There is a selective process involved, based on timing (recognizing opportunities) and knowing when to listen. So listening also requires a certain amount of timing. The next section discusses how vision and time are uniquely linked.

ATTAINING MOTIVATION (VIA TIMING)

It was 1991 and in five years the Olympics were coming to Atlanta, Georgia. Cox Newspapers, parent company of *The Atlanta Journal-Constitution*

(*AJC*), wanted to provide the best Olympics coverage possible—not just to the people of Atlanta, but to the readers of all Cox newspapers. So in 1996, Cox and the *AJC* assembled a 350-member team of journalists, 82 of them from other Cox newspapers loaned to the *AJC* for the project. In return, the team would help compile a six-page section transmitted daily to all Cox papers; most team members would help produce the substantial daily edition of the *AJC* for a month. However, the six-page section would turn out to be much more.

Each night there were two editions of the section, built in a modular style so that on the bottom, inside pages the Cox papers could either run news without time zone references or effortlessly substitute advertisements, news, or other items. The section was transmitted to the newspapers via Cox's still-in-development Wide Area Network (WAN), a high-speed phone link. So not only was Cox providing a service to its employees and testing a new technology, it was teaching its employees teamwork and coordination on a corporate scale (CoxNet, 1999). The technology was created to help each Cox paper browse databases at the Atlanta papers and at other Cox papers via shared software and common pagination systems. Primarily, Cox wanted the WAN system to carry a daily flow of previously gathered pages (e.g., stocks, sports statistics, advertisements, and various special section fronts; Bass, 1999; Rosenberg, 1996).

Not all Cox papers participated in the system at first, but "the Olympics gave us the chance to show this off as something good," CoxNet Director John Reetz said in an interview for this book. "People were treated real well after 'parachuting' in (for the games) and we got everybody in the right frame of mind." A group decision making mentality developed during the games and when the games ended, Cox officials saw an opportunity to put the WAN (renamed CoxNet) to good use as a news tool on a continuous basis. An editorial committee was formed, along with a group of important technical employees at each Cox paper. Then Reetz hit the road, networking with key newsroom and technical personnel, and building support for the CoxNet concept, although the concept itself was in the formative stages. There were ups and downs—simultaneously.

One break came in January 1998 when Cox officials decided to change the Cox Washington, D.C. news bureau's function, transforming it from the clearinghouse of the Cox wire news service to simply a reporting bureau. That meant CoxNet would take over the time-consuming wire service chores—handling copy from all Cox newspapers as well as affiliate wire services (such as that of *The New York Times*). CoxNet set out to improve the quality of the service, particularly the news budget (the computerized presentation of what stories were available) and the story-filing structure itself. On the latter, the goal was to eliminate the large papers' tendency to simply shovel their stories onto wire unedited and to encourage the smaller newspapers to contribute more stories and material.

The bad news was that Reetz faced a lot of missionary work. He said he constantly fought the "what's in it for me?" attitude, logging many air miles to meet with reluctant department heads on a one-on-one basis, working to develop CoxNet's perceived value. Much of the hesitation centered on technical capabilities and compatibility of computer systems, but Reetz also encountered reluctance on a structural scale. He noticed that smaller papers were easier to sell on the system because they needed the help; the bigger papers—although a little spoiled—also were more attuned to the corporate vision for CoxNet. The unwilling participants were in the middle-sized-paper range that perceived CoxNet "as taking more time than it's worth," Reetz said. "We read the newspapers and we see how they use the (CoxNet) content and we ask, 'Will they use it on their own? Will they look at it as a good read?' It's always a struggle. Their bottom line is: 'This is just in my way'—that's what they're thinking."

CoxNet constantly strives to improve itself. In 1999, for example, it created a *budget tool,* a WAN browser that allows section editors (e.g., sports, features, and business) to search across all Cox papers and pull desired materials. If a sports editor's looking for the best professional basketball coverage, he or she can search the budget tool and examine all that Cox papers offer on the subject. CoxNet also initiated a visiting editor program, providing travel and lodging to Atlanta for one visiting Cox staffer at a time for a month-long visit to CoxNet. Probably more importantly, CoxNet began publishing a monthly newsletter. It features, among other items: information on CoxNet software unveilings, profiles of individual Cox papers and employees, roundups of employee awards and distinctions, detailed listings of how each Cox paper is using CoxNet offerings (e.g., "Atlanta story on interest-only loans offering help despite high rates—by Austin"), the latest developments on Internet strategies by Cox papers, and valuable how-to information concerning various professional tasks, from writing to marketing.

The improvements were all part of the selling job that Reetz had envisioned, but not really expected. "With the budget tool," he said, "we thought people would see it and it would sell itself. Once you get some converts, it spreads pretty well. But I thought it would be a top-down sort of things and get done because the publisher said so." The individual Cox papers have had concerns about autonomy, he added. "They want to know 'What does this mean? Do we have to use Atlanta's sports page?' . . . If we (Cox corporate) had mandated this, it wouldn't have worked that well or that fast. There are times I wish we *could* just mandate it, but it doesn't get the use we like. Sometimes I want to ask, 'Can't we just *tell* West Palm (a Cox paper in Florida) to run this?' Well, no, because it infringes on the rights of the local publisher. So you make it so good they don't have a choice."

In tandem with CoxNet, Cox started Cox Academy, an in-house clearing-house for newsroom training. Originally begun in 1996 as "*AJC* University," the concept expanded into a traveling road show featuring up-to-date training conducted by members of the various Cox newspapers. The academy especially attempts to schedule seminars and workshops for employees of smaller Cox papers that are unable—because of the prohibitive cost of travel—to go to Atlanta. The idea now doubles as a retention tool because academy trainers often can provide training for an entire newsroom in one session. For example, the academy tries to schedule sessions at a centrally located newspaper that will enable employees from nearby papers (within four hours' driving distance) to attend. A two-day academy session in Waco, Texas, for instance, drew groups of newsroom staffers from all four Cox newspapers in Texas, and feedback has been positive. "What helps," Academy Director Mike Schwartz said, "is they (attendees) look at us as one of them, not as some outside-the-company consultant. So there's some familiarity. We're not just someone spouting generic stuff. We've been where they are." As with CoxNet, Cox papers do not feel pressured to use the academy. Fred Zipp, the Associate Managing Editor for news at Cox's *Austin American-Statesman,* viewed the academy as "one of three or four options" for off-site training. He said the Austin newsroom is "increasingly mindful" of training and, in the past, has had "a healthy dose of resentment on 'Cox-think.'" There also have been occasions when his paper has been able to ally itself regarding news coverage with the Atlanta papers and the Cox Washington bureau. Although the CoxNet budget tool is a "powerful instrument" and a "good way to get people to buy in to CoxNet," Zipp said he felt it was not being used negatively nor being seen as "corporatization" of the news in Austin.

The Cox experience provides a good example of how timing can affect the motivation of newspaper employees. The Olympics forced more than 300 Cox employees together, gave them a chance to learn teamwork, and become exposed to the beginnings of the WAN. CoxNet has since evolved into the service bureau for all Cox newspapers. Not only does CoxNet provide ready-to-use pages on subjects that some individual Cox newspapers would never have the resources to offer alone, but it handles specific requests for coverage needs from Cox papers (especially in the case of national breaking news) and coordinates sharing of technical resources. Just as importantly, CoxNet seeks new areas of sharing in advertising and marketing. The Olympics provided the trigger event and Reetz has taken the impetus as far he can, continuing to stretch CoxNet's reach and credibility. He needed a quality product, to be sure, but he had to add dependable service, flexibility in adapting to individual papers' needs, and constant networking, continuous monitoring and feedback in order to sell it (J. Reetz, personal communication, November 25, 1999). In effect, he has honed CoxNet into an effective feedback mechanism. In so doing, however, he needed the Olympics as a starting point; it is doubtful that one man could make such an impact without the goodwill push provided by the Olympics. "For us the timing was right because with all this (technological) stuff out there, and people trying to figure out how to reinvent the paper, technology scares a lot of newspapers and managers," Reetz said. "We've been able to take the technology to give them things that have got to be reassuring."

Cox Chairman Jay Smith already had in place a vision to improve Cox newspapers' quality, to adapt to the changing culture of the company, and to achieve efficiencies in organization. CoxNet's seeds were sown by years of preparation—getting the newspapers up to speed technologically, and enforcing a mandate for company-wide pagination. "All of a sudden," Reetz said, "there was a structure to fully capitalize on this infrastructure." To maximize CoxNet, Smith's vision has been open-ended. Reetz said there has been no end-of-the-road mandate. "We've been given latitude to do something—serve newsrooms—that's newsroom driven," he said. "And we're continuously evolving—adding stuff and killing stuff. It just depends on what's needed." This coevolution has had subtle-but-important impact. For example, if a major sporting event is on the horizon, staffing no longer becomes a question of sending the best personnel from each paper but, according to Reetz, sending "the best folks in the company. That's thinking as a team—a huge cultural jump in the company. And that's the kind of stuff we (CoxNet) want to drive."

So the motivation for Cox's newspapers is a combination of external and internal sources. The latter comes from inside, such as doing something for one's own internal reward. The former is generated from the outside and usually driven by an external reward. Cox newspapers can see their own papers' content benefiting from CoxNet (intrinsic) while the extrinsic reward obviously entails being good corporate citizens and the reward of knowing they are helping colleagues at other papers in the company. The key is to achieve the right combination of intrinsic and extrinsic motivation. Timing plays a large part in this combination. It appears, at first glance, that the timing in the CoxNet example seems to be circumstantial or incidental; after all, the Olympics would have occurred and would have been covered with or without the WAN. However Cox's Olympic experiment was primarily geared toward helping the *AJC* boost its coverage. The work of what was to later become CoxNet was not the primary thrust of the huge assemblage of Cox staff. The combination—which translated into "if you do this (help the *AJC*), then we'll do this (published the Olympics section) for you"—was a proposition that held great long-term promise for the smaller Cox papers. It was an opportunity to use current technology to their future advantage, as well as an opportunity for someone such as Reetz to push a vision. By exploring the concept of opportunity, we can make the idea of timing more clear.

The dictionary defines opportunity as a chance, an occasion or opening—a favorable point in time, in which circumstances represent a good chance for improvement or growth. So opportunity has characterized the timing element in each of the cases examined in this book. At *The Dallas Morning News,* the opportunity was a chance to implement an employee-centric pagination system, one sensitive to the needs of its users. It also presented an occasion to do it right, in the sense that previous efforts to implement other editing systems had failed; the process of adoption represented a chance for change in approach. At *USA TODAY,* one opportunity presented itself in the guise of upgrading the newspaper's original journalism of hope to one that would help the publication make its mark and compete more fully. Yet another opportunity involved the viewpoint or the culture of the newspaper itself; in that sense, opportunity is a prospect, an outlook. As cited earlier in chapter 7, the outlook at *USA TODAY* is unique in that it is a reader-centered view that originated with the birth of the paper. So in another sense, the opportunity that changed the paper's news content was a continuation of a reader-focused culture. Lastly, *The Dallas Examiner* saw an opportunity to claim a unique niche and fashion itself as a journalistically credible publication among African-American weeklies. In the process, it also sought to transition from a paper of limited influence to one in which advertisers and readers alike would see the potential for growth and connection to each other.

Three newspapers, three different views of opportunity. Or so it seems. Their varying sizes, audiences, and aspirations make it difficult to discern any patterns. Opportunity appears to be in the eye of the beholder, the person who seizes the chance. This gives the impression that timing (as well as change) is invariably linked to someone's vision. On closer inspection, it is not the eye that determines the opportunity so much as it is the past. *USA TODAY* was shaped in large measure because Neuharth seized upon his failed previous dream (recall from chapter 4 his unsuccessful *USA TODAY* forerunner, *SoDak Sports*). *The Dallas Morning News'* new pagination system was built on the negative experiences (continuing our dream analogy, dare we say nightmares) of *News* staffers with previously unsuccessful editing systems. Finally, Mollie Belt's desire to see her father's newspaper become what he envisioned (after it was apparent that it was not headed that way) prompted all of the change experienced at *The Dallas Examiner*. So in each case, the past and the present offered an opportunity to change and, in turn, prompted a vision and a decision to initiate and enact change. Each of the principal parties sought a break with history and an opportunity—a new outlook, viewpoint, or state. In addition, each case was largely one of internal motivation—the desire to self-improve—with very little help from an external motivation. Although you could argue that, in each case, the profit motive was a form of external motivation, you could not successfully make the case that it was the primary motive.

There is a link between vision, decision making, and timing. An opportunity presents itself, a vision is created based on that opportunity (or timing), which then leads to a decision, which creates subsequent opportunity. The two hypothetically create a continuous cycle (see Fig. 9.3). For newspapers, this means that attaining vision must, by necessity, be preceded by a sequence of events that produce an opportunity. In the context of our earlier dilemma—that is, how does a newspaper create the motivation that helps to deliver the vision—it would seem that, ideally (in the case of intrinsically motivated employees), the environment (in the guise of an opportunity) provides the motivation. When the intrinsic motivation is not present in sufficient levels, then there must be an external factor or factors to prompt action or inspire motivation.

With motivation-inspired timing and vision, then, a newspaper is well on its way to change. That is easier said than done. Some would argue that leadership is much more influential than timing in organizational change. Indeed, organizational leaders often decide on and control the timing of organizational change. In the next section, we examine the function of leadership in organizational change and how timing and vision can be exercised properly and promptly in that regard. We look to our three case studies for specific lessons and suggestions.

PROVIDING LEADERSHIP FOR CHANGE

The following suggestions for facilitating change provide a basic, fundamental approach that draws on the most important elements discussed to this point. It is hoped that editors and publishers will take this list to heart in the spirit in which it is offered—with an eye toward laying the groundwork for improving the chances for positive growth and development of newspapers. Those looking for a quick fix approach to change will be disappointed, since this book has shown that long marches tend to lead to major transformations of the kind needed by many newspapers.

Share Control

Newspaper managers often do not provide vision because they are overly concerned with daily production matters—publishing the paper, editing the content, managing the sales staff, consulting with reporters, and overseeing

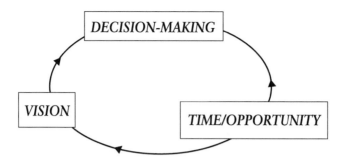

FIG 9.3 The time-vision cycle.

carriers. As a result, there is little time to motivate employees. In addition, constant or continuous control creates the mindset within employees that management sets the tone and therefore it is employees' jobs to follow. In the *USA TODAY* newsroom, the opposite is true. Editor Karen Jurgensen started out with the express intent of getting reporters and editors to feel as if *USA TODAY* was their newspaper, their responsibility. She followed their lead. John Reetz has attempted to do the same thing with CoxNet. He has made a point of selling the service to Cox newspapers as something they can tailor to their own advantage. As a result, his function is more that of coordinator and troubleshooter than of manager.

At this point, the more skeptical newspaper manager might counter that many newspaper employees—especially journalists and ad salespersons—already enjoy considerable autonomy. That may be so, but, again, autonomy should not be confused with creativity; autonomy is a professional concern that allows the employees to do a professional job—itself an act of compliance because that is exactly what management wants them to do. Sharing control also involves establishing mechanisms for feedback; for example providing newspaper carriers freedom to apply new ideas on the distribution level to preclude the carrier's supervisor from getting swamped with the daily details of circulation.

Accomplishing this change will require managers to overcome their fear of delegating control. This shows a lack of confidence, much of it because of uncertainty about the changing industry environment (e.g, see Newspaper Association of America, 1998). Too, editors and publishers feel they bear the burden of responsibility and, thus, should have control. By giving subordinates a comparable, high level of responsibility, the onus shifts. This will involve making employees directly responsible for resources and—ultimately—profits; as a result, this provides direct motivation for employees to be innovative because there will be pressure to perform. As it stands now, all the pressure (created by all the control) is on top management and much of the autonomy (in the case of the newsroom, at least) is with lower-level employees. Of course, no control can be relinquished if employees do not know where and how to apply it, which makes this next recommendation vital.

Clarify Objectives Through Continuous Communication

This may sound obvious, but its self-evidence makes it dangerous because managers often assume it is apparent and, thus, never check to be sure it occurs. In newspapers, for example, it may seem appropriate for the management of *The Dallas Morning News* to tell editors it wants them to adopt a new pagination system. It is quite another, however, to say that a pagination system must meet certain specifications and pass certain user tests and experiments. Management must clearly communicate its intent in such a way that employees have proper direction and guidance regarding the task. This is especially true during a change process.

For instance, *The Morning News* did just that in several ways. Preliminary planning became more solidified and clarified as time went on. First, interested employees were sent to visit other newspapers to compare them with the needs of *The News*. Second, the New Technology Group was formed to help articulate the findings of employees making those trips and to begin a dialogue with senior management regarding what was needed and why. Once the group took root, it developed a communication plan that included several filter mechanisms. A newsletter was created; superusers were trained to help teach the new technology and also to act as a sounding board and hands-on remedy for users' concerns; of course, training sessions were started; and, finally, the new system was introduced in phases that would allow its bugs to get early exposure and treatment before the system was completely installed. Had none of these methods been used and a unilateral adoption urged, it is conceivable the newspaper would have experienced a small-scale mutiny.

In addition, as important as clarification is, it is as important to clarify in a manner that gets the job done with little disruption as possible. For example, when *The Dallas Examiner* hired a new, traditionally trained journalist to be its editor, its two primary reporters departed and had to be replaced. One of the reporters felt angered and betrayed by the new editor's appointment; she and the other reporter also felt the imposition of new standards and stricter definitions of news would have an adverse impact on their reporting styles and that the new editor would be difficult with which to work. The new editor, meanwhile, was distressed by the defections; not only had she hoped for a peaceful transition (complete with appropriate journalistic training), she also had hoped to be able to lead the paper into a new editorial area featuring more hard news and fewer soft, promotional stories. In short, the new editor's vision was viewed as a threat, when in fact it was intended as a professional upgrade.

Institutionalize Commitment to Change

This is a particularly difficult concept to employ, for several reasons. In newsrooms, for example, as news changes, so does journalists' focus. Editors habitually shift gears as the hot topic changes; this is facilitated by the fact that newspapers review and exclude so much news that some news item is bound to gather more attention than other items. In addition, in many newsrooms it is expected that employees will leave after a year or two for larger, more cosmopolitan cities and newspapers. Often reporters are not expected to stay long and, indeed, many smaller newspapers prides themselves in training reporters to the point that they are ready for other, more desirable newspapers. In other words, commitment largely comes in the form of advocacy for professional ideals (such as freedom for the press) and toward the development of a news item (often called getting the story). In addition, newspapers traditionally have not shown much commitment in terms of pay and benefits—the median salary for a newspaper job in 1999 was $22,500 (Brown, 1999); two years earlier, the average pay for teachers—a profession notorious for being undervalued—was slightly more than $38,500 (Education Commission of the States, 1997). Finally, how much commitment can be shown in an ever-changing environment?

The answer lies in the meaning of commitment—an implied obligation, a dedication to one or more persons, a process, and values. When a manager hires people, often he or she feels obligated for pay, benefits, workspace, and no more. Commitment implies more. Since the Watergate era of the mid-to-late 1970s, newspapers have experienced a surplus of job applicants who viewed journalism as a noble cause and crusade. Those good times may be nearing an end; although schools of journalism still have plenty of students, a growing percentage are interested in broadcast journalism, in online fields and in public relations (Becker et al., 1999). Other professions also offer more attractive salaries and benefits. This means that newspapers will have to show a greater commitment in terms of these aspects of the job. Higher pay alone may make the editors' job of providing motivation that much easier because hiring journalists at decent, appealing wages will increase the likelihood of a more self-motivated recruiting pool. The dominant complaint journalists have when asked about job satisfaction: pay (Weaver & Wilhoit, 1996).

Commitment extends to other areas, such as training. The increasingly temporary nature of the workforce will make training a must if newspapers are to succeed in the coming years (Groves, 1997). In addition, with publishers beginning to advocate the delivery of the newspaper in multiple formats—electronic and print, for example—many reporters and editors lack training in how to do so (Newspaper Association of America, 1998). Yet, newsrooms in particular are not providing the training their employees need. For example, few copy editors receive formal training, especially those working night shifts (Davis, 1997). When journalists who have left the profession are asked why, as many say they needed a new challenge as do those who cite salary concerns (Weaver & Wilhoit, 1996)—an indicator that their jobs had gotten stale. Additionally, if today's business environment continues to feature constant, dynamic change—as expected—then training will be all the more important because employees will need training to keep abreast of changes. Perhaps the most significant reason for newspaper managers to exhibit a commitment to training is its perfect fit in the developmental strategy that is vision (Fombrun & Harris, 1993).

For example, we have seen the obvious case of how *The Dallas Morning News* used training to its advantage, providing training to accommodate employees' schedules and jobs. The training prepared them for the changes they were to undergo in using the new pagination system. In this chapter, we also wrote of how Cox Newspapers go the extra step to bring training to the employees, rather than the other way around. Also, we witnessed the not-so-obvious efforts of *USA TODAY,* where training took the shape of the newsroom culture. In that scenario, new employees were inculcated not only in the journalism of hope, but also in the can-do spirit of adapting to reader-driven change. Finally, *The Dallas Examiner* provided reporter and business operations training to its small staff so it, too, could meet changes in content and in managerial direction. So training activity helps newspapers position their employees to not only complete urgent job needs but they also help outfit employees for future tests.

Commitment, then, is more than being consistent. It is an expression of an implied obligation that management has to its employees. In newspapers, training's regular, consistent place at the budgeting table is long overdue. In the new millennium, the changing demographics and economy of the United States will require all companies—particularly newspapers—to put their money where there mouths are if they are to meet the challenge of showing they are serious about change. People will expect jobs to be more meaningful and newspapers—despite their noble First Amendment origins—must enrich their work routines by helping their employees to do so through training.

Teach and Use Continuous Improvement

For several weeks beginning in September 1999, *The Dallas Examiner* labored to get its weekly edition published on time, in working order, and without staff turmoil. Problems cropped up throughout the process, from story idea generation, to reporters making deadlines, to design and production staff being rushed to copy edit and proof pages, to overall low morale.

For example, publisher Mollie Belt claimed stories lacked depth and context; where the reporters saw news, she saw missing sources, incomplete history, and one-sided perspectives. The longtime Dallas resident knew part of the problem was her unique, strong familiarity with the Dallas African-American community. She knew the players of the community's civil rights struggle in ways none of her reporters could. She also was on first-name basis with many of the African-American elite in the city; she had access, of which her reporters could only dream. As a result, when stories would begin to develop after reporters' initial background work, she would often see holes and would suggest changes or additional reporting—changes that took time. Consequently, key stories would be late or incomplete or both, distressing Mrs. Belt as well as frustrating her staff. This had a ripple effect in the production process, which already was working under several other handicaps involving ad solicitation, staff expertise levels, and mutual distrust.

Finally, in November, the publisher took the problem head-on, gathering her staff for a one-day seminar (facilitated by one of the authors of this text) covering all these issues and more. Through discussion, debate, and honest assessment, the staff was able to accomplish several feats. First, story development was kick-started earlier—the day after the paper was published—to assure clarity on what the publisher desired and to make certain that time was allowed for proper, deliberate editing. In addition, the idea of having backup story ideas was introduced to allow for problems with source access. Along those lines, an advance news copy library was prepared to help production staff avoid habitual, last-minute scurrying for replacement materials and thus alleviate a high amount of stress. Second, communication among staffers was given additional structure; routines were established in order to assure everyone knew the status of certain stories and materials. Third, the entire staff was to focus on quality work—from stories, to ads, to design, to production. To do this, staffers were encouraged to spotlight quality. As one wrote in her assessment, "It is better to have one (well-) written story than three shallow stories" in the paper. Finally and most important, the staff learned the value of looking at the entire production process. For the first time, they understood what others did and why. They may not have liked some of their co-workers, but at least they came to respect those colleagues' roles and comprehended the pressure involved.

Similar effects are under way throughout the country. Of the more than 300 newspapers responding to an industry-wide survey, nearly three-fifths have marketing committees that include newsroom representatives. Of those, slightly more than two-fifths have existed for one to three years. Nearly 37%

meet weekly and about a third meet monthly. Newsroom personnel contribute to advertising-supported special sections and other efforts to target readers by submitting ideas, stories, and visuals (Albers, 1998). Such interdepartmental cooperation helps grow readership and generate ideas; still, some publishers are hesitant to do so, especially in light of such scandals as the one involving *The Los Angeles Times,* which had been the most visible advocate of cross-departmental sharing. *The Times* was revealed to have agreed to share the profits from a Sunday magazine special issue promoting a new Los Angeles sports arena with the arena. The incident confirmed many critics' suspicions that corporate news values translates into damaged journalistic credibility (Anonymous, 1999). Newspaper management consultant Geisler (1999) put the journalistic view succinctly:

> Journalists love to point out consistencies: "Two years ago they told us to do just the opposite." "This was not clear in the memo." "Other places never do it this way."
>
> We like to think that by finding these conflicts, we can keep status quo. It rarely works.
>
> Journalists are mouthy, contentious debaters, who love a good argument. We're big on "the principle of the matter," which we often confuse with "my position on the matter."
>
> Journalists are insecure. Yes, for all the power we supposedly wield, many among us have an acute case of "impostor syndrome." We often doubt our own talents. We don't make tangible things like cabinets, don't win big cases in courtrooms, don't heal sick people.
>
> We work with words. We tell tales. We're only as good as our last big story, exclusive, award, or ratings spike.
>
> We worry a lot.
>
> Is it any wonder, then, that change appears as a mortal enemy? (p. 40)

There is no doubt that breaching departmental walls helps the newspaper to improve its content. Newspapers' reluctance in this area—while understandable—may be a classic case of managerial myopia. As renowned management expert Drucker (1999b) observed, the first step in leading change is to free resources devoted to preserving things that no longer play a role in performance and no longer produce results:

Maintaining yesterday is always difficult and extremely time-consuming. Maintaining yesterday always commits the institution's scarcest and most valuable resources—and above all, its ablest people—to non-results. Yet doing anything differently—let alone innovating—always creates unexpected difficulties. It demands leadership by people of high and proven ability. And if those people are committed to maintaining yesterday, they are simply not available to create tomorrow.

In a sense, then, newspapers—particularly newspaper editors—are attempting to maintain yesterday while they simultaneously seek help on achieving tomorrow.

Continuous improvement of newspapers takes more than simply telling journalists to get on the bandwagon and to leave yesterday behind. Too often, the business approach appears to journalists as one more attempt to get the journalists to help do the job of the other departments: "Today, the newsroom helps Dept. X." Managers must frame the issue more positively; the key is for editors and publishers to define interdepartmental cooperation in a context that journalists will understand. It will help them be better journalists. The newspaper is a microcosm of the area it serves. The newsroom must become familiar with certain publics in order to produce news; the same applies for advertising and circulation. Each department has a sphere of influence the knowledge of which will benefit the other. For example, a business reporter can get a better feel for the city's economy by speaking with advertising salespersons, and vice versa. The editor can get a perspective on demographics he or she would not get otherwise by speaking with a circulation supervisor, who can learn a trick or two about distribution incentives from the company marketing specialist.

More importantly, the interaction of all these individuals would produce something greater than the sum of their parts. It stands to reason that having more than one view on a situation provides a basis for comparison; having three or more provides context, not to mention the capability to provide a synergy. In the instance of the newspaper, synergy is the collaborative learning that occurs when representatives of the various departments honestly discuss their objectives and what they know—a mini R&D department that supplies invaluable feedback and generates ideas. This is all the more important when you consider that newspapers traditionally are organized according to departmental function—each department conducts one or two general tasks and organizational units are defined by the nature of their work. While such a scheme allows for specialization within functions and efficient use of resources, it also creates group loyalties and group goal conflict (Rue & Byars, 1983). In a newspaper, this would mean that, for instance, the newsroom would be concerned only with the news content, while the advertising department would be concerned only with the ads, and so on. Even a newspaper's marketing department, which although focused on the entire product, would be concerned solely with doing its job—marketing. As a result, functional departmentation fosters a functional orientation by newspaper employees toward the newspaper itself; that is this orientation manifests itself in the way the newspaper organization positions the newspaper.

The reader concept is an example. Newspapers view their readers as customers. The view is built on the assumption that reading is all a customer can do with a newspaper, that reading is the only activity involved in the use of a newspaper. Of course, this is not true. The public interacts with the newspaper in myriad ways: People buy advertising; view photos; attend newspaper-sponsored events; telephone the audiotex system to hear snippets of news, reviews, and other information they deem important; and they talk to the customer service department or their carriers about delivery issues, to name a few. Yet reading—or, more accurately, subscribing—is the primary action the industry seeks when it attempts to measure success. In this approach, then, the industry views the physical newspaper as its product when, in fact, newspapers produce more than a rolled-up compilation of graphic devices that gets tossed on a porch or a lawn. The industry need not have an outlook that considerably narrows newspapers' potential audience. For instance, why cannot readers be considered news connoisseurs instead? Why does the newspaper industry need to be concerned with people who read or who read on a regular basis? In short, the newspaper should be viewed as an experience, not necessarily just a product. Cross-departmental teamwork would go a long way toward fostering this view among newspaper employees; they would see that their isolated, department-funneled views are not the only frames with which to see the customer.

Fostering continuous improvement among employees allows them to see new markets, create new market space. Kim and Mauborgne (1999) said that doing so requires a different pattern of strategic thinking—this is the vision that newspapers crave. They suggest that challenging an industry's standard understanding about which group of customers to target can help the industry find the new market space. A sub-strategy involves examining how the product appeals to buyers: Rational appeals feature price and function, while emotional appeals highlight feelings. By this definition, newspapers traditionally use rational appeals—the written word is grounded in rational thought, observation, and critical thinking. The most emotion you see in a typical newspaper—if any—might be in its advertising, which most newspapers purposefully set off from the non-advertising content so as not to blur the distinction. Readers know what to expect from newspapers, which might explain why readership has declined. Functional industries (such as newspapers) can find new life by adding a measure of emotion, to kindle new demand (Kim & Mauborgne, 1999). One way of doing so is to allow employees to pool their knowledge about customers and devise new ways of meeting their needs. As they stand now, however, newspapers are largely trapped by their compartmentalized infrastructures.

Cultivate Decision-Making Resources

This suggestion is probably the most important for the newspaper manager typically caught between employee needs, supervisor demands, production problems, and bottom-line concerns. Time is the managerial resource in shortest supply; once given, it cannot be returned. In addition, the constantly changing nature of the business world means that newspaper managers will need to treat time as an organizational resources; that is they will be called upon to develop strategies that do more than simply adapt to external trends. They will have to help shape those trends (Kim & Mauborgne, 1999) to allow their companies flexibility with which to plan and prepare.

Thinking does not simply mean abstract contemplation, intense brainstorming, or random daydreaming. Thinking also involves, in large part, how you make decisions. Typically, for example, decision making is a process that entails collecting information, evaluating and analyzing that information, and then acting on the information. This cyclical process usually includes defining a problem, specifying goals of the decision, developing solutions, selecting a solution, implementing the solution and, finally, monitoring the solution to determine if it is working or whether the process should start anew. Although this is written as a linear process, time determines how much information can be collected, how much analysis can be performed, and the order of the process (Sohn et al., 1999). The process also can be influenced by how the manager approaches the decision to be made. For example, some (e.g., see Hammond, Keeney, & Raiffa, 1998) argue that defining a problem involves more than simply classifying the issue; it also means solving the correct problem—not settling for the first categorization of a problem but, rather, deliberately backing away from it, viewing it in a broader context, and focusing on the essential elements of the situation. Obviously, doing so means an investment of time.

According to Drucker (1999a), successful time investors—and, as a result, the best self-managers—are aware of their strengths, weaknesses, learning styles, and values, as well as having a good sense of their role in business and in life. They must know who they are and why they do what they do in order to be effective. Such self-assessment may appear to border on psychoanalysis—or psychobabble—to the skeptical newspaper manager. After all, newspapers often have to make hurried decisions because they are reinvented on a daily or weekly basis with little time for reflection. However, in each of our featured case study newspapers, successful use of time was made, leading to proper analysis of the particular problem facing the newspaper. The lesson, then, is that time may be in short supply, but in almost all cases it can be allocated for a purpose that the newspaper deems worthy.

Then why bother including it in this list? Newspaper managers are no different than many other managers—they learn to decide based on experiences and training. Decisions are methods by which managers learn to control a problem or an annoyance—the decision is usually viewed as a choice between varying degrees of right and wrong or as an action necessitated by a disagreement (e.g., see Giles, 1988). In short, for a decision to be considered, a problem must exist beforehand. In turn, these problems must be defined, which is code for classified. Once classified, the theory goes, generic or specific solutions–decisions can be made (Drucker, 1983). In short, decision making often is viewed as reactive. Seemingly proactive decision making, often known as planning, also can—in a sense—be reactive if it is conducted with the intent of defending the newspaper against uncertainty or environmental pressure (in itself a problem). To ward off such thinking, newspaper managers must begin to think in terms of the proverbial big picture—no small feat considering the departmental segmentation indigenous to most newspapers.

Taking time is such a simple act, and yet difficult for most managers because it is tied closely to the ideas of efficiency and productivity. Usually this means that the more time the manager spends on an idea or a project, the less productive he or she is. Ironically, however, the more productive an employee is usually is an indicator of how little time she has for things other than work—which is precisely why time is needed if newspapers managers are to meet the creative challenge of change. Reexamining the team concept mentioned in the previous section teaching the business of newspapers, it becomes obvious that any destruction of walls between departments will not be an overnight phenomenon; such changes take time. Walls must come down, communication must reach a comfort level and productive, creative interaction requires considerable time. *The Dallas Morning News* did not develop its pagination adoption plan in a day. Managers are de facto leaders, people to whom employees look for ideas and vision. The leader demonstrates how change should occur and be viewed. In order to do so, leaders must take time to learn and craft their behavior so that they can inspire their followers (Vaill, 1993) to do likewise.

When newspaper managers take the time to think, they not only send a message that they value deliberate, complex decision making, they also signal that they will not succumb to routine and conventional ways of doing things. Such behavior recognizes that time constraints and cognitive limits tend to limit rational decision making in organizations. Complex decision making is a process, yet often a discontinuous one. When Dave Mazzarella distributed his 10 Commandments to the *USA TODAY* newsroom, it was not just to set standards, but to show that things would change. His daily benchmarking sessions and e-mailed critique notes showed that he was not only serious about the standards, but that the standards would be thought about by him and his immediate subordinates on a frequent basis. In other words, this would be no arbitrary or capricious decision. The tradition continued with his successor, Karen Jurgensen, who put the spotlight on thinking about the paper's future. "You have to have someone who can focus on tomorrow," she said. Focusing takes time.

In summary, then, these five suggestions (see Fig. 9.4) should help newspaper leaders provide the necessary motivation as well as strategically and systematically facilitate change. By sharing control, newspaper managers allow subordinates true autonomy and foster creative approaches to job tasks. Clarifying through continuous communication requires newspaper leaders to communicate their vision so employees will know what is expected.

Skill	Skill Attributes
Sharing Control	Follow subordinates' lead; establish feedback mechanisms; allow employees to devise new methods of work; overcome fear of lack of control; gain more confidence.
Continuous Communication	Communicate vision of change clearly and often and through as many means and channels as possible.
Institutionalize commitment to change	Pay employees enough to make them want to stay; train employees for now and for the future.
Teaching Continuous Improvement	Tear down or breach departmental walls; foster synergy; frame cooperation as a positve; challenge employees to create new markets; add emotional component to the newspaper.
Cultivating Decision-Making Resources	Approach decision-making with "big picture" in mind; define problems carefully and within a larger framework; actively set aside time for thinking; make decisions proactively.

FIG 9.4 Newspaper leadership skills to enhance change.

Paying ongoing attention to the change effort is nothing more than caring that employees have the proper tools—mentally and physically—to execute the vision. Teaching and using continuous improvement is an extension of showing commitment; it essentially means newspaper employees must be trained in the knowledge that a good newspaper is more than the sum of the separate departments' outputs—it is enhanced when they cooperate and pool their know-how. Finally, taking the time to think sends the message to employees that change is deliberate, well-structured, and managed—that change is something newspapers create and not something that happens to newspapers. Such steps will allow newspaper managers to provide leadership that will enhance intrinsic motivation, thus creating a learning atmosphere that welcomes and embraces change.

CONCLUSION

At the beginning of this book, we said changing would not be easy for newspapers. Although publishers often see convergent technologies as the driving force of growth, there is a greater force at times opposing growth: newspaper employees. People must embrace and adopt change and its accompanying tools for them to become useful and successful. Within the newspaper, adoption usually occurs for a variety of reasons—behavioral incentives ranging from market incentives to more income to status enhancement. It is the job of newspaper leaders and the readers of this book to understand newspaper employees and how they view change if productive change is to ever occur.

To achieve such change, newspaper managers must understand change. This does not require so much thinking out of the box, trying the latest managerial fad or experimenting with outlandish techniques; there is no magic wand regarding change. Newspapers need to recognize that change is a process, occurring when prompted by changes in the environment, in the motion of the parts of the organization in relation to one another over time, and changes in the organization's internal politics (Kanter et al., 1992).

A newspaper enters its future anticipating unknown results, but also reacting based on its past behavior and expectations. So, as the adoption of pagination at *The Dallas Morning News* showed, the past influences the behaviors and—significantly—the intents, postures, and beliefs of the organization. Although other factors—resources, capabilities, and external pressures—constrain the decision to change, newspapers must understand the role of time in change to succeed.

Time is one concept to which we constantly refer in this book because it is a variable within the change process. Traditionally, newspapers have enjoyed a major role in the development of reasoning and of the American way of life. At the start of the new millennium, however, newspapers have lost touch with many Americans. It is as if time has bypassed many newspapers, which seemingly have settled into becoming a class medium—targeting fewer, more affluent readers instead of being a mass medium. Some cynical critics may tie this to the increasing corporatization of newspapers, that the growing ownership of newspapers by publicly traded corporations caused newspapers to either target more affluent readers or to homogenize news content to the point of turning off readers. Either way, readership is down. Time seems to be running out, these skeptics would say. Is it? In one way, the corporate menace has proven to be a myth and the growing corporatization a blessing: Newspapers do not become less critical of the status quo as they become more corporatized, nor are corporate newspapers the monolithic threat to journalism they are portrayed to be. In fact, the corporate newspaper promotes controlled social change and places greater emphasis on product quality than other newspapers (Demers, 1996b). Such newspapers are in the least danger in terms of survival; time may seem to be more an ally than an enemy.

Nevertheless, there is a continuing need for newspapers to change. Audiences grow and audiences change and they constantly look to see if businesses can keep up; this is better known as demand. As mentioned in the previous chapter, newspapers must adjust to their audience's demands—and they have tried. The time factor has been missing in the approach. For example, one study (Gade, 1999) of newsroom editors reveals three types of managers: critical skeptics who believe changes are leading newspapers to a more market-driven, less journalistic future; resigned pragmatists who recognize profits' supremacy in newspapers while trying to save journalistic standards; and change agents. This latter group sees change as an opportunity for improving newspapers. Meanwhile, the pragmatic editors look at change as an inevitable link in the ongoing chain of efficiency; there is no sense of timing. Finally, the skeptics see change as dumbing down the news. The differences are more than one of word choice; the attitudes reflect varying degrees of commitment as well. Commitment takes time—not necessarily in terms of minutes, hours, or other standard measures of time, but in terms of vigor, motivation, and vitality—in a word, energy—the absence of which are no doubt noticed by the newsroom.

In the previous section, we alluded to the fact that time is in short supply for many newspaper managers. They feel pressured by job demands. These demands also prompt changes. The more changes, the more demands, the less time a manager has. We do not have to single out the newsroom as the only time-deficient department. For example, circulation departments have to literally race to deliver the newspaper at a desirable time. Production departments must follow deadlines in order to allow circulation departments ample time. Advertising departments must deal with time-conscious clients who rely on prompt service to generate a return on their advertisement. So it is likely that editors are not alone in how they view change.

Time is not the exclusive province of the newspaper and its employees. Readers, and potential readers, also are concerned with time. They, too, want more efficient and effective lives. They want information when it is most convenient. They want information when they need it—or sooner. They want the newspaper to provide them with not just news, but with information that will allow them to plan and live their lives to the fullest. The newspaper—in its current print format—largely fails to do this. One major reason has been the dearth of research and development, with the emphasis on the latter. For example, most newspaper departments have sophisticated data management systems—that is pagination in newsrooms, databases in accounting and advertising. However combining these data for a non-department-specific function—for example, if a salesperson goes to an advertiser and needs to see a sales contract and deliver the ad itself—is more difficult to accomplish. Such complex automation takes time to develop. This is made doubly difficult because the newspaper industry largely depends on search and redevelopment, that is newspapers search for existing solutions and adjust them to their own individual situations (Newspaper Association of America, 1998). Newspapers' rate of innovation is sluggish, and American newspapers are particularly slow (D. M. Cole, 1999). As a result, the industry's tardiness in improving the product makes time all that more difficult of an obstacle to conquer—and readers more difficult to attract.

Regardless of whose time is being spent or misspent, the fact remains that time has been misinterpreted by many editors and publishers. The apparent likelihood of technological convergence has made change seem inevitable and, thus, extremely time-sensitive. This gives the impression that time, technology, and audiences are marching in tune and editors have no choice but to follow the wave and attempt to ride the crest. If we are to devise a new way of thinking, we have to start with how we view time in the scheme of managing change. Some view it as a matter of pacing, setting the rate of change within the business, akin to an internal rhythm that relies on choreographed transitions to switch smoothly from one event, product, or process to the next. The key is to synchronize this pace to the momentum of the market (Brown & Eisenhardt, 1998). With newspapers, however, this is particularly difficult to do because of the temporal nature of news and of advertising—a week or a day is not enough time to anticipate change. On the other hand, newspapers typically take six months or a year to even start a new section. Still, with all we know about newspapers, you would think someone would have calculated a newspaper's internal and external metrics by now. Is it possible that they do not exist? Can they when the content typically reflects what happened yesterday?

The answer lies in the very routines of work. Newspaper routines have not changed significantly since 1900. This text has tried to supply various reasons—fear, lack of confidence, lack of feedback, reluctance, and so on. Perhaps that is why so many newspaper proponents eagerly await technological convergence; they see it as dragging the medium into the future—whether it wants to go or not. They reason that the medium is the message and that the message is that newspapers must change their product and their routines (e.g, see Picard, 1998, 1999). If this text has illustrated anything, it is that those routines should not get ignored when change gets considered. Obviously, habits are hard to break. Change is as much social as it is mechanical; it threatens specific social work arrangements that newspaper employees have crafted. Many managers who try to initiate change do not understand this because management usually does not attempt to change its own routines, but rather those of the ones they manage. Newspaper managers such as Tom Curley at *USA TODAY* recognize those routines, cherish them, take advantage of them, and eventually use them in creating new routines. These practices involve not only production-oriented tasks, but also a newspaper's spirit, identity, the conventional ways in which it views itself, its rituals of newsgathering, and its personas—ranging from government watchdog to cultural transmitter.

What does a newspaper's culture have to do with time? The answer is everything. Simply put, a culture determines when a change is viewed as an opportunity or a threat. A culture determines how soon or how slowly an innovation will be adapted, as *The Dallas Morning News* discovered with its pagination system. A culture determines whether reader-centric research gets implemented, as it has at *USA TODAY*. A newspaper's culture influences how and whether a new editor is warmly accepted, as was not immediately the case at *The Dallas Examiner*. A newspaper's culture creates the timeline and routine for any change, as with CoxNet. Knowing the newspaper's culture and how to deal with it helps the newspaper manager decide when to address change and in what form. A culture also may be the reason the change even gets considered because many newspaper cultures provide the origins of a change idea, as *USA TODAY*'s front-page task force did. In sum, newspaper cultures help set the newspaper's basic sense of time and of timing. Even when timing seems to have the upper hand in the relationship—as in the current case of convergence—timing remains a reaction to the scenario, situation, or circumstances created by culture.

So as newspapers seek to change, it is our hope that they take a good look at themselves and their work cultures. In so doing, they will not only give themselves an adequate chance at changing, but also will provide their workforce a fighting chance of growing and learning within their jobs. The success of newspaper change—which occurs through people, technology-task, and the product—depends on people. What roles people take often depends on their characteristics, their knowledge, skills, needs, and preferences as well as their perceptions and expectations. Managers have to consider a change's accompanying degree of doubt, the skill and knowledge required, and to enact its built-in rewards. Only then will newspapers change as they should—and when they should.

References

Albers, R. R. (1995a, April). Back to Boca. *presstime, 17*, 27–30.

Albers, R. R. (1995b, April). New age newsrooms. *presstime, 20*, 31–35.

Albers, R. R. (1998, April). Breaching the wall [online]. *presstime*. Available: http://www.naa.org/presstime/9804/wall.html

Aldrich, L. S. (1999). *Covering the community: A diversity handbook for media.* Thousand Oaks, CA: Pine Forge Press.

Alexander, M. J. (1997). *Net gain?: New England's online newspapers assess benefits and drawbacks of their electronic editions.* Paper presented at the annual convention of the Association for Education in Journalism and Mass Communication, Chicago.

American Society of Newspaper Editors. (1998, December). *Why newspaper credibility has been dropping* [online]. Reston, VA. Available: http://www.asne.org/works/jcp/credibility2.htm

American Society of Newspaper Editors. (2000, April 12). *ASNE's 2000 newsroom census* [online]. Reston, VA. Available: http://www.asne.org/kiosk/diversity/2000Survey/2000CensusReport.html

Anonymous. (1996, July/August). Living on the digital edge. *presstime, 18*, 56–58.

Anonymous. (1998, February 19). Special tribute: Attorney Fred J. Finch, Jr., founder of *The Dallas Examiner. Probe, 1,* (magazine supplement to *The Dallas Examiner*), 12.

Anonymous. (1999, November 13). Editorial independence still one of newspapering's staples. *Editor & Publisher, 132,* 26.

Bachman, K. (1999, March 15). Karen Jurgensen shatters glass ceiling at USA Today. *Mediaweek, 9,* 11.

Bagdikian, B. H. (1997). *The media monopoly.* Boston: Beacon Press.

Bandler, R., & Grinder, J. (1982). *Reframing: Neurolinguistic programming and the tranformation of meaning.* Moab, UT: Real People Press.

Barnard, C. (1938). *The functions of the executive.* Cambridge, MA: Harvard University Press.

Bass, J. (1999, July/August). Newspaper monopoly. *American Journalism Review, 21,* 64–77.

Beam, R. A. (1995, Spring). How newspapers use readership research. *Newspaper Research Journal, 16*(2), 28–38.

Beam, R. A. (1998, Summer). What it means to be a market-oriented newspaper. *Newspaper Research Journal, 19*(3), 2–20.

Becker, G. S. (1993). Nobel lecture: The economic way of looking at behavior. *Journal of Political Economy, 101*(3), 385–409.

Becker, L. B., Kosicki, G. M., Hammatt, H., Lowrey, W., Shin, S. C., & Wilson, J. H. (1999, Autumn). Enrollment and degrees awarded continue 5–year growth trend. *Journalism & Mass Communication Educator, 54*(3), 5–22.

Beckhard, R., & Harris, H. (1977). *Organizational transitions: Managing complex change.* Reading, MA: Addison-Wesley.

Beckhard, R., & Harris, R. T. (1987). *Organizational transitions: Managing complex change.* Reading, MA: Addison-Wesley.

Beckhard, R., & Pritchard, W. (1992). *Changing the essence: The art of creating and leading fundamental change in organizations.* San Francisco: Jossey-Bass Publishers.

Bergquist, W. (1993). *The postmodern organization.* San Francisco: Jossey-Bass.

Bernstein, M. (1989, June). Pressing on. *Black Enterprise, 19,* 142–148.

Bernt, J., & Greenwald, M. (1999). *Enterprise and investigative reporting at Ohio metropolitant newspapers in 1980 and in 1995.* Paper presented at the annual convention of the Association for Education in Journalism and Mass Communication, New Orleans, LA.

Black, F., & Woods, G. B. (Eds.). (1994). *Milestones in Black Newspaper Research.* Washington, DC: National Newspaper Publishers Association.

Bogart, L. (1999, Spring/Summer). Newspapers. *Media Studies Journal, 13*(2), 60–68.

Boyd, H. (1991). The black press: A long history of service and advocacy. *The Crisis, 98*(3), 10–13.

Boyer, T. (1999, July/August). Playing catchup [online]. *American Journalism Review.* Available: http://ajr.newslink.org/ajrboyerja99.html

Brill, A. M. (1999). *New media, old values: What online newspaper journalists say is important to them.* Paper presented at the annual convention of the Association for Education in Journalism and Mass Communication, New Orleans, LA.

Brill, A. M. (1994). *Pagination and the newsroom: A study of implementation of new technology.* Unpublished doctoral dissertation, Minneapolis, University of Minnesota.

Bromley, R. V., & Bowles, D. (1995, Spring). Impact of Internet on use of traditional news media. *Newspaper Research Journal, 16*(2), 14–27.

Brown. C. (1998). Fear.com: On the Web because they have to be, newspapers try to figure out what to do there [online]. *State of the American newspaper.* Available: http://ajr.newslink.org/special/part12.html

Brown, M. E. (1999, October-November). Surveys confirm tight job market [online]. *The American Editor.* Available: http://www.asne.org/kiosk/editor/99.oct-nov/brown1.htm

Brown, S. L., & Eisenhardt, K. M. (1998). *Competing on the edge: Strategy as structured chaos.* Boston: Harvard Business School Press.

Bryant, D. (1989). The psychology of resistance to change. In R. McLennan (Ed.), *Managing organizational change* (pp. 193–195). Englewood Cliffs, NJ: Prentice-Hall.

Carvajal, D. (2000, April 4). USA TODAY trims width and tones down design. *The New York Times, 149,* 10C.

Casale, A. M. (2000, January 3). Papers need to recast for Net. *Editor & Publisher, 133,* 22–24.

Case, T. (1996, March 30). Defending the revolution. *Editor & Publisher, 129,* 8–13.

Charity, A. (1995). *Doing public journalism.* New York: Guilford.

Christie, J. P. (2000, May/June). Sessions, report look at credibility solutions. *The American Editor, 75,* 20–21.

Chusmir, L. H. (1983, Fall). Profile of motivational needs of individuals in the newspaper industry. *Newspaper Research Journal, 5,* 33–41.

Chyi, H. I., & Lasorsa, D. L. (1999, Fall). Access, use and preferences for online newspapers. *Newspaper Research Journal, 20*(4), 2–13.

Chyi, H. I., & Sylvie, G. (1998). Competing with whom? Where? And how? A structural analysis of the electronic newspaper market. *The Journal of Media Economics, 11*(2), 1–18.

Chyi, H. I., & Sylvie, G. (1999, August). *Opening the umbrella: An economic analysis of online newspaper geography.* Paper presented at the Association for Journalism in Education and Mass Communication, New Orleans, LA.

Ciotta, R. (1996, March). Baby you should drive this CAR. *American Journalism Review, 18,* 34–39.

Cole, D. (1999). *News, Inc* [online]. 11:12. Available: http://www.colegroup.com/newsinc/990607SA.html

Cole, D. M. (1995, February). Four approaches to pagination [online]. *presstime.* Available: http://www.naa.org/presstime/96/PTIME/pgpag.html

Cole, D. M. (1996, October). Ch-ch-changes. *presstime, 59.*

Cole, D. M. (1997, January/February). Test your pagination prowess. *TechNews.* Available: http://ww.naa.org/technews/tn970304/p14test.html

Cole, D. M. (1998, October). Horseless publishers. *presstime, 20,* 63.

Cole, D. M. (1999, March). History and the technology race. *presstime, 57.*

Conner, D. (1993). *Managing at the speed of change.* New York: Villard Books.

Compaine, B. M., & Gomery, D. (2000). *Who owns the media?* Mahwah, NJ: Lawrence Erlbaum Associates.

Conniff, M. (1995, February 4). A tangled web for newspapers. *Editor & Publisher, 128,* 4TC-8TC.

Cook, B. B., Banks, S. R., & Thompson, B. (1995). *Copy desk leader behaviors/copy editor job stress—the relationship of copy desk leader behaviors to job stress, hardiness and health factors in copy editors.* Paper presented at the annual convention of the Association for Education in Journalism and Mass Communication, Washington, DC.

CoxNet. (1999). *A guide to the Cox News Service* [online]. Available: http://www.coxnews.com/coxnet.htm#are

Cyert, R., & March, J. (1963). *A behavioral theory of the firm.* Englewood Cliffs, NJ: Prentice-Hall.

Dart, B. (1999, May 4). When a leap of faith pays off in a big way. *The Atlanta Constitution, 130,* 2C.

Davenport, L., Fico, F., & Weinstock, D. (1996, Summer/Fall). Computers in newsrooms of Michigan's newspapers. *Newspaper Research Journal, 17*(3–4), 14–28.

Davenport, T., & Prusak, L. (1998). *Working knowledge.* Boston: Harvard Business School Press.

Davidson, J. (1989, June). An agenda for the 1990s. *Black Enterprise, 19,* 152–158.

Davis, N. M. (1997, November). Honor thy copy editors [online]. *presstime.* Available: http://www.naa.org/presstime/9711/copyeds.html

DeFleur, M. H. (1997). *Computer-assisted investigative reporting: Development and methodology.* Mahwah, NJ: Lawrence Erlbaum Associates.

Demers, D. (1996, Winter). Corporate newspaper structure, editorial page vigor and social change. *Journalism & Mass Communication Quarterly, 73*(4), 857–877.

Demers, D. P. (1995). Autonomy, satisfaction high among corporate news staffs. *Newspaper Research Journal, 16*(2), 91–111.

Demers, D. P. (1996). *The menace of the corporate newspaper: Fact or fiction?* Ames, IA: Iowa State University Press.

Demo, L. (1999). *The shameful delay: Newspapers' recruitment of minority employees, 1968–1978.* Paper presented at the annual convention of the Association for Education in Journalism and Mass Communication, New Orleans, LA.

Dorsher, M. (1997). *Women and "All the news that's fit to print"? A quantitative content analysis.* Paper presented at the annual convention of the Association for Education in Journalism and Mass Communication, Chicago.

Drucker, P. (1999). *Management challenges for the 21st century.* New York: HarperBusiness.

Drucker, P. F. (1983). *Executive success: Making it in management.* New York: Wiley.

Drucker, P. F. (1999, March-April). Managing oneself. *Harvard Business Review, 77,* 65–74.

Drucker, P. F. (1999, June 1). The new commandments of change [online]. *Inc.* Available: http://www.inc.com/articles/details/0,3532,ART804_CNT53,00.html

Durant, T. J., Jr., & Louden, J. S. (1986). The black middle class in America: Historical and contemporary perspectives. *Phylon, 47,* 253–263.

Education Commission of the States (1997). *Average teacher salaries, state by state: 1996–1997* [online]. Available: http://www.ecs.org/ecs/ecsweb.nsf/3826b96034ede7e7872565c50063d6cc/ac62c117f4b62fd6872565c50075ccc7?OpenDocument

Eisenberg, E., & Goodall, H. (1993). *Organizational communication.* New York: St. Martin's Press.

Elkind, P. (1985, July). The legacy of Citizen Robert. *Texas Monthly, 13,* 102–103+.

Endres, F. F., Schierhorn, A. B., & Schierhorn, C. (1999). *Newsroom teams: A baseline study of prevalence, organization and effectiveness.* Paper presented at the annual convention of the Association for Education in Journalism and Mass Communication, New Orleans, LA.

Fair, E. (1985). *Strategic planning in the newspaper industry: Case study of The Dallas Morning News.* Unpublished master's thesis, University of Texas, Austin.

Farhi, P. (1997, August 11). Good news for 'McPaper.' *The Washington Post, 120,* WB12.

Fitzgerald, M. (1990, July 14). Silver lining in ad gloom. *Editor & Publisher, 123,* 26–27.

Fedler, F., Smith, R. F., Marzolf, M. T., & Hines, B. (1995). *Women, three minorities exhibit unique and unexpected news judgment.* Paper presented at the annual convention of the Association for Education in Journalism and Mass Communication, Washington, DC.

Feola, C. J. (1997, March). State of denial for newspapers. *Quill, 85,* 28–29.

Festinger, L. (1957). *A theory of cognitive dissonance.* Stanford, CA: Stanford University Press.

Flatow, G. (1994). Sexual harassment in Indiana daily newspapers. *Newspaper Research Journal, 15*(3), 32–43.

Floyd, D. (1997). The view from within. In E. A. Jefferson (Ed.), *Soapbox: A guide to civic journalism at The Spokesman-Review* (pp. 62–63). Spokane, WA: The Spokane Spokesman-Review.

Fombrun, C. J., & Harris, D. (1993). Managing human resources strategically. In A. R. Cohen (Ed.), *The portable MBA in management* (pp. 252–278). New York: Wiley.

Frame, R. M., Nielsen, W. R., & Pate, L. E. (1989). Creating excellence out of crisis: Organizational transformation at the Chicago Tribune. *The Journal of Applied Behavioral Science, 25*(2), 109–122.

Gade, P. (1999). *Managing change: Newspaper editors' attitudes toward integrating marketing and journalism.* Paper presented at the annual convention of the Association for Education in Journalism and Mass Communication, New Orleans, LA.

Gade, P., Abel, S., Antecol, M., Hsueh, H., Hume, J., Morris, J., Packard, A., Willey, S., Wilson, N. F., & Sanders, K. (1997, August). *Civic journalism: The practitioner's perspective.* Paper presented at the Association for Journalism in Education and Mass Communication, Chicago.

Gade, P., Abel, S., Antecol, M., Hsueh, H., Hume, J., Morris, J., Packard, A., Willey, S., Fraser, N., & Sanders, K. (1998, Fall). Journalists' attitudes toward civic journalism media roles. *Newspaper Research Journal, 19*(4), 10–26.

Gade, P., Perry, E. L., & Coyle, J. (1997, August). *Predicting the future: How St. Louis Post-Dispatch journalists perceive a new editor will affect their jobs.* Paper presented at the the Association for Education in Journalism and Mass Communication, Chicago.

Garneau, G. (1995, April 22). Big-time, online alliance formed. *Editor & Publisher, 128,* 15–16.

Garrison B. (1996). *Newsroom tools for computer-assisted Reporting in 1995.* Paper presented at the annual convention of the Association for Education in Journalism and Mass Communication, Anaheim, CA.

Garrison, B. (1997a). On-line services, Internet in 1995 newsrooms. *Newspaper Research Journal, 18*(3–4), 79–93.

Garrison, B. (1997b, June 21). Computer-assisted reporting (computer analysis has become important tool for gathering and reporting news). *Editor & Publisher, 130,* 40–43.

Garrison, B. (1998). *Newspaper size as a factor in use of computer-assisted reporting.* Paper presented at the annual convention of the Association for Education in Journalism and Mass Communication, Baltimore, MD.

Garrison, B. (1999a). *Journalists and their computers: An inseparable link for the future?* Paper presented at the annual convention of the Association for Education in Journalism and Mass Communication, New Orleans, LA.

Garrison, B. (1999b). *Journalists' perceptions of online information-gathering problems.* Paper presented at the annual convention of the Association for Education in Journalism and Mass Communication, New Orleans, LA.

Garrison, B. (2000a). *Journalists' newsroom roles and their World Wide Web search habits.* Paper presented at the annual Southeast Colloquium of the Newspaper Division of the Association for Education in Journalism and Mass Communication, Chapel Hill, NC.

Garrison, B. (2000b). *Online information use in newsrooms: A longitudinal diffusion study.* Paper presented at the mid-winter convention of the Communication Technology & Policy, Media Management & Economics, and Visual Communication divisions of the Association for Education in Journalism and Mass Communication, Denver, CO.

Geisler, J. (1999, July). Managing change in your work life. *Poynter Report* [online]. Available: http://209.241.184.41/public/Research/lm/lm_different.htm

Gelsanliter, D. (1995). *Fresh ink.* Denton, TX: University of North Texas Press.

Giles, R. H. (1988). *Newsroom management: A guide to theory and practice.* Detroit, MI: Media Management Books.

Goldhaber, G. (1993). *Organizational communication.* Dubuque, IA: Brown.

Graham, G., & Thompson, T. (1997). *Inside newsroom teams.* Evanston, IL: Northwestern University Newspaper Management Center.

Greenwald, M. S. (1990, Winter). Gender representation in newspaper business sections. *Newspaper Research Journal, 11*(1), 68–74.

Groves, M. E. (September, 1997). Newspaper business outlook: Enjoy the latest advertising highs, but remember to prepare for less sunny long-range trends [online]. *presstime.* Available: http://www.naa.org/presstime/9709/forecast.html#top

Gunaratne, S. (1998). Old wine in a new bottle: Public journalism, Developmental journalism, and social responsibility. In M. Roloff (Ed.), *Communication Yearbook 21.* (pp. 277–321). Thousand Oaks, CA: Sage.

Hammond, J. S., Keeney, R. L., & Raiffa, H. (1998). *Smart choices: A practical guide to making better decisions.* Boston: Harvard Business School Press.

Hansen, K. A., Neuzil, M., & Ward, J. (1998, Winter). Newsroom topic teams: Journalists' assessments of effects on news routines and newspaper quality. *Journalism & Mass Communication Quarterly, 75*(4), 803–821.

Hatchett, D. (1991). The black newspaper: Still serving the community. *The Crisis, 98*(3), 14–17.

Higgins, C., Sr. (1980, September). Is the black press dying? *The Crisis, 87,* 240–241.

Hider, J. (1998, June 20). The trouble with newspapers. *Editor & Publisher, 131,* 40–46.

Huseman, R., & Goodman, J. (1999). *Leading with knowledge.* Thousand Oaks, CA: Sage.

Jennings, M. (1999, March 27). Editors need to listen up. *Editor & Publisher, 132,* 70.

Johnson, P. (1977, June). Publishers' message: Change or be changed. *The American Editor, 130,* 16.

Johnson, S. (1993, March). Newsroom circles. *Quill, 81,* 28–30.

Joseph, W. F. (1985, July 25). Identity crisis hurts minority press. *Advertising Age, 56,* 51–52.

Jurczak, P. R. (1996). *Newsroom cultures, newspaper acquisitions and the community: A case study of Pittsburgh newspapers.* Paper presented at the annual convention of the Association for Education in Journalism and Mass Communication, Anaheim, CA.

Jurgensen, K. (1999, July 27). *A simple message: Value diversity.* Speech presented to the Nancy J. Woodhull Forum on Diversity and Media, Arlington, VA.

Jurkowitz, M. (1998, April). A staff interviews its boss in Hartford. *The American Editor* [online]. Available: http://www.asne.org/kiosk/editor/98.april/jurkowitz1.htm

Kanter, R., Stein, B., & Jick, T. (1992). *The challenge of organizational change: How companies experience it and leaders guide it.* New York: The Free Press.

Kanter, R. M. (1983). *The change masters: Innovation for productivity in the American Corporation.* New York: Simon & Schuster.

Katz, D., & Kahn, R. (1966). *The social psychology of organizations.* New York: Wiley.

Katz, J. (1998, January 10). Clueless in the newsroom: Can newspapers make it? *Editor & Publisher, 131,* 28–29.

Kees, B. (2000, May/June). Shifting demographics mandate change. *The American Editor, 75,* 16–18, 19.

Kim, H. (1999). The rising tide at USA TODAY [online]. *Mediaweek.* Available: http://www.mediaweek.com/buzz/articles/bzarticle19991029–174707.asp

Kim, W. C., & Mauborgne, R. (1999, January-February). Creating new market space. *Harvard Business Review, 77,* 83–93.

Kimberly, R., & Quinn, R. (1984). *New futures: The challenge of managing corporate transitions.* Homewood, IL: Dow Jones-Irwin.

Kirsner, S. (1997, July/August). Web of confusion. *American Journalism Review, 19,* 34–39.

Kirsner, S. (1998, March 28). Inside the WSJ interactive edition. *Editor & Publisher, 131,* S4–9.

Kodrich, K. (1998). How reporters react to Knight-Ridder's 25–43 Project. *Newspaper Research Journal, 19*(3), 77–94.

Konrade-Helm, J. (1995, April). Dallas paper can wait to paginate. *Newspapers & Technology, 7,* 6.

Korchersberger, R. C., Jr. (1990). Staff consolidation: A newsroom with a view. *Newspaper Research Journal, 11*(1), 26–39.

La Brie, H. G., III. (1979). *A survey of black newspapers.* Kennebunkport, ME: Mercer House Press.

Lacy, S., & Ramsey, K. A. (1994). The advertising content of African-American newspapers. *Journalism Quarterly, 71*(3), 521–530.

Lacy, S., Davenport, L., & Miller, C. (1998, March). Women in newspaper newsroom management: 1949 to 1979 [online]. *Web Journal of Mass Communication Research, 1*(2). Available: http://www.scripps.ohiou.edu/wjmcr/vol01/1–2a-B.htm

Lacy, S., Sohn, A., & Wicks, J. (1993). *Media management.* Hillsdale, NJ: Lawrence Erlbaum Associates.

Lacy, S., Stephens, J. M., & Soffin, S. (1991). The future of the African-American press. *Newspaper Research Journal, 12*(3), 8–19.

Lallande, A. (2000, June). More for the money. *presstime, 22,* 58–63.

Landry, B. (1987). *The new black middle class.* Berkeley, CA: University of California Press.

Lanson, J., & Fought, B. C. (1999). *News in a new century: Reporting in an age of Converging Media*. Thousand Oaks, CA: Pine Forge Press.

Lawrence, P. R. (1954, May-June). How to deal with resistance to change. *Harvard Business Review, 32,* 49–57.

Lawrence, P. R. (1989). Why organizations change. In A. M. Mohrman, Jr., S. A. Morhman, G. E. Ledford, Jr., T. G. Cummings, E. E. Lawler, III, & associates (Eds.), *Large-scale organizational change* (pp. 48–61). San Francisco: Jossey-Bass.

Lee, B. (1999). *Online weekly newspapers' contents and their strategies to meet challenges.* Paper presented at the annual Newspapers and Community Building convention of the National Newspaper Association, Boston.

Lewis L., & Seibold, D. (1998). Reconceptualizing organizational change implementation as a communication problem: A review of literature and research agenda. In M. Roloff (Ed.), *Communication Yearbook 21* (pp. 93–152). Thousand Oaks, CA: Sage.

Lewis, R. L. (1995). *Transformed work organization in newspaper firms.* Unpublished doctoral dissertation, University of North Carolina, Chapel Hill.

Lewis, R. L. (1997). How managerial evolution affects newspaper firms. *Newspaper Research Journal, 18*(1–2), 103–125.

Liebler, C. (1994, Summer). How race and gender affect journalists' autonomy. *Newspaper Research Journal, 15*(3), 122–130.

Lisheron, M. (1997, July/August). Big time in The Big Easy. *American Journalism Review, 19,* 26–32.

Logan, J. R., & Schneider, M. (1984). Racial segregation and racial change in American suburbs, 1970–1980. *American Journal of Sociology, 89,* 874–888.

Logan, R. A. (1986, Spring/Summer). USA TODAY's innovations and their impact on journalism ethics. *Journal of Mass Media Ethics, 1,* 74–87.

Manning, R. (1991). *Last stand: Logging, journalism, and the case for humility.* Salt Lake City, UT: Peregrine Smith.

Manning-Miller, C., & Dunlap, K. B. (1999). *Diversity in journalism and mass communication education.* Unpublished report to the Oversight Committee on Diversity of the Association for Education in Journalism and Mass Communication, Columbia, SC.

Martin, S. (1994). External information databases in small circulation newsrooms. *Newspaper Research Journal, 15*(2), 154–159.

Martin, S. E. (1998, Spring). How news gets from paper to its online counterpart. *Newspaper Research Journal, 19*(2), 64–73.

Massey, S. W. (1997, September). *Community newspapers: What price for the future?* Paper presented to National Newspaper Association/Huck Boyd National Center for Community Media, Fort Worth, TX.

Mastin, T. (2000, Spring). Media use and civic participation in the African-American population: Exploring participation among professionals and nonprofessionals. *Journalism & Mass Communication Quarterly, 77*(1), 115–127.

Masullo, G. (1997). *Newspaper nonreadership: A study of motivations.* Paper presented at the annual convention of the Association for Education in Journalism and Mass Communication, Chicago.

McCartney, J. (1997, September). USA TODAY grows up. *American Journalism Review, 19,* 18–25.

McGill, L. T. (2000). *Newsroom diversity: Meeting the challenge.* Arlington, VA: The Freedom Forum.

McManus, J. H. (1994). *Market-driven journalism: Let the citizen beware?* Thousand Oaks, CA: Sage.

McMillan, S., Guppy, M., Kunz, B., & Reis, P. (1996). *A defining moment: Who says what about public journalism.* Paper presented at the annual convention of the Association for Education in Journalism and Mass Communication, Anaheim, CA.

Merritt, D. (1995). *Public journalism & public life: Why telling the news is not enough.* Hillsdale, NJ: Lawrence Erlbaum Associates.

Merritt, D., & Carter, H., III. (1996). *Civic journalism: It's more than just good journalism.* Washington, DC: Pew Center for Civic Journalism.

Merskin, D. (1996, August). *The daily newspaper and audiotex personals: A case study of organizational adoption of innovation.* Paper presented at the Association for Journalism in Education and Mass Communication, Anaheim, CA.

Meyer, P. (1995). *Public journalism and the problem of objectivity* [online]. Speech given to the conference of Investigative Reporters and Editors, Cleveland, OH. Available: http://www.unc.edu/~pmeyer/ire95pj.htm

Morgan, H. (1993, March). Orchestrating news coverage. *Quill, 81,* 25–27.

Moses, L. (1999, April 10). Papers ponder how to integrate Web sites. *Editor & Publisher, 132,* 28–29.

Moses, L. (2000a, February 7). If you build it, they will come. *Editor & Publisher, 133,* i47.

Moses, L. (2000b, June 26). Gannett Co. ramps up to replace NEWS 2000. *Editor & Publisher, 133,* 5–6.

Mueller, J. E. (1997). Delivery system disaster: Circulation problems of the St. Louis Sun. In C. Warner (Ed.), *Media management review* (pp. 115–125). Mahwah, NJ: Lawrence Erlbaum Associates.

Mueller, J. E. (1998). *Sun sawed in half: The brief life of Ralph Ingersoll's St. Louis newspaper.* Unpublished doctoral dissertation, University of Texas, Austin.

Mueller, J. E. (1999). *Web community building concepts applied to online newspapers: A case study of a four-state region.* Paper presented at the annual Newspapers and Community Building convention of the National Newspaper Association, Boston.

Murdock, I. (2000). Developing a newspaper Internet strategy [online]. *American Society of Newspaper Editors.* Available: http://www.asne.org/works/interactive/asne1.htm

Murphy, J. (1990, August 8). *The Dallas Morning News.* Unpublished case study, University of Texas, Austin.

Nadler, D. A. (1988). Organizational frame bending: Types of change in the complex organization. In R. H. Kilmann & T. J. Covin (Eds.), *Corporate transformation: Revitalizing organizations for competitive world* (pp. 66–83). San Francisco: Jossey-Bass.

Nadler, D. A., Gerstein M. S., & Shaw, R. B. (1992). *Organizational architecture: Designs for changing organizations.* San Francisco: Jossey-Bass.

Nadler, D. A., & Tushman, M. L. (1995). Types of organizational change: From incremental improvement to discontinuous transformation. In D. A. Nadler, R. B.

Shaw, & A. E. Walson (Eds.), *Discontinuous change: Leading organizational transformation* (pp. 15–34). San Francisco: Jossey-Bass.

Najjar, O. (1995, Fall). ASNE efforts increase minorities in newsroom. *Newspaper Research Journal, 16*(4), 126–140.

Nanus, B. (1992). *Visionary leadership.* San Francisco: Jossey-Bass.

National Advisory Commission on Civil Disorders. (1968). *Report of the National Advisory Commission on Civil Disorders.* New York: Bantam.

Neuharth, A. (1989). *Confessions of an S.O.B.* Garden City, NY: Doubleday.

Neuzil, M., Hansen, K., & Ward, J. (1999, Winter). Twin Cities journalists' assessment of topic teams. *Newspaper Research Journal, 20*(1), 2–16.

Newspaper Association of America. (1998, September). *International Newspaper Operations Leadership Forum.* Vienna, VA: Author.

Nicholson, J. (2000, June 19). Living large, but too well. *Editor & Publisher, 133,* 58–60.

Noth, D. P. (1999, October 30). Portal envy: Why the newspaper industry is spending millions to build local gateways to the Web. *Editor & Publisher, 132,* 16–19.

Nutt, P. (1986). Tactics of implementation. *Academy of Management Journal, 29,* 230–261.

Osborne, D. M. (1998, November). The devil might be an angel. *Brill's Content, 1,* 96–101.

Pease, T. (1989, Fall). Cornerstone for growth. *Newspaper Research Journal, 10*(4), 1–22.

Peng, F. Y., Tham, N. I., & Xiaoming, H. (1999, Spring). Trends in online newspapers: A look at the U.S. web. *Newspaper Research Journal, 20*(2), 52–63.

Perry, E. L. (1996). *Media use habits of African-Americans in a small Midwestern city.* Paper presented at the Association for Education in Journalism and Mass Communication, Anaheim, CA.

Petersen, B. K. (1992). The managerial benefits of understanding organizational culture. In S. Lacy, A. B. Sohn, & R. H. Giles (Eds.), *Readings in Media Management* (pp. 123–152). Columbia, SC: Media Management Division of the Association for Education in Journalism and Mass Communication.

Pew Research Center for The People & The Press. (1999). *Striking the balance: Audience interests, business pressures and journalists' values.* Washington, DC: Author.

Pfeffer, J., & Salancik, G. (1978). *The external control of organizations: A resource dependence perspective.* New York: Harper & Row.

Phipps, J. L. (1999a, July 31). Local is everything on newspaper Web sites. *Editor & Publisher, 132,* S23–26.

Phipps, J. L. (1999b, July 31). Superfast Internet access will change reporting and broadcasting. *Editor & Publisher, 132,* S28–34.

Picard, R. G. (1998). Interacting forces in the development of communication technologies: Business interests and new media products and services. *European Media Management Review, 1*(1), 18–24.

Picard, R. G. (1999, Second quarter). Implications of the changing business model of the newspaper industry. *International Newspaper Financial Executives Quarterly Journal, 5,* 2–5.

Picard, R. G., & Brody, J. H. (1997). *The newspaper publishing industry.* Needham Heights, MA: Allyn & Bacon.

Pogash, C. (1995, July/August). General Mills' gift to journalism. *American Journalism Review, 17,* 40–44.

Pogash, C. (1996, June). Cyberspace journalism. *American Journalism Review,* 26–31.

Polansky, S. H., & Hughes, D. W. W. (1986). Managerial innovation in newspaper organizations. *Newspaper Research Journal, 8*(1), 1–12.

Prichard, P. (1987). *The making of McPaper: The inside story of USA TODAY.* Kansas City, MO: Andrews & McMeel.

Pride, A. S., & Wilson, C. C. (1997). *A history of the black press.* Washington, DC: Howard University Press.

Rappleye, C. (1998, January/February). Cracking the church-state wall [online]. *Columbia Journalism Review.* Available: wysiwyg://32/http://www.cjr.org/year/98/1/church/asp

Reddick, R., & King, E. (1995). *The online journalist: Using the Internet and other electronic resources.* Ft. Worth, TX: Harcourt Brace & Co.

Reed, R. (1998, September). Giant: The eyes of the nation are on Texas and the thriving survivor in Dallas [online]. *American Journalism Review.* Available: http://ajr.newslink.org/special/

Rich, C. (2000). *Writing and reporting news: A coaching method.* Belmont, CA: Wadsworth.

Rieder, R. (1999, January/February). Getting back to basics [online]. *American Journalism Review.* Available: http://ajr.newslink.org/ajrremjan99.html

Ritt, G. (1995, December). Five commandments of the new media. *The American Editor, 70,* 6–7.

Robinson, K. (1991). *Women newspaper managers and coverage of women.* Unpublished master's thesis, Michigan State University, East Lansing, MI.

Rogers, E. (1986). *Communication technology: The new media in society.* New York: The Free Press.

Rogers, E. (1999). Anatomy of the two subdisciplines of communication study. *Human Communication Research, 25*(4), 618–631.

Rogers, J. (1999, December 14). Five ways to prepare now for CCI. *Interface, 1,* 1.

Rose, H. M. (1976). *Black suburbanization.* Cambridge, MA: Ballinger.

Rosen, J. (1996). *Getting the connections right: Public journalism and troubles in the press.* New York: Twentieth Century Fund Press.

Rosen, J., & Merritt, D., Jr. (1994). *Public journalism: Theory and practice.* Dayton, OH: Kettering Foundation.

Rosenberg, J. (1996, February 24). Cox readies network for Olympics. *Editor & Publisher, 129,* 34–35.

Rue, L. W., & Byars, L. L. (1983). *Management: Theory and application.* Homewood, IL: Irwin.

Russial, J. (1994). *Pagination and newsroom organization.* Paper presented at the annual convention of the Association for Education in Journalism and Mass Communication, Atlanta, GA.

Russial, J. (1997). Topic-team performance: A content study. *Newspaper Research Journal, 18*(1–2), 126–144.

Russial, J. T. (1994). Pagination and the newsroom: A question of time. *Newspaper Research Journal, 15*(1), 91–101.

Schein, E. H. (1985). *Organizational culture and leadership*. San Francisco: Jossey-Bass.

Schein, E. H. (1992). *Organizational culture and leadership* (2nd ed.). San Francisco: Jossey-Bass.

Schein, E. (1989). Planned change theory. In R. McLennan (Ed.). *Managing organizational change*. Englewood Cliffs, NJ: Prentice-Hall.

Schultz, T. (1999). Interactive options in online journalism: A content analysis of 100 U.S. newspapers [online]. *Journal of Computer-Mediated Communication*. Available: http://www.ascusc.org/jcmc/vol5/issue1/schultz.html#Conclusions

Shearer, M. E. (1999, July). Taking time out to make the picture whole. *The American Editor, 74*, 4–17.

Shenk, D. (1999, January). Why you feel the way you do. *Inc., 21*, 58–68.

Shepard, A. C. (1994, September). The gospel of public journalism. *American Journalism Review*, 28–34.

Shepard, A. C. (1998, May). The change agents. *American Journalism Review, 20*, 42–49.

Sherman, H., & Schultz, R. (1998). *Open boundaries: Creating business innovation through complexity*. Reading, MA: Perseus Books.

Sims, B. (1999, May/June). The new rules of pagination. *TechNews: The NAA Magazine of Newspaper Operations, 5*, 8–13.

Singer, J. B. (1997, Winter/Spring). Changes and consistencies: Newspaper journalists contemplate online future. *Newspaper Research Journal, 18*(1–2), 2–18.

Singer, J. B. (1999). *The metro wide web: How newspapers' gatekeeping role is changing online*. Paper presented at the annual convention of the Association for Education in Journalism and Mass Communication, New Orleans, LA.

Snyder, B. (1998, March 16) Advertisers scramble in wake of NCN demise. *Advertising Age, 69*, 32–33.

Sohn, A. B., Ogan, C. L., & Polich, J. (1986). *Newspaper leadership*. Englewood Cliffs, NJ: Prentice-Hall.

Sohn, A. B., Wicks, J. L., Lacy, S., & Sylvie, G. (1999). *Media management: A casebook approach*. Mahwah, NJ: Lawrence Erlbaum Associates.

Smith, A. (1979). *The newspaper: An international history*. London: Thames & Hudson.

Smith, A. (1980). *Goodbye Gutenberg: The newspaper revolution of the 1980s*. New York: Oxford University Press.

Smith, A. W., & Moore, J. V. (1985, December). East-West differences in black economic development. *Journal of Black Studies, 16*, 131–154.

Squires, J. (1993). *Read all about it: The corporate takeover of America's newspapers*. New York: Times Books.

Steele, B., & Cochran, W. (1995). Computer-assisted reporting challenges traditional newsgathering safeguards [online]. *ASNE Bulletin*. Available: http://www.poynter.org/Research/car/car_chal.htm

Stein, M. L. (1990, February 3). Black publishers' perspective: Newspaper execs meet to discuss the state of their business. *Editor & Publisher, 123*, 11, 43.

Stein, M. L. (1997, October 25). Public journalism loved and hated. *Editor & Publisher, 130*, 31.

Stempel, G. H., Hargrove, T., & Bernt, J. P. (2000, Spring). Relation of growth of use of the Internet to changes in media use from 1995 to 1999. *Journalism & Mass Communication Quarterly, 77*(1), 71–79.

Stepp, C. S. (1995, April). Reinventing the newsroom. *American Journalism Review, 17,* 28–33.

Stepp, C. S. (1996, April). The new journalist. *American Journalism Review, 18,* 18–23.

Stepp, C. S. (1999, September). Then and now. *American Journalism Review, 21,* 60–75.

Stepp, C. S. (2000, July/August). Reader friendly [online]. *American Journalism Review.* Available: http://ajr.newslink.org/ajrcarljul00.html

Stohl, C. (1995). *Organizational communication, connectedness in action.* Thousand Oaks, CA: Sage.

Stolberg, D. (1989, March). Some daily newspapers are working with high schools on plans to "grow their own" minority journalists. *ASNE Bulletin, 64,* 22–24.

Stone, M. L. (1999a, May 8). Sulzberger tells newspapers how to survive digital age. *Editor & Publisher, 132,* 36.

Stone, M. L. (1999b, July 31). Print to Web: It takes teamwork. *Editor & Publisher, 132,* S8–14.

Sullivan, S. (1999, April 16). Remarks made at University of Texas Department of Journalism Symposium on Online Journalism, Austin, TX.

Sylvie, G. (1995). Editors and pagination: A case study of management. *Journal of Mediated Communication, 10*(1), 1–20.

Sylvie, G. (1996, Spring). Departmental influences on interdepartmental cooperation in daily newspapers. *Journalism & Mass Communication Quarterly, 73*(1), 230–241.

Sylvie, G., & Brown-Hutton, L. (1999, August). *Black newspapers: In search of an advertising strategy.* Paper presented at the Association for Education in Journalism and Mass Communication, New Orleans, LA.

Sylvie, G., & Danielson, W. (1989, May). *Editors and hardware: Three case studies in technology and newspaper management.* Austin, TX: The University of Texas.

Tagiuri, R. (1968). The concepts of organizational climate. In R. Tagiuri & G. Litwin (Eds.), *Organizational climate: Explorations of a concept* (pp. 11–34). Boston: Harvard University Press.

Tarleton, L. (1996, October). Pagination: It's hard, it's painful, it's worth it. *The American Editor, 71,* 4–5.

Taylor, F. (1911). *Principles of scientific management.* New York: Harper & Row.

Terry, C. (1993, November). The color(s) of power. *presstime, 15,* 36–41.

Thomas, R. (1993). Managing diversity: Utilizing the talents of the new work force. In R. Cohen (Ed.). *The portable MBA in management* (pp. 315–339). New York: Wiley.

Thompson, M. (1995, June 26). Times Mirror tries to deliver its future. *Mediaweek, 36,* 46–50.

Tichy, N., & Ulrich, D. (1984). Revitalizing organizations: The leadership role. In R. Kimberly & R. Quinn (Eds.), *New futures: The challenge of managing corporate transitions* (pp. 240–264). Homewood, IL: Dow Jones-Irwin.

foresaw the coming of World War II and warned that: 'Our civilization will go too, and it may be nearer the end than we think... '; 'The one gigantic problem which threatens to drag us down is the problem of establishing justice and order in place of chaos which reigns in the world of international affairs....' He asked: 'Is it possible to set up an international government?'

One could interject that the question is still pertinent, but the problems to be solved by united action are now expressed in such studies as *The Limits to Growth* in terms of over-population, exhaustion of natural resources, destruction of our natural habitat, and so on – but it is time to encourage you to turn to the preface and to the full story which Professor Thomas tells so well.

7 MARCH 1974   ROLAND MICHENER

Preface

The objective of this work is to present an impression of the thought and career of an historian well known in his day in Canada and the United States, Alfred LeRoy Burt (1888–1971), who taught at the University of Alberta from 1913 to 1930 and at the University of Minnesota from 1930 to 1957. As such, it is hoped that it will be regarded as a useful contribution to the intellectual history of Canada, for historians have always occupied a prominent but as yet largely unrecognized role in that history. In the definition of the Canadian identity, historians have occupied a strategic position as the interpreters and custodians of the collective memory of Canadians.

Burt was not the founder of a school of historical interpretation, but he was a key figure in the renaissance period of Canadian historical scholarship which spans the second and third decades of the twentieth century. His *Old Province of Quebec*, published in 1933, was the first fruit of the intensive cultivation of the primary sources assembled over the years in the Public Archives of Canada by the Dominion archivists Douglas Brymner and Arthur Doughty. In his teaching at Alberta and Minnesota, Burt was also a formative influence on the thinking of successive generations of students.

Extensive extracts from Burt's letters to his wife and from his public lectures and articles have been reproduced in this study. The letters to Mrs Burt were written twice a week whenever he was away from home, and hence have a diary-like quality. Each letter begins with a reference to family matters or other concerns not germane to this inquiry. The total collection has been carefully perused, and references to public affairs, contacts with professional colleagues, and reading and research activities have been included in the extracts.

The project originated with a suggestion by Mrs Joan Jenness of Ottawa, Professor Burt's youngest daughter, who has presented the correspondence to the Public Archives of Canada.

I am greatly indebted to Mrs Jenness for encouragement and advice, for renewing an association which began when I was a student of her father in Minneapolis, and for demonstrating that she maintains the tradition of warm-hearted hospitality which her parents extended to me and to many other students at the University of Minnesota.

Mrs Forrest Johnson and Mrs Mary Leinbach, Professor Burt's other two daughters, read the manuscript and made helpful suggestions. Among those who supplied valuable information or criticism were Professor Herbert Heaton of Minneapolis, a former chairman, and Miss Louise Olsen of Sioux Falls, South Dakota, a former secretary, of the Department of History, University of Minnesota, my colleague Professor L.G. Thomas of the University of Alberta, Professor Carl Berger of the University of Toronto, Professor Roger Graham of Queen's University, the archives staff of the University of Minnesota Libraries, and Mr Frank Strowbridge, former sales manager of Gage Educational Publishing Limited of Toronto. Mr James Parker, Archivist of the University of Alberta, arranged for access to the records in his custody and contributed personal information on the Burt family relationships. I am indebted to Miss Jean Wilson of the University of Toronto Press for expert editorial assistance. The secretarial staff of the Department of History, University of Alberta, aided in the typing. My wife's proofreading and preparation of the index is gratefully acknowledged. I am also grateful to the Right Honourable Roland Michener for his perceptive foreword.

This book has been published with the assistance of a grant from the Humanities Research Council of Canada, using funds provided by the Canada Council, and with the assistance of the Publications Fund of the University of Toronto Press.

LHT

THE RENAISSANCE OF CANADIAN HISTORY

A BIOGRAPHY OF A.L. BURT

1

Family Roots and
Educational Experiences

The year was 1913 and the University of Alberta in Edmonton was beginning its sixth session in September, housed in its first two buildings, Athabasca Hall and Assiniboia Hall, overlooking the tree-clad banks of the North Saskatchewan River, with a student enrolment of 425 and a teaching staff of twenty-five in the Faculty of Arts and Sciences. The campus must have seemed graceless and crude to the new lecturer in history, Alfred LeRoy Burt, familiar with the ordered solidity of an eastern Canadian university and the mellow perfection of an Oxford college. Only the impressive campus plan in the President's office revealed the vision of a well-landscaped symmetry of buildings, towers, and quadrangles.

But everything was new in Alberta in that year, and the province, organized only eight years previously, had no settled traditions and no firmly established organizations of power and patterns of life. Large-scale immigration was still continuing; thousands of pioneer homesteaders were engrossed in 'proving up' their lands. As in the other prairie provinces, there had been a frenzied speculation in town lots which had collapsed earlier that year, but the promise of uninterrupted economic progress was guaranteed by the finest-ever wheat harvest, the petroleum discoveries south of Calgary, and flourishing lumber, coal, natural gas, livestock, and fur production. Over forty-seven hundred miles of railways were under construction.

Edmonton had a population of about 60,000 in 1913 and, like other prairie cities, seemed to be in the vanguard of urban growth in Canada.

The population was youthful, energetic, optimistic, sociable; and proud of its freedom from the restraining habits, traditions, and attitudes of the custom-hardened East. A perceptive English observer was struck by the heterogeneity of the place at this time:

On the pavement, rough railway men, miners, and odd customers of every kind jostle well-dressed women and smart business men. It is just as much a curious mixture as the buildings. Imposing looking banks, small wooden shacks, and virgin bush, one next to the other, are still to be seen on some of the main streets of this wonderful city. ... Edmonton strikes me as a pleasanter place to live in than most provincial towns in England. It is certainly every bit as civilized, with its broad asphalted streets, large churches, banks, shops, and excellent tram service.[1]

Across the river from the university campus, the Lieutenant Governor had moved into a handsome residence which, with the imposing Legislative Building still under construction, symbolized the emergence of the capital city and province from the primitive stage of frontier development. It was an exciting setting for a new university and, to young academics, a stimulating environment for personal achievement.

A profound transformation could also be detected in the nation itself at this time. Although the eastern provinces had long passed the stage of pioneer agricultural settlement, it was only in these first years of the new century that industrialization and urbanization could be regarded as significant facts of life in Canada. Factory production, extensive new transcontinental railway construction, trade union organization, town-planning activity, women's rights agitation, and the Canadian Club movement were some of the visible portents of a new era in Canadian history. Less tangible but no less revolutionary was the burgeoning consciousness of national identity and national destiny, which was particularly noticeable in the West.

The literary event of 1913 was the completion of the 22-volume historical work *Canada and Its Provinces*, the largest co-operative effort ever undertaken by Canada's leading Anglophone and Francophone intellectuals. Among the contributors were a number of university teachers, but by no means the majority, for Canadian history was still of peripheral interest in university departments of history and there was still no national organization of professional historians.

There were additional contributions to Canadian literature in the same year by Charles G.D. Roberts, Sir Gilbert Parker, Stephen Leacock, Arthur Stringer, Sir George W. Ross, Marjorie Pickthall, Beckles Willson,

Hector Garneau, Arnold Haultain, Colonel William Wood, J.S. Ewart, N.E. Dionne, the Honourable Thomas Chapais, Isaac Cowie, Lawrence J. Burpee, and others. Among works singled out by the editor of the *Canadian Annual Review* as 'the chief Canadian books of the year' was one by the young lecturer in history at Edmonton, entitled *Imperial Architects*. 'This book,' the editor of the *Review* wrote, 'fills its own place in the greatly growing roll of Canadian publications ... It deals with the problem of Imperial construction, with the growth of the Empire, with the schemes of closer union – Defence, Tariffs, Federation, Imperial Council, etc.'[2] Even more important than this tribute was the brief but favourable reaction in the *Review of Historical Publications Relating to Canada*, whose stern application of high standards had challenged so much shallow scholarship. 'It is to be hoped,' wrote the reviewer, 'that Mr Burt will deal later with proposals subsequent to 1887,' the terminal point of the study.[3]

Alfred LeRoy Burt was born on 28 November 1888, at Listowel, a town of about 2600 inhabitants, in the northern part of Perth County, Ontario. The area had a population of mixed origin – English, Scottish, German, and Irish. His father, Christian Kimpel Burt, was a drygoods merchant in Listowel, in partnership with his half-brother John Croft Burt. Their father, Johann Bört (his children spelt it Burt), was born in Oberant Ehringer, Württemberg, Germany, and had migrated as a young man to Canada in 1846, where he settled on a farm at Gowanstown in Wallace Township. He was twice married, and his second wife, A.L. Burt's grandmother, Salome Kimpel, was also of south German origin. A.L. Burt's father married Sarah Large, a girl of Irish extraction, the daughter of a furniture factory owner. She was a determined young woman who worked in her father's factory to finance her studies in music and art at Hamilton Ladies' College. A gifted pianist, she nourished in her son a lifelong love of music and gave him the training which permitted him to find inspiration and relaxation at the keyboard of the piano.

Like many other distinguished Canadians of his generation, Burt's earliest education was in a small-town school. He attended the elementary school in Listowel, but about 1898 the family moved to Toronto, where in due course C.K. Burt became head buyer in the Canadian firm of Tip Top Tailors. A.L. and his brother Arthur attended city schools, and in 1906 he graduated from Humberside Collegiate, winning the first Edward Blake scholarship in mathematics and science. That year Burt enrolled in Victoria College at the University of Toronto, but after a year in science he switched to the honours course in modern history. His courses included Roman history, medieval and modern history, English and Canadian constitutional history, economics, and German and English literature. A student of George M. Wrong, he became a member of the History Club which Wrong had founded in 1904 to promote informal contacts between staff and students, of the type which Burt was to organize later at the University of Alberta. Other extracurricular activities included piano performances, tennis, and the presidency of Victoria's largest student organization, the Union Literary Society. One contemporary remembered him as 'a poet with a gift for thought and the firm technique of a mature mind.'[4] A handwritten notebook of his efforts in the composition of verse survives in his personal papers.

Tragedy touched the Burt family when the younger son, Arthur, was drowned in a swimming accident during his first year at university. A.L. thus became an only child, bearing that emotional burden as the supporter of the parents' hopes which the only child alone can comprehend. At this time his mother's influence was particularly intense, and she encouraged him to compete for the most coveted prize available to Canadians, the Rhodes Scholarship. In 1910 he was the unanimous choice of the University of Toronto's selection committee from among the graduates of that year. A press notice of this event deserves quotation:

'In view of the oft-heard condemnation of musical study and athletics as being a waste of time and energy and as distracting with disastrous results the minds of young people from more practical things, it is interesting to record the fact that Mr. Alfred LeRoy Burt, the brilliant young graduate of the Ontario Provincial University, to whom has fallen the honor of being selected as Rhodes Scholar from the institution, is both a trained athlete and an accomplished musician. Since a mere child he has been an enthusiastic student of music, and he acted as accompanist for the Alexandra Choir of Toronto, a chorus of 400 voices, for over a year. When Gipsy Smith was in Toronto last May at Massey Hall, Mr. Burt was the pianist. He often appears in concerts, and his playing has been spoken of very highly by competent critics. He has had a number of flattering offers to enter upon a musical career, but prefers the studious life of a scholar. In athletics he has always taken a prominent part, being one of the bright particular stars of the university gymnasium and an active worker in committee and on the field and ice. Lawn tennis is his forte, however, he having been in the finals several times, but losing the championship by narrow margins....'[5]

It is probable that his university experience was already leading Burt beyond the normal thought pattern of middle-class Victorian Ontario and the narrower tenets of his parents' Methodist faith. But he remained a loyal and affectionate son, and he never abandoned the best qualities of the family tradition – a strong commitment to high principles and to the disciplined life.

In winning the Rhodes Scholarship for Ontario, Burt joined the highly select group of young Canadians who had received this award since 1904 under the terms of Cecil Rhodes' will. In the mind of the founder, a period of study at Oxford would have the great advantage to young colonists, irrespective of race or religion, 'for giving breadth to their views, for their instruction in life and manners, and for instilling into their minds the advantage to the Colonies as well as to the United Kingdom of the retention of the unity of the Empire.'[6] Though the passing years have destroyed Rhodes' hope of Empire unity, it was a goal supported by many English-speaking Canadians at the time, for they did not regard it as incompatible with their growing sense of nationality.[7] Burt shared Rhodes' ideal only in the sense that he was to adopt a practical-minded view of the desirability of a multinational political association of which the Empire was the sole example before World War I.

The university authorities assigned Burt to Corpus Christi College, one of the smallest in Oxford, founded in 1517. It had been his first choice, and had an excellent scholarly reputation. The register for the Michaelmas term in 1912 records seventy students in residence, including four Rhodes scholars, Burt being the only Canadian. His tutor at Corpus Christi was a Fellow of the College, Robert B. Mowat (1883–1941), a young Scot who began as a specialist in medieval English history and subsequently produced numerous works on European diplomacy and on the history of Britain. In later years Mowat devoted much time to popular exposition of the themes of the League of Nations and the contributions which the English-speaking peoples could make to the problems of political organization. Two older scholars whose lectures Burt attended were H.A.L. Fisher (1865–1940), Fellow of New College, and H.E. Egerton (1855–1927), of Magdalen. The former was the leading English-speaking authority on the French revolutionary period and also on modern Europe; both were fields which engrossed Burt's attention for many years. Egerton was the first Beit Professor of Colonial History at Oxford, a chair established by Alfred Beit, close friend and associate of Cecil Rhodes. He was best known for his *Short History of British Colonial Policy*, and for a study of federations and unions in the Empire which was used in the Oxford syllabus in modern history. Years later Burt recalled his work with Egerton in the following terms:

On proceeding to Oxford, I was surprised to find that one of the special subjects offered by the School of Modern History was a rather intensive study of a short period of Canadian history. I did not choose it. My tutor chose it for me, and I still remember a smothered feeling of resentment at the thought of having to learn about the history of my own country from a man who had never lived in it. That feeling, of course, was an unconscious reaction of nationalism. But I was soon grateful to my tutor for sending me to sit at the feet of that ripe scholar, the late Professor Egerton, who introduced me to the source materials of Canadian history. He also made me look at the history of other parts of the British Empire ....[8]

Burt's extracurricular activities included piano music, voice training, and tennis. His associations with other Canadians at Oxford were close, particularly with three other 1910 Rhodes scholars. There was D.C. Harvey[9] from Prince Edward Island, a Dalhousie graduate. Then there was John E. Read from Nova Scotia, who was educated at Dalhousie and Columbia universities. J.T. Thorson of Manitoba, like Read, was specializing in law while Harvey and Burt were enrolled in modern history. Read has written of Burt that 'of all my friends, there is none who had greater gifts for friendship,'[10] a tribute which is echoed by many of Burt's professional colleagues and students. He and Read spent six weeks in the summer of 1911 travelling in Italy, each with £25 in his pocket. 'Florence,' Read recalls, 'gave us both an insight into the march of civilization which we have never lost.' On another occasion Burt and Thorson spent a holiday together on the Isle of Wight. His most intimate English acquaintance was Arthur Forrest, from Bath, who was later killed in the Gallipoli campaign, and after whom he named his first child, his daughter Forrest Burt.

Burt's continued enthusiasm for music is substantiated by the article 'The Relation of Music to the Other Arts,' which appeared in the college's *Pelican Record* in 1913. It is a sophisticated and analytical discussion of the nature of music and its historical development.

The other arts [he concluded] speak to us in terms of this world, and appeal to us indirectly through what we have seen with our physical or intellectual eye. Music's appeal is direct; it speaks to us not in terms of this world; it tells us what we have never seen or heard. The soul may be lifted up by a noble poem or exalted by a masterpiece of painting or sculpture, but it can never rise beyond a certain height, and there it stays. Under the spell of music, however, it seems to be freed from the chains of earth and to soar ever upward. ... as music ... discards the principle of imitation for the great principle of creation; as it possesses a mysterious power over the soul unknown to any of the other arts; as it is the purest expression of beauty; is not this, the youngest art, at the same time, the noblest art?[11]

Oxford University prizes, wrote one don in 1912, 'tempt the more ambitious'; they were not numerous, 'and are the reward of exceptional ability.'[12] The Alfred Beit Prize, established in 1905, was awarded annually for an essay on some subject connected with the advantages of 'Imperial Citizenship,' or with colonial history. The subject for 1913 was 'Proposals in the direction of a closer union of the Empire before the opening of the Colonial Conference of 1887.'[13] Burt competed for this prize, and he and Lewis Bernstein Namier of Balliol College (who was to become one of the most influential historians of the present century in Britain) were co-winners. Burt also won the Robert Herbert Memorial Prize, established in memory of a former Under-Secretary of State for the Colonies, awarded on the result of the competition for the Beit Prize.

Burt's essay was published in Oxford with an introduction by Egerton, under the title *Imperial Architects*. The work deals with an aspect of Anglo-American intellectual history. Although the relationship between the self-governing colonies and Britain had been a major preoccupation of Canadian and British historians and political thinkers for a generation, the subject had been treated hitherto primarily in terms of the events of the struggle for responsible government, or as a subject for partisan debate on imperial unity. Burt's book was essentially a dispassionate analysis of the philosophy of imperial relationships, although it is clear that the author sympathized with the ideal of a multinational political structure to promote commonly accepted objectives. The first third of the study is concerned with the schemes of American and British political thinkers for the maintenance of the unity of the Empire prior to the American Revolution. The balance of the work deals with the revival of British interest in the Empire, from its hesitant beginnings in the second quarter of the nineteenth century to its full-blown expression in the Imperial Federation League of 1884 and the Colonial Conference of 1887. 'The opening of the first Colonial Conference,' Burt wrote in his concluding paragraph, 'closed the door on *ideal* Imperialism and ushered in *practical* Imperialism. The era of ideal Imperialism was very fruitful of paper plans. The age of practical Imperialism is not less concerned with the ideal, but more engaged in its fulfilment – the attempt to build a far greater political structure than the world has yet seen.'[14] For a twenty-five-year-old student, the publication of this essay was a remarkable achievement, displaying the maturity of his mind and his firm grasp of the essentials of historical analysis.

Apart from the stimulus of the Beit Prize, one can assume that there was another reason for Burt's interest in this subject. The question of Canada's relations with Britain was vigorously debated in his native land in the pre-war years. Imperial preference and imperial defence were issues of practical politics, and the usually strident utterances of the proponents and critics of the idea of imperial unity were widely discussed. In this situation, Burt viewed the role of the historian as one who contributes to public enlightenment by relating current ideas to their earlier manifestations and to their implications for contemporary society. He undoubtedly was influenced by the widespread view in English-speaking Canada that the country was emerging to nationhood under the British monarchy, and that she should cultivate an association with Britain based on the principle of equality. Burt had no strong emotional commitment to the ideology of imperialism, a fact which probably explains his early conversion to the League of Nations ideal during the war years. Nevertheless it is interesting to note that he returned to the theme of empire in his last book, *The Evolution of the British Empire and Commonwealth from the American Revolution*, published in 1956. The subject, he wrote in his foreword, 'began to intrigue me forty-five years ago, when I was a student of the late Professor Egerton and lived in daily contact with other students drawn to Oxford from all over the empire.'[15] Nearly half a century had passed since the composition of his first work, but despite the revolutionary changes in British imperial relationships in the intervening years, one can justify his inclusion of the earlier work in the 'Suggestions for Further Reading' in the 1956 book. From first to last, he remained the moderate and pragmatic observer, who rejects both English-Canadian and French-Canadian isolationist nationalism.

As his Oxford career neared its close, having won his BA degree in the autumn of 1912, Burt naturally began to look for a teaching appointment in Canada. He wrote to the President of the University of Alberta, Henry Marshall Tory. 'An appointment in Edmonton would be very acceptable to me,' he stated, 'for outside of Toronto I have not so many friends and relatives in any place as Edmonton.'[16] Tory replied that there was no opening; but the situation had changed by the time Burt returned to Toronto and in August he was offered and had accepted a position as lecturer in history at Alberta. He certainly met the criterion of Tory's appointment policy, derived from President Remsen of Johns Hopkins University who, Tory noted, 'realized that it would be difficult to get distinguished men to come to a new institution because such men would ...

be settled in ... but that the choice must be for young men of promise who, if not great at the moment, had the possibility of becoming great in the future.'[17]

As with all new institutions, the character of the University of Alberta was being shaped by the ideas and personality of its first president, who held the position for twenty years.[18] Born on a pioneer farm near Guysborough, Nova Scotia, his childhood circumstances were not markedly different from those of the young lecturer in history whom he appointed in 1913. Moreover, like A.L. Burt, he had a mother of singular intelligence and force of character who encouraged her sons to educate themselves for careers in the mainstream of Canadian life. By dint of hard work Tory had accumulated funds to attend McGill University, and after a brief career as an ordained minister of the Methodist Church he was appointed to the teaching staff at McGill. During the following seventeen years his abundant energy and initiative won him a position of prominence as a teacher and administrator. In 1907 he accepted the invitation of the Premier of Alberta, the Honourable A.C. Rutherford, to become the president of the new provincial university.

Tory was singularly well suited by long experience and convictions to head the University of Alberta in its formative years. He had already expressed his devotion to the principle of extending high standards of university education throughout Canada, particularly in the West; he was (despite the official policy of his own church) equally firm in his opposition to denominational colleges and to the proliferation of institutions which would be unable to offer the benefits of a true university. Moreover, in his view the scholar should not lead an ivory tower existence. 'The fact is,' he wrote on one occasion, 'one can hardly take an abstract idea like the truth and separate it out as unrelated to life, and say it is the only thing worth while.'[19] This philosophical principle was particularly important for a state-supported institution of higher learning in a democratic society. In his first convocation address in October 1908, Tory expounded this doctrine:

The modern state university has sprung from a demand on the part of the people themselves for intellectual recognition, a recognition which only a century ago was denied them. The result is that such institutions must be conducted in such a way as to relate them as closely as possible to the life of the people. ... This should be the concern of all educated men, it should never be forgotten.

He must have been thinking of his own youth, as he continued:

It is the glory of our Canadian institutions that they have directed from the homes of those we are accustomed to call the common people, a steady stream of men into positions of responsibility among us. Without that which the university has to offer this would never have been possible.[20]

But Tory's adherence to this principle did not mean that exclusive priority was to be given to applied science and professional education. When the first term opened, the Faculty of Arts and Science consisted of a staff of five (including the President, who taught mathematics and physics) comprising professors of classics, English, modern languages, and civil engineering. In later years new faculties appeared, offering a variety of professional studies, and the humanities were overshadowed; their prestige, but not the quality of instruction, was impaired. The program of the Extension Department, created in 1912 to serve the rural area and smaller urban centres, to which Burt was to contribute, nevertheless stressed the humanistic as well as the practical interests of the pioneer population.

Of classroom teaching in Alberta, the first professor of classics wrote: 'The plan which we followed from the start was to fix our standard of instruction on an equality with that of the older institutions of the country.'[21] The principle of appointment reinforced this standard – no one was to be given professorial rank who had not been trained in at least two universities.[22]

The first few years of Tory's presidency were not easy: there were financial stringencies and pressures from ambitious towns to decentralize the university by locating some faculties in other centres; the effort to establish a rival university in Calgary; the feeling in some quarters that the creation of a university was premature; the uncertainty created by Rutherford's resignation as Premier in 1910; the suspicion in the minds of some of the members of the Senate that Tory would be unduly influenced by McGill traditions. By the time Burt joined the staff, however, most of these issues had been resolved by the determination and diplomatic skills of the President and the prospects for steady expansion seemed highly favourable.

The history department which Burt joined in 1913 consisted of Gordon Stanley Fife and the President, who in the early years, when time permitted, lectured on British and Canadian political and constitutional history; occasionally his lectures were given by Dr J.M. MacEchran, head of the Department of Philosophy and Psychology. Fife, a Rhodes Scholar of 1908 and a native of Peterborough, had attended Queen's University. He was appointed to the university in 1911 as the first lecturer in history and English. When Burt joined the staff, six courses in history were listed in the calendar. In his first year he taught European history.

In 1914, following the end of the spring term, Burt proceeded overseas to pursue post-graduate studies at the ancient University of Freiburg, in the beautiful upper Rhine region near the Black Forest. Here he took a course on 'The French Revolution and the Wars of Liberation.' The French Revolution was his major historical interest at this time. He also wished to make a first-hand assessment of the situation in Germany, for the growing tensions in Anglo-German relations had produced widespread concern in Canada and other parts of the Empire. Discussions with German students were revealing. He would have been interned in Germany had he not been tipped off by a friend who had received his army call-up. Hastening to the border, Burt found it closed, but being fluent in the language he was able to discover another exit point and a man who could be induced to accompany him with a wheelbarrow to transport his books. He crossed into France in the nick of time. Fife, who was also travelling in Germany that summer, had a comparable experience.

During the academic year 1914–15 at Alberta the teaching of political economy became one of Burt's responsibilities, and the department was renamed history and political economy. He offered general history (an introductory course), European history from the Renaissance to 1648, and a general introduction to political economy; one suspects that his University of Toronto courses in this latter subject and Alberta's financial position during the war years dictated this combination of disciplines, which continued until 1920, when the two departments were separated.

Burt and Fife lived in apartments on the third floor of Athabasca Hall, and near the beginning of Burt's second year they organized the History Club on the University of Toronto model, which still flourishes today as the oldest undergraduate society on the campus. The two young bachelors took turns entertaining the Club, whose membership over the years has included many Albertans who have subsequently distinguished themselves in various careers.

Before the beginning of Burt's third term in Edmonton, an event occurred which was to have a profound influence not only on his personal happiness but also on the success of his academic career. This was his marriage, on 18 August 1915, to Dorothy Duff, a Master of Science in biology from McGill, who had been appointed to the University staff the previous year. Her grandfather, a Scottish Congregational minister, had migrated with his family to the Eastern Townships in 1856. Dorothy's father became a well-known hardware merchant and subsequently a chartered accountant in Montreal, where he lived for sixty-four years. Charming, firm-minded, and comely, Dorothy Duff had been a brilliant student in high school and university. The fact of her appointment to the university, even though it was in a junior capacity, was indicative of her intellectual qualities, for this was an era when few Canadian women were given university appointments. The fact that Burt could regard his wife as his intellectual equal was a stabilizing element in their marriage. This circumstance is implicit in the language and content of his letters, which provide clear and ample evidence of his philosophy and of his attitude to public affairs and to the study and teaching of history. Throughout their life together he relied on her as a severe and constructive critic of his prose style.

Burt's teaching assignment appears to have been heavier in 1915–16, probably because of Fife's enlistment in the spring of 1915 in the Third Universities Company. Not long after, Fife was transferred to the Princess Patricia's Canadian Light Infantry and a year later he was dead, killed in the Battle of Mount Sorrel, not far from Ypres, one of the many potential intellectual leaders of which the nation was robbed by World War I. During the 1916–17 term, Burt was promoted to assistant professor of history and economics, and it was in this year that he offered, in addition to courses in British and European history, the lecture course in Canadian political and constitutional history, which had first been listed by the department in 1914.

The following year the first honours courses were introduced, and Burt gave a seminar in seventeenth-century English constitutional history. His first students were Aileen Dunham, Lillian Cobb, and Alan Harvey. The former two subsequently had distinguished academic careers in the United States, and the last was an Alberta Rhodes scholar. The course was based on S.R. Gardiner's works, and each student prepared a half-hour paper every week, to be read and discussed. Professor Cobb[23] recalls:

How hard he worked, and how hard he worked us! On January 28, 1918 word got around that Mr. Burt would probably not meet his 9:00 o'clock class, because his first child had been born that morning. None the less he met us. Once, when we thought we couldn't stand the pressure, we drew lots as to which of us would ask him for a day off. He seemed very surprised, but said readily: "I had planned for a day off at the end of the course. You may take it now if you wish." We did!

'It was ... the major inspiration which later led me to graduate school and a life-time career in History,' Professor Dunham declares.[24] Burt's students were frequently entertained in his home, where his wife's domestic skills and personal interest in the young people complemented her husband's efforts to overcome institutional impersonality in faculty-student relations. Since the History Club was an all-male preserve, Mrs Burt had organized the Bluestocking Club for women students. These initiatives were among the enduring influences which the Burts had on those students who took up academic careers.

Invited in 1917 to contribute an article to the monthly edition of *The Gateway*, a student publication, Burt wrote 'Is Life Worth Living?,'[25] a concise statement of his approach to university education. Referring to the bitter experience of war, the disillusionment with old forms of religion, and the obvious incompetence of governments, he urged his readers to avoid 'misplaced beliefs' and to lead society by giving 'a truer meaning to life' than that provided by materialistic standards.

The University [he wrote] aims to teach its students two things – to do something and to be something. It turns out young lawyers, doctors, teachers and engineers inspired to do their best in their chosen professions. But that is not all. The University imparts another training, another inspiration – to be something ... to have a large mind and a strong character. This is the product of no single university course, but of the whole atmosphere of the institution – lectures, laboratories, reading and companionship in all. ... This is the vision, the light that dawns upon the University student....

This declaration expressed the essential elements in Burt's philosophy of life and of higher education.

2

The Tank Battalion

The first year of the war did not have much effect on the university, but from 1915–16 on the reverse was true. Before the war ended enrolment declined, many students interrupted their studies to enlist, and nearly half the members of the faculty had joined the army. Both staff and students, including Burt, participated in the Canadian Officers Training Corps program on the campus, and in the summer at Sarcee Camp near Calgary; in 1916 he was commissioned as a lieutenant in the active militia but was rejected for the infantry because of flat feet when he tried to enlist the following year. In 1917 the University of Alberta contributed a company to the Western Universities Battalion, and medical students joined the 12th Field Ambulance. Late in the year the President left the campus to organize the work of the Khaki University in the United Kingdom. Having completed basic officer training, Burt was able to join the First Canadian Tank Battalion when it was established early in 1918, with the rank of lieutenant.

The First Tank Battalion was exclusively recruited from Canadian universities,[1] presumably because the military authorities assumed that young men of proven intelligence would quickly master this new and complicated form of weaponry. The two officers in the Alberta contingent were lieutenants Burt and George H. Steer, a Queen's graduate and barrister in Edmonton. Since there were no tanks in Canada, training in the use of this new instrument of war had to be postponed until the troops arrived in England. The Alberta contingent of seventeen men left Edmonton in the last week of April 1918, and arrived in Ottawa on the 30th.[2]

Despite the fact that the great German spring offensive of 1918, which began on 21 March, was scoring notable successes against the British and French forces and reached the Marne River only 37 miles from Paris by 30 May, no sense of urgency seems to have been conveyed to the men of the Battalion. Training in the theory of this most difficult of tactical arms was delayed until well after the unit arrived in England.

Burt's first day in Ottawa is described in one of his regular twice-a-week letters to his wife:

Ottawa, April 30, 1918

...We had a pleasant train journey. ... At Winnipeg ... D.C. Harvey of Wesley College, a friend of Oxford days who taught you remember at McGill for a year, came to the station and cheered my soul by his chronic grousing.

...Dinner was to have been ready in the station here on our arrival 7:52, but the train was late and the chef gone. Coventry (Lieut.) (Oxford and Toronto. Biology) met us and said the Russell House had a good cafeteria. So there I marched the men and persuaded the man in charge to accept my coupons on the G.T.R. for 18 meals, to the surprise of Coventry who feared I should have to pay. ... 139 men and some officers are already here. The Toronto Company which I hear is over strength is not yet arrived. There is a whole batch of Laval students under a man named Bourassa, no relative or any affinity of the infamous. ... The general talk is that we will be away in a fortnight. We report tomorrow morning to assist in giving the men some elementary drill. It is now 10:30 and we have been unsuccessfully trying to see the o.c. [Major Macfarlane] since breakfast. He must be, like you, a great friend of his bed.

We expect to get two or 3 days leave at most, if we can get that; I am writing mother I am trying to get it next weekend.

Now I must off to see if we can get a glimpse of the o.c. who I hear has distinguished himself in France and is not yet 30, a fine fellow.

Burt's reference to Bourassa is typical of contemporary English-Canadian reaction to the Nationalist leader. In later years Burt was to write perceptively on the reasons for French-Canadian opposition to conscription, but not sympathetically of Bourassa. What he regarded as extreme nationalism in all its manifestations was repellent to him. The following three weeks were occupied with drilling and meetings with his parents and friends, including Vincent Massey, a contemporary at Toronto and Oxford, then secretary of the Dominion War Cabinet. The highlight was the arrival of Mrs Burt and Forrest, who came to Ottawa for a few days' visit. From the Women's Patriotic League of Listowel he received handmade accessories for his outfit. For reading matter on the voyage, his kit held *The Thoughts of Marcus Aurelius* and Palgrave's *Golden Treasury*.

During the first week of June the Battalion boarded ship in Montreal and arrived in England a little over two weeks later. Although the danger of German submarine attack was almost non-existent by this time, the usual precautions were still in force. The following letter summarizes the events of the voyage.

Rolling on the billows
June 20, 1918

At last our long voyage is just about to close unless a submarine intercepts us very shortly and there is some real danger yet. We have all worn our life belts all the way across, and in obedience to orders have slept in all our clothes during the last few nights. It was really very comfortable.

The days on board have passed very lazily. They were so much alike one might almost question if there was such a thing as time. Each morning I rose at 7 a.m. bathed, dressed and had a short walk on deck till breakfast at 7:45. The next event in the day was p.t. at 10:30–11:30 and it has been great fun balancing on one leg when the ship was rolling well. There were only two other regular events in the day, lunch at 12:30 noon and dinner at 6 p.m. The lacunae were filled in by learning and practicing the semaphore system of signalling, (I have also learned but not yet used the Morse Code.), a very little bridge, a little more reading and shuffleboard, still more conversation, even more musing and a great deal more of sleep. All through I have never been as lazy in my whole life before. The total result I feel to be distinctly good.

I have not played much bridge because practically everybody plays for money and then I hate it. I have only played twice for money, each time unsuspectingly losing and gaining 80¢ and 25¢ respectively. I do not anticipate playing much more.

My reading has been more patchy than this letter is and will be, for I never knew when I sat down with a book what I would be doing in fifteen minutes – still reading, playing shuffleboard, talking, idly dreaming or soundly sleeping. Under such conditions I finished Morley and Kipling's Tales and have read much of Marcus Aurelius. In the past I have several times approached M.A. but somehow it never went as I expected, but now – I suppose because of the new manner of life I have undertaken for a short while – I find myself revelling in it. It is not a book to be swallowed in big gulps, but to be chewed slowly in small morsels; I know nothing like it. Of course the stoic philosophy in its entirety is not acceptable to me. I refer particularly to its fatalism. But the rest of it is strong meat to the soul. It teaches me that whatever my environment may be, yet I have full control over myself – that while the body lasts the spirit should not fail – that no matter what may come it matters not, for I may be self-contained, serene and even happy. ... I was quite amused the other day when Capt. Gerrie of the Y.M.C.A., said to me "I never see you but you are wearing the smile that won't come off." I think you might like the stoic Emperor now though like myself you might not have relished him very much not long ago. I am greatly anticipating in the days to come the ever fresh moral treat I carry in my pocket. I will send you some of the passages that appeal particularly.

Conversations on board have been delightful. ... With quite a number of our own officers too I have had many good serious chats. Their company is going far to offset my dislike for military life.

As for the externals of our journey, it has been much pleasanter than I anticipated. After the first two nights on board, and we sailed within 24 hours of when I last saw you – Steer and I have had the cabin all to ourselves. The other two officers were badly bitten and chased out by bed bugs which have left us unmolested. The weather has been nearly perfect. I have had a strong sunburn which took the skin off my manly brow – so genial was the sun. The boat is so steady and the sea so very calm that although some of the men below were seasick the officers were all immune. Our convoy was a good-sized one and the camouflage paint made it difficult to tell whether the ships were floating nightmares or cubist or futurist illusions. More interesting even is the sight of destroyers scurrying hither and thither. We of course had boat drill every day and wore our life belts constantly. The last few nights a few have tried to whisper wild rumours but we have not seen any submarines. A cloud has been cast over us today by the disappearance of one of our officers. I understand he was invalided home from the front suffering from shell shock and when last seen was in very low spirits. A court of inquiry is now sitting upon the case.

We have a good idea of where we will land but naturally may not tell and our letters may be held some time after we land. Our further destination is unknown. All we know is that we will be in quarantine for about a fortnight after landing as is usual with troops reaching England. ...

The Alberta boys are all as usual. I see quite a bit of them visiting them usually at every meal time except breakfast. Old Bill Sykes has taken to playing whist with great gusto. Fife[3] has very much improved and Archie McGillivray is into every fun that is going. Marsden[4] is now called nothing but Bishop and is I think a most wholesome influence. I like all the boys much better even than when we pulled out of Edmonton.

Burt's letters from the training camp in England are in essence a personalized diary of the Canadian tank training program, which lasted for four months. Since no comparable accounts seem to exist, they are a unique historical record. For about six weeks the Battalion was housed at a segregation camp at Frensham Pond, near Aldershot and Farnham, Surrey, putting in time until they could move to Bovington Camp in Dorset for tank training. The time was spent in squad drill, sports activities, swimming, and listening to lectures on map reading, motor mechanics, and infantry attack tactics. There was time for some long walks about the country, and for reading. Marcus Aurelius was a familiar companion. Those who knew Burt later as a teacher and friend can imagine him savouring some such passage of the philosopher-emperor's as the following:

Suppose that men kill thee, cut thee in pieces, curse thee. What then can these things do to prevent thy mind from remaining pure, wise, sober, just? For instance, if a man should stand by a limpid pure spring, and curse it, the spring never ceases sending up potable water; and if he should cast clay into it or filth, it will speedily disperse them and wash them out, and will not be at all polluted. How then shalt thou possess a perpetual fountain and not a mere well? By forming thyself hourly to freedom conjoined with benevolence, simplicity and modesty.

'I have found an equilibrium of spirit such as I did not know a few years ago,' he wrote to his wife.[5] But all was not serious. Describing a picnic under the trees with Edmonton men, with Steer producing cakes of chocolate from his trunk, Burt remarked, 'Now you will think from this that I am no stoic but an Epicurean which I hope you *know* is not true.'[6]

A short leave in London permitted Burt to attend a performance of J.M. Barrie's *Dear Brutus* at Wyndham's Theatre, and to visit R.B. Mowat, his Oxford tutor, who was working in the Intelligence Department of the Admiralty, and who promised to try to find another one of his students as a temporary replacement in the Alberta history department. One evening was spent reading about the Montague Report on the Government of India, 'which interests me very much.'

...If carried out, as seems most likely, it will effect one of the greatest reforms and be one of the greatest experiments in government in modern times. The report, though very lengthy, has a simple, short principle, the careful extension of responsible government in India until ultimately after a long period the government will be on a par with that of the Dominions.[7]

Around mid-July the Battalion moved to its permanent training quarters, the Imperial Tank Training Camp (Bovington Camp) near Wareham, Dorset – on the edge of the heathland beloved of Thomas Hardy. Bovington was a great improvement over Frensham Camp, where eating at the mess involved a half-mile walk and 'where we never got enough to eat and what we got was seldom properly cooked and invariably gritty with sand and dirt.' 'I learn,' Burt continued, 'that our experiences at Frensham – which was not so terribly bad but seems so by comparison, will have been the most uncomfortable in our whole army life. ... They say life in France for us will be better than here – at least so far as food goes ... The W[oman's] A[uxiliary] A[rmy] C[orps] are settled here and are responsible for the good cooking.'[8]

The episodes of the training program are best described in the following extracts from Burt's letters home:

July 20, 1918
Until yesterday we had easy work i.e. the officers in the same group as myself. But yesterday we found we had done with the snap courses and that laborious days had begun. We have barely an hour for lunch, which is less than it seems, as we have to march back to our quarters, doff our overalls – scrub up and after lunch dress again for toil and march back. We were plunged into the intricate theory and working of large engines and find it confusing but even more interesting. The preliminaries over – we are now in the beasts themselves, but I fear the awful censor would frown dark blots if I ventured into any descriptions. When this particular course is over we switch on to gunnery on which Steer was put first. Each lasts a few weeks. It feels good to be really at work after we have been pottering about for so long at squad drill, etc. I find that study after the day's work will not be too strenuous for the pleasure of life, and I anticipate many enjoyable hours reading....

July 28, 1918
Thursday we began to drive our awful beast in the open. (It is called a bus in ordinary language among us) – each taking his turn. We are divided up in groups of five. It is not bad fun, but it is inconceivably dirty. We have to do all the work [of] cleaning and keeping it greased, oiled, etc. I have never been so dirty in my life before. I am sure you would have difficulty in recognising me returning from work. I lack only the tin dinner pail. My overalls are already black and shiny – the oil has come through, staining my underwear, and my hands! They are like a mechanic's, and in spite of any soap, promise never to be really clean again till the war is over. Friday afternoon we had an intersting time. Our instructor told us to

get out and have a smoke, then he got busy dickering with the works. After a while he emerged and told us to start the bus. Of course it would not work, and we had to puzzle out the various troubles and straighten them. But we succeeded in the end. I will be able to *run* our motor [car] after the war. Yesterday morning we spent the whole time cleaning – from 8:30 to 12:15 working like Trojans. When noon came we were all played out and glad to have a half holiday....

August 11, 1918

This week finished up one section of our work. Wed[nesday] night and Thursday we were examined on our driving. Clames and I were best of our class of 10. Friday we were examined in the shops on the engine, etc., and I came out all right. Yesterday we spent an extra day on the new engine.

Steer returned from Lulworth Cove Friday night, having finished his gunnery. I have a week yet, on repairs in the shops and then turn on gunnery....

Wednesday orders came out that we must each select a batman from our tank crews. ... My new man is a young French Canadian – Barrette – a law student from Laval. ... He is a tremendously clever boy and possesses wisdom as well as knowledge. I have many good chats with him. Last evening I spent most of the time discussing the French Canadians and the Roman Catholic Church with him. He is very liberal in his views. Of course he is hardly French Canadian. His mother is from Paris and his father's mother was also and he has been in France a number of times.

A Quebecer with such views was a rare bird at a time when the conscription controversy was raging, and Burt recognized that he was hardly representative of Canadian opinion.

August 25, 1918

Friday was another day full of surprises but of a different kind. We were shooting "classification" *i.e.* to be classified as shots good or bad. To my astonishment I led the class with 188 out of 200. The next was 178 by Capt. Gardiner – an attached officer. Then Clames got 163. We three were thus made Marksmen. Five were first class *i.e.* between 130 and 160, and four 2nd class shots *i.e.* between 100 and 130. 80% is necessary for markman. I cannot tell you how it happened. The major was quite bucked with my performance. That night was mess night. Several big officers down from London were our guests and the concert in the messroom lasted till after 10 p.m. It was excellent – there were no piano solos to ruin it. The old general, who was the chief guest, moved the Col. to relax the rule against pipes after dinner, which made many of us happy. These concerts are always in the mess room itself – which is the dining room hut – not the ante-room, a hut which is our sitting room.

A few days later there were several examinations, including one on the use and care of the machine-gun. About the middle of September Burt and his party marched about five miles from Bovington Camp to Lulworth Camp near the south coast, for the first of several sessions of tank combat training. The countryside here is beautiful, particularly near the chalk cliffs of Lulworth Cove. 'The country here,' he wrote, 'is very rolling, the hills high and cut away in steep cliffs to the sea. The hills look like great green velvet masses.'[9] They remained here for about a week before returning to Bovington Camp, and he described their activities as follows:

September 18, 1918

...Monday morning we did a little practice laying guns on targets. That is from a moving tank. A lecture or so filled up, with some messing about, the first day. Yesterday we began the actual firing of the six pounder. The shell and cartridge together must be about 18" long. The bore of the gun is 2¼". It has a great bark and flash. But curiously the noise inside the tank is very small compared with the noise outside. The flash reaches about 10 feet out of the muzzle and sometimes there is a back flash in the tank when loading rapidly. The actual projectile weighs six pounds and explodes on contact. Yesterday I was unfortunate. By my third shot I had found the range and hit the target. But the tank was away around and there was danger of sending a round into the cove so I was commanded to select a new target. But it needs three shots to get a target and I had only two left. So my average error was 11 yds. 10 yds. is necessary for a 1st class shot and this morning my name was read out among those who must do better. So I set to and in this morning's practice had an average error of 2 yds. which is not very easy to beat. I had imagined I would be afraid of the gun but I like it. They will not let us wear anything in our ears and it is well. The noise is not very much.

By 25 September they were back at Bovington Camp. The training program during the whole period in England was not so exhausting that Burt was unable to find time for a considerable amount of reading, of both history and fiction. The works of Thomas Hardy and George Meredith were his favourite novels, although he also devoured *Jane Eyre*, *Don Quixote*, and some of Kipling. Studies by A. Fournier on Napoleon and F.V.A. Aulard on the French Revolution were among the books he ordered from Blackwell's: 'I prefer to spend my spare money in that way than in bridge or poker debts and wine treats, as quite a number do.'[10] William O'Brien's life of Parnell he found 'a very biased work, but interesting reading.'[11] Guglielmo Ferrero's *The Greatness and Decline of Rome* was 'enlightened as great history should be with general observations of a pointed nature.'[12] But although cards failed to attract, and books were a solace, he was not unsociable, supervising the construction of a tennis court and always in demand as a pianist. Steer and Marsden were his close friends and they spent much time together.

The next three weeks were spent at Bovington Camp.

September 25, 1918

Life is very sweet especially at afternoon tea when I have my rapidly diminishing store of honey with perhaps a couple of friends. I have been thinking of late how foolish many of us – selfish indeed and myself quite so – really are. We have plenty to eat and yet we encourage those at home to spend on parcels of foodstuffs amounts foolish in comparison to the quantity sent. Really we are greedy spoiled children and nothing else – like boys at boarding schools who are all stomach. So please do not spoil me and instead of wasting your good money on sending me superfluities spend it on something you yourself need – or something nice for Forrest. I am just beginning to realise the terrible extent to which you have spoiled me...

October 2, 1918

...Monday morning I began a fortnight's course on reconnaissance which promises to be quite interesting. It is chiefly a study of ground so that we may be able to visualize ground from a map, and recognising its different qualities know how to use it. We have some lectures but more practical work. For example we drew an enlargement of a square on a map of this locality. Took it out yesterday morning and examined the ground, inserting everything in pencil on the map. Then in the afternoon we finished it all in india ink. This morning we had some lectures and again this afternoon we spent examining a small section of country on either side of a road for a 'road traverse' which must be finished and handed in Friday morning. I wish I had your artistic eye and deft hand here to give me a little help. The tennis court is all finished now but the marking of the court, the erection of the net and of the big net around the court. Yesterday after tea we had a lecture by the General of this camp telling us he wanted an improvement in discipline etc. of which he said there was a noticeable falling off among officers and men. Indeed it is very true and natural when there are no regular parades, and all – officers, N.C.O.'s and men are off at schools all day. So saluting grows lax and men slouch around etc....

October 6, 1918

...I am quite busy. The reconnaissance course is no snap. I have been working overtime every day. Thursday after dinner I went back and worked the whole evening, Friday after tea again, and then yesterday afternoon and to-day also. We are busy finishing up a panoramic sketch and a river reconnaissance. I find I am no great artist for my maps get only fair average marks – a necessary humiliation to my pride. We have this week still on the course. The company goes off to Sherford Tuesday for a week's tank manoeuvres and then to Lulworth for a week's gunnery. As I am on this course I stay here and when finished go to Lulworth. Steer returns at that time and most likely we will go together. In my last letter I mentioned a reduction of establishment. The result is not finally settled and will not be published for some time so please don't mention this abroad....

It is beastly hard to write, for everybody is now talking and several will discuss the war with me. There is a widespread general expectation. One of our section commanders returned from the front last night and says we have the Germans on the run and will keep it up. To my mind everything hinges on Turkey. As the allies practically demand her extinction she will fight on as long as she can. Then Austria will be open to the south and she likewise will collapse. Germany still has 4 million men on the west front and could fight on – but a losing battle. The German people will then see the futility of their much vaunted military government, and the latter to stave off revolution will conclude peace and yield somewhat (or appear to) to the people's demands. The point is how long can Turkey resist – not long I think, for her sole source of supplies of munitions and large source of foodstuffs are cut off unless the Germans made a sudden eruption to the south and seize the Constantinople railway. Thus the war may end this year quite precipitately, but if not will be brought to a close in a great spring campaign. This conclusion seems generally held among the men here and in France....

Burt's observations are shrewd, for the Allies were able to advance only very slowly in Belgium and France, and the German armies were never destroyed in battle.

October 13, 1918

...My course on reconnaissance finished yesterday. By strenuous labour I managed to get a first again. Two tied at 90. I averaged 84. There were about three of around there. It was very interesting. Thursday morning, Friday all day, and yesterday we spent upon a problem of finding a course for tanks over a couple of miles, and establishing necessary posts for them – of course drawing a careful map for the whole. I may send home some books wrapped up in one or two of my splashes. The comment on my panoramic sketch is most amusing....

By this time, the question of the abdication of the Kaiser had become a subject of public discussion in Germany and various rumours were circulating. If Wilhelm II had abdicated promptly in favour of his grandson's installation as a constitutional ruler, the monarchy might have survived World War I. President Wilson's first communications with the German government culminated in a Note which was reported in the London *Times* on 16 October 1918. This stated that Germany must change her constitution to eliminate arbitrary power, that the Allied military advisers must determine the conditions of an armistice, and that any armistice must safeguard Allied military supremacy.

October 16, 1918

...I received in a letter from father a P.O. order to buy myself a chamois vest for my birthday – so you need not be afraid of my taking pneumonia, consumption, or anything like that if I should go to France this winter. By the way, a wire came to the orderly room here this evening stating that the Kaiser has abdicated in favour of his grandson. If that be true peace is very much nearer by that stroke. Pres. Wilson's reply was very pleasing. Steer and I have had a few great arguments over the matter. He inclined to believe and I to distrust the *bona fide* of Germany in her recognition of Wilson's 14 points. But the Kaiser's going is most significant.

October 20, 1918

...Saturday morning [at Lulworth Cove] I was with a party loading ammunition and cleaning M.G.'s (machine guns). ... Today I expected to be on a fatigue party in charge of men digging trenches for the royal 'show' [for King George V] but the lot fell to others. It was cold and rainy so I spent the morning by the fire in the hut reading a little but most of the time chatting with the major and a few other officers. This afternoon from lunch to tea I went for a long walk over the cliffs and exploring a cave. I climbed over 500 ft. and had a great view. At the end of my climb I found a secluded nook commanding one of the loveliest valleys running down to the sea that I have ever seen. The wind was high and it was spitting rain more or less, but it was a beautiful afternoon. The leaves are falling fairly fast now....

Our plans are changed. We leave here Oct. 28 for a week's manoeuvres at Sherford Bridge. We go to France Nov. 18 as a unit. The intervening fortnight we spend at Bovington. I hope to get some leave then....

Early in November the unit had a few days' leave, which Burt spent in Bradford, Yorkshire with Mrs Burt's uncle, Professor Archibald Duff, a distinguished Old Testament scholar at the University of Leeds. Here he received the news of the armistice. Writing on 10 November, he commented:

...The great news is crowding in these tremendous hours. Last night we learned of the Kaiser's abdication. Amidst the general joy and sense of relief I cannot help feeling sad and somewhat shamefaced that though I am in khaki I have not served in France and in all probability will not be able to. Though I have satisfied my conscience I feel something lacking – I suppose a sort of consciousness of public opinion. I now want to tear off the khaki lest I be mistaken for one of those who suffered in France. ... I had intended getting my picture taken when I next got leave – but now I think not – I don't want to have it taken in my uniform.

In the normal course of events the armistice would have been the termination of Burt's military career, and there were rumours that the Battalion was to be shipped back to Canada within a week or two and discharged on arrival. But the demobilization arrangements were obviously confused, since at the same time an education officer had been appointed and a survey of the educational qualifications and interests of the men had been made, which indicated the possibility that the unit would be remaining in Britain for some time. Then, on 24 November, Burt received a letter from President Tory, in London, asking him to transfer to the Khaki University.[13] On 20 November he wrote home as follows:

Sunday night the few of us interested in Education discussed plans for work in the B[attalion] here. We expected the Col. but he did not appear. So the plan that I should go up with him to London did not materialize. But I decided to go, paying my own way. I left at 9 a.m. and arrived 1:30 p.m. and found Dr. Tory in his new quarters, the old Alberta Government offices – very luxurious indeed. He had just received my letter – but it was in a pile of mail he had not yet read. When I told him my application to be transferred had gone to Argyll House (Canadian Headquarters) he said he would see it was put through at once as he needed me in the worst way. He was very busy so I did not remain long. ... I then proceeded to the old headquarters of the Khaki University to see what could be done immediately in the line of books and courses for our unit. I had a very pleasant time with Capt. Cameron[14] – collected quite a mass of literature of the K.U. and arranged for a parcel of text books to be sent up at once....

I do not know what to think or say. It is clearly my duty as well as my interest to stay here and work in the K.U. As I cannot fight in France it is the next best thing to do....

November 24, 1918

Yesterday afternoon Dr. Tory came down for the weekend as Col. Mills' guest.

(Col. Mills is an extremely able and most charming man). A Khaki College Canadian Tanks is being founded here where the unit expects to remain for some months until the general demobilisation after the signature of peace. He departed this afternoon just before tea, having made quite an impression – I like him more and more and apparently he reciprocates. ... He thinks a lot of you. He was surprised I had not already reported in London and is impatient my transfer is not through yet. He says he must have me right away and so has arranged with Col. Mills that I be sent to London at once, if necessary on leave till the transfer is through. So off I go tomorrow or the day after. ... Dr. Tory is in a further difficult position because the Alberta Govt. offices are only loaned to him. He has to go to France immediately and needs a good Alberta province man to take charge of his office during that time and selects me particularly because Miss MacAdams,[15] who is likely to cause trouble has, he says, a very high opinion of me. Then he wants me to go in and out of London organizing the work in different centres and later – if the bulk of the Canadian army is to be kept in France, I may have to go through [sic]. I almost tremble at the responsibilities he is thrusting upon me but at the same time am inspired by the opportunity of greater work. I am astounded at the confidence he places in me.

Burt spent the next seven months in London occupied with the affairs of the Khaki University, and was to justify Tory's confidence in his knowledge, administrative abilities, and good judgment.

3

The Khaki University

Apart from the enlistment of University of Alberta students and staff in the armed forces, the most important contribution which the university made to the nation during the war years was in releasing its President from his normal duties to serve overseas as head of the Khaki University of Canada. The organizational principles for this institution had been formulated by President Tory in the summer of 1917 at the request of the Canadian YMCA.[1] The YMCA and the Chaplaincy Service had been providing reading matter and sponsoring informal lectures for the troops, and these were so well received that the idea of providing an organized educational service had emerged. Tory was selected to survey the situation in France and England and propose a specific scheme. He arrived in England in July and his report was published in September. This recommended that the service should have personnel support and sponsorship by the army authorities, with the YMCA providing financial assistance; the universities of Canada were to co-operate by establishing an advisory board and by recognizing university level work undertaken by the men. In the end, the program covered the whole spectrum of educational interests – elementary school subjects, instruction in agriculture, commerce, applied science, theology, and regular courses in British universities. The work began in a limited way in the autumn of 1917, but was stepped up in 1918 following Tory's return at the beginning of the year as Director of Educational Services, with the rank of Hon. Colonel. Area study centres were established in fourteen locations in England, and

Battalion schools were created for illiterate soldiers and others wherever servicemen were stationed.

The administrative aspects of this project were formidable, and frequently contentious, involving the differing views and personalities of army officers, YMCA officials, the chaplains, and university authorities in England. By the time of the armistice, Tory was overburdened with organizational details – hence his desire to obtain Burt as his personal assistant in the central office in London. The following letters describe Burt's initiation in this activity.

November 27, 1918

Well, here I am presiding in Dr. Tory's offices while he is spending the day at Whitley Camp. Monday my transfer did not arrive, so Col. Mills as agreed sent me to this institution "on command" i.e. temporarily attached for duty till my transfer was actually through. ... He [Dr. Tory] was much relieved to see me and sent me up to Bedford Square to straighten out the history courses – which were just going to press in the calendar of the K.U. It was lucky I did not wait for the train Tuesday morning for the courses were a bad jumble and it took me the morning to straighten them out and make sure the necessary books were available. The afternoon I spent trying to find a place to lay my head. ... I had just time to call on Frank [Underhill][2] for 5 m[inutes] and arrive at the Central Hall Westminster where Dr. Tory was lecturing under the auspices of the R[oyal] Col[onial] Inst[itute]. ... At the lecture (Dr. Tory spoke very well) I was much struck by Sir Charles Lucas[3] who presided. He looked a frail and very unfashionable old gentleman but betrayed himself in his words as president to be a remarkably incisive intellect and an attractive master of style. Mrs. Tory of course was there looking as well as ever. After the lecture Dr. and Mrs. Tory, Lt. Col. (Dean) Adams,[4] Marsden and the future Mrs. [Marsden] and your humble husband drove up here in Dr. Tory's official car and indulged in an unofficial cup of tea. I met Col. Adams only yesterday morning – submitting my report to him – and find him a most charming person. ... I had a few words with Dr. Tory in which I received orders to take charge of this office during his absence and to take any action immediately necessary that might arise in his mail or with the advent of callers. It is really a roving commission to sit in a chair before a large desk in a large beautifully furnished room with two ticking stenographers in two rooms, one on each side. He tells me he is going to keep me quite close to him until the New Year anyway....

...there was another incident today. You see these are still nominally the Alberta Gov[ernment] Offices – the K.U. name is not advertised on doors or windows at all. So benighted or prospective Alberta people are liable to drop in.

One such appeared this afternoon finding me ensconced in the erstwhile chair of the Agent-General for Alberta, and I was faced with the necessity of behaving as much as possible like the original occupant. (Keep this quiet – this is one reason I am here – to save trouble and a possible awkward situation). He was a poor devil of 55 or so who was doubly steeped in sin, and so caught in the mesh of the devil. To wit. His first wife refused to go to Canada to live with him so he sought, found and bound a more amenable partner, and slept in prison 15 mos. as a bigamist. His second sin was to dabble in Calgary oil stocks. In fact he is a real live stock promoter over here. Now for the mesh. He is contracted to return to Canada but is having difficulty with the immigration officials. I looked tremendously wise – as you know I can – and gave him a little advice from the abundant fountains of my wisdom. He threatens to return in a week if his problem is not solved.

December 1, 1918

My work in London keeps me very busy. I am doing all sorts of things from outlining courses in history – in considerable detail – for the guidance of students, and attending to benighted Albertans who need the assistance of the Agent-General of Alberta. My chief duty at the present is to fulfil the latter function (Breathe it not in Gath). Miss MacAdams has been very worried over the situation. The Agent General – Reed – was hopelessly incompetent and she is greatly relieved to know I am there to protect Albertan interests from being neglected. It is a tremendous joke. She [Miss MacAdams] insists to me that I have the proper qualities for the Agent General's function, and that I am not a political heeler [and] should have the job. Indeed she swears by all the serious gods that she is going to move it in the house when she returns.

The Khaki University plan for the admission of Canadian servicemen to British universities had not been implemented so far, and Tory directed Burt to solicit the co-operation of the university authorities. This involved him in considerable travel during the next few months. His first visit was to Oxford, which he described in the same letter:

Friday and yesterday Dr. Tory was at Seaford, leaving me in charge of the offices and any business that arose needing immediate attention. I am up here [Oxford] this weekend on his orders to see what arrangements can be made to send senior students here from January till the summer. I expected that the reactionary University authorities would do nothing, and that I would have to fall back upon arrangements with the different colleges. I am fairly sure of the latter now in any case, and have good hopes of getting something out of the university. A.L. Smith, the greatest historical tutor Oxford has had – the present head of Balliol – has been kindness itself. I spent the greater part of the time from two till 11:30 – coming back here [Corpus Christi] to dine pleasantly with the dons. He even insisted on coming out with me and going around Oxford to see a number of people who might give valuable assistance. I have a number of appointments to-day which will take up the most of my time, I expect. It is a great treat to mingle again in a scholarly atmosphere. For example last night I dined here with Schiller – the leader of the pragmatic school of philosophy, Plummer the church historian, Dr. Grundy, the ancient historian – my own tutor Mr. Mowat, and Clarke, Corpus Professor of Latin. We had a great chat in the senior common room over wine afterwards – before I rushed back to Balliol. I interviewed that old beast Tommy Case – the president of Corpus – to get permission to sleep in college. All he could say was that the war had ruined Europe. He has very few if any friends, for though he has a pleasant social manner he insults everybody. I counted myself lucky to escape in a few minutes unscathed. I had a pleasant 15 min[utes] chat with Wylie and his wife yesterday before I found the Master of Balliol in. Wylie is Oxford secretary of the Rhodes trust. They are great friends of mine. I go to tea with them to-day. At the Master's last night I met ... MacInnes – he is quite blind but has an alert mind and is a good scholar[5] – he wants to get a university post somewhere in Canada. I told him how he might manage it at Queen's and suggested b.c. as a good chance....

In a few minutes I am to go for a walk with my old tutor – then I meet Capt. Fife who has charge of imperial soldiers sent here for study by the British gov[ernment]. After lunch I have another appointment with the Master of Balliol and then I must see Barker,[6] the historian, author of Plato and Aristotle on our shelves. I hear he is keen.

In London, Burt had a modest room at the Red Court Hotel, Bedford Place. The guests were sprightly, and their activities would have been a continuous distraction to a less serious-minded person.

December 8, 1918

...This is really a very comfortable hotel. ... In the drawing room is a very good Bechstein piano. Many of the guests are kind and flattering and insist on my playing for them every evening. Some of them are extremely nice people – a few are not – particularly a creature called Mrs. Bland. She has a soldier husband who is here this weekend. It would be well if he were here always. She gets on my puritanical nerves. I sit at a table with three American [privates] – one a grad[uate] of Yale. I don't mind their consuming every dinner with the aid of a fork firmly grasped in the right hand, but their kind friendliness has a difficult job sometimes to make up for their perpetually talking shop. ... But the nice people are considerable....

Later on, Burt frequently took his meals with Hugh McLaughlin,[7] for whom he had arranged accommodation at the Red Court. McLaughlin, a Toronto graduate and student-at-law, had also been with the Tanks, and was now secretary of the London College of Khaki University.

On 9 December Burt was named head of the Khaki University's Department of History, and thus became a member of Tory's Advisory Council.[8] Early in January 1919, he visited Glasgow and Edinburgh universities. His departure from London and trip north is described in a letter of 8 January, written in Edinburgh:

Monday I had a severely busy day. I was getting Dr. Tory off to Seaford in the morning and had to "shoo" off a lot of people to get the necessary business done. The rest of the day I was rushed with correspondence and students at British Universities –which is largely in my hands – and later with making arrangements for my trip up here. In the morning Killam[9] walked in. It was good to see him again. Directly after going to France in July he was taken away from the artillery and attached to the intelligence corps, spending most of his time questioning German prisoners. He came across several of his old friends. He has come to take charge of Mathematics. ... I left 11:30 p.m. from Euston for Glasgow. It was impossible to get a berth but I secured a whole seat for myself on which I had a good sleep. I arrived 9:30 a.m., had breakfast and a bath and interviewed Sir Donald MacAlister head of the univ[ersity], and the registrar, and after lunch the head of the Royal Technical College. Everything was plain sailing. I arrived here a little after 5 p.m. and visited every hotel on Princes St. until I found a bed in a room with another officer. I met a South African officer with whom I chatted till 9 p.m. and then read till midnight. Then I slept – till quarter to ten. I hastily shaved and dressed and rushed off to the Univ[ersity] (it was too late to get breakfast) and thence to the residence of Sir Richard Lodge, prof. of history and dean of the faculty of Arts, with whom I had a very pleasant interview and then back to the university. ... I expect to spend tomorrow and perhaps the next day at Cambridge. We are getting excellent arrangements here also....

I like Dr. Tory better every day, and I think he likes and trusts me, so the future looks good. I have suggested to him that MacGibbon (economics) who was in the Tanks and is now with the k.u. of c. would be an acquisition for Alberta. He seems to think so too, and we may see Mac. in Edmonton next fall.[10] He is a very keen studious fellow who has written some good things, esp[ecially] a book on the Railroad problem of Canada.

On 12 January Burt noted that the Khaki University 'is going not badly though military authorities do not make the way easier.'

...I am off early to Cambridge to make arrangements there for students who may never go. Friday after we had been told to go ahead we received a letter from an authority at Argyll House (Can. H.Q.'s) which threw a heavy shower of cold water on our scheme for studying at British Universities. But we expect it still to go through. The college camp for matriculants, 1st and 2nd year Univ[ersity] students is starting at Bramshott the latter part of this week. Killam is going there to take charge of mathematics and I perhaps in history – such is the uncertainty of life.

By mid-January this issue was resolved:

January 19, 1919

The question of sending men to British Universities has been finally settled. We can select 100 from France and England each and I have the matter in hand. The actual selection rests in the hand of a committee composed of Dr. Tory, Dean Adams, Maj. Gill[11] and myself – any three can act. I am secretary of the works – which kept me busy all yesterday afternoon and which will keep me busy most likely until next June. I may have to do a couple of days teaching each week in Bramshott into the bargain.

By 25 January Burt was able to write that the worst of his organizational work was nearly over, and that he might go to Ripon to teach, along with Killam. However, in the end Frank Underhill, who had enlisted in 1915 from the University of Saskatchewan history department, was assigned to this position. Burt remained in the London office, where he wrote as follows on 19 February:

...Since Sunday I have had my nose to the grindstone – in the office all day except for 20 min. or so for lunch round the corner. The great pressure of work just at present – the men are swarming from France to attend universities here – has entailed extra long hours. To-day I was up to my ears in work from 9:20 a.m. till nearly 7 p.m. My correspondence for three days had been almost neglected but to-day I caught up a great deal and expect tomorrow morning to get up to date. Many men are simply shipped over from France with imperfect papers by ignorant c.o.'s for education. The poor men are quite at sea, know nothing of British educational institutions and would sit all day asking advice. Then there are constantly other distractions, Dr. Tory asking me this and that, and now and again I have to abandon everything else to help him bring forth a report or an article. It is almost a turmoil I live in, and when I get home I will do nothing but breathe constant sighs of relief that it is all done.

The pressure of work here continued for another three or four weeks. His letter 2 March detailed further activities:

The Khaki University is thriving mightily in spite of many difficulties internal and external. Sometimes I am tempted to get mad with some people who are actuated by petty jealousies and animosities....

Canada's Khaki University was a unique educational venture which attracted much public interest. Tory was in constant demand as a speaker and writer of articles on the subject, as Burt noted in the following letter of 25 March 1919:

I am really in a villainous temper for I have a filthy cold and my head feels exactly like a block of wood. Colds, however, are very fashionable around here now – due I believe to very unseasonable cold weather. Col. Tory is not immune. He was down only from lunch till tea. He had promised an article for the Empire Review and forgot about it till the last moment. I saw he was in no state to manage it so I took over the task. ... It was quite amusing – Dr. Harrison head of MacDonald College walked in in the midst of it, and the last time he saw me I was wrestling with a similar task – last December – when Dr. Tory on the eve of his departure for France remembered he had promised Galsworthy an article for his paper. Don't mention this business of article writing outside, for Dr. Tory is supposed to be the writer and signs them....

The record of servicemen in the universities proved highly satisfactory. 'Several of our students at British Universities,' Burt wrote, 'are covering themselves with glory – heading class lists, being drawn by professors into special research, etc.'[12] He must have found this result of his efforts a compensation for laborious days, uncomfortable train travel, and above all the homesickness and restlessness to which he refers in almost every letter to Mrs Burt. By the end of June his work, and that of the Khaki University, was over, and he was able to leave for home. President Tory and his associates had the satisfaction of having created a service which contributed to the development of similar work among the armed forces of New Zealand, Australia, the United States, and Great Britain, to the maintenance of morale during the confused process of demobilization, and to the encouragement of many young Canadians to complete educational programs at home which they might not have undertaken without the stimulus of this opportunity.[13]

4

London Days

Burt's months in London with the Khaki University coincided with the period of the Peace Treaty negotiations and with a year of marked political and industrial unrest in the United Kingdom. These public issues were very much in his mind, and the constant references in his letters reveal much of his political and social philosophy at this time. He found relaxation and stimulation in visits with English and Canadian friends with similar interests. Other evenings were spent in extensive reading.

The Britain of 1919 had changed greatly from that of post-Edwardian times when Burt had studied at Oxford. The war and its aftermath had deepened class conflicts in the country and had produced a ferment of reformist and revolutionary attitudes which were beyond the capacity of the coalition government to comprehend. No consistent and comprehensive program was developed by Lloyd George's ministry to cope with labour unrest, and the conflict between corporate economic interests and those who sought a greater degree of social and economic equality. The general election of 1918 was conducted by the government on the basis of such conflicting slogans as 'A Country Fit for Heroes to Live In,' 'Hang the Kaiser,' make Germany bear 'the Whole Cost of the War,' and 'the Menace of Bolshevism.' The curious mixture of Conservatives and unprogressive Liberals who comprised Lloyd George's cabinet was incapable of devising an industrial policy which would be fair to the working class. The Labour party achieved its greatest electoral success to date, with over 2 million supporters, 22 per cent of the total votes cast. Its campaign was based for the first time on a program, *Labour and the New Social Order*, compiled by the Fabian, Sidney Webb. But although it became the largest opposition party, its parliamentary performance was indifferent.

In many industrial centres labour resorted to direct action. There were alarming strikes in the Clyde area where the engineers and shipworkers demanded a 40-hour week. Even policemen were sufficiently dissatisfied that strikes or threats of strikes occurred, and in Liverpool the government called in the troops. More formidable was the threat of a strike by the coal miners. The government threatened the use of troops, then appointed a royal commission and promised to implement their recommendations, but subsequently repudiated this promise. The railwaymen were also restive and resorted to strike action later in 1919. The Red Scare, which so alarmed the Establishment, coupled with the resentment of the workers over inadequate housing, meagre and poor food, the high cost of heating, and low wages, produced an explosive mixture.

Burt's assessments of economic and political conditions in Britain at this time are to be found in the following letters, which indicate that his observations were radicalizing him to a marked degree.

January 29, 1919

Conditions in England are now and will be quite serious, for labour unrest is deep and widespread. Some fear a real revolution shortly. The general feeling seems to be that there must be a very radical change in the whole scheme of things in the immediate future. If this is not accomplished by regular means it will in all probability be brought about by force, but I do not think accompanied by violence. The old system of the distribution of wealth and the conditions of labour are doomed, and if statesmanship is exercised no one will be injured really and the working world will be regenerated. The toiler must labour fewer hours and under more liberal conditions. He will not be ruled autocratically as he has been by his employer, but must have some governing say in the environment and manner of his work. The wages system is only a makeshift and strikes and rises in wages are no solution because the level of prices fluctuates. Some solution by which 'real' wages are substituted for 'nominal' wages must be found (nominal – money wages, real – what they are worth in purchasing power) by establishing a fixed relation between a set and recognised standard of living and the remuneration necessary to sustain it. This is a most difficult problem and will be followed by another – the readjustment of this equation from time to time. Then there is also the problem of accumulated wealth – inherited fortunes and large incomes. A readjustment here would give our old society a new lease of life. Ideally inheritance and bequest should be abolished, but there are many practical difficulties. They could be limited much more than they are at present. Profits and large incomes must be taxed very much more heavily than at present. Indeed confiscation may be necessary to a certain extent. The present distribution of wealth is too uneven. Land of course in England is a crying problem. The owners of land in the future must regard themselves less as absolute owners and more as trustees for the nation. Do you think I am a Bolshevik? Really however such a revolution peacefully carried out will alone save English and other societies sooner or later from Russian Bolshevism....

March 9, 1919

...I am experiencing a curious conflict. On the one hand I sympathize heartily with the pressing desire of the working class for the elevation of their standard of living. It is unjust that such a large portion of mankind should have such a disproportionately small amount of pleasure. There should be more compensation for their work being a task. Moreover the existing distribution of wealth is unjust. The disproportion is greater than the difference of merit. But on the other hand a fear battles with this sympathy. In the past you see again and again in an ever recurring cycle, liberty awakening, struggling painfully, conquering, misusing its victory, descend into license and end in dissolution, out of which in turn a new power arises creating order. Is it not the same as ever? The present is only a little point in the continuous stream of time. The rising of the lower classes under the inspiration of a more or less developed socialism is largely materialistic – a search for happiness in a readjustment of material things and conditions. Will their reign, which is inevitable, not be unfavourable to the finer things which are not practical in the vulgar sense – which are a nobler adornment of real life than the luxury of worldly goods? I fear for the ideal, the intellectual. The vast machine of the modern world is ever more complicated till it is almost impossible to regulate it consciously, and yet this is becoming every more necessary with the appearance within – here and there – of new formidable forces which if not controlled and adjusted in harmony with the whole, will surely wreck it. So I fear the coming dissolution but have no forshadowing of the power that is to emerge from it. Do you call me a pessimist? I hope not, for in spite of it all life is worth living, for it is like a work of art that may be improved....

Thus, like most intellectuals, Burt was uncomfortable in a society dominated by materialist values, whether the domination was a product of middle class aquisitive capitalism, or of proletarian welfare statism. Nor has the dilemma been resolved in their minds during the last half century.

To Burt, at this time, parliamentary institutions seemed incapable of dealing with the contemporary economic crisis and with increasingly complex forces in modern industrial society; party politics and the existing political structure had become irrelevant. On both sides of the Atlantic before and during the war years there was much theorizing by critics of the democratic state as it existed at this time – the chief targets of criticism being the party system, unbridled individualism, and majority rule. Various remedies for the complaints were advocated, and some liberal-minded thinkers preached the virtues of the pluralist state, where interest groups would have greater autonomy. In his home province the leader of the United Farmers of Alberta, Henry Wise Wood, under the pressure of agrarian discontent, was articulating his idea of group government, which shortly thereafter was to destroy the system of bipartisan politics in the province.[1] Burt expressed his own views in the following terms:

March 23, 1919

...The greatest need of the day is for organizing genius and the greatest problems are no longer political but economic. Government is of necessity coming to regard its greatest problems to be those of the production and distribution of wealth. To this end the existing form of government, a relic of the past, patched and remade in parts, is far from being able to cope with the situation. Our house of commons is a relic of days long ago when the districts represented by the members were each distinct, more or less self-sufficient units of society. The basis was geographical, the town and the country each with its corporate existence. But with generations have appeared new and more vigorous and vocal units which quite overshadow these old moribund ones. The new units are those bound by common economic interests and the most pressing present day problems arise out of the relation between these units. A great industrial parliament, in which the professions as well as the trades and business would be represented as such, would square very much more closely with existing needs. In fact what we want is an industrial parliament to replace our moth-eaten political parliament. But we are the slaves of our forefathers because inertia is as important a factor in human life as in physical. The task ahead is a stupendous one. In the past our economic life resembled a machine which regulated itself automtatically in some respects very well – particularly in determining what goods and how much of each would be produced. With countless competing producers this was the natural result of each seeking his own gain. But this is no longer possible. The labour world has organized with sufficient strength to throw the machine out of gear and now we face the appalling task of adjusting and regulating this stupendous machine in full consciousness. How it can be done the Lord only knows. Whenever I have had too much dinner I fear the result will be failure and chaos. It would be easier if there were not so many prejudices current in society. Miss Bowers nearly made me say "damn" to her face. She was very loquacious and disdainful of the lower class – they were getting good wages and as they did not know how to spend their money, should not have any more – their whole moral standard was infinitely lower than that of the middle and upper classes. She was aghast when I asked her what was going to happen to her dear England if it were true that the vast majority of the nation were such as she depicted them. I was nearly rude enough to ask her how she would like to have to keep a family on the mere existence a "tommy's" wife has been getting through the war. I am sure she thinks I am a Bolshevist...

For a time he had high hopes of Lloyd George, but soon became disenchanted. He was initially pleased by the Prime Minister's attack on Lord Northcliffe, who was advocating harsh peace terms for Germany. Northcliffe was the first press lord to substitute interestingly presented news for long reports of political speeches and weighty editorials, and this was what the working and lower middle classes wanted, although only slightly over half of English households subscribed to a daily newspaper of any type.[2]

April 20, 1919

...Lloyd George's attack [on 16 April] on the Northcliffe press is the thunderclap which promises the present freeing of a surcharged atmosphere. Northcliffe deserved it and more. The syndicated press which he personifies is a standing menace, for it creates public opinion and deceives the public into believing they thought it out themselves. But more than this. Ll[oy]d G[eorge] has been wandering into a far country with unnatural companions. His present government is a pasteboard structure in no way representing the people or their needs of today. The people are radical and in their hearts are crying for radical reforms – a peaceful revolution. I think his blow from the shoulder means that at last he has seen it and is going to slough off the present unnatural government of worn out or incapable or unknown politicians, to organize a strong national government that will build strong from the foundations. England needs to pass through changes as great as France in 1789. He will do it....

Beginning in 1919, the British worker was caught between the millstones of rising prices and lagging wage increases, combined with a severe housing shortage, which aroused Burt's humanitarian sympathies:

June 29, 1919

...The next chief interest of the hour is the Labour Conference where they voted for direct action i.e. strikes to force the government into a policy of 'hands off Russia.' Many are alarmed at this threat of using unconstitutional methods to gain political ends. Some of the papers are not kind to the Labour World. They do not see that every large effective measure of reform in England since Catholic Emancipation 1829 has been carried as a result of the use or threat of force. It is nothing new. That is the madness of it. Another thing they fail to see is that the present government which was based on grand election promises has been comparatively marking time. The Government is responsible for much. If the people were crazy enough to transform the election into an orgy of vengeance, the elected of the people should have realized the situation of the country and set about bravely to effect some very necessary reforms. But the world is going to the Dogs. The complexity of society and government has completely outgrown the development of human ability to manage it and we are like to come a cropper as a result. ... Of course capital is necessary but the holding of it in large blocks by private individuals for selfish ends is not necessary. ... Violent revolution and seizure would be bad, so would full compensation (such as for land and mines) for it would only transform not remove the evil. The best way I think is by progressive taxation – leaving some fruits to individual enterprise but taking more and more for the state. Death duties should be heavier and if direct heirs fail, property in case of intestacy should revert to the state. But this is only the dull machinery. We need a new spirit of service for the state. We have, due to the form of our political development, over-emphasized rights at the expense of duties. We need to emphasize that duties are proportional to ability....

This humanist position was in part a product of his own spiritual quest as a young man, and in part a disenchantment with contemporary institutionalized Christianity. Reporting a conversation with London friends, a disillusioned clergyman and his wife, he declared:

... The Church has suffered by the best men leaving it. Up to a certain point this is cowardice. But a time may be reached when this ceases to be – when the balance of good lies outside and it ceases to be worth while remaining in to save it.[3]

This was a common reaction of many British and Canadian intellectuals at the time, as the experience of James S. Woodsworth and others indicates. On 29 June Burt returned to the topic:

In a few conversations of late I have poured out my scorn upon the Churches – shipwrecks of the past because they could not navigate modern strange waters. I have analyzed the church of today and extracted the following formula 2 parts spiritual – 1 part gregarious instinct, all in a solution of perverse self-deceit. But poisons may do good sometimes. It would be folly to shake the faith of those who lack the vigour or ability (excuses valid almost solely in middle or old age) to find a better. I think Christianity as we have known it is rapidly dissolving and that before we reach old age it will play a very much smaller part in the great game of life than since its foundation.

Yet despite his strictures, Burt was not unaware of new life stirring in the Church. Commenting on an address by Dr William Temple, he described him as 'one of the greatest forces in the new and rising generation of the Church of England' – an accurate prediction.[4] It is clear that throughout his life he was never a sterile sceptic; rather, religion in its philosophical dimension was always a vital element in his thinking. Half a century later, Malcolm Muggeridge was to express himself in almost identical terms:

For me the only great joy is understanding. This means being attuned to God, to the moral purpose of the universe, to the destiny of the human race that I belong to, to the things that are good – this is joy, and it is of course experience.[5]

On the position of women in society, Burt had shed most of the vestiges of Victorian middle class ideology, if indeed he ever possessed them prior to his marriage. Writing on Christmas Day 1918, he commented:

Your letter of the 19th raised the question ... of the economic position of woman. I agree with you that the conditions that have subsisted are not good or right, and also that the solution is difficult, for making a home and raising a family is something hard to combine with making money to keep the family. Some say that the solution lies along the line of paying someone, a nurse, etc. to look after the children. But this may be good for some. It certainly does not suit me, for I think it eliminates one of the most beautiful things in life. Certainly I agree that no woman on marrying should be obliged to give up her career and that every woman as every man should be trained for a career, also that it might often be wiser for the woman to be the wage earner and the man the home maker. Though I think the reverse condition will always be much commoner....

As an historian, Burt had a special interest in the momentous decisions which were being made in Paris during 1919. He had approved Wilson's 4 July (1918) speech at Mount Vernon, where the President had sum-marized allied war aims: 'What we seek is the reign of law, based on the consent of the governed and sustained by the organized opinion of mankind.'[6] On 16 March 1919, Burt wrote as follows:

The chief interests here are Paris and the investigation into the coal mining industry. Feeling here is not at all like that of the Bulletin editorial you sent or your diatribe against Wilson and the Americans. All here look to him to hasten the coming of peace and its establishment upon the justest foundation. For here at closer range people see the terrible difficulties that may easily arise from the clash of national interests and aspirations within the ranks of the allies. An independent disinterested arbiter is necessary. England is tremendously unfortunate and handicapped in that several of her colonies are receiving considerable additions of territory. ... More than any other man perhaps, Wilson is possessed of the general confidence.

A week later he returned to the same theme:

...People here are now beginning to worry a bit over Paris and the European situation since the turning over of Hungary to the Bolshevists. The whole mess is simply the result of what comparatively few people have been able to see – the almost impossibility of making the interests of the different states to coincide even for an appreciable time. The present trouble is a healthy shock to the empty headed fools who have thought it would be easy to straighten out the world's problems in a short while at Paris, and a partial awakening to the fact that larger politics are so tangled and involved by geographical conditions and the mixing of races, that in undoing one wrong you only make another. ... Compromise is necessary. It is also perhaps a shock to the faith in a league of nations. I fear few in America, France or England would be willing to fight to straighten out the Roumanian boundary of Hungary, and very naturally. You cannot make a new heaven and a new earth in one day. National characteristics grow, they are not made and remade. It is a question of time, time, time!

A conversation with family friends of Mrs Burt living in Finchley aroused his unspoken ire ('Rest assured I was very polite'), and prompted these observations:

April 6, 1919

...Imperialism – the instinct of one nation to dominate over others – is inherent in all peoples. Sometimes it breaks out here and sometimes there. All have been guilty. Moreover nations differ so vitally in character and interest that the mass of one race cannot understand that of another to which it may be opposed or even connected by alliance. People cannot see this – they think other people must be like themselves and when they find they are not, they put the difference down to wickedness. The clash of interests and ambitions at Paris today finds a very close parallel in the Congress of Vienna – the same desires for increased territory and punishment of the victim – the same deadlock due to conflict of interests and desires. In fact in some ways the situation is worse. There is perhaps as great if not greater eagerness for vengeance as in 1815. But it would require the return of the Kaiser and a terrible renewal of the war to present the same justification.[7]

Burt saw very clearly that the dynamic nature of modern society precluded 'permanent' solutions in international affairs, and that constant adjustments of the peace settlements of 1919 would be necessary in the future. 'There are fundamental clashes of desires and interests and imagined interests,' he wrote, 'which cannot be definitely solved.'

You can solve them one way, but you only create by that solution new and difficult problems. ... Paris will give us peace in our time I hope, but not for all time.[8]

Unfortunately, British, Canadian, and French political leaders in the twenties made the maintenance of the status quo the chief article of their political faith, with disastrous results for mankind.

Burt was not affected by the growing hysteria over Communism.

April 30, 1919

...The Russian situation is very suspicious. The newspapers are unanimously loud in their condemnation of Bolshevism. They announce the Bolshevist power tottering to its fall, but at the same time we retire before it – withdrawing from Odessa and planning to evacuate Archangel and the Murmansk coast. There is a vigorous life in Russia which is too sustained to be explained by the tirades of the press. Coleman's brother told me a friend of his had travelled, after living a while under the supposedly bloodthirsty Bolshevists, from Moscow to Vladivostock and had been treated only with courtesy. Indeed there is internal war but of a particular type – a war on all who are not engaged in any labour which may be directly or indirectly useful to society but who are living "independently" that is upon their money – really parasites. ... Of course in some ignorant minds the cry is simply against capital and is interpreted as heralding the destruction of society. Capital however is fundamental – the real question is the ownership and control of it. This in the past has been too much in the hands of individuals and too little in those of the state or society....

About the time he penned these lines the Winnipeg General Strike began. The strike had overtones of revolutionary rhetoric, but in reality was a struggle for jobs and a peaceful readjustment in the relations of labour and capital. But to the Canadian economic élite and to the political establishment it was Bolshevism, and they reacted by suppressing civil liberties and smashing the strike, but not its objectives, which were to be almost universally accepted in the years to come.

As the date of the publication of the Treaty of Versailles drew near (9 May 1919), Burt described the state of opinion in Britain.

May 4, 1919

...Every interest here seems in breathless suspense awaiting the publication of the peace terms and the action of Germany. I think I detect the growth of a juster frame of mind though some still make a parade of ridiculous demands. No adequate reparation can be made for war. The greatest danger is that too much will be taken, to the material injury of Germany, which will reflect injuriously upon us, to the creation of a spirit of revenge, and to our own moral injury. I am afraid that the present settlement will be relatively less just than that of France a century ago. But behind Germany lies an extremely complicated Europe with unalterably conflicting rights. ... The acts of nations are almost entirely pure selfishness. For the most part they try to clothe them with motives of broad justice and right. But it is more self deception than general deception. Because each is different in character and interests each is bound to suspect the others. England is very unfortunate. She cannot help herself in appearing as the head of an Empire that has gained more territory than all the rest put together. ... Yet as time goes on and the bonds of alliance relax there will appear peoples on the continent to accuse England of being always Napoleon's "perfidious Albion" – pretending to fight for the justice of Europe but really reaping a great harvest overseas.

His final words on the subject, as he prepared to depart for Canada, were prophetic: 'Well, the peace is signed at last – a rotten peace that will cause much trouble unless it is soon mended by the League of Nations.'[9]

Burt's reading during his sojourn in London was almost exclusively in the field of French history, particularly in the period of the French Revolution and Napoleon, for which he purchased numerous multi-volume works.[10] These included Albert Sorel ('He is most penetrating and brilliant – an extremely difficult matter in a sustained work'),[11] Lavisse and Rambaud, Vandal, Chateaubriand, Lanfrey ('written 50 years ago and yet perhaps the best life of Napoleon by a Frenchman'), Taine, P.P. Segur ('It is good to read partial accounts if they are well written – and of course one reads both sides'), Thiers, and Gustav Le Bon. The latter's *Psychology of Revolution* he found 'very suggestive.'

The working of psychology, especially mass psychology, has not been sufficiently recognized by writers of history. ... We need more of this method of approach. The mere study of documents is insufficient. The historian of the future must know more of the principles underlying the working of the human mind and human conduct.

Of the various biographies of Napoleon he wrote: 'The extreme difficulty of forming a tempered judgment about Napoleon is due to the old conflict of state or political morality with personal and individual morality, complicated by the clash between liberty on the one hand and prosperity, order and glory on the other.' This intensive study program perfected his reading knowledge of French and heightened his enthusiasm for European history during the period 1789–1815.

Why should I not tackle this period [he wrote on 20 April] which attracts me so, and for a few years devote the most of my time to it? It has the supreme value over other periods of presenting a highly concentrated history of all Europe in a few years. There is a tremendous mass of printed material available.

This inclination received the encouragement of Professor George Wrong, who was visiting Britain at this time on Khaki University business.[12]

Burt's views on historiography are expressed in a letter of 9 March 1919, prompted by his reading of Sorel:

...He takes long views of history and connects up distant but similar effects by unearthing deep and permanent causes. That grander style of history appeals to me more and more. The present American tendency – it was common also in Germany before the war – of digging in one little corner should be left for the painstaking but unenlightened toiler – the kind that denies the existence of any inspiration except perspiration. Big minds should essay big tasks. These of course demand much more knowledge and require much wider and more reading. But the rewards are infinitely greater. ... This, the synthetic view, appeals greatly to me. ... So the ambition is growing upon me to know more and more of history in the wider sense, and to postpone to a riper period the distillation of this knowledge into published work....

April 30, 1919
...We in America are at times impatient with these beastly European peoples who apparently intentionally misunderstand each other and hate each other so cause perpetual strife. But the same mental attitude so strongly condemned is just as

strongly entrenched at home. What is the outlook of this old world! We talk so loudly about education doing so much. We prescribe it as a panacea for all ills. But the people supposedly the most educated – taking things largely – are no better. I suspect that we have made a great mistake in prescribing so beatifically without examining the quality of our medicine. It is a material education that we have developed and we are trusting blindly in a great God to bring all right, forgetting that the real and true God is in our minds and spirits. Education today could take many a good lesson from classic times, from Greece, Rome and the Renaissance, when character and mind in the broadest manner were prominent ideals. We have got lost in the mechanism of life, the nobility and beauty of life have faded from our vision. It is our duty to restore these as much as possible...

As is the case with most thoughtful graduates of Oxford and Cambridge, Burt felt that these communities of teachers and students most clearly approached his ideal, and he coveted something of their spirit and organization for the University of Alberta.[13] A conversation with one of his former Oxford lecturers who had been in intelligence work during the war is revealing.

May 4, 1919
...We discussed the new tendency so stimulated by the war for the government to call in trained minds for advice and assistance. He says they gave them quite a free hand. One thing very interesting was the value of the broadly trained mind as against the highly specialized trained man. They were able to approach and solve almost any problem that came up and were not cramped in their view by a narrow training. All said and done, I think the Oxford don the best of his type. He knows so much of so many things and does not make a parade of it. The atmosphere is exactly as Dr. Parkin[14] once described it to me – one of intellectual luxury, and it was a great treat to breathe it once more...

Though there was little hope that the University of Alberta, or any Canadian university for that matter, could be reconstructed on Oxford lines, Burt returned home in a positive frame of mind, committed to doing his best for the students and the institution as a whole.[15] He also brought home from his London experience and reflections an intense interest and concern for international relations, which remained a dominant concern in his subsequent academic career.

5

Scholar and Commentator

When Burt returned to Edmonton, the Department of History and Political Economy consisted of himself, Professor D.A. MacGibbon, and Morden H. Long. Long, a graduate of McMaster and a Rhodes Scholar of 1908, had been teaching at a high school in Edmonton before his appointment as lecturer in the history department in 1918.[1] Between the two historians a warm friendship developed. There was a sharp upturn in university enrolment in 1919–20, with nearly five hundred more students than the 618 who were on campus the previous year. History registrations reflected this over-all increase, and Burt taught three courses – British history beginning in the Tudor period, Canadian political and constitutional history, and an honours seminar on Europe from 1789 to 1815. During the year the honours program was revised to include seven or eight courses in history and a reading knowledge of French or German. Burt's course on Canadian history required four texts: Sir Charles Lucas's history of Canada from the discoveries to 1763, Egerton's *Canada Under British Rule*, Lord Durham's Report, and W.P.M. Kennedy's *Documents of the Canadian Constitution, 1759–1915*.

In the following year the departments of history and economics were separated, and Burt was promoted to associate professor. Tory remained the nominal head of the department. Burt offered four courses – two covering the entire period of British history, the Canadian undergraduate course, and an honours seminar on British history from 1603 to 1660. There were no graduate students – a university library of only 17,000 volumes was patently inadequate for this purpose.

In March 1921, Burt contributed a brief article to the student magazine, *The Gateway*, entitled 'Thoughts on the Russian Revolution.'[2] This article was a typical example of an activity which became a distinguishing feature of his career – to challenge students in other disciplines and the lay public with the practical value of historical knowledge and with the opportunities which historical study can provide in developing the faculty of judgment. This strongly-felt obligation to public service conjoined his personal inclinations with one of the basic principles upon which Henry Marshall Tory had established the provincial university. Throughtout the twenties Burt accepted speaking engagements in every corner of the province, and he was the chief contributor, outside the faculty of agriculture, of articles in *The Press Bulletin*, published by the Department of Extension. These articles dealt with such topics as the League of Nations, international affairs, and French-English relations in Canada.

The article on the Russian Revolution revealed his insight, sense of proportion, and commitment to the value of the historical approach to contemporary issues, which had been deepened by his wartime experiences in London. Writing at a time when 'the Red Scare' was still a powerful influence on public opinion in Canada and the United States, he urged his young readers to adopt a more objective and historically informed attitude.

The Russian Revolution [he wrote] is an epoch, perhaps the greatest, in modern history. ... Those who possess treasure and are possessed by fears see the red doom of our civilization stalking westward, while those who are burdened with little property or fear acclaim the rising of a new day.

But it was the phenomenon of revolution, and particularly the characteristics of the French Revolution, which would enable the observer to view the events of the Russian Revolution in proper perspective.

The great paradox of the French Revolution was the intimate conjunction of an ethereal idealism with a crass materialism. It exalted the best and debased the worst in men.

There was the same intellectual ferment and unrest, he noted, in the last half-century of Russian history as in France in the eighteenth century, the same rooted antipathy to monarchial absolutism, the same reliance on government to create new men and a new society, the same aspirations of an ignorant and oppressed peasantry, the same outbreak of mob violence, the same messianic zeal in exporting the revolution to neighbouring countries.

The Bolsheviks with the soviets are the Jacobins with their clubs. ... Their strength lies in three things; their fanaticism, their use of force, and last but not least patriotism roused by the hostility of foreign powers.

The outcome will be different and yet the same....

The year 1921 was a major turning point in Burt's career. It was obvious that further intellectual satisfaction and professional recognition would depend on research and publication, no matter how effective and brilliant his performance as a lecturer presenting 'the synthetic view' of the broad vistas of European and British history, of which there was ample evidence in the popularity of his courses. Despite his earlier strictures against 'the mean scholar who sorts out and arranges neatly the small details of a dark corner,'[3] he had come to realize that work of this type had its value and its scholarly rewards. The best historiography, he realized, combines the two elements. Wide acquaintance with historical forces and movements is vital in the selection and elucidation of a theme chosen for laborious, detailed investigation. At the same time, Burt never abandoned his enthusiasm for the broad perspectives of history, and this was expressed in the form of popular articles and public addresses, of which his article on the Russian Revolution was a typical example.

Since research in the primary sources of British and European history was impractical because of the inadequacies of the university library and the expense of overseas travel, he directed his attention to the investigation of a Canadian theme, 'the dual nationality of Canada, where public questions have so often been seen out of focus because viewed with only one eye – French or English.'[4] It was a congenial subject, since it possessed the philosophical dimension which Burt so much admired in European historical scholarship. But he was soon confronted with the limitations of the existing accounts on which his generalizations could be based. 'The inadequacy of the secondary authorities on the crucial period [of the conquest and post-conquest years] drove me to the Public Archives of Canada,' he wrote.[5]

Burt first visited the Archives after the end of the spring term in 1921, spending a month in research on the beginnings of British rule in Canada. By this time the acquisitions program of Arthur G. Doughty (1860–1936), Dominion Archivist since 1904, and of his predecessor, Douglas Brymner

(1823–1902), had built up a large body of significant source material relating to pre-Confederation Canada. But comparatively few historians had yet made use of the ore in this rich mine. Doughty had also 'worked out a system under which the Public Archives of Canada remained open all day and all night to accredited historians and research workers.'[6] This was to be a boon to Canadian historians. University teachers were not well paid, and there was no Canada Council to assist their research activities.[7] The arrangement was particularly significant in the depression years, which otherwise would have seen few if any significant publications in the field of Canadian history. With a growing family, Burt was often hard put to make ends meet during the 1920s, and his visits to Ottawa were in the plain living and high thinking tradition.

May 21, 1921

When I scribbled my last I had just secured but not got possession of my room. It was then being decorated. By evening I got in. It is much like a student's room in the U. of A. except that it has running water. My meals I get at a boarding house 'round the corner where hosts of clerks eat three times a day. The substance is much better than the style. The respectability of the place is guaranteed by 15 Y.M.C.A. lodgers who board there. I have added eggs and bacon to my usual breakfast. The terms are most reasonable as they would need to be after the way my money has disappeared. I ... pay $5. a week for my room. The board is $7. per week.

I plunged into the Archives yesterday afternoon at 2 p.m. and stayed till after 5. I was back after dinner for another three hours. Today I worked morning and afternoon. ... At the Archives I met an interesting French Canadian [Gustave Lanctot] who was just ahead of me and overlapped me at Oxford.[8] He has a post here – I believe second in command to Dr. Doughty the Archivist. He is writing books on the French Régime and spends his days and nights at the Archives. Though the hours are 9–12:30 and 2–5, I can work all night and Sunday too. I merely have to be sure I get enough books out in those hours. Your father and I are going round tomorrow morning and Lanctot is going to show us the whole place.

Before leaving Edmonton I made a list of the Archives Publications in the Alberta Library and have characteristically lost it. I enclose a full list of their publications. Would it be too much trouble to give it to Miss Calhoun or to Cameron[9] with a request to note on it what we have not got and return it to me as soon as possible? Some things are scarce and a few days may determine whether we secure or miss some of the lacking volumes. Dr. Doughty has promised to do what he can.

May 26, 1921

...Working away in the Archives this morning I was also accosted. Looking up I saw a strange face. It was that of Chester New, an old Toronto man who took his graduate work in Chicago with a year abroad. [10] He has been known to me and I to him for some time through MacGibbon and Long, after both of whom he warmly inquired. He has been some years collecting material for a Life of Lord Durham and will now be sitting across the table from me every day. We lighten our labours by little breaks discussing phases of Canadian history. I am pleased he has turned up, for I like him.

My task is mountainous. I have been writing for over nine hours today securing facts for only one detailed incident. Walker, a magistrate of Montreal and one of the English minority that followed the Conquerors into Canada, was assaulted in his own home by some carefully disguised soldiers in December 1764. There is no end of letters, writs, positions and legal examinations. The affair was never sifted out at the time and is still referred to as a mystery by modern writers. It caused Murray's recall, however, and is intimately linked up with the strained relations of English and French immediately after the Conquest. The last thing I copied tonight was a long document inspired by Walker. It is a thorough going indictment of Governor Murray and his whole Government, charging him with ruling tyranically and setting race against race. Of course it is violently biased. Tomorrow morning I dig into Murray's reply paragraph by paragraph.

...I do not expect to get much reading done for I can work nights and Sundays at the Archives, and I must make the most of having come so far for such a short time.

...I have a pleasant walk of about 10 minutes from here to the Archives....[11]

May 29, 1921

...It is very pleasant now sitting across the table with New. We have frequent minute chats and having a great deal in common, these little breaks are not vain conversation. He commends my purpose in digging through the sources of Canadian history....

I am really getting a lot of valuable material. It is slow work – I shall not be able to finish collecting the material for General murray's period of Government which is only to 1766. I think I will be able to clear up much that has been doubtful.

The next letter records the formation of the League of Nations Society in Canada, an event of considerable importance because Burt became deeply involved in the work of the Society in Alberta throughout the decade. It also led to his friendship with Sir Robert Borden, Sir George Foster, and the officers of the national organization in Ottawa.

May 31, 1921

I have just returned from an organization meeting of the League of Nations Society for Canada, which passed off very well. I will enclose a clipping in the morning if there is an account in the paper. I there met Dr. Tory who has just reached Ottawa from Toronto....

...I had a delightful chat with Mr. Adams, a most charming Scot. He says the abolition of the Conservation Commission, of which they were a part, was a piece of party politics. It was an important body with a number of highly paid specialists who aroused the jealousy of lesser-paid civil servants in the regular departments and also of the politicians who had little control over the Commission. We had also a good chat on Architecture in Canada....

The Conservation Commission had been created in 1909 with Clifford Sifton as chairman. It held its first meeting in 1910 and inaugurated a far-reaching program of scientific investigations on natural resources conservation, land use, industrial development, water pollution, and other matters, working in close co-operation with experts from the municipal, provincial, and federal governments and the universities. It issued recommendations for government action and published voluminous reports. Sifton resigned as chairman in 1918, and the Meighen ministry abolished the Commission early in 1921, despite the protests of the supporters of the Commission's work.

May 31, 1921 (continued)

Harvey from Winnipeg appeared yesterday in the Archives and we have now a pleasant trio. Of course I know and like Harvey of old. I am getting to know New better and begin to feel as if here were a good old friend. It adds delight to the work.

...I am collecting some good stuff which I think will enable me to produce a good article this winter on the beginnings of my problem right after the conquest....

June 3, 1921

It is true I have been sticking very close – but it is necessary if my short stay here is to allow me to utilise the material I collect without letting it lie suspended in mid-air for a year or so. I am limiting myself to Murray's Government. He succeeded to the command on Wolfe's death and became Governor on the conclusion of Peace. Three years later he was recalled. Those three years from the peace to his recall 1763–66 are about the most critical in Canadian history. He sought to win the hearts of the French to British rule, and at the same time saw rise up against him the bitter opposition of the few hundred British merchants in Canada. The latter in their desires to crush the French and treat them as a subject people planted the seeds of the conscious racial strife. Their relations with Murray are at present only vaguely known. I am tracing the origin of this clash and have discovered some valuable material which will enable me to clear up much that has been in doubt. To me Murray is standing out more and more as a real statesman and I have unearthed one very clear cause of quarrel which has hitherto been unnoticed and have been able to fix a pretty close date for its origin. But I would not be able to produce these results in an article until I had examined all the available material. This I can do I believe in my stay here – but only by spending every available hour upon it. I have gone through about 15 huge folio volumes of correspondence already. I have to plan it so that I will have several days at the end searching for loose strands that I have missed by the way. The bulk of the material I am examining is neither calendared, i.e. summarised roughly in the printed archive reports, nor indexed, i.e. having a table of contents for each volume. Thus I have to go through it all letter by letter. I should be able to produce a good article for the Canadian Historical Review. It is now 11:20 and I am fairly weary having worked there every evening this week but Tuesday....

June 18, 1921

...Yesterday noon New took me to lunch at the University Club where we had a good meal and a delightful chat with several others. So my noon hour was prolonged guiltily into the afternoon and we three stopped early for a chat and a stroll back to the city together. ... I returned to the Archives [this morning] to find that Underhill had been looking for me and that I had been demanded on the telephone. New insisted on my lunching with him again to meet Underhill that we might arrange a date for returning together....

June 21, 1921

...Yesterday I worked in the Archives till 1:30 when I went to dinner, read a little, wrote a note to Toronto and then met the trio at the University Club. We took the car to Rockliffe – walked round a little lake, found a pretty nook looking out over it, and indulged in light historical conversation. We all know each other pretty well and are very congenial, and so we had a most delightful time. The three of us in the Archives have really had a great time imparting our discoveries and view to each other and having many a laugh. On our return Harvey went off to have supper with his brother-in-law whose guest he is in Ottawa. He is a Deputy Minister. Frank Underhill entertained New and myself to supper in a pleasant Japanese restaurant. ... This morning we went through the Mint. Frank was to have come but did not appear. It is a great place. They melt the metal and purify it in crucibles heated by oil, then they pour it out into ingots an inch or two wide, a couple of feet long and as thick as your finger. These they put through tremendous rollers which roll it out into long ribbons just the thickness of the coin. From these the coin is punched. They are then softened by heating and being suddenly plunged into cold water. Then they are stamped by the dies. Finally they are all weighed and sounded carefully (except the coppers and 5¢ pieces) one by one. The balance for weighing is remarkable. We saw 25¢ pieces going through. The scales are manufactured in the mint in England and are as delicate as the finest chemical scales. They work automatically 3 sec. for each piece. The light, heavy, and exact weight coins are automatically separated. They all have to be sounded by hand. If there is a blister or crack they ring like lead.

June 23, 1921

...Tonight I am going back to the Archives in a last mad rush to finish. I fear I cannot get off tomorrow night. I have much material and am determined on one article at least. I have solved one mystery (the Walker affair) I think very neatly and fully, and have my judgment confirmed by a conversation with Wm. Smith the secretary of the Archives, who is a keen student of Canadian history.

William Smith (1859–1932) was educated at the University of Toronto and in 1913 was appointed to the Archives staff as deputy keeper of the public records. He was the author of three historical works of which the best known is his *History of the Post Office in British North America*. Burt developed a great admiration and affection for him, and Smith became his closest friend on the Archives staff.

Returning to Edmonton, Burt completed his first article for the *Canadian Historical Review* during the summer, which was published the following year under the title, 'The Mystery of Walker's Ear.' In this year (1921) he was promoted to full professor and, although Tory retained his connection for one more term, Burt became, in effect, the head of the department in 1921. In addition to carrying a full teaching load, he gave himself unstintingly to the life of the university as musical director of the choir for the Sunday morning services in Convocation Hall, as one of the lecturers for the Philosophical Society on the topic of international relations and the League of Nations, and as a member of the national subcommittee of the League of Nations Society for promoting its work in Canadian universities.[12]

Burt did not visit Ottawa in 1922, and during the 1922–3 academic year he was much involved in League of Nations Society activity. In an Armistice Day address, and in a speech delivered at one of the Sunday services in Convocation Hall in the spring of 1923, he presented cogent reviews of the functions and problems of the League and of actions taken during its brief existence which had solved a number of acute problems. These addresses,[13] the editor of *The Gateway* noted, 'are attracting much attention in the city,' and corrected impressions conveyed in the daily press.

The nature of the League [Burt declared] is often misunderstood. It is neither a superstate nor a powerless body. The Covenant is simply an agreement whereby the various member states forego some of their fullest freedom in the future for the good of themselves and the welfare of the world at large....

The difficulties of the League have been tremendous – enough to destroy it, were it not the sole hope of a shipwrecked world. It was born into an atmosphere surcharged with national hate and mistrust, an atmosphere arising out of the war and the peace settlement....

...More and more we are coming to see how faulty was the settlement of Europe effected at Versailles.

Burt stressed that naïve optimism and negative pessimism were equally inappropriate in estimating the prospects of an institution which 'represents the world as no other body ever has.' There was evidence, he thought, that universality of membership would ultimately be achieved.

But there is a grave danger. In these democratic days the breath of life of all government is public opinion. What is true of ordinary government is equally true of the League of Nations. Only in so far as it has the backing of a continuous and intelligent public opinion throughout the world can it hope to succeed. Here then lies a tremendous moral responsibility upon everyone of us. We must work out our salvation through the League; it will not work our salvation for us. If we fail to shoulder this great responsibility, we will stumble along the same old way which we all know leads to disaster.

In addition to his public addresses, Burt published two articles in the Extension Department's *Press Bulletin*,[14] reiterating this argument. In these and subsequent articles and addresses during the 1920s Burt was performing the function which today is almost monopolized by the newspaper columnist. The recent emergence of this class of journalist has overshadowed the former influence of the editor and of the few academics who assumed the role of commentators on national and international affairs.

Devotion to the interests of the League of Nations Society was expressed in travels around the province, and in the spring of 1924 the Extension Department published a booklet which he had prepared, *A Short History of the League of Nations*, which was suitable for use in schools or in discussion groups. Burt received an appreciative letter from Sir Robert Borden:

I have just read your "Short History of the League of Nations" and I hasten to send my warm congratulations. It is admirable in every way. ... You are entitled to the sincere thanks of all those who take an interest in the purpose of the League and who have some confidence in its usefulness.[15]

Burt viewed the League of Nations as a constructive force in the modern world, and he did not hesitate to stress its achievements in resolving potentially dangerous disputes. But he was quite aware of its limitations and did not believe that mankind had moved into a new era of perpetual peace. The pursuit of national interests and the emotional power of mob psychology were realities which he analyzed in an article entitled 'The Horoscope of Mars,' published in 1923 in *Queen's Quarterly* – in which his talents as a commentator on international affairs were never better displayed. The theme was the nature of war in the modern world – its endemic character, its effects on civilization, and the prospects for its elimination. The 'dark half of the horoscope of Mars' was evident, he argued, in deeply rooted characteristics of the society of sovereign states. There was the hard fact that the devices of arbitration, international conferences, and international law had not triumphed over resort to force, where vital interests were at stake. History was replete with examples of a great power or group of powers intervening to settle disputes, and would have to be accepted unless an international organization existed to prevent war. The principle of the sovereignty of the state was still operative, with the consequent 'unwillingness of states to curtail their full freedom of action.' The divergence of national interests might be mitigated to some extent, but differences based on ethnic and geographic factors were permanent. It was usually impossible 'to fix a frontier which does not violate some fundamental principle, racial, economic or military,' and compromise arrangements often became obsolete.

There were other threats to peace, among them mob psychology, which 'may be even more powerful in the future.' 'In proportion as governments are controlled by the mass of the people, it is possible that foreign relations will be guided less by cold calculation than by hot

passion, by mob impulse.' Still another consideration ignored by inter-
nationalists was 'the danger that any system of perpetual peace will lead to
the establishment of a static world' – a comfortable arrangement for the
beneficiaries of the status quo, but a grievous vexation to the discon-
tented. 'We have not yet learned to solve,' he pointed out, 'the gigantic
problem of harmonizing the vital element of growth with an artificial
system of order.' 'The pacifist ideal opens out the prospect of justice
sacrificed on the altar of peace.' Finally, on the dark side of the horoscope,
was the fact that war was 'an age-old instinct.'

It is a human institution older than private property and more ancient than
marriage. As its roots are deeper, is it not probable that it will outlive the sacred
right of private property and the honourable state of marriage?

Despite the pessimistic prognostication which it was possible to make,
with abundant historical evidence to support it, there was also the 'bright
half of the horoscope of Mars,' which was struggling for predominance.
The increasing destructiveness of modern weapons, the involvement of a
nation's whole population in a war effort, the increasing cost of arma-
ments, the danger of national bankruptcy, all suggested that 'war has been
approaching the point where it must swallow up civilization, or be
abolished by it.' Moreover, Burt argued, increasing economic interdependence provided a powerful self-interested motive for avoiding war.
Reinforcing this influence was the growth of international voluntary
organizations representing the common interests of scientists, scholars,
and trade unionists. Humanitarian activity and concern was also growing.

In so far as our feeling and our thought are focussed upon the problems of human
suffering and human betterment, we are evolving an ideal that takes precedence
over the limited and lower ideal of national welfare.

These influences were affecting men's ideas. The thought of war as a
glorious thing 'has been buried deep in the mud of Flander's fields.' The
sense of international morality that was beginning to grow and the increasing acceptance of the concept of a divided sovereignty were hopeful
signs. 'A final solution may not be attainable, yet something can be accomplished,' Burt claimed. Progress could be made by reducing trade barriers
and by revising school curricula to curb national prejudice, to demonstrate the relation between the evolution of warfare and the rest of life,
and to stress humanitarian ideals.

6

The Old Province of Quebec

The spring of 1923 found Burt again at the Public Archives, for nearly two months of continuing research on the theme which he had begun to investigate in 1921 and which in following years was to result in seven significantly original articles in the *Canadian Historical Review* and the *Transactions of the Royal Society of Canada*. The culmination of this effort came in 1933 in *The Old Province of Quebec*, which his distinguished student, Dr Hilda Neatby, a noted specialist in this field, has described as 'a work so thorough and detailed that it is still without a rival as the standard work of reference for the period.'[1] 'Had I known how many years it would take,' the author noted in his foreword, 'I might not have begun it. But I could not leave off once I had started.'[2]

As before, his letters to Mrs Burt gave a detailed running commentary on his activities and relationships in Ottawa.

June 18, 1923

Here I am at the above address [the YMCA] for the present. It is not exactly what I would desire in every respect, but it is good, and I have saved the time and trouble in looking for a room in a private boarding house....

This morning I met Dr. Tory right after breakfast, and with him attended the annual meeting of the League of Nations Society, which sat both morning and afternoon. Sir Robert Borden presided in the morning and Sir George Foster in the afternoon session. The meeting gave a great reception to the account of our doings in Edmonton, and requested Dr. Tory to prepare a detailed account to be laid before the Executive Committee, for they said that a knowledge of the work we had done and were doing would be of great value to the rest of Canada. Sir Robert Borden took me to lunch in the Rideau Club and put me up there for a week; in the afternoon he had my name added to the list of the General Committee for Canada....

Beside the people mentioned the only other person whom I have met so far is McArthur, Morison's[3] successor at Queen's as professor of colonial history. As he is running the Queen's summer school at the Archives, I will see more of him, and will be able after a while to give you a better impression of him.

Duncan McArthur (1885–1943) became an intimate friend whose scholarship Burt greatly admired. He had been educated at Queen's University and was a member of the staff of the Public Archives from 1907 to 1912. In this capacity he had assisted Doughty in editing *Documents Relating to the Constitutional History of Canada, 1791–1818*, one of the large volumes of primary sources being published by the Archives. He left the Archives to practice law for a number of years, and then accepted an appointment as professor of history at Queen's in 1922. In this capacity he inaugurated a summer school course in Ottawa, where his students used the collections in the Archives. Following McArthur's appointment as Deputy Minister of Education for Ontario in 1934, Queen's continued to offer the course till 1940. In addition to the widely-used school history of Canada, to which Burt refers in subsequent letters, he contributed chapters to *Canada and Its Provinces* and to the Canadian volume in the *Cambridge History of the British Empire*.

June 22, 1923

After finishing my last epistle, I went over to the House of Commons and heard Sir Lomer Gouin move the second reading of a bill on the Lake of the Woods waterways, and the Hon. Arthur Meighen deliver an incisive speech against it....

Last night I returned after supper for the first time to the Archives and got in a good evening's work. New was here as he usually is....

The Archives are busy now. McArthur has 9 or 10 students here in the Queen's summer school, George Brown[4] whom I knew in the Tanks has just turned up, and Innis[5] a new man on the economics staff at Toronto, is working here with the assistance of his wife. He is huge and youthful, his wife square and likewise – both pleasant people. But I like New best. We do not breakfast together, for we both rise at uncertain hours, but we have our lunch and supper together, and this makes the great capital city seem much less formidable.

June 25, 1923

Here I am again at my accustomed seat – I have a big book on the chair to get the right height for my machine, and to keep my trousers pure and undefiled from the cheap varnish on the chairs. I have just returned from supper and my accustomed rest thereafter with a pipe and book, and the place is delightfully quiet, – though uncomfortably hot, as it has been almost all the time since I arrived in this corrupt capital.

After meals I have been stretching out on my bed and spending a little while reading Chapais, Cours d'Histoire du Canada, and am at present finishing the first volume. Chapais is professor at Laval, Quebec, and, so I am told, was made Senator on the strength of this book.[6] They should have made him Premier, I find myself in such agreement with him.

I have been pounding away on my machine so much and so hard that I have split one of my fingernails, as I used to do when thumping the piano for Gypsy Smith in Massey Hall. But this means that I am finding some good stuff. For a day now I have been working through 100 pages of documents bearing on the beginnings of strife between the civil and the military authorities in Quebec, and it is very amusing. It began with an Ordinance that all persons must carry a lantern at night in the streets. All went well until one merchant disobeyed, Allsopp was his name. He was accosted by a sentinel and asked for his light. He pointed to the Moon, according to one evidence. In another document, he finally produced a paper folded up like a lantern, and said, as he took this from his pocket, that he was obeying the Ordinance, because the latter did not say that the lantern must be lit – which was true. It was amusing also to find that Quebec had speed laws in 1764. No one could gallop on horseback, or drive vehicles faster than a walk. The fine was 10/, and if this was not paid, the offender had to work four days in repairing the highways. In the same Ordinance I found a reference to the origin of sleigh bells, which I thought were wholly poetic or something like that. This Ordinance required 'at least six horse bells to be affixed to the horse harness, or the said sled or slay' – the honk of the silently approaching motor! Already I have 80 pages of notes typed as close as this neat little machine will let my Scottish-? soul do it.

I am losing some of my friends here. New is off to Toronto tonight. He has been here since early in May. Innis and his wife go at the end of this week...

Today is election day in Ontario, and the elections are a great gamble. No one seems certain of what will be the next government. The results are to be announced tonight at the Y. where they will be gathered by a private wire and put on a big bulletin board. There is to be music too – I suppose to smooth over the political discords and make people take what comes without too much bitterness of thought. Really the situation is most unfortunate. Drury[7] is the best man, but his chances are about as small as I feel some times when you get mad with me.

June 27, 1923

After writing my last to you, I went to the House of Commons, where I heard Meighen baiting Graham, the Minister of Railways, and drawing upon himself the ire of the veteran Fielding. I am told that as long as that Fox Terrier who leads the Conservative Party remains leader, the Liberals are sure to remain in power. He is so cocksure, so carping, so irritating. McArthur, New and I had a good political argument the other night, and we were all agreed that if the Conservatives got another head, the Liberals might split, the Quebec Liberals being reabsorbed into the Conservative fold, and the real Liberals joining with the Progressives to make a hopeful party. Then came the results of the Ontario elections. They put great heart into the Conservatives in the House here, for here they are a small band. I am not pleased with the results....

Though New has gone, and Innis is going tomorrow, I am at no loss for friends ... McArthur, too, is quite a jolly fellow. I see quite a bit of him and we have good fun together. Somehow or other he ever tempts me to jolly him, and we hit it off quite well. Like most other Queen's people, he is an incorrigible Liberal, and that gives us an opportunity of great argument. Another good friend is Mr. Smith, the Secretary of the Archives. He is somewhere in his "sixties," is small of stature and very dull of hearing. But he has the spirit of perpetual youth, is very large by nature and penetratingly acute in mind. He is one of the best natured men that I have ever met. Unlike most deaf people, who are morose, he has an ever bubbling sense of humour. When he laughs, which is very quietly, his eyes close and his mouth becomes like Forrie's when she is in the same mood. He is a wonderful talker, and it is a delight to listen to him, for his knowledge is stupendous. For a quarter of a century he has spent much of his time just steeping himself in Canadian history. I doubt if there is anyone else living who is so familiar with the manuscript material of our history. Even the minor characters, that flit now and then across the stage, he has traced, and he can talk of them as if they were his bosom friends. ... In the evening, when I had just got to work again, in he dropped, "Well here you are again!" No smoking is a rigid rule here, but Mr. Smith is wedded to his pipe. "If you're not busy, let's just close this door and have a smoke." He did it and we lit up, and talked and talked, and when we woke up it was 11:10. He is greatly concerned, as I am about the prospects of Canadian history. ... "You know, New, McArthur and you are my hope" he said as we were walking home together. For more than two years he has been spending all his time in collecting and writing a history of Labrador. It is for the Department of Justice, which has charge of the boundary dispute between Canada and Newfoundland. ...

Then he is going to tackle a Constitutional History. I believe he is due to retire soon, so that his scribal ambitions may ere long have freer scope.

June 30, 1923

I am very glad that I did not attempt to use all the material that I gathered a couple of years ago, for the continuance of the search is throwing new light on the fragments which I gleaned two years ago. Moreover it is all soaking in, a most important thing, for the only way to write history is to steep one's self in the documents of the period. Already, however, I see an article or two that I may throw off in my nebular flight.

All this afternoon, I was going through the case of a Jew, Eleazer Levy.[8] It was so interesting that the afternoon went by before I knew it....

...I also collected quite a lot of material on the beginnings of trouble under Carleton, and have reversed my judgment on one famous case of Carleton's action. All the texts speak of the opposition on his arrival as factious, but after examining all the material, I have come to the opinion that he was wrong, indeed that he was very high-handed and unjust. I discussed the matter with Mr. Smith and he agrees with me. Perhaps I will write an article on this before I write on anything else.

So here I am glorying in the riches of this place. It is far from being dull. It is often quite exciting, searching through documents tracing something out and wondering where it will end. Will Levy get justice? I am itching to know. It is also quite amusing. Every volume brings a laugh. Complaints about "Hoggs" running about the streets of Quebec to the distress of many good citizens, the advertisement of the bone of a whale that had been "wrecked" in the Gulf, etc. are as good as Punch or Life.

...I was the guest of Mr. Biggar[9] at dinner in the dining room of the Houses of Parliament. Biggar is a cousin of the Edmonton man, and is the European representative of the Canadian Archives. Just at present he and Dr. Doughty have exchanged jobs. The restaurant is in a most glorious place – above the House of Commons. We had a table by the window, and from our chairs we could look down on the surging Ottawa and over many miles of beautiful country. After dinner, the session bells clanged everywhere through the buildings, and we rushed down to the House of Commons, to hear the debates which had just begun. Till nearly half past eleven, we listened to a debate upon the coming imperial conference. Some of it was most amusing. S.W. Jacobs (Member for the Holy Land – Montreal) wanted the Prime Minister at the conference to promise the vote to the Hindoos in Canada and press for it elsewhere. But this suggestion only let loose a storm from the Western Mountains....

July 2, 1923

The placid routine of my life goes on, my only excitement being in that routine. I find my digestion greatly assisted by a rest for half an hour after every meal – I frequent a restaurant near the Y.M.C.A. There in one of the topmost rooms I stretch me out after meals, light up my old friend, and read. At present I am busy with a book lent me by Mr. Smith – Dix Ans. It is the history of 1840 to 1850, and was written shortly after the time by one of the most modest authors of whom I have heard – Gérin-Lajoie.[10] It is a wonderfully fine piece of work, and would have been published when it was written, had not a friend, who had a poor book coming out on the same subject, requested him to hold his back so that the sale of the other work might not be hurt. So the manuscript remained locked up in a drawer for more than a generation, known only to a few. Then in 1888, it was given to the public by his widow. I would like to be able to do two things like that, but I fear that I can do neither. As it is a big volume, I expect that I will be reading it for some time, but I am not impatient to finish it – it is so good.

Burt was too modest in his estimate of his capability in comparison with Gérin-Lajoie. His *Old Province of Quebec* and *The United States, Great Britain and British North America from the Revolution to the Establishment of Peace After the War of 1812* are monumental achievements of historical scholarship, based on a painstaking examination of thousands of documents and supporting a narrative distinguished by balance, clarity, and vigour.

The rest of the time [he continued] I spend here, and every day I glean some more sheaves. Yesterday and today (it is now 4:20) I have been copying some documents from the Shelburne Papers. They are unsigned and bear no date, but they are valuable. Here is why. For a long time, ever since the American Revolution, there has been a theory, only now and then protested against, that the Quebec Act was the product of the coming of the American Revolution. In short, it is this, that the British Government, seeing the coming trouble with the American Colonies, passed the Quebec Act, which gave the French their laws and religion, with an eye to placating the French in order that they might be used, if necessary, against the English Colonists to the South. In other words, the motives behind the Act take away all the virtue that is in it. Now I have gone through practically all the correspondence right up to the passage of the Act in 1774, and find no evidence to support the American Revolutionary view. These documents which I have just copied reinforce my distrust of the old theory, which by the way Kennedy[11] repeats as if it were the gospel. They were papers of advice given to Shelburne when he was on the Board of Trade and Plantations, and outline an American policy. They were written between the conquest of Canada and the passage of the Stamp Act. They start from the thesis that further emigration to the colonies should be discouraged, for already the colonies are so populous that they constitute a danger. The problem then is how to keep them in proper dependence upon the mother country. The author would check all further spreading westward of the population in America, for it must be kept to the sea coast and not allowed to grow inland. His reasons for this are ingeniously involved. If they spread inland they will be driven by the cost of transportation to develop their own manufactures – which of course would compete with those of the mother country. They will also become more independent in spirit. If they are kept to the seaboard, they will remain dependent upon English goods and will always be under the shadow of English guns. But more is necessary than this, he said. The British Government should use the Indian as a counterpoise to the British Colonists. By preventing the colonists spreading over the Mountains, the Indians will find their hunting grounds preserved, and will be bound more closely than ever to the British interest as against the colonists who would like to despoil them. ... There is a suspicious parallel with the policy which was actually followed, and it has an unpleasant look about it. But what of the Quebec Act? Well here it is. The American Revolutionary theory cannot be correct, for if anyone was at that time actuated by the motives it presupposes, the author of these documents would have been the first among them. But he is utterly innocent of any suggestion of using the French in Canada as a counterpoise to the English to the South of them. It cannot be out of delicacy that he omits mention of it, for he talks quite freely about using the Indian – which is a thousand fold worse. I have become quite excited over the problem, and not a day passes without some discussion or argument upon it. Shortt, who has a violent prejudice against the French Canadian, believes the old theory with all the persistence of a hopeless Presbyterian, and McArthur, of whom by the way, I am very fond, follows him in this. But they cannot produce any documentary evidence in support of it....

Adam Shortt (1859–1931) to whom Burt refers in the preceding letter, was educated at Queen's University, and the universities of Glasgow and Edinburgh. He taught at Queen's from 1885 to 1908, when he was appointed a civil service commissioner. He was the leading pioneer worker in the field of Canadian economic history. He collaborated with Doughty in editing the first great co-operative work of Canadian historical scholarship, the 23-volume *Canada and Its Provinces: A History of the Canadian People and Their Institutions*. His first formal connection with the Archives was in 1907 when, in association with Doughty, he edited a volume of documents on the constitutional history of Canada. From 1918 until shortly before his death he was chairman of the board of publications of the Archives.

July 8, 1923

Yesterday, I was here steadily, though not working all the time, for I had several chats with Mr. Smith. He told me some good tales. One was about a prisoner in Newfoundland, who wrote to the government complaining of the dampness of his cell, and threatening, if they would not do something, that he would not stay. ... I have just returned to write this and a letter to Wallace,[12] and do a little more on an article I am writing. A few days ago I dropped Wallace a line suggesting that I could supply him with a short article on the beginning of the Carleton regime for the September number. He has asked for it and requested that I let him have it by the 20th at the very latest. Already I have broken the back of it, and it is so intensely interesting that I grudge the time necessary to go out for meals. I fear the article may kick up a rumpus, for there are many worshippers of Carleton and this material I have discovered presents him in a most damaging light, not only as a tyrant, but also as a shifty politician. He had a row with his council, and it was so serious that he dared not meet them for more than two months, and then he was able to do it only because events played into his hands. He fired two leaders of the Council and frightened the rest of the majority who were opposed to him into submission. But he carefully obscured all this from the home government. It is really quite a shocking affair.

July 11, 1923

Monday night I finished the article over which I was so wrought up...

Do you remember Benvenuto Cellini's wild excitement in the process of casting his bronze statue? My excitement was much the same. For several nights I had very restless sleep...

July 15, 1923

My article on Carleton has run the gauntlet. McArthur came back from Kingston Wednesday night, and when he came in the next day I gave it to him to read. He has been a great admirer of Carleton. He read it carefully, and agreed with me on the whole thing and that it was an important revelation. Then he suggested that I bring it to Shortt, wondering what would be his reaction. So we went over to the latter's office across the street and sat while he read it. He also accepted it and said it was a very fine piece of work. That night I sent it to Toronto, but I have not yet heard from Wallace. A nice touch of irony was added by a letter which Dr. Doughty, who has just returned, received from the present Lady Dorchester. (She holds the title in her own right). The burden of the letter was pious hope that the study of the Canadian Archives would only add lustre to the memory of her famous ancestor.

Burt's article, 'Sir Guy Carleton and His First Council,' was published in the December 1923 issue of the *Canadian Historical Review*, but it is not apparent that her ladyship (if she read it) found it as much of a revelation as it was to Burt's professional colleagues. His letter of 15 July resumes:

For the last two days I seem to have been more social than industrious. Thursday I must have spent an hour and a half in Dr. Shortt's office talking to him – rather being talked at, for he is a most wonderful talker – I can only with the greatest difficulty squeeze in a very little word every fifteen minutes. ... The morning [Saturday] was not over before McArthur came in and asked me to come over to see Dr. Shortt. McArthur and I had been talking about the state of Denmark and I had suggested that there was only one man in Canada to set it right – Dr. Shortt. I urged him to press the matter on him, but he preferred that I should do it. So he came for that purpose. I have been quite concerned, and I found McArthur the same, when I talked to him about it, over the state of historical study in Canada. There are a number of local societies organized for local antiquarian research, but nothing can be hoped for from them. Then last year the Landmarks Association and the Battlefields Association combined into the Canadian Historical Association. It will never be a *real* Canadian Historical Association, for it has been started on the wrong lines and the best students of Canadian history are not taking it seriously. Indeed, it threatens to prevent the formation of a real Canadian Historical Association, which would be a clearing house for ideas on the study of Canadian history. Then there is the Canadian Historical Review, run independently by the University of Toronto. This it seems to me, ought to be the organ of a real Association. But Dr. Shortt thought the time had not yet come for such action, and I am afraid he sees truly. The centre of any such association would be the Archives here, but at Toronto they have no one who knows the Archives, and the same is true of McGill. ... This means that Queen's is the only University which has taken a real interest in the Archives, and the rest will hold back or out. He suggests that the only practical thing to do now, is to get as many as possible back of the Review to use that as an organ of all students of Canadian history. The difficulty there is that the French Canadians have no contact whatever with the Toronto Review, and I fear that the Toronto people will not make a move of themselves, and of course the French will not ask to be allowed to come in on the Review. So I asked Shortt, if he would not try his hand at bringing them together. He agreed. He promised that he would speak to Wallace and try to persuade him that the Review should be a medium of expression for French Canada, and he also promised to approach the French Canadian historians to prepare them for the invitation, if he can extract it.

The Canadian Historical Association had been founded by the Historic Landmarks Association at its annual meeting in May 1922. Its first president, L.J. Burpee,[13] stated that the reorganized society would broaden the scope of its activities beyond the promotion of interest in historic sites and buildings to include 'the encouragement of historical research and of an intelligent public interest in the history of our country, as well as the co-ordination of the efforts of provincial and local historical societies,' and to bring 'into more perfect harmony the two great races that constitute the Canadian people.'[14] To this latter end English- and French-language secretaries were appointed, but the officers of the Association were predominantly English-speaking. Membership was open to laymen as well as professional historians and, contrary to Burt's deprecatory remark, a number of distinguished historians had joined. But he did not become a member until 1926, when he was elected to the Council. He apparently felt initially that the organization should be more restricted in membership and objectives, comprising only persons who were actively engaged in historical research in French and English Canada.

The *Canadian Historical Review*, established in 1920 as the successor to Wrong's *Review of Historical Publications Relating to Canada*, was published and financed by the University of Toronto. Although it reviewed publications by French-Canadian historians, it was not until 1962 that an article in French appeared in its pages. Three years after Burt wrote, it was arranged that all members of the Association would receive a subscription to the *Review*.

The letter of 15 July continues:

So we talked till it was after 1 p.m. and then I rushed back to get my hat and slip out for dinner. But when I came in to the room where I work, I found Mr. Smith entertaining Judge Latchford,[15] and I had to be introduced. I tried to slip away, but Mr. Smith said, "Just wait a minute, I'll go with you." Now it happens that Judge Latchford is an old man and has his mind packed with the greatest mass of antiquarian lore about Ottawa that is to be found in the compass of one small cranium, and Mr. Smith is very much afraid that he is going to take it all to heaven, where it will not be needed. So the conversation went on for over an hour, and on the way to town we had to make a detour to see the stone erected on the site of Col. By's house – which Judge Latchford says was never there at all. ... He [Smith] has a hundred books filled with typewritten notes on Canadian history, the work of many years. He hopes to use the material, and he will use some of it. But he is worrying, for he says that he has done a lot of digging and has left his material in perfect shape, so that another may use it. ...

In our conversation we drifted on to the troubles of 1827, and to William Lyon Mackenzie. ... Do you know the romance of the unpublished life of Mackenzie, [of which] I think I have told you some time? When the Makers of Canada Series was being compiled, a man named LeSueur[16] was set to work on the life of Mackenzie, and for a long time he worked in the home of the rebel's grandchildren with all the family papers. He got the book all ready for the press, and the first proofs were struck off. Then it was stopped. I had understood generally that the family objected and blocked the publication of the book. But last night Mr. Smith told me that it was Mackenzie King himself who was responsible. I do not blame the poor harassed prime minister, for certainly it would do him a great deal of harm if his grandfather's life were really published. It would be a gross injustice, for he would have to suffer for another man's sins.

July 18, 1923

I have been working on the regular despatches between the Governor and the Home Government and am down to 1778–79. The manuscripts were arranged so that a natural stop comes in the middle of 1781. So I should strive to reach there. But if I am to get the full meaning of all the material which I gathered I should round it out from the other sources available, and these I find are more extensive than I had imagined. So I am working hard to get over this ground, and have been hoping I might do it in the two months I had counted on spending here.

As we have already seen, Burt's work with the League of Nations Society in Alberta had brought him into contact with Sir Robert Borden during his visits to Ottawa, where Sir Robert was an active member of the national organization. Burt greatly admired Borden's qualities as a man and as a statesman. In later years in conversation with students, he would often refer to the fact that Borden's role in the evolution of dominion status had been ignored by the Liberal establishment of political scientists, journalists, and historians. It is not surprising that his *Short History of Canada for Americans,* first published in 1942, is unequivocal on this point. Borden's activity in forcing the British government to grant the dominions a voice in the conduct of the war and the peace negotiations and to support their claim to be independent members of the League is incisively presented. Likewise, in winning the right to the independent conduct of relations with foreign states in 1920, 'the British government,' he wrote, 'yielded before the insistence of the one man who, more than any other, forced the transformation from the British Empire to the British Commonwealth of Nations.'[17]

July 23, 1923

Yesterday I had a most delightful time when I went to tea with Sir Robert and Lady Borden. Somehow or other, they made me feel as if I were an old friend. I like them both immensely. Lady Borden is bubbling over with fun. Beside Dr. Doughty and myself, the only guests were a Mr. and Mrs. Blake. He is vice-consul or something like that for Australia. ...

The Bordens have a most beautiful place at the East end of the city. The house was designed by the late Stanford White, of Thaw fame,[18] and the ground runs right down to the Rideau River in the most picturesque manner. We had tea on a big tiled porch at the back of the house and from there the view is one of the most beautiful I have seen in Canada, and reminds me of many a charming little bit in England. Thirty feet in front of us, the garden ended in a low wall through which a path disappeared. Then we looked through the tops of trees of all varieties to the river and the rolling wooded country beyond. Through the tops of the trees a church spire peeped up. After tea was over, we walked down to the river – a drop of about sixty feet. We went down by lovely winding paths through a mass of wild vegetation. Once we descended over the brow of a hill, it looked as if we were miles from civilization. Only the asphalt paths betrayed the civilization all around us. Three little valleys, each with a spring and a rill down to the water's edge and the several paths wind in and out of these little dales. I was strongly reminded of the Gorge at Niagara. Sir Robert said that he had been told by a forester that the variety of the trees and shrubs there was so considerable that he really had an arboretum. Among the trees was one I had never seen before. It is the Striped Maple. The leaf is very large – about twice the size of the ordinary maple. The bark is very smooth, but two feet off it looks as if it were split all along it in very distinct white cracks. But when you put your hand on it, it is as smooth as paper; the white is a stripe in the grey colouring of the bark. From the front door, there is another beautiful view. Across the street is a park, and far beyond loom the spires of the Parliament Buildings and Library. We all had such a delightful time that it was nearly seven before we departed....

I am just finishing the official correspondence down to 1781, and then I am going to fill it out from various series of papers – the Shelburne Correspondence and the Dartmouth papers....

The present Lansdowne family I could curse with bell book and candle. The Earl of Shelburne became the first Marquis of Lansdowne, and so in Lansdowne House the Shelburne Papers reposed. While there they were copied by hand (a few only by typewriter) for the Canadian Archives. Unfortunately most of the papers are unsigned, but no note was taken of the handwriting. It would be very valuable to know what of these were written by Shelburne himself, but it is impossible to find out now, for the Lansdowne family have since sold this collection, which really ought to have been considered as belonging to the English nation, and these papers have disappeared somewhere into the black night of the United States.[19] Will you not join me in a good round curse?

It was at this point, in the mid-summer of 1923, that Burt visualized the final form of his first major historical work, *The Old Province of Quebec*, but many weary hours of labour were to intervene before that objective was attained.

August 1, 1923

Already my mind is clearing to the view that while I may strike off an odd article, my chief purpose must be to write a real history of the period after the Conquest. Another visit like this to the Archives, will probably enable me to fill out to the Constitutional Act of 1791, and I had thought of writing the History of Canada to 1791, in which I should make an entirely new estimate of Carleton. This new estimate is greatly needed, for there is a mass of detail covering the period of his stay in Canada which leads me to believe that the interpretation which has been accepted to the present is quite wrong. It is true that he saved Quebec and in doing that saved Canada in the winter 1775–76. But more and more I am coming to the view that the difficulties which surrounded him, were to a very considerable extent the result of his own actions towards the English element in Canada, and towards the lower class of the French Canadians. Despite all that has been said, he did not know them. His outlook was limited to the seigneurs and the upper clergy. But when I come to write, I think that I would prefer to bring my work down to 1806, instead of stopping at 1791. My reason is this. I am coming to the conclusion that the common division of Canadian history into periods – the Conquest – The Quebec Act – The Constitutional Act – The Act of Union – Confederation – is all wrong. It is a superficial and even artificial analysis. Digging underneath the surface I begin to see more and more clearly that there are three great periods in the history of our country; (1) The French Period; (2) The period when the English ruled the French, 1760 to 1849; (3) the period including the present time, when the English and French together rule themselves. The middle period is more and more attracting my attention, as the great protracted turning period in the fate of our country, and it divides itself into two equal halves. The first goes down to 1806. During this time the relations between the two races were on the whole fairly harmonious, and the government was carried on largely in the interests of the French. But the second half was entirely different. It was the troubled period in our life. The American civil war was a concentrated struggle, but our strife was painfully protracted. From 1806 to 1849, the government was carried on by the English, no longer in the interest of the French, but against them. For over forty years their backs were against the wall. To me it is a remarkable thing, that right on top of this prolonged fight for their existence, the French stepped out and marched hand in hand with the English from 1849....

August 4, 1923

Yesterday ... McArthur arrived back from that place [Kingston]. I had just settled down here to a good evening's work when he arrived at the door. I did not think of any more work that night. We went outside, it was a very hot night, and we stretched out on the grass, lit our pipes, looked out over to the Laurentian Hills, and talked and talked. I have discovered a document which I think hits on the head his pet theory of the Quebec Act – he is loath to admit it as yet. Well we discussed that for a while. Then the methods of writing history, the proper divisions of Canadian history – he agreed with me in my heresy which I confessed to you the other day. I also propounded my idea of a board, backed by a number of moneyed men, to encourage and supervise scholarship in Canadian history. He thought it was a great idea, and asked my permission to mention it to Burpee. I told him to tell all the world. It seems that it may be very apropos, for there has already been a step taken to commemorate the Centenary of Parkman's birth, and no definite ideas that are generally satisfactory have been broached. Scholarships had been suggested, but McArthur thinks that this is infinitely better.

Burt envisioned an organization which would provide financial assistance to scholars who would spend their summers, or a sabbatical year, in the Archives, where the results of their research could be shared with the group and their writing subjected to critical evaluation. Burt's proposal was not adopted by the Parkman centennial committee, but two years later William Smith was hoping that 'the round table idea applied to university teachers' could still be implemented.[20] The basic issue remained unresolved – how was the scholar and the artist to find support for the free expression of his insights and discoveries? Canada, having neither an hereditary aristocracy nor an overly-generous plutocracy could not provide the patronage so common in Britain and Europe. Nor were the meagre budgets of universities of much help. Burt's idea was realized in part when the Canadian government established the Canada Council in 1957, financed at the start by substantial returns from death duties on the estates of two multi-millionaires – Isaac Walton Killam and Sir James Dunn.

August 8, 1923

...In the same mail with yours, I received a letter from the Edmonton branch of the Canadian Authors Association, requesting me to give the opening address of a series of public lectures to be given in the Public Library this fall and winter. They want me to speak on Francis Parkman on September 17th. It will be a sort of centenary celebration, for he was born on September 16th 1823, I believe. Be prepared to help me write my address!...

I have made another friend here, Russell[21] from the University of Michigan. He is working here to collect material for his thesis, which is on the Western Posts under the British rule, i.e. from the conquest of Canada to the Peace of 1783, or more properly to Jay's Treaty of 1796. I have gone past much of the material he needs without paying very much attention to it, but I am familiar with the way about, and with the history of Canada at that time, so that we have quite a little to talk about on our work. He has been studying under Van Tyne,[22] who holds a unique place. He is one of the small group of outstanding American historians who have reversed the old tradition of the American Revolution. This, by the way, is one of the most interesting things in the history of scholarship. British historians have been too polite, and have in the past accepted the traditional American view of the Revolution, and have repeated it in their writings upon that period – they gave the American version. It has been left to American historians to return the compliment by investigating the period thoroughly and giving the British version. Thus today, if you want to see the American side of the quarrel, you have to read a British writer, and if you want to see the British side you have to read an American writer. Sometimes people smile at the American Historical school, but if it has done no more than this, it has thoroughly justified itself, and made one of the most important contributions in the world to the state of historical knowledge.

During the 1923–4 academic year, eight courses were offered by the history department at Alberta, Burt and Long sharing them equally. But in addition to this heavy teaching commitment, Burt also imparted to the public the results of his reflections on contemporary issues, both national and international. In an article in *The Press Bulletin* entitled 'The Need for a Wider Study of Canadian History,'[23] he wrote simply but forcefully on the value of a knowledge of the past as it pertained to the dual nationality of Canada, Canadian-American relations, the future of the British Commonwealth, and sectionalism in Canada. He believed the youthfulness of the western Canadian population to be a valuable asset, but it had a drawback in that 'the steadying influence of experience, of a knowledge, of the past' was lacking.

What experience is to the individual, history is to a people. There are some individuals who take all their many mistakes and call them experience, and they go on with their experience. They never learn....

English Canadians, he argued, often ignored some of the simplest facts of Canadian history: that the country had been French for about as long as it had been British; that for a century after the conquest the French remained the majority; that until 1849 the French, although the majority, did not control their government and consequently there was bitter racial strife – 'French Canada was fighting with its back to the wall, fighting for its life. ... This chapter of Canadian history is one which should never be forgotten, for it is packed with object lessons of tremendous import...'

Turning to relations with the United States, he stressed that every Canadian should know something of the history of that country, for there had been 'a most intimate action and reaction going on' between the two countries from the earliest times to the present. The impact of the Civil War on Canada was one of many examples of this process.

...The development of Canadian national consciousness since Confederation, insofar as it has developed, has been largely a reaction from contact with the United States. As it has been, so it will be....

The future of the Commonwealth, he believed, was uncertain, but its guiding principle of autonomous self-governing dominions had been Canada's historic contribution to an institution which was 'the combined product of Englishmen and Canadians wrestling with the almost baffling difficulties of colonial government.' Similarly, sectionalism in Canada was a continuing problem 'and the best weapon in this fight will be a knowledge of the common past.'

... If it be true, as some aver, that Canadians know less about the history of their own country than do most any other civilized people, our situation is most perilous. We may break asunder.

On 1 February 1924, Burt elaborated on one of these issues in an address to the Edmonton Board of Trade, entitled 'Canada's Dual Nationality.'[24] This required some courage in view of the bitter feelings towards French Canadians which survived in the post-war period in English-speaking Canada. It is clear that he believed that the transplanting of French culture to the New World was as much an element in the definition of the Canadian identity as the transit of British speech, customs, and law, and hence both components were worthy of patriotic pride.

... At various times in many lands [he declared], races have been assimilated. But this has occurred only when the assimilated did not possess an old and fixed civilization, or where they were in a hopeless minority and scattered. Neither of these fundamental conditions existed in Canada. The French belonged to a civilization as ancient and as established as that of the English and, far from being a small minority, they actually outnumbered [for many years] those who desired to absorb them. Nationality resembles gunpowder. The greater the pressure on it, the greater is its power....

His observations were not only apposite but also prophetic:

... We must remember that our national problems of today and tomorrow are shot through and through with this principle of dual nationality. ... We talk of the industrial development of Canada. Quebec has the greatest unexploited labour market in our country. Already several industries are slipping down from Ontario, and if this continues, may not the old spectre of racial strife arise once more clothed in a newer economic garb?...
... The balance of our constitution, between French and English rights, rests upon the supposition that the French are largely confined to Quebec. What if this ... numerical and geographic balance of our population shifts? ... Suppose this movement continues, what will happen to our constitution? Should it, can it, be erected into a 'dead hand' to keep French rights cooped up in Quebec? ... Is not a constitution an artificial creation, and nationality a law of nature? If a constitution is to survive must it not be in general accord with the underlying conditions and forces? In the days to come, Canada will most likely be brought face to face with this grave question. ... Let us make the most of this happy time, by getting to know each other better, by peering out upon the world through each other's eyes, so that when the day of trial comes, we may not fall out and rend our country as in the past, but pull together to make this a greater and better land!

The historical analysis in this address was largely confined to the period before 1867 and did not grapple with the complexities of dual nationality in the Confederation movement and in the Canadian West, but it was directed to laymen, not historians. The rejection of the 'black letter' school of narrow constitutional interpretation in favour of a philosophy which accommodated the changing characteristics of Canadian society was the most valuable feature of the address. As might be expected, it was welcomed by the small and vulnerable French-speaking community in Edmonton and was translated and published in the periodical of the Collège des Jesuites.[25] The Quebec nationalist politician, Armand Lavergne, also offered his congratulations:

Your idea of Canadian patriotism has been my life long ideal, and I believe it is only by its practical realization that we can achieve the prosperity and happiness of our beloved country.

You have done a good deed for Canada and I beg to be allowed to offer you my sincere thanks and the expression of my highest admiration.[26]

Burt was instructing his hearers on facts of Canadian history which Anglophones frequently forgot. But it was a stance unpopular in the West, where French was regarded as a foreign language. Few western-Canadian Anglophones accepted the dual nationality concept. Lavergne's letter suggests that had more English-speaking Canadians possessed Burt's insight and capacity to peer out upon the world 'through each other's eyes,' the future relations of French and English would have evolved in a very different manner during the next half century.

Burt did not return to the Archives in 1924 or 1925. Always a devoted and affectionate husband and father, he disliked the months of separation from his family, now numbering three children, Forrest, Mary, and John Arthur. The fourth and last child, Joan, was born the following year. Moreover, his salary did not permit annual visits to the Archives.[27] Under these circumstances, he had to draw on the 'capital' of the notes and copies of documents accumulated during his first two summers in Ottawa. In 1924 he produced 'The Tragedy of Chief Justice Livius' for the *Canadian Historical Review*. His reputation as an authority on the post-Conquest period was growing. He was selected by the editor of the 1926 anniversary edition of The Makers of Canada series to update and correct A.G. Bradley's *Lord Dorchester* and Jean N. McIlwraith's *Sir Frederick Haldimand*.[28] He completed this assignment in the summer of 1925 in twenty-eight pages of lengthy notes and comments, based on hitherto unused primary sources and contemporary research.

There were no changes in the history department's teaching program during the years 1923–6. During the mid-twenties there was little growth in university enrolment, the total number of students being about 1300. Professor C.S. Burgess (1870–1971) of the Department of Architecture, who taught the history of architecture in his own department, was pressed into service as a lecturer in history for several years, limiting Burt's and Long's teaching responsibilities to three courses each.

The History Club was flourishing and met regularly at the Burts' home for their sessions. Many of his former students look back to these years with nostalgia. One of them recalls the annual social meetings where Burt would play the piano for dancing, and in addition to the current popular tunes would produce sprightly improvisations.

In a small university such as Alberta during these years, it was not difficult for students to establish a personal relationship with their professors. One of them, William R. Watson, who did not have the use of his hands, had developed unusual skill in using his feet for all the purposes which the missing members provide. He describes in his reminiscences[29] Burt's kindness in making him feel at ease during his frequent visits with the Burt household. 'I later came to realize,' he wrote, 'that the greatest gift that the university can bestow is the possibility of personal contact with men such as these: widely read and with extensive intellectual interests. ... many of them have one thing in common: they invest their subjects with their characteristic personalities, and the size of the University is, quite happily, such as not to submerge their personal influence.'

Burt followed current developments in international relations closely, contributing informative articles to *The Press Bulletin* on reparations, disarmament negotiations, the Geneva Protocol, and the Locarno Pact.[30] While not minimizing the obstacles to international amity, he was hopeful that the League of Nations would soon move toward universality of membership and that an era of peace was in prospect. He was less optimistic on Canada's future, in an article entitled 'What Is Canada?'[31] Sectionalism, and any failure to recognize the dual nationality of Canada, were capable of tearing the country asunder, he declared.

... In all attempts to secure justice for any section of Canada, we dare not think of our own part alone. If it was worth fighting for, it is worth making some sacrifices for, and each must be willing gladly to face any sacrifice that seems necessary in the interests of the whole. Surely we would not sell our national birthright for a mess of provincial pottage!

Another threat was the Americanization of Canada:

...We are so overshadowed by the very greatness of the United States that we tend to have an inferiority complex. We cannot escape the tremendous contrast in development and are forever making comparisons at our own expense. This has been eating our heart away. ... To say this implies no disparagement of that great and wonderful people to the south of us. It simply means that we have not been left to be ourselves and to develop our own personality. American capital, to which we owe a great deal of our material development, has brought with it American business to such an extent that some are already troubled by the spectre of economic annexation....

...There are two forces which have long been acting upon us and will most probably continue to act – [British] imperialism and Americanism pulling us in opposite directions till we often know not where we are or what we are.

There are some who have a child-like faith that in His own good time, or perhaps before, God will mould this people into a great and good nation. He will never do it ... unless we face our difficulties frankly and surmount them bravely. If we are to make anything of this country we must remember that it is French as well as English. ... There are a few who would like to make Canada an Anglo-Saxon and a Protestant land, but such an attitude of mind, if widespread, would wreck this country in a generation. A frank and full recognition of our dual nationality must be at the very foundation of the Canadian mentality....

Our heritage is much greater than we often realize. We have the makings of a wonderful national spirit. We are compounded of two of the greatest races in the world, French and English. This need not give rise to internal strife, but rather to a richer national life...

Burt held tenaciously to this conviction over the years. Unfortunately he was too sanguine in his assessment of Anglo-Saxon attitudes, even though forty years later the Royal Commission on Bilingualism and Biculturalism reaffirmed the principle which Burt had articulated so forcefully in 1924 and 1926. Most Canadians are still unaware that the enjoyment of cultural diversity is more rewarding and more exciting than the dull homogeneity of a conformist society.

7

Constitutional Issues
Old and New

In 1926 Burt arrived in Ottawa about mid-June. Earlier in the year he had accepted an invitation from Cambridge University Press to contribute a chapter, which was to be entitled 'The Problem of Government, 1760–1774,' to their Canadian volume in a new history of the British Empire.[1] This would require him to provide a definitive narrative of the results of his examination of the earlier part of the history of the old province of Quebec. It was evident that after five years of effort he was recognized as the leading authority in this important field of Canadian history.

He roomed again at the YMCA. New, Harvey, Brown, Underhill, and Morton[2] were already in town. William Smith arranged a guest membership for him in the University Club, which enabled him to take meals and meet friends there. To his academic associations he was able to add the political, due to his friendship with the Conservative Member of Parliament for Edmonton East, A.U.G. Bury.[3]

At the general election in the autumn of 1925, no party had gained a majority of the seats. The Conservatives, led by Arthur Meighen, were the largest group. The Liberals under Prime Minister Mackenzie King had held office since 1921 on the strength of Progressive support, and were now even more dependent on it, for the Progressives, though reduced in numbers, held the balance of power. Since the beginning of the session in January the struggle for office between the two major parties had been intense; as the Progressives were not all of one mind, the government could never be sure of their support on a confidence motion, and the

Conservative opposition was relentless in pressing its attacks. It was one of the most exciting sessions in the annals of Canadian political history. It was therefore not surprising that Burt was constantly diverted from his study of the political and constitutional issues of a century and a half earlier. His comments reflect a lack of sympathy for both old parties, and a qualified approval of the Progressives, both nationally and in his adopted province.

June 16, 1926

Monday evening [June 14] instead of returning to dead men's words, I turned to hear those of some live specimens. The debate was just interesting enough to hold me until bedtime. But yesterday!!! As Bury had not seen the Archives, I thought I would make an appointment with him, and immediately after lunch sought him out at the House. He agreed to come this morning and then lunch with me. But we have not lunched here [the University Club] yet, though it is now 8:20 p.m.

Just as I was about to leave him [Bury], having refused his invitation to the gallery, I inquired if there might be anything interesting coming up in the debate. He nibbled at the line I thus threw out, so I went up into the gallery and caught a whale. Parliament waited until I had taken my seat and then Davis, Bury's roommate from Calgary, introduced his motion of want of confidence in the government.

Davis' want of confidence motion condemned the government for its failure to implement the legislation promised in the Speech from the Throne. One of the measures promised had been the ratification of the agreement with the government of Alberta for the transfer of natural resources to provincial control. The natural resources question was one of the long-standing grievances of the prairie provinces, and ever since the establishment of Saskatchewan and Alberta in 1905 federal control of public lands and all the resources associated therewith had been a lively political issue. Since all the other provinces of Canada controlled their resources, the prairie provinces regarded the situation as an unjust discrimination against them.

The air became electric and it was 12 hours before the thunderstorm had passed. There were many bright bolts and much heavy thunder. A kink in the rules of the house prevented all discussion of the real cause of the motion – the general question. From first to last, the Speaker – Lemieux – was frequently invoked to keep the various debaters in the path which was not straight and narrow, but wide and tortuous. To quote the words of the Minister of Agriculture, Motherwell, "many members ate of the forbidden fruit" and he pled to be allowed a nibble. He is a big man with shining pate and snowy goatee. His vigor of body and tongue suggest the cattle drover. When the members of the crowded opposition benches developed from verbal hectoring to bovine booing, he stopped his address and booed back at them as loud as he could bellow. Then no one could boo, for they all doubled up. Even the packed galleries rocked with laughter. The battle was so intense that the imperturbable Charlie Stewart lost his temper and foamed at the mouth in his effort to tell Meighen, without saying so, that he was a liar. Meighen never lost his equanimity. His enemies may have thought that he seemed to be rejoicing devilishly over the way he toasted the fat Premier on his fork. You could almost hear the victim sizzling. Bourassa, whose countenance recalls the Devil, and whose seductive words strengthened that impression in the beginning, grew very excited and began to scream like a mere mortal. For an hour and a half he fought for the white government against the orange opposition. When one Alberta progressive, and then a second, rose and declared against the government they had hitherto supported, it seemed as if the roof was about to fall or the floor to blow up. By dinner time, it was becoming apparent that the government was playing a waiting game – to stall off a vote until they could recall absent members to Ottawa. Outside the house, the government was busy courting the coy Progressives and browbeating the timid ones. Toward midnight the debate sank into weary words dropped on dull ears, till R.B. Bennett with a torrent of wild words whipped it into a frenzy. Without dropping the bitter party man, he rose to be the noble champion of his calumniated province. To the very last, the poison worked. Lucien Cannon, the Solicitor General, in parliamentary language, called Meighen a liar and the latter made him withdraw. Then the vote was called, and while the division bells rang for ten minutes to call the members, those present forgot their animus in spirited songs – jollier choruses than our undergraduates can sing. At the last moment, a dozen men marched in, two by two, past the bar of the house; and as they entered, keeping close military step they suggested policemen coming to arrest the government, for they all entered opposition seats amid strong cheering. Order was called and the atmosphere was that of a great court where a great judge was to pronounce great sentence. No one could tell what the sentence was to be – life or death – as the members rose one by one and their names were called off, first against the government and then for it. Cahan of Montreal refused to vote with his party against the government. Had he risen and three more Progressives joined the two who battled in the afternoon, the game would have been up. Why did they not? There were several reasons. One was the fear of leaping from the Liberal frying pan into the Conservative fire. The other was the $4000 sessional indemnity which would have been imperilled by an election, for King had openly shaken that big stick in the afternoon. Great was the government cheering which was deadened in the packed galleries, for the government had weathered a greater crisis than had been experienced during the session for perhaps many years....

It was nearly 3 a.m. before I tumbled into bed. I was as tired as if I had fought the whole battle myself, and I slept as soundly as if the victory or the defeat had been my own.

June 18, 1926

Since my last letter, I have had little parliamentary experience. Last night I dropped into the gallery to see an almost empty house engaged in dull committee work. Hearing that the report of the Customs probe was to be tabled this afternoon, I walked up the hill dragging Pearson[4] (Rollie's Oxford and Toronto friend) [Roland Michener] at my heels. Bury smuggled us into the member's gallery where we heard most of the report read. We did not remain long, for after setting the debate down for next Tuesday, the House went into committee on estimates – a matter as dull and uninteresting as other people's money.

Though I have been here a week, I have accomplished little at the Archives – gathered in a few peppery letters of Governor Murray. I have been on a vain search for further light upon the administration of justice during the military regime 1760–1764. Those four years attract me very much – they were the nuptials of French and English Canada. The former were much more prosperous and much happier than ever under the French rule. It is almost unique in the history of conquered territories.

The Customs Inquiry Report to which Burt refers had been prepared by a special committee of the House of Commons which was established in February to investigate charges of corruption in the Department of Customs and Excise made by the Hon. H.H. Stevens, a Conservative member from British Columbia. The committee held 115 sittings and examined over two hundred witnesses. It submitted a report on 18 June which was highly critical of the administration of that department. Consequently it provided fresh ammunition for the Conservatives, who had maintained a deafening barrage of criticism of King and his colleagues throughout the session. The debate on the report began on 22 June and lasted till Saturday morning, 26 June. During the debate the government was defeated on several procedural votes, but not on a formal want of confidence motion. Burt's letters of 23 and 25 June deal with the tense and emotion–charged proceedings in the House, which he was able to observe first hand.

June 23, 1926

I was up to the House last afternoon and night for the debate on the Customs report. It was very exciting. This afternoon I tried it again, but was bored by a very prolix speaker from Vancouver[5] who was apparently trying to tire the House.

In a few minutes I am going in to dinner, after which I shall try it again in the hope of hearing the leaders.

June 25, 1926

At the present moment I am very wide awake though not sure of myself, for I did not get to bed till 6 a.m. and I rose at 8.45. It has been the most exciting experience in my life since I scrambled out of Germany at the outbreak of war. At 7.20 last evening Bury gathered Pearson and myself under his spreading wing in a sardine crowd outside the members' gallery. 7.30 saw the doors open, and us flow tumultuously in. From 8 p.m. till 9 p.m. bills. Then Cahan, who was speaking when the House rose for dinner, resumed his arraignment of the government and continued it for over an hour. He is an old gentleman with white hair and pointed beard, powerfully built and with a commanding address. Though his shoulders are bent, they leave the impression not of weakness but of the ability to carry a tremendous load. He has neither the mental nor the verbal agility of Meighen. But if he lacks his power, yet he is more effective. Meighen commonly overshoots the mark, Cahan hits it. He won considerable sympathy by professing his personal regard for Boivin, and thus made his charges against his administration of the Customs Department more telling. D.M. Kennedy of Peace River, who has been bitterly attacked by the Conservatives on the ground that he was sitting in Collins' seat[6] and has consistently voted with the Liberals, was as dramatic as an undramatic individual seldom can be. He turned on the government and has virtually turned it out. His refusal to vote for the Woodsworth amendment which would have exculpated the government came as a startling announcement. A thrill ran through the house and its galleries – "The Government is lost." Now let me remind you that since Confederation, no government has been overthrown on the floor of the house. All but one government were lost in the elections. The one exception was Sir John A.'s administration in 1873 when it was wrecked by the Pacific Scandal and then it was not defeated on the floor of the house. It resigned because defeat seemed probable....

There were four divisions. First the Woodsworth sub-amendment was lost 117–115. Then a new sub-amendment was introduced by Fansher. It was the same as Woodsworth's except that instead of replacing the condemnation of the government in the amendment, it added something to it. At once Speaker Lemieux ruled it out of order. He had enough technical right on his side to justify it – but to me it seemed a violation of the spirit of the rule he invoked. At once Meighen appealed to the house against the speaker's ruling. It was startling to all present. So a second division was held on the ruling of the speaker and it was rejected by 118–116. So far as I am aware this is the only time such a thing has occurred in this Dominion.

Certain of defeat if the vote were then taken, the government started obstruction by putting up some of its members to kill time while the premier called a cabinet meeting. During the interval to the next division there was some obvious lobbying – right on the floor of the house. When the Premier returned to the house it was obvious that something was about to happen. It did, but not as the government hoped. A progressive moved the adjournment of the debate and a fear shivered through many of his hearers that the progressives might wish to postpone a decision. Of course the government voted solidly for adjournment so that they might continue negotiations over the weekend. But they were beaten 115–114 in the third division of the night. Again they played for time and opened their wind bags while a second cabinet meeting was held. This lasted till 5 a.m. [June 26th] and after jockeying for position by fusing the sub-amendment with the amendment so that they might advance a sub-amendment of their own, the government again supported adjournment – this time successfully, 114–113.

But the government has gained really nothing and lost a great deal. Firstly by clinging to power by their finger nails they are impairing their moral prestige in the country. Any other government in the same position would have resigned. Secondly, the government violated a pledge. The whips of the parties had solemnly agreed on a division to settle the debate last night, and the Liberals repudiated their whip's pledge by voting to adjourn. Thirdly, they have done some dirty work behind the scenes. It is generally understood that King demanded from Byng the promise of a dissolution should he be defeated, and has been refused. He has, during the fevered hours of the crisis, appointed E.M. Macdonald, who is minister of militia to the senate, and Tremblay, Lapointe's private secretary to the civil service commission.[7] There are rumours of other appointments, but these are taken as certain. These "death-bed" appointments are likely to be King's death warrant. I do not see how he can face parliament at 2 p.m. Monday, for this action must have disgusted several more Progressives who have hitherto supported him. His resignation over the week-end is the most likely denouement.

The interest was so intense that few seemed to feel sleepy – the galleries were almost full to the end. Agnes MacPhail was to have sailed from Montreal. Some wondered why she delayed until they heard that King had had the sailing postponed some hours and had promised her a special train to catch her boat. Immediately she cast her vote at 5.15 a.m. she bolted – the only one in the house.

The time killing speeches were for the greater part of the time quite amusing. Motherwell, half angry half humorously roared like a bull...

The Conservatives were in gay mood, but not too jubilant. They vented their feelings in songs, and did the others – while the division bells were ringing to gather the members – and in tearing up and throwing their order papers at each other.

I was interrupted in this by Dr. Tolmie[8] who is living at this club. He used to be minister of agriculture when Meighen was premier and now has charge of the organization of the Conservative party. He tells me that Bury has been a surprise. From being written down as a candidate who had no possible chance of election, he has risen to be a successful member and one "who stands in well with Mr. Meighen." I told him one or two pleasant things about Bury and he thanked me for them, because as he said, it was his business to get all the information he could about their own men. Now I have rambled on and on about the political crisis. But really, last night and this weekend are certain to be long remembered in Canadian history. There has been nothing like it since 15 years before I was born.

Although Burt had expected that King would resign, the latter clung to office, and without waiting for the House to pronounce its judgment on the Stevens committee report, advised Lord Byng, the Governor General, to dissolve Parliament so that his ministry could contest another general election. Lord Byng refused to accept this advice on the ground that Meighen, as leader of the largest party in the House, should have an opportunity, if he wished, to form a government and complete the work of the session. King thereupon resigned on 28 June. King, in his fit of anger with Lord Byng, took the unprecedented action of relinquishing office before a successor was chosen, thus depriving the country of a government and creating a constitutional vacuum. Byng thereupon called upon the leader of the opposition to form a government and Meighen, after much anxious consideration, agreed. Politically, it proved to be a mistake, but from a constitutional point of view it was correct.[9]

June 29th, 1926

Yesterday Pearson and I were just struggling into the Members' Gallery as the house adjourned after King had announced his resignation. After much argument in the rotunda in front of the chamber – with Bury, Gershaw, Liberal of Medicine Hat, and Tobin, I carried Bury off to the Archives, where Doughty graciously placed himself at our disposal till 6 p.m., unfolding all the treasures of that wonderful place....

This afternoon Pearson and I went up to the house again and saw that the members had all exchanged seats and heard Drayton make his speech on behalf of Meighen. When Rinfret, F.[rench] Liberal, resumed the debate on the customs report, we departed.

The Liberals have been very steeped in both strategy and tactics. They were expecting a defeat and wanted it to come on a matter of principle, on which they could appeal to the country. They had their chance a fortnight ago and they threw it away by forbidding any discussion of the natural resources. Now they have retired under a cloud – a vote of censure [the 29 June vote condemning the administration of the Department of Customs and Excise]. And their tactics have been in keeping. Their speakers have been very inferior to those of their opponents. They contradicted themselves and each other and they were not honest. King himself was the worst offender. Neither French nor English have much good to say of him now. Indeed you everywhere hear talk of a successor. Dunning and Lapointe are the two most mentioned, and Dunning seems to have the advantage. As Lanctot said just before I left dinner, "We would rather have Dunning, for we fear that Lapointe would sacrifice us to get English votes."

For one thing every Alberta man must condemn King. By prohibiting the discussion of our resources problem until our legislature would agree to the Bourassa amendment,[10] he prevented his English-speaking followers from understanding the real nature of that clause and Lapointe purposely deceived them. I wondered why he yielded to Bourassa's influence when he must have known that Archbishop O'Leary was opposed to the amendment. But now, looking back, I think I see his reason, – that it was not the power and insistence of the French members – but a political parachute to ease his inevitable descent.

One nasty thing may happen. The investigation into the customs administration which Inspector Duncan[11] carried on and formed the basis of the recent parliamentary investigation uncovered a hole of abominable immorality, worse than that of Sodom and her sister city. The stench was so nauseating, they had to put the lid on. Part of Duncan's report was officially stated to be too indecent to print. It was open to members to examine, however, and it turned even Agnes McPhail and Woodsworth against the government yesterday morning.[12] I don't much care what the policy of the Conservatives is. We had to have a change, and if the new government does not cleanse the Augean stable, they will have to go too.

Here I am running on at weary length about the politics of this country. But it is one of the crises in our political history and we may never see the like again. The progressive movement is performing the great function for which it was inaugurated – the purification of our politics. They have induced an energetic competition between the old parties to elevate our political morality.

These comments demonstrate how difficult it was for the Progressives to continue supporting the King government.

My work at the Archives [he continued in the same letter] has gone slowly. Parliament's storm is not alone to blame. I have been caught in a tangle in the very beginning of my chapter. The explanation hitherto given for the system of justice in Quebec differing from that of Three Rivers and Montreal during the military regime does not satisfy me. I may not find the way out, but I am going to do a deal more struggling yet. The passage of time and the halting of my work is beginning to alarm me. I may not be able to do much of the writing here, but may have to content myself with collecting more material to work up after I return. These kinks are most exasperating, especially when they force me to read through countless pages of xviii Century French in mss., as I am doing now.

Burt's industry in these years was laying the foundation for his legendary reputation among his associates, including the staff of the Archives. He is reputed to have read and mastered the contents of the 'Q' series for a sixty-year period – a massive collection running to several hundred volumes. One of his students recalls a facetious story which L.B. Pearson claimed was making the rounds in the Archives, that 'Professor Burt was planning to copy all the National Archives and then set fire to the building, so that he would have a complete monopoly.'[13]

July 2, 1926
...I have been going through records of cases tried in the military courts between 1760 and 1764 to find some gleam of light to lead me out of the darkness. The records are all in French, xviii Century French, and the writing is at times abominable. It has been dreary ploughing – all in vain. It is hard to see ahead in this work of research and it is quite possible that I will spend my time searching and collecting rather than writing. I can do the latter after I have finished here, for it does not have to be in till next February....

The Commons met on 30 June and 1 July, with all of the big guns of the two major parties firing continuous salvos across the floor of the House for hours at a time. The Liberal opposition chose the constitutionality of Meighen's ministry as the main target of their attack. Burt's friend Bury was one of the last speakers on the confidence motion and gave a cogent defence of the Conservative position. But the motion was carried by a one-vote majority at 2 a.m. on 2 July. The Governor General thereupon assented to Meighen's request for a dissolution.

So the political duel has been suddenly ended for the nonce! Everybody here is discussing the action of the Governor General, Liberals condemning him for granting Meighen what he refused King, and the Conservatives replying that King was given his chance and only sought a dissolution to escape the vote of censure that was hanging over his head and finally descended upon it. I have not been up on the Hill since Tuesday, when I heard Drayton make his statement in the house for Meighen. It has been interesting, but I was physically incapable. I have been going off to bed early and lying in as late as I could. ... When I went into the bathroom to shave, I found myself beside Woodsworth, who remarked to me "Well that was the strangest Dominion Day celebration I ever saw," and on my questioning him told me how the government had been defeated early this morning by a majority of one. At noon, feeling better, I went to the house only to hear the announcement of the dissolution....

July 3rd, 1926

Now I am settling down in the Archives – except when I spend the hours chatting with that dearest friend William Smith. I feel very sad to think of his sailing a week from today. When I am his age, I pray you and Heaven may have combined to make me half so sweet in disposition and stimulating in mind. Every day he sends up for me – sometimes several times – to go down for a smoke and a chat, and we discuss everything from the customs probe and the constitutionality of the governor general's action, down to amusing anecdotes and up again to the philosophy of St. Paul or the Roman Church....

July 6, 1926

Bury explained a mystery that had been troubling my mind. Why had the Progressives supported Meighen in two divisions in the house – on matters of policy – later ratted, precipitating the Dissolution? It was incongruous. ... According to Bury, the Progressives were expecting the Conservative government to approach them for a bargain. They were disappointed. Then King approached them, suggesting that Meighen if defeated would be refused a dissolution, which would of course mean that King would come back. Then he promised to form a coalition with the Progressives who would no longer be in the outer chamber of power. It is a scandalous business, for before Byng called upon Meighen to form a government, he was assured by Forke that the Progressives would co-operate to finish the business of the session.[14] Certainly the coming election is going to be a hot fight. The Liberals will try to obscure the issue by talking of constitutional rights – all bosh because King was going to do the very thing Meighen has done had he been given a dissolution. And what is the outcry against Byng for giving Meighen what he refused King? A smoke screen. The Governor General was right. No government has the right to demand a dissolution in order to avoid a vote of censure of parliament. There is the central point upon which the Conservatives will try to focus and from which the Liberals will try to distract them by a smoke screen of voluminous words. For the life of me, I cannot see where there can be any considerable change in the complexion of the house of commons. The Liberals may lose a few seats in Alberta over their bungling of the resources, and there is talk of the Conservatives winning some seats in Quebec now that Patenaude has come under Meighen's umbrella....

...Bury dropped in to see me at the Archives and we had another session in Smith's office. It has been a great pleasure to have Bury here and I was sorry to see him go. Poor Bury! He has had six strenuous months here. Now, instead of a rest, he returns to his law practice and another election fight. He is a poor man, and it is as hard on his purse as it is on his body. I do hope he is returned,[15] for he is a representative to be proud of. He is head and shoulders above most of his fellows....

This afternoon I finished writing an account of the military regime 1759–1764. I am rather pleased with the way it is shaping. But I shall not be satisfied with it until you have combed it over. I have decided to do the final writing in Edmonton. The only other writing I may do here is a little on the Royal Proclamation of October 7, 1763, which laid the basis of civil government in 1764. Then I think I will spend the rest of my time examining the minutes of the Council down to 1791 with a view of writing something on the actual government of the country, pointing out the development toward parliamentary procedure in Canada and the political struggle that went on within the Council. In conversation with such people as Smith and McArthur, I gather that I have some stuff that others have not seen and that I may make some contribution to our history in that other important corner of it.

July 9, 1926

McArthur has been tearing around at a great rate, instructing his research class in their beginnings, and visiting professional and amateur politicians to glean a harvest of information. He confirms what I have heard that Skelton[16] has been advising King very closely in this whole constitutional crisis. I fear he had been a poor friend to King and to himself. He has pushed King into a difficult position and himself into another. It may go hard with him if the Conservatives come back from the country, for he has violated the tradition of the civil service in giving political advice beyond the borders of his official province....

I have plunged into the minutes of the Legislative Council and am working my typewriter like a threshing machine. It is going much faster than when I was here last and I am in hopes of collecting fairly complete reports of its doings and procedure before I depart. With that treasure trove, I hope to produce a good study. In reality it presents a foreshortened picture of parliament. When civil government was set up, the Council began wholesale legislation. Soon experience slowed them down, for they made many mistakes. Then they gradually adopted the parliamentary practice of reading a bill three times and the Governor withdrew from the meetings, except on formal occasions when he gave his assent to the legislation that was passed. There was also the problem of admitting the public to the debates, but the Councillors were opposed successfully. But most interesting to me is the political history which has been quite ignored by writers hitherto – the appearance of parties within the council and the consequent party struggle. To several with whom I have discussed the subject, it has appeared an attractive study which ought to be published.

Today the Archives presents a contrast with what it was five years ago. For some while then I was the only visitor digging in the mine of the manuscript room. Now there are about a dozen. Morton is busy on the North West, gathering some illuminating material. Harvey is continuing his work on P.E.I., hoping to reach confederation, the end of its separate history, before he has to leave later in the month. Pearson is quite intoxicated by his study of the Loyalist settlement in Upper Canada, and is bringing his wife down this evening to introduce her as an assistant in the hunt. She arrived in town only this morning. Underhill comes up in the afternoons – his mornings he spends in the Parliamentary Library. McDougall[17] whom MacGibbon was appointing to Alberta until Toronto snapped him up, is here also. ... There are several others whom I know not – but that is nothing against them.

There is always a knot of us at the University Club, lunching and dining together and sometimes we drag in members of the club to join in a good discussion. One of these is a cousin of Jack Read of Dalhousie. He was a freshman when he [Jack Read] and Harvey were seniors. Another was a year after me in Toronto and is now an official in the Justice Department here ... It is very pleasant because we are welcome guests. In the summer many of the members of the club travel through the Dominion on scientific and other work and the club has hard sledding...

July 11, 1926

...J.S. Ewart K.C.[18] you may remember is the man who wrote the Kingdom Papers which advocated the elevation of Canada into a separate kingdom under the present sovereign. For some time he has been back of the Progressives, perhaps inspiring their wider views – which are a bit narrow.

Conversation here is getting a bit stale on the political issue. But soon the campaigners will whip up the tired jade and make her gallop and froth at the mouth. It will be amusing to see the antics. One most interesting bit which may come out during the fight is that King himself appealed to Byng to consult Downing Street – he appealed himself to the authority he pretends to repudiate.

8

The Flowering of
Canadian History

The mid-1920s saw the first flowering of Canadian history based on
scientific methods as modern historians define that term, with its exhaustive search for evidence and critical evaluation of primary sources. It was
an exciting period for ambitious young men and others in their prime of
life – an intoxicating time of continuous discoveries.

> Attempt the end, and never stand to doubt;
> Nothing's so hard, but search will find it out.[1]

might well have been their motto. Most of the research and writing was
designed to improve the accuracy, scope, and depth of the existing accounts of Canadian political and economic development. Burt's work was
a notable example of this. There was a strong, almost exclusive emphasis
on the pre-Confederation period, on the history of the various regions of
Canada, and on the earlier period in imperial and Canadian-American
relations. Post-Confederation national development attracted less attention, as did biography and social and intellectual history. The reasons for
this preoccupation with the remoter past are not entirely clear, but there
were at least three predisposing circumstances: the shallowness of earlier
work provoked the younger men to undertake revisionist studies; the
historiographically conservative conviction that recent history could not
be treated objectively; and finally the inadequacy of source material on
the post-Confederation period. The Public Archives had few collections
of papers of prime ministers and other leading political figures of the

recent past; the holdings of post-Confederation federal departmental records were limited, and complete files of many newspapers were almost inaccessible. Nevertheless, the activities of these archives-oriented pioneers of the 1920s were highly significant, and provided a sound foundation for the treatment of national history in future years.

'It is very interesting to see the actual renaissance of Canadian history in course of preparation,' Burt wrote on 13 July 1926:

In the old building it would have been impossible to accommodate the number of researchers that are now busy here.[2] Beside those I have earlier mentioned, Morton, Harvey, Underhill, Pearson and his wife, there are General Cruickshank,[3] Mackintosh,[4] (Economics at Queen's) Wilson[5] (History at Dalhousie) Armstrong (an old Queen's man teaching in a middle west u.s. college) Fife (who went over in the tanks with me and is now teaching in a Vermont college). Then there is McArthur and his regular class. I forgot to mention Brebner,[6] who appeared today and is already half buried. In addition, I hear that two other members of the Toronto history department are due here this month, as well as Chester Martin from Manitoba.[7] We may foregather at a dinner next week where we may focus some of our separate conversations. There has been considerable talk of coming to some understanding about being here in July as much as possible to get the maximum number here at the same time. Then we would have a sort of clearing house of research information and gain much by mutual criticism and suggestion. Certainly all the professional historians in Canada are turning their eyes on the Archives during the summer and a revolution is bound to come about as the result. It is a great change from five years ago when I came down here with your encouragement to find that I was almost alone. Of course this growing interest will affect the Archives, directing them in the channels where they should seek new material and enabling them to get more money from the government.

These impressions are reinforced by Professor W.M. Whitelaw's recollections of these years. With characteristic vivacity he describes the relationships which developed in the relaxed atmosphere of summer days and evenings in the building on Sussex Street:

I would fain ... recall the long, gaunt figure of General Cruikshank, off in a corner of the student's room at the Archives, pecking out, year by year, with one bony finger on a typewriter almost as worn, but quite as dauntless as himself, the story of the Niagara Frontier: In the center of that same room (itself the center of Canadian Historiography) I can see Mr. Burt, driving home an argument with the small end of his trusty briar....

The Archives, Whitelaw recalled, was 'more than a mere repository and disseminator of information.'

It became the Mecca to which there came an ever increasing number of scholars from an ever widening circle. Here in unhurried and easy intimacy we discussed our mutually interlocking problems, often with considerable heat, but never so far as I can remember, with bitterness. Here was education at its best, international, interprovincial; education without tears, without examinations, without lectures.[8]

On 18 July Burt described a visit with colleagues on the Archives staff which gave him much pleasure:

After a light supper here – for tea and heat reduced our appetites – McArthur and I went out to Marion's[9] where he and Fee[10] were awaiting us. Fee is in charge of the Map Room of the Archives. ... Marion is a French Canadian who took his degree in Paris. For five years he was professor of French at R.M.C. Kingston and now is official translator of the archives. Now you know the four of us who sat down to smoke and talk – first. We kept pretty well within French Canada and all the time were fairly close to Bourassa. Marion has a great admiration for him but can never forgive him for his alliance with the Conservatives against Laurier in 1911. He and the Conservatives in that warm summer campaign certainly sowed the political wild oats that are choking the national field today. Marion says that Bourassa laughs when any Tory accuses him or Quebec of disloyalty and replies "Your money did it." Indeed Atholstan[11] gave him $15000. He refused to take it but A. insisted. Thereupon he said "very good, you do not give this to me but to my cause. You pay for 15,000 subscriptions for my paper, and I will pick out a list of names all over the province to receive it." From Bourassa we passed to Sam Hughes – as he appeared in Quebec. Let us hope for Sam's sake that the doorkeeper above was not from French Canada. Finally we were lifted up by a discussion of Laurier, and we were all of one sweet accord. McArthur told us the story of how he threshed out his contribution of Papineau to Canada and its Provinces in a short series of interviews with Laurier just after his defeat in 1911.

I cannot tell how long we talked. It must have been a long while – judging by the sequel. At last we called a truce on politics and Marion produced three bottles of wine. We had a glass of each and then voted unanimously in favour of no. 3. Then he raided the cellar, in which the bottles were counted by the hundred, and produced several of no. 3. It was a delicious sparkling red wine – home made. We drank each other's healths, pledged France and Canada, and plunged into bridge, – for love....

...Morton, I am getting to know and like better all the time. My first impression of two years ago – that he was tedious – has quite melted away as I have broken through the barrier of his deafness. He is a plain-looking man of fifty or more with iron grey hair, a merry mouth half concealed by a grey moustache, and blue eyes that twinkle most of the time. He is a wide scholar with a rather rich background of Trinidad, Edinburgh, Pine Hill College (Halifax), and Knox College (Toronto). He is an old friend of President Murray and is much consulted by him. He knows the West and its history as few know it, and will some day write something of great value. He has no side – he is all substance – and light withal. You would wonder who were those two old cronies, if you could see us daily walking to and from the archives arm in arm.

Harvey too, I am enjoying very much. ... His volume on P.E.I., which you will find in the study, has been well reviewed – even in the London Times Literary Supplement. Every year we get together the friendship we formed years ago in Oxford grows richer – I suppose because we have certain confidence in each other and know each other pretty well. He has to leave on Friday for P.E.I., where he is to deliver some addresses on Whelan, one of the fathers of Confederation. I shall miss him very much....

I have had several good conversations with McArthur about the period on which I hope to write. A chance remark the other day made me fear that we were far apart on the Quebec Act, and that our chapters might present a clash to the reader. But I seized the bull by the horns and found that it was no bull and had no horns. At 2 a.m. when we parted after two nights' discussion, we discovered that we stood on practically the same ground.

His history of Canada for high schools is coming out and I promised to read all the proofs he has here, the first 32 galleys. I began it last night and have been at it all day except for the pleasant time at Underhill's. I have promised to finish it this weekend while he is in Montreal and Kingston. It is now 10 p.m. and I have still 10 galleys to scour and cut before I retire. His substance is excellent but he needs a wife like you. You have revolutionized my style. His is not so bad as mine was, but I hope to effect some improvement.

July 20, 1926

...Instead of digging into McArthur's proofs, I had him himself. ... We roamed all over from his proofs to the history of Canada and on to educational policy generally. He feels as we do that our chief problem is the student who comes up for the asset of a couple of letters after his name instead of development within....

Yesterday at noon, Harvey, McArthur and I lunched together and got deeply engrossed in a discussion of several problems in Canadian history – how the Englishman writing on colonial affairs knows too little of local conditions, and the Canadian writer is too ignorant of the important background of British politics and government – how the French developed an entirely different empire in

America from what the English built up – and the fallacy that the exclusion of the Huguenot was chiefly responsible, a fallacy born of ignorance of European conditions. Then we drifted off into a discussion of P.E.I., Harvey asking our advice on the work he was doing. Inseparable as yet, we retired to McArthur's and continued for half the afternoon. Here's the great value of foregathering at Ottawa. We who are attempting to do work are scattered. Here we meet in close contact and discuss our problems with each other. It must lead to us submitting our results to others who are competent to judge before we dare forth into print. Harvey had not done this with his volume on the French period, fearing it would be an imposition because he thought few would be interested in it. I am glad that McArthur asked Harvey to send him the ms. of the new book he is preparing and he insisted that it would be to his benefit to submit it to me also. We have all been too much inclined to stick our heads in our own holes, and we have suffered.

Last night at dinner we had a little informal meeting with Morton added to our number. In a general way we laid plans for the dinner which is to be held in the Rideau Club. I am to lead off with a little appreciation of Doughty. Morton is to raise the question of publications, and McArthur is to present the problem of closer co-operation of us professional historians in a group around the Archives. The purpose of the dinner is twofold – to thresh out our own general problems and to strengthen Doughty's hands. All of us who are doing research here and a few others such as Doughty, Skelton, Senator Haydon, and perhaps Sir George Perley or Sir Robert Borden, are to be present....

I came across a very interesting document on Saturday – or rather two of them – by John Gray who died in 1768. He was a trader in Canada and was deeply engaged in the fur trade. In his long account of the conditions of the trade and discussion of the policy which ought to be adopted, I came across a contrast between the personnel of the French and the English traders. There he laid his finger on the cause of much of the trouble after the conquest. The French traders coming from a better social class, were imbued with a sense of honour which the English traders, coming from a lower class, had little of, and thus the English were more unscrupulous in their dealings with the natives.

Burt's letter of 23 July describes the dinner for the Dominion Archivist, Dr Doughty, given by Sir George Perley, former High Commissioner for Canada in London, and Secretary of State in the Meighen ministry formed after King's resignation. It was an appropriate gesture on the minister's part, for Doughty experienced many frustrations in his period of service as Dominion Archivist, and in view of these his achievements were remarkable. Sound principles of archives administration, close working relationships with federal government departments, and spacious physical facilities, now taken for granted by researchers in the Public Archives of Canada, existed only in rudimentary form, or in the mind's eye of the chief archivist.

The principal obstacle to archival progress was government indifference, which was reflected in budgetary and administrative limitations. It was not Doughty's fault that so many post-Confederation departmental records and ministerial papers were not in archival custody. In 1920 he drew Borden's attention to the failure to implement the report of the Royal Commission on Public Records, which in 1912 had proposed that the Archives assume the role of a public records office, having the same function as the British Public Record Office.[12] In the following year he emphasized how far ahead of Canada the United States was in archival activity, and in the resultant quality of historical scholarship and university teaching. 'This will in course of time,' he wrote to Meighen, 'have a very serious effect on Canadian development, and it is certainly worthy of the most earnest and careful consideration by those who are entrusted with the Government of this country.'[13] In subsequent years he renewed his plea for the establishment of a policy regarding the disposal of departmental records.

Despite staff limitations, service to university staff and students, and the general public, was liberally extended, and Doughty was generous with his own time in dealing with requests for assistance – often spending ten to fifteen hours per day at his desk or in the manuscript room. He was a tireless and resourceful collector of private records in Canada and the United Kingdom and was particularly interested in the development of the picture division, for he was convinced that historical works would attract greater public interest if suitably illustrated. He hoped that the universities could be encouraged to assist their professors of Canadian history to prepare collections of documentary sources of the same type which he and his staff were selecting and editing for publication, and pled with Wrong to encourage Toronto staff and students to make more use of the growing collections. 'The digging and delving is a very tedious process,' he wrote, but 'the fact is that there is not a chapter in Canadian History that can be properly written with a knowledge obtained from books.'[14]

George Smith,[15] who is next to Wrong and was one year ahead of me at Oxford, and Glazebrook,[16] a junior member of the history dept. at Toronto, came up specially for the occasion....

The Country Club is a beautiful place up the river a few miles – on the Quebec or club side of the 'great divide.' About 22 sat down to dinner – McArthur's class and all the rest of us that are digging here. I was very delighted over the whole affair because of one thing. Several years ago George Smith was very scornful about my going to the Archives – so much so that I did not care if I ever saw him again. Just before the Hart House dinner this summer, he hailed me for a minute, and was very friendly. Then he sent a still friendlier message after me here and yesterday and today, he impressed us all with his keenness to get to work here and me with his very friendly attitude. I gather that he had a sort of "complex" about the Archives. He has wanted to come but feared to come lest the initiation be humiliating. I think that he was very pleasantly surprised. He is to be back for a real session on August 8.

Well, after the dinner we adjourned to a bright room with easy chairs and talked. I led off with a few words of appreciation directed at Sir George and Dr. Doughty, both of whom replied. Then we got down to discussing our problems generally – cooperation around the archives and the publication of the results of research. This morning, to continue the discussion, McArthur, Smith, Morton and I breakfasted together here and then retired to a quiet room. We decided that a committee should be selected at a dinner to be held after Smith returns next month – when Kennedy will be here also. By the way, Kennedy has suddenly landed back in Canada and he is now a full professor in Toronto with a department all to himself – Constitutional History. The other decision which we reached was that we workers in the Archives should work towards being an interuniversity faculty or rather committee to guide research here in the summer – an extension of the Queen's work. Everyone's of the opinion that we should place ourselves freely at the disposal of advanced students who resort hither.

It was probably as a result of these discussions that, beginning in 1927, the *Canadian Historical Review* commenced publishing an annual list of MA and PH D theses dealing with Canadian history, which had been completed or were in course of preparation. The first list was compiled by George Brown.

July 25, 1926

During the last couple of days I have been helping another novice [Glazebrook] get his feet wet. ... He has begun to dip in the stream at the point where I plunged in. This is merely to assist in a lecture course he has to deliver this year. He hopes to return about the middle of August and may bury himself in the post-Loyalist settlements of Upper Canada, which will dovetail in well with the work Pearson is undertaking. Pearson is a daily joy. Such a contrast to the dejected fellow I met in

Toronto! He has found his feet and is as happy as a lark digging up materials on the Loyalist settlement in Canada. He has to return to Toronto to prepare for next winter's work.

While going through some newly acquired material yesterday I came upon a most touching series of letters – between Pitt and Henry Wolfe. Pitt is consoling the latter, who is heartbroken over the death of his son and is fondly treasuring his box of papers just sent in. I felt as if I were there.

The other evening at dinner Morton told an amusing story about an old elder whom he once knew. This elder, who was on most intimate terms with the Almighty, was called upon to pray at a church meeting. He had suffered heavy business losses during the week. This was known to the community in a general way. During the course of the prayer they learned some of the particulars, until he dismissed the subject by concluding "O, Lord, with all thy faults we love thee still."

July 29, 1926

...My alarm at the mass of stuff still ahead of me has set me typing furiously. I must have taken over 10,000 words of documents today and I will get a few thousand more before I go back to bed....

McArthur is like the flying Dutchman. He is here, there and everywhere all at once. Now he is off to Kingston again, eternally busy over this endowment campaign. He is great company. The night before last Marion asked us out to his house to discuss the Alberta School and Natural Resources question. He is a great worshipper of Bourassa and wanted an opportunity to convert me. But instead of this, he drew a double attack from McA. and myself. The amusing thing is that we all have the same end in view – harmony and equality of French and English in Canada, but temporarily break harmony in discussing the means of establishing it. We played a few rounds of bridge and drank some of his good wine and said that we were going to retire early. That was a rash statement, for when we dropped bridge we fell back into the general discussion of French and English in Canada and talked and talked. It is very good, for Marion is an ardent churchman and also a man who appreciates old France....

It was during this summer of 1926 that Burt met J.S. Ewart, then seventy-seven, the tutor of the Canadian public on constitutional issues, who had been preaching the doctrine of national independence for over twenty years. Ewart believed that it was in the best interests of Canada to extend the powers of self-government, won in domestic affairs during the nineteenth century, to embrace all the powers which a nation-state possessed in a world of independent nation-states. Throughout most of his long career as a propagandist, he favoured a continuing relationship with

Britain and the other dominions only in the form of a common sovereign, defined as a Personal Union with each dominion having the name and status of a kingdom, although for a time during and after the Great War he shifted to the more radical position of proposing that Canada become an independent republic.

July 31, 1926

This afternoon I took off quite unexpectedly. Yesterday Morton fell in with J.S. Ewart and when he told him of the various people working here, Ewart sent a message for me to lunch with him at the Rideau to-day. There I went at 1 p.m. and then, as the day was hot, we motored out to the Royal Ottawa Golf Club to lunch there. We talked and talked of everything from the causes of the great war to the mistakes of King and Meighen and back again to the results of the war. Then he told me of a map of Europe which he had prepared to show in a graphic manner the complicated troubles of the old world. He wanted very much to show it to me, so he ran me back to his house, where we arrived just in time for tea. After that we retired to his study to examine the map and discuss Canadian history. It was nearly six before I could tear myself away and then he insisted on driving me back to the Archives where I salved my conscience by getting in an hour's work.

Ewart is an old man, though he looks little more than sixty. He showed me a photo of the lacrosse team which won the championship of Canada in 1875 – of which celebrated team he was a member.

Though he has many friends – everyone spoke to him at the Golf Club – he seemed to me quite lonely and a little out of touch with life. Years ago he started to dig in the Archives and worked up the materials down to 1818 in about 6 volumes. Then the war interrupted his Canadian historical studies and drew him off into European politics. His recent work on the causes of the European war has been highly reviewed. He has just received a very eulogistic letter from W.H. Dawson,[17] the author of several good books on recent Germany, but cannot read it. Dawson writes an abominable hand, and I spent most of the lunch hour trying to decipher it.

He [Ewart] has been an eminently successful counsel and has had a great influence behind the scenes of politics – though he will line up with neither political party. He agrees that there is little practical difference between the parties though there may be great talking differences, and he places his hopes in the Progressives. There I think he is sound, for the imaginary difference between the two old parties really demands an independent jury to hold the balance between them. Really, I should not be surprised at a larger Progressive contingent this election.

He says that King was quite sound in his remarks about not being in fear of the result of the vote on the customs report. He, Ewart, had some doubts upon that point, and therefore he approached Forke and some of his followers, who confirmed King's statement that he would have pulled through on the vote. Then I asked him why King did not forge ahead to the vote. To this he replied that King was uneasy about the Alberta Resources and really feared a motion on that subject. Whereupon I asked him if King has not erred – that the Alberta Resources would make a better election cry than the customs report. ... He agreed, and said that this was a tremendous error on King's part. Meighen, however, made his mistake, according to Ewart, and I think he's right. He says that Meighen should have refused to assume the reins of government and King would have been forced to the country on the customs probe without any covering mantle of a constitutional issue. Meighen's over-eagerness may be his own undoing.

Ewart was assessing Meighen's decision in the context of purely political considerations, and in this respect his judgment was correct, as the 1926 general election results were to show. Meighen, however, had based his decision to assume office on the constitutional principle that Byng 'had properly declined to follow most improper advice,' and that there was 'no honourable alternative to the acceptance of office.'[18]

I asked Ewart how was a poor independent to vote – who agreed with King on the constitutional issue but believed his government was responsible for corruption on a dangerously large scale. He doubted whether there were any such independent individuals. When I suggested that I thought I knew many, he seemed to catch at this as a substantial hope – that many men were not hide-bound to a party or a formula. I was rather amused at this, for he [Ewart] is generally regarded as a slave to his formula of independence. The refusal of a dissolution by Byng is almost a nightmare to him. We seem plunged back in the medieval days of Canada – when Governors really governed and the people obeyed. He cannot see that there is little difference – we have the election anyway. He quoted Borden's words to support King and I quoted Asquith's[19] to uphold Meighen.

That Burt had little sympathy for the views of the imperialist Tory establishment in Toronto and Montreal is abundantly clear from his next comment on Ewart's ideas:

But underneath it all, he is tremendously sound in his placing Canada first for Canadians and his desire to make them think of Canada as a self-respecting nation. On one point I had misunderstood him and I was glad to be corrected. He is commonly suspected of an anti-British prejudice. It has been said that hatred of

Britain – or mistrust of Britain – is the mainspring of his thought. When I suggested by way of repeating the story of Chancellor Stuart's[20] talk to our British Universities Club, that the champions of Canadian nationalism can win if they pay a generous tribute to England, what she has done and what she stands for, he came through handsomely. Indeed he almost repeated Justice Stuart's phrases.

But all said and done, Ewart is a theorist who impresses me as up in the clouds, his feet hardly touching the ground.

August 2, 1926

I have been in the "slough of Despond" for some days past. The unmastered – ungathered – material is so mountainous, and the open questions so numerous, I despair of approaching a satisfactory study – much less any finality. I shall just have to content myself with gathering what I can and doing the best with it. Yesterday, I spent a number of hours with McArthur going over my rough draught on the military regime. He has "raked it fore and aft" and I am extremely grateful to him. Everytime I discuss Canadian history with him, the more profound is my respect for him. His knowledge is wider and intenser than Smith's. Indeed he is the only one who may be regarded as a sort of master of Canadian history. When I get my chapter written, I am going to send it down to him to criticize and he is going to do the same with his two chapters which follow on mine.[21] It is a great joy to have such a friend. If he passes anything I do, I need not care what anyone else may say. At times there is the reverse of the coin sitting uppermost, and I despair of ever getting to know the elusive history of this country. I am really an ignoramus and wonder if I am any good at all....

Saturday, I think I told you, I had an interesting experience with John S. Ewart. Yesterday afternoon, I had another when McArthur and I called on Sir Robert Borden. There were no other guests for tea and we had a very delightful time. We discussed the European dislike of America, the Mexican situation and the Roman Church, the Maritime probe, the Progressives, and gardens. You see I nearly spelled the last with a capital letter – because the Bordens are such keen gardeners and it is a real subject with them – and I have much enthusiasm though little intelligence. Lady Borden was quite amusing in her denunciation of the Progressives. They upset things so! If they were all straight Liberals, it would not be so bad, for then you could know where you are! Of course I had to draw her on by apologizing for them and their supporters who find no difference between the two historic parties except talk. Very mischievously, but sincerely, I suggested that the coming elections might strengthen the disturbing contingent. I really think that likely, because one of the outstanding lessons of the last session was the power which a balancing third party may exercise. There must be such a party till the average voter can cast an intelligent and honest vote for either of the old parties.

We talked also of the investigations into the condition of the Maritime Provinces.[22] Sir Andrew Race Duncan, the Chairman, is an extremely able man, according to Sir Robert. The two others are a Nova Scotian judge and Cyrus Macmillan. The only opinion about the last which I have heard here is that he is a lightweight. It is expected that the report will be a Duncan report. Sir Robert thinks that the people in the Maritime provinces are themselves to blame for many of their ills. They do not work so hard as men do in other parts of the Dominion – or in the u.s. He [Borden] says that Nova Scotia is preeminently suited to sheep-raising and yet the Nova Scotians have not sufficient enterprise to undertake it. He suggests that they might make a great deal of the tourist traffic if they would only set out to capture it – but they are lazy....

My last days here are apt to be busy and interesting. Kennedy arrives this evening and next Sunday George Smith and George Brown return. Then we are to have more meetings. One thing we are now discussing is a survey of printed sources for Canadian History. Many American state historical societies and other organizations have published large collections of documents as a foundation for their own history. In them is a great deal of most valuable material for Canadian history. The plan is that each man will take a block of this and work through it carefully to index all bearing on Canada. It makes me feel hopelessly ignorant and even helpless – for our poor library has nothing. They have much more in Saskatoon...

Having trod these highways and byways of scholarship and politics, Burt returned to Edmonton in August. As indicated in his letters, he hoped and expected that the Progressives would retain their position of influence in Canadian politics. While he was in Ottawa the Alberta wing of the party, the United Farmers of Alberta, had won a second sweeping victory in the provincial general election of 1926. In the federal election, held at the beginning of the fall term, on 14 September, the voters of Alberta returned eleven UFA members, three Liberals, and one Conservative. Although the popular vote was much closer than these figures indicate, UFA success in federal politics was more decisive than in 1925. However, the national result gave the Liberals their first over-all majority in the House of Commons since 1921.[23]

9

Last Years at Alberta

The 1920s in Alberta was a period of slow and sporadic growth in the provincial economy in contrast to the boom years preceding the war. Farm income fluctuated with varying climatic conditions and market prices. Private capital investment was still chiefly directed to extractive industries such as coal mining, and to disappointingly capricious oil discoveries in Turner Valley, and had not created extensive industrial employment. Throughout the decade the population was predominantly rural – 62 per cent of the 1931 total of 731,000. Although the rate of population increase was larger than in the other two prairie provinces, it lagged behind British Columbia. In general, the buoyance and optimism of the pre-war years had evaporated.

The victory of the United Farmers of Alberta in provincial politics did not revolutionize the economy or the administration of public affairs – the cabinet was cautious and conservative in outlook, and there were more innovators in the Labour and Liberal parties and among the rank and file of the farmers' organization. The most significant development occurred outside the ambit of government initiative – the creation of the Alberta Wheat Pool – and this involved action by the farm movements of the three prairie provinces.

The public debt inherited from the Liberal government was large and provincial finances were chronically precarious. For most of the decade the provincial government pursued a policy of rigid economy in educational expenditures. The annual grants for operating expenses of the University of Alberta increased only slightly, despite a 40 per cent increase in enrolment between 1919 and 1929. Salary scales were lower than those of many universities in Canada. Since public demand stressed the vocational value of a university education, the chief developments in the twenties were the creation of additional professional faculties, and the university made much of its extension services to the rural population and its participation in the activities of the Research Council of Alberta. It was not an encouraging period for scholars in the humanities and social sciences – no new departments were created in the Faculty of Arts and the University library had only about 33,000 volumes by 1930. There was practically no increase in the number of graduates in Arts during these years.

In the department of history, C.S. Burgess continued to provide part-time assistance until 1928 when two young scholars, Miss Jean Murray, MA,[1] and Mr Wallace Sterling, BA,[2] were appointed, the former as an instructor and the latter as a sessional lecturer. But there was no increase in the number of students enrolled in history courses.

During these years Burt continued to accept public speaking engagements and to participate actively in League of Nations Society affairs. In February 1927, he spoke to the Calgary Board of Trade on the 1926 Imperial Conference,[3] whose deliberations, he declared, had produced fewer changes in the imperial relationship than many people believed who were unacquainted with the arrangements arrived at during the previous decade. The most important result of the Conference, he asserted, was that while it had 'given us practically no new liberty ... it had added a mighty responsibility.'

Our international notes will bear no endorsation by the government in Britain. We will have to bear full responsibility for our own signature. We can no longer shut our eyes to the question of defence. ... If we trust to the Monroe Doctrine rather than to ourselves, we are accepting a position of inferiority. We likewise degrade ourselves if we rely on the British navy without doing our utmost to provide for our protection in time of danger. Some think that it is good business to take this advantage of Great Britain and of the United States, but it is not and cannot be good business, for it is bad morals. ... We need to grow up to our voice, and it is not the body but the mind and character that make the man.

It has been claimed that Mackenzie King's creation of an external affairs bureaucracy in Ottawa and a few legations abroad after 1926 was 'a daring innovation ... which would end dependence on British diplomacy and make equality of status something more than a convenient fiction.'[4] But

most people. And you have triumphantly solved the problem that defeated poor Knaplund – of combining the treatment of topics with a chronological narrative that preserves the sense of movement which is of the very essence of history.[21]

McDougall's prediction of the popularity of *The Evolution of the British Empire and Commonwealth* was borne out by its adoption within a year by over forty universities in the United States. This was partly the result of the sweep and range of the work, for this last of his major publications was the type of historical exposition which he had so admired in Sorel in 1919:

He takes long views of history and connects up distant but similar effects by unearthing deep and permanent causes. That grander style of history appeals to me more and more.[22]

Burt's career at the University of Minnesota ended with his retirement in 1957. Professor Heaton, then chairman of the department, recalls that he cited Burt and E.S. Osgood, who retired the same year, as up-daters of the Turner thesis – men who had begun life as easterners who had moved to the far west, subsequently turning back as far as the Midwest – 'living examples of the Turnaround Theory.'[23]

Burt's retirement did not terminate his scholarly activities; during the following academic year he was visiting professor at Carleton University, Ottawa, which had been founded by Dr Tory fifteen years earlier. In addition to his university duties, he delivered a series of six public lectures in Ottawa on the Commonwealth, sponsored by the English-Speaking Union. In 1958–9 he was visiting professor at the University of Chicago. In 1960–1, at the age of seventy-two, he taught at the University of Manitoba. Professor Carl Berger recalls the course which Burt offered that year, in which he displayed the same stamina in a three- or four-hour seminar which Professor Lillian Cobb had noticed 43 years before in Edmonton. And his characteristic emphasis on clarity in composition as the essence of the historian's craft continued undiminished. 'He was the first teacher I ever had,' Professor Berger claims, 'who went through an essay word by word, line by line, paragraph by paragraph to show me exactly how it could have been put together more effectively and like everybody else who came into contact with him I have never forgotten that experience.'[24]

After the end of the term Burt suffered a stroke, which limited his capacities, despite a gradual recovery in subsequent years. In 1963 he wrote a preface for the Carleton Library's edition of Professor Aileen

Dunham's *Political Unrest in Upper Canada 1815–1836*. The reprinting of this work after the lapse of nearly forty years was a signal recognition of the scholarship of one of his first honours students at Alberta, and his participation in its reissuance was a happy epilogue to his long teaching career.

The late sixties were a quiet time spent happily in Minneapolis, with regular summer sojourns at Kirk's Ferry (Larrimac) on the Gatineau. In 1966 he returned to Edmonton to receive the University's honorary degree of Doctor of Laws, and to renew acquaintance with many distinguished Albertans who, as senior members of the History Club, organized a banquet and presentation in honour of the Burts. During the following year the Minneapolis home was sold to permit a move to Wellesley, Massachusetts, where Arthur and his wife were anxious to have his parents nearby. Unfortunately this arrangement was to benefit A.L. only, for Mrs Burt died rather unexpectedly in 1967. This blow he accepted with sorrowful resignation. Dorothy Burt, in addition to the contribution she had made to A.L.'s literary endeavours, had been an affectionate wife and mother, a generous hostess, and an active community worker, particularly in the affairs of the local Anglican (in the United States, Episcopal) congregation. Her wisdom and tact were decisive elements in fifty-two years of married life, while endearing her to friends young and old.

Fully alert in his mental faculties, though handicapped in his ability to communicate, Burt's last years were spent tranquilly in Wellesley, and with his other children. His music record collection remained a solace to the end, which came quietly on 21 June 1971. Those who had known him were reminded of the last words of Bunyan's Mr Valiant-for-truth:

My sword I give to him that shall succeed me in my pilgrimage, and my courage and skill to him that can get it. My marks and scars I carry with me, to be a witness for me. ... So he passed over, and all the trumpets sounded for him on the other side.

[John Bunyan, *The Pilgrim's Progress. The Second Part*]

12

Committed Scholar and
Dedicated Teacher

There can be no disputing that A.L. Burt was one of the leaders of the group of historians who revitalized Canadian history in the 1920s and 1930s by establishing it on a firm basis of exhaustive documentary research. Younger scholars in the years since World War II have inaugurated important work in new directions – social, economic, and intellectual history, as well as political – which were ignored or passed over lightly by these pioneers. Yet it is noteworthy that revisionism has not seriously modified the contributions to the discipline made by Burt and his contemporaries. Their concentration of effort was both necessary and, in its end products, creative.

In assessing Burt's role in the intellectual life of his time, it is essential in the first place to refer to his role as a teacher. His effectiveness on the rostrum in front of a large class has been noted previously. His object was to arouse the interest of the students, to convey to them something of his own love and enthusiasm for the subject. He succeeded because he was a bit of an actor, and by gesture, declamation, and embellishment of phrase clothed the abstractions of historical fact with a rich texture of realism. To prepare for these appearances he insisted on an uninterrupted hour before class time. His lecturing technique involved a close observation of the reactions of his class. If he sensed that they were not getting the point, he tackled it again from a different angle; conversely, if they had grasped the point quickly, he cut short his illustrations and explanations.

In contrast to these undergraduate lectures, Burt's seminars on Canadian history were informal and intimate, as he discussed the implications of a particular document, or the students' interpretations of some episode of the period under consideration. On one principle only he was authoritarian: 'Reserve judgment till you can get all the evidence – get to the source.'[1]

Without exception, his graduate students found him 'a very warm man, generous, friendly, even fatherly,' as one of them has described him.[2] 'More than one hungry young man was fed at Mrs Burt's table, and benefited by Mr Burt's conversation and sage advice,' recalls Miss Louise Olsen, an MA in history, the omnicompetent and perceptive departmental secretary. 'Some of the graduate students simply gorged themselves with both food and drink.'[3]

On one occasion I was able to accept Mrs. Burt's invitation to Thanksgiving dinner, when the board was loaded with all kinds of good food. We stood while Mr. Burt said grace (in Latin, and wearing his Oxford jacket). We were a large group of family and graduate teaching assistants. Mr. Burt carved the turkey, while Arthur cut slices from a slab of roast bacon.[4]

Burt's conversations with his graduate students extended beyond the realm of mutual professional interest, notably in the field of music. Visitors at his home soon became aware of his competence at the keyboard of the family piano, and his infectious enthusiasm for the orchestral works of the classical composers was one of their enduring memories of his friendship.

Although his own research was concentrated on political, constitutional, and diplomatic history, Burt welcomed scholarly contributions in other fields of historical study, as his book reviews testify. Strongly convinced of the social function of history, he stressed the importance of literary style in establishing communication with the reader. He applied the same standard to his own work: 'I fill my scrap basket several times with discarded drafts before I can complete a chapter. It is like sweating blood....'[5]

The thrust of his thinking exhibited a consistently liberal bias – for he was an ideologue of neither the right nor the left. He can best be described as a pragmatic democrat, with a basic sympathy for the economically weak and underprivileged. Nationalism, imperialism, *laissez-faire* capitalism, socialism, and communism were human concerns, deserving of analysis and understanding in their historical context, but he was committed to none of them. However, his dislike of authoritarianism and blind prejudice is abundantly clear in his books and public addresses. This was a corollary of his oft repeated dictum that a democratic society could survive only if it possesses an informed public opinion.

His democratic and humanitarian instincts, which were so clearly evident during his sojourn in London, coupled with his experience of life in the Canadian West, are vigorously expressed in an analysis of the Social Credit victory in Alberta and of the origins of the Union Nationale in Quebec, which he published in the New York monthly, *Events*, in 1937.

Premier Aberhart of Alberta has done more for Canada than for his own province. This wild man of the West has taught the wise men of the East a much needed lesson. The economic collapse gave fantastic proportions to the debt structure of the Canadian West, making readjustment imperative, but the financiers of the East were blindly stubborn until the Premier of Alberta shook them. He did it because they made him. As eager lenders, they shared with the equally eager borrowers the responsibility for the "extravagance" of the West, but they were so determined to make the West pay the whole bill that they contributed more than a little to the political victory of the Social Credit party in Alberta. ...

Burt was undoubtedly correct in claiming that 'If the legislature were dissolved today for another election, his party would win again, for he has given the people something and there is no alternative government visible.' Turning to Quebec, he wrote:

Down East, French Canadian nationalism is insurgent once more and, incidentally, has given another shock to the financial interests already hit by the rise of Aberhart in the West. Whether Liberals or Conservatives were in office in Quebec, there was little doubt that the seat of power was St. James Street, Montreal, the Wall Street of Canada. But the election last August [1936] saw a great upheaval. Liberals, Conservatives and St. James Street were all routed at the polls by a racial movement organized under the name *Union Nationale*. ...

Instead of reacting against the economic system, French Canadians have reacted against the unquestionable economic domination of the British, and thus the radicalism born of hard times has in French Canada taken on a distinct racial and political form. They will be masters in their own house. Some of them have been talking and more have been dreaming of a day when they will form a French and Roman Catholic republic on the shores of the St. Lawrence.[6]

A few months later in an article in the same periodical, 'Stress and Strain in Canada,' he wrote

Another feature of this ... movement has been the failure of the traditional parties, seated in the East, to understand the new society growing in the West, and here lies what may be a valuable lesson. For the present predicament of Alberta, the historic political parties are much to blame. Liberals and Conservatives alike, and even the United Farmers who held office for fourteen years, have been too absorbed in playing the game of politics to have much concern for the political education of the electorate. ...[7]

As an Ontarian who had lived in western Canada during a period of rapid cultural change, Burt was interested in the applicability of Turner's thesis as an explanation of what had been distinctive qualities of Western life. As we have noted in a previous chapter, he explored this theme in a general way in a public address in 1930. Other Canadian historians, particularly A.R.M. Lower and Frank Underhill, were finding the thesis applicable to some strictly circumscribed developments in Canada, while Walter N. Sage had delivered a general endorsement in 1928. Burt's approach was both subtle and selective. In the region west of the Great Lakes he stressed the impact of frontier conditions on a population who 'were not an average representative of the society which they left behind.'

They were a picked lot, selected by conditions. They were the poor who had a hope of becoming richer and [with] the ability and the energy to realize their hope if it was at all possible.[8]

Like the more perceptive British travellers who published their impressions of the western mentality before World War I, Burt stressed the distinctive qualities of responses which are convincing to anyone who has lived in the West:

The new life which they created was crude and material. Conditions made it so. But it was redeemed by a peculiar idealism – an intense belief in what man can do and a tremendous faith in the future. It was free of the feeling of restraint which the growing past throws over a man. It was emancipated; it was creative. ...

Thus we have had in North America, in Canada as well as in the United States, a life with little leisure or culture, a life that is intensely practical and concerned with material things, a life in which emphasis is laid on growth and quantity, and on the future instead of the past.[9]

'But all this is a tale of yesterday,' Burt observed, turning to an elucidation of the new conditions which had transformed Western society – the mechanization of agriculture, the declining size of the farming population, the influence of machine-made, mass-produced goods, the growth of an urban industrial society.

Reverting to the past again, it is interesting to note that in his 1932 address to the Minnesota Historical Society Burt first propounded what became one of his settled convictions, although it was not one which went unchallenged by some of his colleagues in later years: that Turner's hypothesis was confirmed by the history of New France.

Feudalism lost all its strength on being transplanted into Canada; and the government of the colony, though autocratic according to the letter of the law, was very far from autocratic in practice. The eyes, the ears, and the mouth of the government in every parish were those of the local militia captain; and he, though formally appointed by the governor, was substantially the elected leader of the people. From the earliest days of New France, the breath of liberty entered into the lives of the French Canadians to a degree which has been little appreciated except by themselves. ... It was physically impossible to hold down the habitant as the peasant was held down in old France. America emancipated him. The woods were at his very door and liberty was forever beckoning him through the trees. ...

This thesis Burt developed more fully in a paper read in 1940 at the annual meeting of the Canadian Historical Association. He repeated it in 1957 in a chapter entitled 'If Turner had Looked at Canada, Australia, and New Zealand When He Wrote about the West,' in the book *The Frontier in Perspective*. Australia on the other hand, he observed, exhibited a sharp contrast in development as compared with North America; on that continent the small independent farmer was almost non-existent, and hence of little influence in shaping politics and society; in New Zealand the farmer or rancher emerged only after fifty years of subservience to a pastoral oligarchy of large estate owners.

Turner's and his disciples' failure to discover that the frontier was not peculiar to the United States, Burt concluded, was the most serious criticism which could be leveled at their work.

They have studied and written as national historians without realizing that the besetting sin of national history, in this as in every other country, is too exclusive a concern with what has happened within its own borders. To avoid this insidious snare is not easy, for nationalism by its very nature is introspective and given to self-glorification. If Frederick Jackson Turner and his followers fell into this sin, they are not alone. They have plenty of company.

Burt's views on French-English relations in Canada have been frequently referred to elsewhere in this work, and it remains to note his attitude to the Francophone historiographical tradition. His closest French-Canadian friends were Gustave Lanctot and the Abbé Arthur Maheux, who in the 1970s would be labelled federalists. There is no evidence of any contact with the Abbé Groulx, whose uncompromising nationalism and hostility to British influence in Canada were being transmitted to successive generations of college students during his long career as a teacher and prolific writer. As a moderate critic of the ideology of nationalism, there was no possibility of a productive dialogue; avoiding direct confrontation, Burt confined himself to lamenting the tendency of those French-Canadian historians and writers who sought 'to preserve their national integrity by withdrawing within themselves, indulging in self-pity over their hard lot, and nursing their prejudices.' He approved Maheux's use of history 'pour inspirer à la jeunesse la très positive notion d'égalité entre les deux groupes du Canada.'[10]

As a professional, Burt gained the respect of other professional historians. He was tireless in the search for facts in the documentary sources, discriminating in weighing them as evidence, acute in his conclusions and generalizations, and tireless in striving for effective literary expression. His major works were in the mainstream of contemporary historiography. Like other historians whom Professor Arthur Marwick has labelled the 'straight line professionals of the inter-war years,' his two major works were concerned with 'the obvious centrality of institutions and political activity.'[11] Considering these skills and interests, one must ask why his productivity was relatively limited. The answer is to be found in Burt's concept of the range of his commitments.

Reviewing his career as a whole, it is obvious that Burt sought continuously to relate his professional labours to the needs and concerns of contemporary society as he saw them. Serious-minded from his earliest years, he did not take his responsibilities as a citizen lightly. War service, activities for the League of Nations Society, participation in the Canada-United States Committee on Education, and the Canadian Institute of International Affairs, were time-consuming. Above all, his ready acceptance of numerous speaking engagements in Alberta and Minnesota to advance the cause of international understanding were an expression of his conviction that the scholar in a democratic society has an obligation to share his insights and knowledge with the public.

The same motive was involved in the time he devoted to popular articles and to writing books for school and college students. In these works, his knowledge of history was explicitly used as an instrument to advance such causes as a better understanding of Canada's dual nationality, improvements in Canadian-American relations and, above all, the construction of a peaceful world order. From first to last, by perceptive assessments of individual and group character, he combatted irrational fears and prejudices. In these writings he did not shun moralizing.

Like other historians, Burt must be judged in the light of the fact that 'each age writes its own history,' each age has its evaluations of what is significant in its past, and 'will tend to see the past in the light of its own preoccupations.'[12] World War I had a profound influence on his thinking, and the prevention of a similar catastrophe was his chief imperative – indeed it almost became an obsession. The mobilizing of public opinion in support of the League of Nations concept was a 'tremendous moral responsibility.' 'If we fail to shoulder this great responsibility, we will stumble along the same old way which we all know leads to disaster,' he had declared.[13]

Had he eschewed what for him was the scholar's responsibility as an activist, and the obligation to communicate, Burt would undoubtedly have produced a larger corpus of original contributions to historical knowledge, but this was the price he was ready and willing to pay for a conscience which, had he overruled it, would have left him restless and unsatisfied – a hollow man.

Men exist for the sake of one another. Teach them then or bear with them.
[*The Thoughts of Marcus Aurelius*, Book VIII, No. 59]

APPENDICES

1 'On the Study of History'

Extracts from two lectures
delivered to the students in the first year of
the Faculty of Arts and Sciences,
University of Alberta, October 1927

Before discussing the value of studying history, I wish to protect you and me from a possible misunderstanding. I have not the slightest wish or intention to decry any other subject. Some people have the notion that every professor thinks his own subject the only one worth while. Personally, I doubt the existence of such bespectacled mental monstrosities, but I quite understand how a man who sets out to spend the most of his life in delving deeper into one particular subject may sometimes leave such a false impression. I hope that I will not. I merely want to give you a peep into the reasons why we study history.

It often happens that we attempt to explain what we take for granted, that we find a most inadequate justification. We take life for granted. Who of us could sit down and write out a convincing argument to prove that life is worth living? Most of us would make a sorry mess of it. ... As a student of history speaking to other students of history, I feel that I am very likely to advance reasons for the study of history which may seem hopelessly inadequate or even trivial. If you condemn me for this, I will agree with you most heartily, for I have never yet been able to find a fully satisfactory explanation of why I have undertaken to spend my life in the study of history. I fear that I will never find it, but I am confident that I will be able to analyse the inner urge a little better as life goes on. As I see it now, the value of the study of history is both practical and ideal. Let us concentrate first on the practical value, on the study as a means to an end in our everyday life.

It provides us with a stock of knowledge which is necessary to intelligent reading and conversation. Surely it is of some real practical value to know what other people are speaking and thinking about, for otherwise we would be cut off from our fellows. Somebody mentions Sir John A. Macdonald and some political trick which he played, or perhaps the great part he took in making this fair country of ours. He might as well have spoken in Chinese, if we have no knowledge of the history of Macdonald and his time. We read some reference to Abraham Lincoln, but it means nothing to us if we are ignorant of the history of the United States at one of its supreme crises. Someone talks of Oliver Cromwell, but we must be dumb if we have never read or heard of that great man who ruled over the destinies of Great Britain when they were trembling in the balance. ... Someone may speak of the religious difficulties faced by King Feisal today in Mesopotamia, but the meaning of what he says is locked up in the history of over a thousand years ago when the Moslem world split. We may hear that England by her conquest of India was threatened with the fate of Rome. But what does that mean unless we recall how Rome's military conquests reacted to injure Roman character? ... Almost all intelligent conversation and thinking is coloured by the past, and unless we are tolerably familiar with it, we are perpetually at a loss.

Other subjects are equally valuable as a sort of stock in trade of educated conversation, but history is as important and as necessary as any of them. A knowledge of history is one of the marks of an educated man whatever be his profession or business. ... There are other and more compelling reasons for turning our eyes backwards – without running any danger of imitating Lot's wife.

It is impossible to turn our back upon the past without coming to grief. There are some who purposely shut their eyes upon the past as all bad and useless – something to be discarded. Let us see what happens to those who trust to their own blind wisdom. After the 'wisest fool of Christendom' came down from Scotland to rule England, he did not make the success of it that other Scots have done. The times grew more and more out of joint, till at last the Great Rebellion broke forth, and England was torn by civil war. The Roundheads won on the battlefield and then they tried to set matters right so that they would never go wrong again, and they did it thoroughly. They cut off the head of the king, they abolished the church of Archbishop Laud, they swept away the old House of Lords, and they radically remodelled what they had left of the ancient institution of parliament. By these simple operations, they sought to make a new and a

better England, and indeed they foreshadowed many of the great reforms of the nineteenth century. But did they succeed then in doing what
they were trying to do? No! They found that Charles I when dead was a
more powerful enemy than he had been when alive. ... And the result?
Only a few months after Cromwell was laid in his grave, the king came
back in the person of Charles II, the House of Lords returned, and the
established church was restored – and all with such wild enthusiasm that
the naive Charles II observed that it must have been his own fault that he
had stayed out of his own realm so long.

Another example occurred a century and a half later. When the
French Revolution broke out, men were carried away by their hatred of
the past. They destroyed their old institutions in a night, and they tried to
create a new heaven and a new earth in a day. But they could not, for they
were not Gods but only men. What happened? The Revolution turned
and devoured her own children. Then came Napoleon, a more tyrannous
master than any king had been, and at last the French restored the
monarchy which they had guillotined. And the Church which they had
thought they abolished came back too. They could not help it.

Very recently, the Russians have also tried the glorious experiment of
taking the Golden Jerusalem by storm. The Bolsheviks abolished almost
everything but themselves, and they even made a beginning at that. But
what have they done? The Czar is dead, but tyranny is not.

Of course later generations have benefitted from the English Civil War
and the French Revolution, and, very possibly, Russia may be a better
country in the future for the events of the last years. But the significant
fact is that the revolutionaries all failed for the most part in what they were
trying to do at that time. They were baffled by some unseen power that
held them in its mysterious grasp. What was it? It was the past which rose
up against them and defeated them. No individual at any moment of his
existence can cut loose from his past, for that is himself. So it is with any
people. It cannot shut the door upon the past, and cut itself off from its
history, for that is its essence.

...Here lies a grave danger, for every so-called reform or 'step in
advance' will be in vain and may very probably bring trouble unless the
past is taken into account....

At present there is a good deal of discontent and unrest with parliamentary government as it exists, not only in Italy but in many parts of
the world as well. Again I would suggest that a sense of the past is
indispensable. Parliamentary government has been working best in that

country where the history of that institution is best known – in England. It is only by a study of the past that we can see that our laws and our parliaments are not dead but living things which are changing all the time....

But while we are learning the nature of the present by a study of the past, at the same time we develop our mental faculties, we develop our judgment. The study of history is much more than learning a story or a lot of events. That is the 'A.B.C.' of history. It is the attempt to find a connection, a cause for things. Why did the Reformation in England come under Henry VIII? Why was America discovered when it was? Why did the Crusades come when they did? Why were they a failure, and why did the movement die out in the 13th century? Why did Rome conquer Carthage? Why did that home of individual liberty, Greece, become enslaved? Why did civilization arise in the Nile valley? Sometimes we find the answer easily, even though it very seldom lies on the surface....

Sometimes the answer long eludes our prying search. Not until about 30 years ago did we really understand why Carthage fell. Sometimes we never find the answer. But we hope to do so some day. Meanwhile, the inquiry into the working of cause and effect in human affairs, whether it leads to a definite conclusion or not, is extremely valuable to our minds. We are developing judgment. Here the study of history is of great practical value. Our judgment upon present day problems is keener and sounder in proportion as we exercise it upon the problems of the past....

History is not a simple science; it is a most complicated business. But how can it be applied if there is no certainty to it? Our judgment is aided by some particular qualities of mind and by several general conclusions which we may deduce from the past.

One quality of mind which is sadly needed today is imagination. The absence of this has been one of the greatest causes of wars. People in one country cannot understand the people of another. They live their daily lives largely in ignorance of them, until suddenly they are confronted by some serious clash of feeling and interest, and then, on the spur of the moment, they condemn the other people as wrong and bad, simply because they think and feel in a different way. They give full vent to their tempers, and think that they are doing the work of God. If only we had more imagination, to project ourselves into the lives of people different from ourselves, to think their thoughts, to experience their feelings, to peer out upon the world through their eyes, how much more tolerant, how much more peaceful would we be! Here is one of the greatest uses of the study of history, the study of the life of other peoples, of other conditions of living, of other ages. It is more than just reading about them, it is living with them. There is no better way to train this imagination which is necessary if we are going to live in any harmony with other people both beyond and within our own borders.

Closely linked with imagination are other mental qualities which are necessary for the welfare of our society and which may be greatly developed by the study of history. One of the commonest sins of youth, and even of maturer age, is the forming of hard uncompromising opinions. Even when we do not form them ourselves, we catch them from others. For this prevalent disease, the best antidote by far is the study of history, which ever inculcates a largeness rather than a narrowness of view. Another valuable mental quality which it gives is a sense of proportion. Two illustrations of this will suffice. Almost every people, at one time or another, has thought that it was the chosen of Heaven. If this continent understood a little more history, we would hear less about God's country, and the biggest talkers in the world would tell us less about all the biggest things in the world, including themselves. We would also have a sounder sense of proportion about the age in which we live. It is only a moment of time in the life of mankind, and we should not be impatient because we cannot do in a few years more than has been done in centuries in the past.

From the past, also, we may draw some very practical general conclusions. In this, however, we must be most careful, for history, like the Bible, can be made to teach anything which people want it to teach. For the most part, the lessons of the past are very broad, and are forced home time after time without any possibility of mistaking. Incidentally, we have already discovered one of the most important of these – that we cannot cut ourselves off from the past, for if we try it will rise up against us. But while there is this law of permanence, there is also the law of change. One of the first things to strike the student of history is the successive fall of empires. ... Each was great in its age, because it was adapted to existing conditions. But they could not stand still and the times changed. Then each in turn lost the faculty of clinging to life by a new adaptation to the world around us. Whose turn is next?

These are not the only lessons which the past holds in store for us. There is the law of interdependence. This operates in many ways. One of the simplest is the reaction of the conquered upon the conqueror. ... Still another lesson is the value of individual initiative. People are like children. They are much better when they do things for themselves.

And so we might go on, but let us look back to see what all this practical value of history means. Our greatest heritage today, is not the wealth of our natural resources. It is our past, the experience of generation after generation, without which these resources would be of no more value than nature is to the utter savage.

In the present state of our civilization, there is a greater need to delve into this wonderful storehouse of the experience of mankind than has ever existed before. We often flatter ourselves because we live in the most democratic age that the world has seen. Indeed we have raised democracy up into a sort of dogma or religion. Now there lies a very grave danger right here. As never before we have given the power of government into the hands of the people, but are the people able to shoulder this mighty responsibility? No answer to this question can yet be given, for our democracy is very young. It has developed within the last hundred years. We are in the midst of a great experiment, upon which the fate of our society rests. Whether this fate will be further human development, or the doom of our society, will depend in large part upon how far our masters, the people, will take to heart the experience of the past. The future will be dark without a much wider study of history than there has ever yet been.

Apart from this practical purpose, there is another great reason for the study of history. It is an end in itself. If properly approached, it becomes an ever-growing joy, for it enlarges our being. ... There are some people whose lives are bound about closely by time and place, the twin tyrants of mankind. But we may burst through their close restraints, and the process of expansion is one of the greatest and finest joys that we can win. We may grow until our lives reach out over time past, and even penetrate somewhat into the future, and though our bodies may be in one little place, our minds may rove over space. The curiosity with which nature has endowed us all, is the magic charm which may set us free. We want to know the why of everything, and so we pursue many studies. But of them all none is more fascinating, more noble than history – the growth of mankind. But of this I will say no more. For if you have this great vision of the study of history as an end in itself, my words would be stale and unprofitable; and if you have it not, they would be unavailing, for this is a vision that is caught only by trying to penetrate into the wonderful mystery of the world of man.

2 A.L. Burt: A Bibliography

Abbreviation UAED, University of Alberta Extension Department

1913
Imperial Architects: Being an Account of Proposals in the Direction of a Closer Imperial Union Made Previous to the Opening of the First Colonial Conference of 1887 (Oxford: B.H. Blackwell)
'The Relation of Music to the Other Arts,' *The Pelican Record* (Corpus Christi College), XI, 5 (March 1913) 153–63

1917
'Is Life Worth Living?' *The Gateway* (University of Alberta Students' Union), (May 1917) 17–19

1921
'Thoughts on the Russian Revolution,' *The Gateway* (March 1921) 8–12

1922
'The Mystery of Walker's Ear,' *Canadian Historical Review* III, 233–55

1923
'Sir Guy Carleton and His First Council,' *Canadian Historical Review*, IV, 321–2
'The League of Nations. I: Its Organization,' *The Press Bulletin*, UAED, VIII, 10 (19 January 1923) 1–4

'The League of Nations. II: Its Working,' *The Press Bulletin*, UAED, VIII, 11 (26 January 1923) 1–4
'The Need for a Wider Study of Canadian History,' *The Press Bulletin*, UAED, IX, 5 (23 November 1923) 1–4
'The Horoscope of Mars,' *Queen's Quarterly*, XXX, 3 (January–March 1923) 273–96

1924
A Short History of the League of Nations: Its Origin, Organization and Problems (Edmonton, UAED)
'The Tragedy of Chief Justice Livius,' *Canadian Historical Review*, V, 196–212
'Canada's Dual Nationality,' *The Press Bulletin*, UAED, IX, 9 (15 February 1924) 1–4
'Le Dualisme canadien,' L'Echo du Collège d'Edmonton, II, 7 (25 mars 1924) 1–7
'The Stumbling Block of Europe – Reparations,' *The Press Bulletin*, UAED, X, 1 (3 October 1924), 1–6
'Disarmament and the Fifth Assembly,' *The Press Bulletin*, UAED, X, 4 (24 October 1924) 1–4

1925
'Shall Canada Accept the Protocol?', *The Press Bulletin*, UAED, X, 11 (26 February 1925) 1–4

1926
Introduction and appendices to A.G. Bradley's *Lord Dorchester*, and J.N. McIlwraith's *Sir Frederick Haldimand*, The Makers of Canada Series, anniversary edition (London and Toronto: Oxford University Press)
'Peace in the Heart of Europe,' *The Press Bulletin*, UAED, XI (22 January 1926) 1–4
'What is Canada?' *The Press Bulletin*, UAED, XI, 4 (8 February 1926) 1–4
'The Policeman: A Story for Young People,' *The Bulletin of the League of Nations Society in Canada*, IV, 6 (December 1926) 8–10

1927
'Who was the "Com[man]d[ant] de la Troupe dans chaque coste"?,' *Canadian Historical Review*, VII, 227–30
'The Imperial Conference,' *The Press Bulletin*, UAED, XII, 7 (25 March 1927) 1–4
A New World or the League of Nations (Ottawa: League of Nations Society in Canada)

1928

High School Civics: A Brief Treatment of the Civics Section of History 3. (Edmonton: School-Book Branch, Department of Education)
'Governor Murray and the British Government,' *Transactions of the Royal Society of Canada*, 3rd series, XXII, sect. ii, 49–56
'On the Study of History,' *The Press Bulletin*, UAED, XIII, 3 (14 March 1928) 1–4

1930

The Romance of the Prairie Provinces (Toronto: W.J. Gage and Co. Ltd.)
Manitoba High School Civics (Toronto: Educational Book Co. Ltd)
'The Problem of Government, 1760–1774,' in *The Cambridge History of the British Empire* (Cambridge: Cambridge University Press) 146–72 (chapter 6)
Lord Dorchester. Ryerson Canadian History Readers (Toronto: Ryerson Press)
'The Quarrel between Germain and Carleton: An Inverted Story,' *Canadian Historical Review*, XI, 202–22
'Our Dynamic Society,' *The Press Bulletin*, UAED, XVI, 3 (12 December 1930) 1–4

1931

'Guy Carleton, First Baron Dorchester (1724–1808),' *Encyclopaedia of the Social Sciences* III (New York: The Macmillan Company) 227–8
'A New Approach to the Problem of the Western Posts,' *Canadian Historical Association Annual Report* 61–75

1932

'Our Dynamic Society,' *Minnesota History*, XIII, 1, pp 3–23

1933

A New World or the League of Nations, revised edition (Ottawa: League of Nations Society in Canada)
The Old Province of Quebec (Minneapolis and Toronto: The University of Minnesota Press and Ryerson Press)

1935

'Guy Carleton, Lord Dorchester: An Estimate,' *Canadian Historical Association Annual Report* 76–87

1937
The Romance of Canada (Toronto: W.J. Gage and Co. Ltd)
'Canadian Cross Currents,' *Events* (New York) I (February 1937) 131–4
'Stress and Strain in Canada,' *Events* (New York) II (July 1937) 69–73

1940
The United States, Great Britain and British North America from the Revolution to the Establishment of Peace after the War of 1812. In the series The Relations of Canada and the United States (New Haven, Toronto, and London: Yale University Press, The Ryerson Press, Oxford University Press)
'The Frontier and the History of New France,' *Canadian Historical Association Annual Report* 93–9

1942
A Short History of Canada for Americans (Minneapolis and Toronto: the University of Minnesota Press, The Educational Book Company of Toronto, Ltd)
'The American Key,' *Revue de l'Université d'Ottawa*, XII, 153–66
'The United States from the Depression to the Second World War' (Part VII), and America's Involvement in the War (Part IX): nine chapters in Allan Nevins and Louis M. Hacker, eds., *The United States and Its Place in World Affairs, 1918–1943* (Boston: D.C. Heath and Company)

1944
A Short History of Canada for Americans, revised and enlarged edition (Minneapolis and Toronto: The University of Minnesota Press, The Educational Book Company of Toronto, Ltd)

1946
Canada: Our Oldest Good Neighbor, EM47, GI Round Table (Washington: US Government Printing Office)

1947
'American Cooperation with Britain and the Canadian-American Marriage,' *The United States in the Postwar World*, addresses given at the 1945 Summer Conference of the University of Michigan (Ann Arbor) 81–94

1950
'Broad Horizons,' *Canadian Historical Association Annual Report* 1–10

1955
Guy Carleton, Lord Dorchester, 1724–1808, revised version, Canadian Historical Association Booklets, No. 5 (Ottawa: Canadian Historical Association)

1956
The Evolution of the British Empire and Commonwealth from the American Revolution (Boston: D.C. Heath and Company)

1957
'If Turner had Looked at Canada, Australia, and New Zealand When He Wrote about the West," in W.D. Wyman and C.B. Kroeber, eds., *The Frontier in Perspective* (Madison: The University of Wisconsin Press) 59–77

1961
'Peter Mitchell on John A. Macdonald,' *Canadian Historical Review*, XLII, 3, pp 209–27
'British America,' in American Historical Association, *Guide to Historical Literature* (New York: Macmillan and Company) 697–708

1964
'The Problem of Nationalism,' in L. Bryson, L. Finkelstein, and R.M. MacIver, eds., *Conflicts of Power in Modern Culture* (New York: Cooper Square Publishers Inc.) 590–6

3 A.L. Burt's Ph D Students

1934 Hilda Neatby, 'The Administration of Justice under the Quebec Act'

1947 Gerald M. Craig, 'The Influence of the American Background on the Struggle for Self-Government in Upper Canada'

1947 Paul F. Sharp, 'The American Revolt in Western Canada: A Comparative Study Showing American Parallels'

1948 Gerald S. Brown, 'The Policy of Lord George Germain toward the American Revolution, 1775–1778'

1953 Alvin C. Gluek, Jr, 'The Struggle for the British Northwest: A Study in Canadian-American Relations'

1953 Lewis H. Thomas, 'The Struggle for Responsible Government in the North-West Territories, 1870–1897'

1954 P.C.T. White, 'Anglo-American Relations from 1803 to 1815'

1957 Galen Broeker, 'The Problem of Law and Order in Ireland, 1812–1836'

1957 Roy C. Dalton, 'The Jesuit Estates Act (Quebec)'

1957 G.G. Hatheway, 'The Indian Neutral Barrier States'

1957 Leslie L.F. Upton, 'William Smith: Chief Justice of New York and Quebec'

1960 Alan H. Lawrence, 'The Influence of British Ideas in the British North American Revolution'

1968 Wilfred I. Smith, 'Canadian Representation Abroad to 1896'

Notes

CHAPTER 1   FAMILY ROOTS AND EDUCATIONAL
EXPERIENCE

1 J.B. Bickersteth, *The Land of Open Doors: Being Letters from Western Canada* (London 1914) 105, 106
2 *Canadian Annual Review* (1913) 702
3 *Review of Historical Publications Relating to Canada*, XVIII (1913) 16. The work was also praised as 'a timely and valuable contribution to a subject that is becoming increasingly important,' in a long review by 'H.P.' in the *Oxford Times* 28 June 1913, and was also favourably reviewed in *The Spectator* and *The Scotsman*.
4 See review of *The Romance of the Prairie Provinces, The Mail and Empire* (Toronto) 26 April 1930, by William Arthur Deacon.
5 *The Sudbury Journal* 9 June 1910
6 G.R. Parkin, *The Rhodes Scholarship* (Toronto, etc. 1912) 91
7 See Carl Berger, *The Sense of Power: Studies in the Ideas of Canadian Imperialism, 1867–1914* (Toronto 1970).
8 A.L. Burt, 'Broad Horizons,' Presidential Address, *Canadian Historical Association Annual Report, 1950* 1
9 D.C. Harvey (1886–1966), after his studies at Oxford, taught at McGill and the universities of Manitoba and British Columbia. In 1931 he was appointed Archivist of Nova Scotia, and retired in 1956.
10 J.E. Read to John Arthur Burt, 2 July 1971

11 *The Pelican Record* XI, 5 (March 1913). Reprinted in *The Gateway*, 27 November 1923, University of Alberta Archives, hereinafter cited as UAA

12 F.J. Wylie in Parkin, *The Rhodes Scholarship* 175–6

13 The Head Registry Clerk, Oxford University, to the author, 19 March 1971

14 *Imperial Architects: Being an Account of Proposals in the Direction of a Closer Imperial Union Made Previous to the Opening of the First Colonial Conference of 1887* (Oxford 1913) 225

15 *The Evolution of the British Empire and Commonwealth from the American Revolution* (Boston 1956), foreword

16 Burt to Tory, 4 February 1913, H.M. Tory Papers, Academic Appointments File, UAA

17 Tory autobiography, unpublished, 'Going West,' 9, H.M. Tory Papers, XXIX, Public Archives of Canada, hereinafter cited as PAC

18 For an account of Tory's career, see E.A. Corbett, *Henry Marshall Tory, Beloved Canadian* (Toronto 1954).

19 H.M. Tory to W.H. Alexander, 21 July 1934, Wallace Papers, UAA

20 Quoted in Corbett, *Henry Marshall Tory, Beloved Canadian* 100

21 W.H. Alexander notes (undated), Wallace Papers, UAA

22 *Ibid.*

23 Professor Lillian Cobb to the author, 5 February 1971

24 Professor Aileen Dunham to the author, 2 February 1971

25 *The Gateway* (May 1917) 17–19

CHAPTER 2   THE TANK BATTALION

1 See *Report of the Ministry, Overseas Military Forces of Canada 1918* (London, nd) 377. 'The 1st Tank Battalion was authorized by General Order 64 of 1 May 1918. ... The unit remained there [in England] until its return to Canada on 18 May 1919 and was subsequently disbanded' – Director, Directorate of History, Department of National Defence, to author, 5 April 1971

2 See University of Alberta Soldiers Comforts Club, *Weekly News Letter*, 20 April 1918, UAA

3 H.M. Fife, a private in the University of Alberta contingent

4 The Rev. Tom Marsden was a Cambridge graduate who had come to Edmonton as an Anglican missionary in 1915. He lectured in history and English in the 1917–18 term, and remained in England after the war.

5 A.L. Burt to Mrs Dorothy Burt, 29 June 1918

6 *Ibid.*

7 *Ibid.*, 9 July 1918

8 *Ibid.*, 17 July 1918
9 *Ibid.*, 18 September 1918
10 *Ibid.*, 20 July 1918
11 *Ibid.*, 25 September 1918
12 *Ibid.*, 6 October 1918
13 *Ibid.*, 17 November 1918
14 See below, p 171n9.
15 Miss Roberta MacAdams, a nursing sister who had been active in Women's Institute work in Alberta, was one of the two members of the Assembly elected by the overseas service voters in 1917. See L.G. Thomas *The Liberal Party in Alberta: A History of Politics in the Province of Alberta 1905–1921* (Toronto 1959) 166, 179.

CHAPTER 3   THE KHAKI UNIVERSITY

1 See *Report of the Ministry, Overseas Military Forces of Canada 1918* (London, nd) 472–82; H.M. Tory Papers, VI, PAC.
2 Frank Underhill (1889–1971), was on the teaching staff of the Khaki University. A graduate of Toronto and Oxford, he taught history and political science at the University of Saskatchewan from 1914 to 1927, when he moved to the University of Toronto, retiring as professor of history in 1955.
3 Sir Charles Lucas (1853–1931), civil servant and historian. Lucas, a graduate of Oxford, produced several works on the history of the Empire following his retirement in 1911 as first head of the Dominions Department of the Colonial Office.
4 F.D. Adams (1859–1942) was Dean of the Faculty of Applied Science, McGill University.
5 C.M. MacInnes (1891–1971) was born in Calgary and educated at Dalhousie and Oxford universities. He did not secure a post in Canada; but was appointed to the staff of the University of Bristol in 1919, and became Professor of Imperial History there in 1943. He was the author of several works on the history of the Empire and on the history of Bristol. In 1930 he published *In the Shadow of the Rockies*, the first scholarly treatment of the history of the western plains region of Canada, which remains a standard reference.
6 Ernest Barker (1874–1960), at this time Fellow and Tutor of New College, Oxford, author of standard works on the political thought of the classical world, with a world-wide reputation
7 Hugh J. McLaughlin (1892–1972) of Toronto subsequently became a prominent barrister and Queen's Counsel, and was a Bencher of the Law Society of Upper Canada.

8 Tory Papers, VI, PAC, 'Instructions,' 9 December 1918
9 S.D. Killam (1888–1923) was Assistant Professor and later Professor of Mathematics at the University of Alberta.
10 D.A. MacGibbon (1882–1969), a graduate of McMaster and Chicago, was Professor of Economics at the University of Alberta from 1919 to 1929.
11 J.L.W. Gill (1871–1939) was Professor of Engineering at Queen's University.
12 A.L. Burt to Mrs Dorothy Burt, 6 April 1919
13 See 'Khaki University,' *Encyclopedia Canadiana* v (Ottawa 1958) 400–1; E.A. Corbett, *Henry Marshall Tory, Beloved Canadian* (Toronto 1954) ch. 13

CHAPTER 4 LONDON DAYS

1 See M.P. Follett, *The New State: Group Organization the Solution of Popular Government* (New York and London 1918); on Henry Wise Wood's view of group government, see W.L. Morton, 'Social Philosophy of Henry Wise Wood, the Canadian Agrarian Leader,' *Journal of Agricultural History* XXII (1948) 114–22. The clearest presentation of group government theory was provided by William Irvine in *Co-operative Government* (Ottawa 1929).
2 See A.J.P. Taylor, *English History 1914–1945* (Oxford 1965) 187
3 A.L. Burt to Mrs Dorothy Burt, 28 May 1919
4 *Ibid.*, 30 March 1919. William Temple (1881–1944) became Archbishop of York in 1929 and Archbishop of Canterbury in 1942. As a church leader and writer, he identified himself with the Labour party and was an inflential champion of social justice, church union, and of a reasoned exposition of the Christian faith.
5 Malcolm Muggeridge, *Jesus Rediscovered* (London 1969) 180–1
6 See report in the *New York Times*, 5 July 1918
7 A.L. Burt to Mrs Dorothy Burt, 20 April 1919
8 *Ibid.*, 20 April 1919
9 *Ibid.*, 29 June 1919
10 He was also completing his collection of nineteenth-century political biographies.
11 A.L. Burt to Mrs Dorothy Burt, 19 January 1919. Succeding comments on French historians are taken from letters in April, May, and June.
12 *Ibid.*, 12 May 1919
13 *Ibid.*, 22 May 1919
14 Sir George R. Parkin (1846–1922), the leading Canadian advocate of imperial federation and organizer of the Rhodes Scholarship administration. Author of *The Rhodes Scholarships* (Toronto, etc. 1912)
15 A.L. Burt to Mrs Dorothy Burt, 2 June 1919

CHAPTER 5 SCHOLAR AND COMMENTATOR

1 Morden H. Long (1886–1965). Long was promoted to Professor of History in 1935 and headed the department from 1946 to 1952.
2 *The Gateway* (March 1921) 8–12
3 *Sup.*, 46
4 Foreword, *The Old Province of Quebec* (Minneapolis and Toronto 1933)
5 *Ibid.*
6 Norah Story, 'Sir Arthur George Doughty,' *The Oxford Companion to Canadian History and Literature* (Toronto, etc. 1967) 220
7 Professor D.G. Creighton's experiences a decade later were similar to Burt's: see his 'The Decline and Fall of the Empire of the St Lawrence,' *Canadian Historical Association Annual Report, 1969* 14–16.
8 Gustave Lanctot was educated at the University of Montreal and at Oxford. He joined the staff of the Public Archives of Canada in 1912. He succeeded Sir Arthur Doughty as Dominion Archivist in 1937, retiring in 1948.
9 D.E. Cameron (1879–1946) was a graduate of the University of Edinburgh, and studied theology at New College, Edinburgh, and at Gottingen. A chaplain in World War I, he was on the staff of the Khaki University. He was chief librarian at the university from 1921 to 1945. Miss Calhoun was also a member of the library staff.
10 Chester New (1882–1960) was a Professor of History at McMaster University from 1920 to 1951. His biography of Lord Durham appeared in 1929.
11 The Archives was then housed in a substantial stone structure on Sussex Street, next to the Mint. It was subsequently enlarged in 1926.
12 See H.M. Tory Papers, League of Nations Committee, UAA
13 *The Gateway* (14 November 1922 and 21 April 1923)
14 *The Press Bulletin*, UAED, VIII, nos. 10 and 11 (19 and 26 January 1923)
15 Borden to Burt, 17 June 1924, Sir Robert Borden Papers, PAC

CHAPTER 6 THE OLD PROVINCE OF QUEBEC

1 Hilda Neatby, introduction, Carleton Library reprint of *The Old Province of Quebec* I (Toronto 1968) x. Dr Neatby was Burt's first PH D student (1934). From 1936 to 1944 she taught at Regina College, and subsequently at the University of Saskatchewan where she was head of the Department of History from 1958 until her retirement in 1969.
2 Foreword, *The Old Province of Quebec*
3 J.L. Morison (1875–1952) was born in Scotland and educated at Edinburgh and Glasgow universities. He was Professor of History at Queen's from 1907 to 1922 and at King's College, Newcastle on Tyne, from 1922 to 1940.

4 G.W. Brown (1894–1963) graduated from the universities of Toronto and Chicago, and was appointed to the history staff of Toronto in 1925.

5 Harold A. Innis (1894–1952) graduated from McMaster and the University of Chicago, and in 1920 was appointed to the Department of Political Economy at the University of Toronto.

6 J.A.T. Chapais (1858–1946) was active in law, politics, and journalism, and as professor of history at Laval. In addition to his eight-volume history of Canada he produced biographies of Talon and Montcalm. He was appointed to the Senate in 1919.

7 E.C. Drury was a leader of the United Farmers of Ontario and was premier of Ontario from 1919–23 heading a government supported by farmer, labour, and independent members.

8 For a concise description of Levy's difficulties see *The Old Province of Quebec* 109n.

9 H.P. Biggar (1872–1938) was educated at the universities of Toronto and Oxford. From 1905 to 1938 he was chief archivist for Canada in Europe. He edited several documentary publications of the Public Archives and also the Champlain Society's six-volume work on Champlain. His brother, O.M. Biggar, had practised law in Edmonton, see *inf.* 113.

10 Antoine Gérin-Lajoie (1824–82), lawyer, journalist, librarian, and historian. The book Burt was reading was *Dix Ans au Canada, de 1840 à 1850*, an impartial account of the movement for responsible government.

11 W.P.M. Kennedy (1881–1963) was at this time a member of the Department of History at the University of Toronto, and had published *Documents of the Canadian Constitution: 1759–1915* (1918) and a textbook, *The Constitution of Canada: An Introduction to Its Development and Law* (1922).

12 W.S. Wallace was educated at the universities of Toronto and Oxford. He taught history at the universities of Western Ontario, McMaster, and Toronto and was librarian of the University of Toronto from 1923 to 1954. He edited the *Canadian Historical Review* from 1920 to 1929.

13 L.J. Burpee (1873–1946) was appointed to the federal civil service in 1890 and was secretary of the International Joint Commission, 1912–46. He was a prolific writer of well-researched works on Canadian subjects, particularly the history of exploration. He was the first president of the Canadian Historical Association.

14 *Canadian Historical Association Annual Report, 1922* 8

15 F.R. Latchford (1854–1938) at this time resided in Toronto, but was educated in Ottawa and practised law there before his career in politics and on the bench. He became judge in 1908 and was appointed Chief Justice in appeal, Supreme Court of Ontario in 1923.

16 W.D. Le Sueur (1840–1917) was a civil servant, journalist, and author. His biography, *Count Frontenac*, was published in The Makers of Canada Series, 1906.

17 *A Short History of Canada for Americans*, 2nd ed. (Minneapolis 1944) 249

18 Stanford White (1853–1906), American architect and designer of several important buildings including Madison Square Garden, where he was murdered by Harry K. Thaw.

19 The Shelburne (Lansdowne) Papers were purchased by Wm. L. Clements from Sotheby and Co. in 1921, and subsequently presented to the library of the University of Michigan.

20 Smith to Burt, 18 August 1925, RG 37, PAC

21 Carl P. Russell (1894–1967) received his PH D in history from the University of Michigan and became a member of the staff of the US National Parks Service.

22 C.H. Van Tyne (1896–1930) taught at the University of Michigan from 1903 until his death. An influential teacher, he was the author of many important works on United States history.

23 *The Press Bulletin*, UAED, IX, No. 5 (23 November 1923)

24 *Ibid.*, IX, No. 9 (15 February 1924)

25 *L'Echo du Collège d'Edmonton*, II, No. 7 (25 mars 1924)

26 Lavergne to Burt, 10 April 1924, Burt Papers, PAC

27 Burt to Tory, 12 December 1927, Tory Papers, UAA

28 In 1966 the University of Toronto Press reprinted one of these volumes with Burt's notes, under the title *Sir Guy Carleton*.

29 William R. Watson, *My Desire* (Toronto 1935) 40

30 *The Press Bulletin*, UAED, XI, No. 4 (8 January 1926)

31 *Ibid.*, XI, No. 4 (8 January 1926)

CHAPTER 7 CONSTITUTIONAL ISSUES OLD AND NEW

1 *Cambridge History of the British Empire* VI (Cambridge 1930) ch. 6, 'The Problem of Government, 1760–1774'

2 A.S. Morton (1870–1945) was educated at the University of Edinburgh and in Berlin. He was head of the Department of History at the University of Saskatchewan from 1914 to 1940.

3 A.U.G. Bury (1869–1951) was educated at Trinity College and King's Inn, Dublin, and practised law in Edmonton. He was Member of Parliament for Edmonton East 1925–6 and 1930–5, and mayor of Edmonton 1927–9.

4 L.B. Pearson, Prime Minister of Canada 1963–8. Pearson was educated at the universities of Toronto and Oxford, and taught history at the University of Toronto, 1924–8.

5 D. Donaghy, Liberal member for Vancouver North

6 Collins was the Conservative candidate in the Peace River riding in the election of 1925 and was defeated by a narrow margin. With the support of the Conservative opposition, he petitioned the House of Commons to set aside the result because of proven irregularities in the conduct of the election, but no action was taken prior to the dissolution of the House. See *House of Commons Debates, 1926*, 'Peace River Election.'

7 Burt's information was incorrect insofar as Macdonald was concerned, but two other Liberal appointments to the Senate were made: see *House of Commons Debates, 1926* 5098.

8 S.F. Tolmie (1867–1937), Member of Parliament for Victoria, BC, federal Minister of Agriculture, 1919–21, and subsequently premier of British Columbia, 1928–33

9 See W.R. Graham, *Arthur Meighen* II (Toronto 1963) 419–23, and E. Forsey, *The Royal Power of Dissolution in the British Commonwealth*, 2nd impression (Toronto 1968), chs. 5 and 6, and pp xix–xxiv.

10 The King ministry and the Alberta government had negotiated an agreement for the transfer of the natural resources to the province, but when King subsequently succumbed to pressure by Bourassa to include a proviso that the Roman Catholic minority be given specific guarantees of a share of the proceeds from the sale of school lands, the Alberta government demurred and the agreement was not ratified.

11 Walter Duncan, a confidential inspector in the Department of Finance

12 Woodsworth, however, continued to vote with the Liberals.

13 J.J. Saucier to L. Ogden, 29 June 1969, History Club Records, UAA

14 Bury was in error so far as the time of Lord Byng's interview with Forke is concerned – it was after Meighen had agreed to form a government.

15 Bury was defeated in the 1926 general election by a narrow margin.

16 O.D. Skelton (1878–1941) was educated at Queen's University and the·University of Chicago. He was Professor of Political Science at Queen's from 1908 to 1925, and Under-Secretary of State for External Affairs from 1925 to 1941.

17 J.L. McDougall was educated at the University of Toronto, the London School of Economics, and Harvard. He was an instructor in economics at Toronto in 1926–7, and taught at Queen's from 1932 to 1966.

18 J.S. Ewart (1849–1933) practised law in Toronto, Winnipeg, and (after 1904) Ottawa. An advocate of Canadian independence, he wrote a number of books and articles, including *The Kingdom Papers* and *The Independent Papers*. He was also the author of *The Roots and Causes of the War 1914–1918*. For a discussion of his ideas, see F.H. Underhill, 'The Political Ideas of John S. Ewart,' Canadian Historical Association, *Annual Report* (1933) 23–32.

CHAPTER 8   THE FLOWERING OF CANADIAN HISTORY

1 Robert Herrick, *Seek and Find*
2 The new wing of the Public Archives building was opened in 1926.
3 E.A. Cruikshank (1853–1939) was educated at Upper Canada College and began his military career in 1877. After overseas service in World War I, he was appointed director of the historical section of the general staff. He was the author of numerous historical studies and was also the first Chairman of the Historic Sites and Monuments Board of Canada.
4 W.A. Mackintosh was educated at Toronto, Queen's, and Harvard universities. He was Professor of Economics at Queen's, 1925–7, and Principal, 1951–61.
5 G.E. Wilson was educated at Queen's and Harvard universities and was Professor of History at Dalhousie 1919–69, an unequalled period of service in a Canadian Department of History. He is the author of a biography of Robert Baldwin.
6 J.B. Brebner (1895–1957) was educated at Toronto and Oxford universities, and taught at Toronto from 1921–5, and at Columbia University, 1925–57. He was the author of several significant studies on the colonial history of Nova Scotia and on the exploration of North America. *The North Atlantic Triangle* is his most important work.
7 Chester Martin (1882–1958) was educated at the University of New Brunswick and was the first North American Rhodes Scholar at Oxford. He taught at the University of Manitoba for twenty years, and was head of the Department of History at Toronto from 1929 to 1952, succeeding George M. Wrong. His publications include several pioneer studies (the earliest appearing in 1914) on the history of the Canadian West.
8 W.M. Whitelaw, 'Canadian History in Retrospect,' *Canadian Historical Association Annual Report, 1956* 38, 40. Whitelaw was born in 1890 and was a graduate of the University of Toronto, Union Theological Seminary, and Columbia University. He had a peripatetic university teaching career, and was the author of the brilliant and original work *The Maritimes and Canada Before Confederation*, published in 1934.
9 Séraphin Marion was educated at the University of Ottawa and the Sorbonne. He was the French editor in the Archives. Mr Norman Fee informed the author that the visit referred to here was in the home of Marion's father, who was an employee of the architect's branch of the Department of Public Works.
10 Norman Fee joined the staff of the Public Archives in 1907. He served in various capacities until 1929, when he became Director of the Map and Picture divisions. From 1938 to 1956 he was Assistant to the Dominion Archivist, and acting Dominion Archivist in 1948. He retired in 1957.

11 Sir Hugh Graham, Baron Atholstan (1848–1938), founder and publisher of the *Daily Star*, the *Family Herald* and *Weekly Star*, and the *Montreal Standard*, and prominent member of the Conservative party

12 Doughty to Borden, 30 November 1920, RG 37, PAC

13 Doughty to Meighen, 28 April 1921, RG 37, PAC

14 Doughty to G.M. Wrong, 13 May 1921, RG 37, PAC

15 G.M. Smith (1888–1947) was educated at Toronto and Oxford universities. He was a specialist in modern European history and international relations. He came to Edmonton in 1931 as Burt's successor as head of the department, and continued in this position until 1946.

16 G.P. de T. Glazebrook was educated at Toronto and Oxford and taught history at the University of Toronto from 1925 to 1941 and subsequently. He was on the staff of the Department of External Affairs, 1949–56.

17 W.H. Dawson (1860–1948), British author of numerous works on the history of Germany

18 W.R. Graham, *Arthur Meighen*: Vol. II *And Fortune Fled* (Toronto 1963) 420.

19 This was probably a quotation from the former prime minister's speech to the National Liberal Club in the United Kingdom on 18 December 1923, which is referred to in Forsey, *The Royal Power of Dissolution of Parliament in the British Commonwealth* (Toronto 1968) 89.

20 Mr Justice C.A. Stuart, Chancellor of the University of Alberta, 1908–26

21 McArthur wrote Chapters 7, 8, and 9 of the *Cambridge History of the British Empire*, VI.

22 On 7 April 1926, Prime Minister King announced the appointment of a royal commission to investigate the 'Maritime Rights' question, composed of Sir Andrew Duncan, Hon. W.B. Wallace, and Professor Cyrus Macmillan of McGill University.

23 In the general election held in September the Conservative strength declined from 116 to 91. The results were Liberals 128, Conservatives 91, Progressives 20, Others 6. Mackenzie King again became Prime Minister.

CHAPTER 9 LAST YEARS AT ALBERTA

1 Miss Jean Murray subsequently received her PH D from the University of Chicago, and taught at the University of Saskatchewan from 1931 to 1968.

2 J.E.W. Sterling was a graduate of the University of Toronto who received his MA degree in history from the University of Alberta in 1930, and his PH D from Stanford. He has had a notable academic career in the United States, and was President of Stanford University, 1949–68, and on his retirement was appointed Chancellor of that university.

3 'The Imperial Conference,' *The Press Bulletin*, UAED, XII, No. 7 (25 March 1927)
    1–4
4 H.B. Neatby, *William Lyon Mackenzie King, 1924–1932: The Lonely Heights*
    (Toronto 1963) 195
5 Graham Spry was a Rhodes Scholar from Manitoba in 1921, and has had a long
    and distinguished career in business and government administration and as a
    writer on political and economic subjects. From 1927 to 1932 he was living in
    Ottawa as national secretary of the Association of Canadian Clubs and was a
    member of the national executive of the League of Nations Society.
6 C.P. Meredith was General Secretary of the League of Nations Society in
    Canada.
7 The Judicial Committee of the Privy Council gave its decision on the respective
    claims of Canada and Newfoundland on 1 March 1927. The Canadian gov-
    ernment had argued for a boundary which would have confined Labrador to a
    narrow strip one mile inland from the high-water mark on the sea coast.
    Newfoundland's claim, with some minor modification, was accepted by the
    Privy Council.
8 *A New World or the League of Nations* (Ottawa 1927) 12
9 Lionel Groulx (1878–1967), cleric and historian, with a long and productive
    career as a teacher and author; founder (1947) of *Revue d'Histoire de l'Amérique
    française* and the author of many works on French-Canadian history and
    contemporary affairs. A vigorous defender of the nationalist cause in Quebec,
    Groulx had a profound influence on several generations of students.
10 H.H. Love, president of W.J. Gage and Co. from 1919 until his retirement in
    the 1940s, was responsible for Gage's specialization in school textbook publish-
    ing.
11 A.L. Burt Papers, PAC
12 The Royal Society met for the first time in western Canada at Winnipeg in May
    1928. Burt's paper, 'Governor Murray and the British Government,' was
    presented by Chester Martin, a Fellow of the Society. See *Transactions of the
    Royal Society of Canada*, 3rd series, XXII, section ii (1928) 49–56.
13 *The Press Bulletin*, UAED, XIII, No. 3 (14 March 1928) 1–4. Selections from
    this apologia are reproduced as Appendix I of this work.
14 A.L. Burt, *High School Civics: A Brief Treatment of the Civics Section of History* 3
    (Edmonton 1928) 81 pp. Authorized for use in the schools of Alberta by the
    Honourable Perren Baker, Minister of Education
15 Herbert Heaton (1890–1973) was born in England and educated at the univer-
    sities of Leeds and Birmingham, and the London School of Economics. He
    taught in Australia, 1914–25, at Queen's University, 1925–7, and was profes-
    sor of economic history at the University of Minnesota, 1927–58.
16 A.L. Burt to Mrs Dorothy Burt, 22 April 1928

17 R.G. MacBeth, *The Romance of Western Canada* (Toronto 1918)

18 A.L. Burt to Mrs Dorothy Burt, 27 April 1928

19 Herbert Heaton to the author, 24 March 1971, describing the observations of his daughter who took courses from Burt

20 A.L. Burt to Mrs Dorothy Burt, 2 June 1928

21 J.C. Saul was editor-in-chief of W.J. Gage and Co. from 1919 to 1939.

22 Lorne Pierce, editor of the Ryerson Press, 1920–60

23 W.N. Sage (1888–1963) was educated at the universities of Toronto and Oxford and taught history at the University of British Columbia from 1918 to 1954, and was head of the department, 1932–53.

24 D.R. Michener was born in Lacombe, Alberta, and was selected as Rhodes Scholar from the University of Alberta in 1919. He practised law in Toronto, 1927–57 and was elected to the Ontario legislature and later to the House of Commons, where he served as speaker. He was appointed Governor General of Canada in 1967 and retired from that post in 1973.

25 James Malcolm (1880–1935) was Minister of Trade and Commerce from 1926–1930.

26 A.L. Burt to Mrs Dorthy Burt, 3 May 1928, a letter written from Minneapolis

27 L.H. Gipson (1880–1970), was Professor and Head of the Department of Government and History, 1924–46. He is the author of the monumental 14-volume work *The British Empire before the American Revolution*.

28 J.W. Schulz (1859–1947), author of *My Life as an Indian, The Story of a Red Woman and a White Man in the Lodges of the Blackfeet* (New York 1907) and numerous other works on western Indian life in the United States

29 J.P. Pritchett was educated at Stanford and Queen's universities. He subsequently taught at Queen's, the University of North Dakota, and, from 1938 to 1950, at Queen's College of the City University of New York.

30 The Russell, at the corner of Sparks and Elgin streets, was the chief Ottawa hotel from the earliest days of the capital until the turn of the century. It was destroyed by fire in 1927, and the property was expropriated by the government.

31 B. Claxton (1898–1960), was educated at McGill and practised law in Montreal and taught commercial law at McGill. Liberal member of Parliament, 1940–54, and a prominent member of the federal cabinet 1944–54

32 A.L. Burt to Mrs Dorothy Burt, 19 July 1928

33 Review of Corbett, *Henry Marshall Tory, Beloved Canadian*, *Canadian Historical Review*, xxxv (1954) 348–9

34 'The Quarrel Between Germain and Carleton: An Inverted Story,' *CHR*, xi (1930) 202–22

35 *The Press Bulletin*, uaed, xvi, No. 3 (12 December 1930) 1–4

36 See above, 107

37 W.L. Morton, *The Progressive Party in Canada* (Toronto 1950) 267

38 See above, 38, A.L. Burt to Mrs Dorothy Burt, 9 March 1919

CHAPTER 10 FIRST YEARS AT MINNESOTA

1 A.L. Burt to Mrs Dorothy Burt, 27 April 1928

2 *Ibid.*, 29 April 1928

3 'For Guy Stanton Ford, A Debt Only History Can Pay,' *Minnesota Alumni News* (February 1963) 10

4 A.L. Burt to R.C. Wallace, 24 April 1930, Wallace Papers, UAA

5 Burt to Wallace, 2 April 1931, *loc. cit.*

6 A.L. Burt to C.K. Burt, 27 January 1944, Burt Papers, PAC. Subsequent references to Burt's letters to his father are all from this collection.

7 Professor H. Heaton to the author, 24 March 1971

8 *Canadian Historical Review* XV (1934) 196

9 G.M. Wrong to A.L. Burt, 4 January 1934, Burt Papers, *loc. cit.*

10 R. Coupland to A.L. Burt, 10 November 1937, Burt Papers

11 Michel Brunet, *Les Canadiens après la Conquête, 1759–1775* (Montreal 1969) 18

12 *Canadian Historical Review* XLI (1960) 330–1

13 *Canadian Historical Review* XVII (1936) 74–6

14 *American Historical Review* LVIII (1952–3) 961

15 *Minnesota History* XVIII (1937) 83

16 *Canadian Historical Review* XXXVII (1956) 177–8

17 A.L. Burt to C.K. Burt, 11 October 1936

18 *The United States, Great Britain and British North America* 184

19 *American Historical Review* XLVII (1941–2) 87

20 See, for example, B. Perkins, ed., *The Causes of the War of 1812: National Honour or National Interest?* (New York 1962); G.R. Taylor, ed., *The War of 1812: Past Justifications and Present Interpretations* (Boston 1963).

21 A.L. Burt to C.K. Burt, 11 October 1942

22 See A.L. Burt to C.K. Burt, 31 May 1945. Abbé J.T.A. Maheux (1884–1967) was educated at Laval University and Paris. He taught at Laval for over thirty years, and in 1938 was appointed archivist of the Quebec Seminary. He was a strong advocate of a better understanding between French-speaking and English-speaking in Canada.

23 *A Short History of Canada for Americans* (Minneapolis 1942) 250

24 A.L. Burt to C.K. Burt, 19 March 1942

25 A.L. Burt to C.K. Burt, 11 October 1942
26 W.L. Mackenzie King to H.H. Love, 12 December 1942, Burt Papers, *loc. cit.*

CHAPTER 11   INTERNATIONALIST

1 Undated offprint, *St Paul Sunday Pioneer Press*, 'Can Modern Civilization Be Saved?'
2 A.L. Burt to Forrest Burt, 8 February 1938, Burt Papers, *loc. cit.*
3 A.L. Burt to C.K. Burt, 8 April 1944
4 Burt Papers, *loc. cit.*
5 Allan Nevins and Louis M. Hacker, eds., *The United States and Its Place in World Affairs, 1918–1943* (New York 1943) vi
6 A.L. Burt to C.K. Burt, 13 February 1943.
7 Nevins and Hacker, *The United States and Its Place in World Affairs, 1918–1943* 392–3
8 Herbert Heaton to the author, 26 May 1972
9 Burt Papers, *loc. cit.*
10 L. Bryson, L. Finkelstein, and R.M. MacIver, eds., *Conflicts of Power in Modern Culture* (New York 1964) 596
11 See A.L. Burt to C.K. Burt, 12 April 1942 and preface to C.F. Kraenzel *et al.*, *The Northern Plains in a World of Change* (Canadian Association for Adult Education 1942).
12 See brochure of the Canada-United States Committee on Education, October 1951, Burt Papers, *loc. cit.*
13 See offprint from *The United States in the Postwar World: Addresses Given at the 1945 Summer Conference of the University of Michigan* (np 1947).
14 A.L. Burt to C.K. Burt, 27 April 1944
15 A.L. Burt to C.K. Burt, 21 February 1946 *et passim*
16 *Transactions of the Royal Society of Canada, 1946*, Proceedings 51
17 See letters to Miss Louise Olsen, secretary of the Department of History, copies in the possession of the author.
18 A.L. Burt to C.K. Burt, 29 July 1943
19 J.A. Walden (D.C. Heath and Co.) to A.L. Burt, 19 February 1943, Burt Papers
20 *Canadian Historical Review* XXXVIII (1957) 62–4
21 Charles Mowat to A.L. Burt, 19 September 1956, Burt Papers, *loc. cit.*
22 See above, p 45
23 Professor Herbert Heaton to the author, 24 March 1971
24 Professor Carl Berger to the author, 24 July 1973

CHAPTER 12   COMMITTED SCHOLAR AND DEDICATED
TEACHER

1 *Ottawa Journal*, 28 September 1957, 'Carleton's Burt Rewrites History'
2 Alvin C. Gluek, Jr to John Arthur Burt, 7 July 1971, Burt Papers, *loc. cit.*
3 Louise P. Olsen to the author, 4 January 1971
4 'Unpublished Reminiscences' of Louise P. Olsen: selection of material on A.L. Burt and Mrs Burt supplied to the author
5 A.L. Burt to C.K. Burt, 15 November 1945
6 *Events* (February 1937) 131–2, 133–4
7 *Ibid.* (July 1937) 70
8 *The Press Bulletin*, UAED, 12 December 1930, 'Our Dynamic Society'
9 'Our Dynamic Society,' *Minnesota History* XIII (1) 6
10 *Canadian Historical Review* XXII, p 437
11 Arthur Marwick, *The Nature of History* (London 1970) 180
12 *Ibid.* 19
13 See above, p 56

Index